THE
SEARCHERS

Contemporary Approaches to Film and Television Series
A complete listing of the books in this series can be found at
http://wsupress.wayne.edu

GENERAL EDITOR
BARRY KEITH GRANT
Brock University

ADVISORY EDITORS
PATRICIA B. ERENS
School of the Art Institute of Chicago

LUCY FISCHER
University of Pittsburgh

PETER LEHMAN
Arizona State University

CAREN J. DEMING
University of Arizona

ROBERT J. BURGOYNE
Wayne State University

TOM GUNNING
University of Chicago

ANNA MCCARTHY
New York University

PETER X. FENG
University of Delaware

THE SEARCHERS

Essays and Reflections on
JOHN FORD'S CLASSIC WESTERN

EDITED BY
Arthur M. Eckstein and Peter Lehman

WAYNE STATE UNIVERSITY PRESS   DETROIT

Copyright © 2004 by Wayne State University Press,
Detroit, Michigan 48201. All rights reserved.
No part of this book may be reproduced without formal permission.

08 07 06   5 4 3 2

Library of Congress Cataloging-in-Publication Data

The searchers : essays and reflections on John Ford's classic western / edited by Arthur M. Eckstein
and Peter Lehman.
 p. cm. — (Contemporary approaches to film and television series)
ISBN 0-8143-3055-X — ISBN 0–8143-3056-8 (pbk.)
1. Searchers (Motion picture)   I. Eckstein, Arthur M.   II. Lehman, Peter.
III. Title.   IV. Series.
PN1997.S3197S43 2004
791.43'72—dc22
2003023827

∞ The paper used in this publication meets the minimum requirements
of the American National Standard for Information Sciences—
Permanence of Paper for Printed Library Materials, ANSI Z39.48–1984.

Brian Henderson's essay was previously published as
"*The Searchers:* An American Dilemma." *Film Quarterly* 34 (1981): 9–23.
It appears here courtesy of *Film Quarterly.*

Richard Hutson's essay was previously published as
"Sermons in Stone: Monument Valley in *The Searchers*" in
The Big Empty: Essays on Western Landscapes and Narrative, ed.
Leonard Engle (Albuquerque: University of New Mexico Press, 1994).
It appears here courtesy of the University of New Mexico Press.

Douglas Pye's essay "Miscegenation and Point of View in The Searchers"
was previously published in *The Book of Westerns,* ed.
Ian Cameron and Douglas Pye, copyright 1996 by Movie.
It is reprinted here by permission of the Continuum International Publishing Company.

For Jeannie Rutenburg and Melanie Magisos

"Sure as the turning of the earth"

CONTENTS

Acknowledgments ix

Preface: A Film That Fits a Lot of Descriptions
Peter Lehman xi

Introduction: Main Critical Issues in *The Searchers*
Arthur M. Eckstein 1

The Searchers: An American Dilemma
Brian Henderson 47

John Wayne and *The Searchers*
William Luhr 75

Sermons in Stone: Monument Valley in *The Searchers*
Richard Hutson 93

"Typically American": Music for *The Searchers*
Kathryn Kalinak 109

Homer's *Iliad* and John Ford's *The Searchers*
Martin Winkler 145

What Would Martha Want?
Captivity, Purity, and Feminine Values in *The Searchers*
Gaylyn Studlar 171

Contents

Incest and Miscegenation in *The Searchers* (1956)
and *The Unforgiven* (1959)
Arthur M. Eckstein 197

Double Vision: Miscegenation and Point of View
in *The Searchers*
Douglas Pye 223

"You Couldn't Hit It on the Nose":
The Limits of Knowledge in and of *The Searchers*
Peter Lehman 239

"That Don't Make You Kin!": Borderlands History
and Culture in *The Searchers*
James F. Brooks 265

Re-searching
David Grimsted 289

Native American Reactions to *The Searchers*
Tom Grayson Colonnese 335

Film Credits 343
Selected Bibliography 345
Index 355

ACKNOWLEDGMENTS

The origins of this volume of essays lies in a 1996 conference held in the Department of History at the University of Maryland at College Park to celebrate the fortieth anniversary of the release of *The Searchers*. We thank the University of Maryland for its financial support of the conference. We also thank Wayne State University Press for its continued interest in the project, and especially Barry Grant and Jane Hoehner for their contributions toward making this collection of essays even better than it was. We also thank the University of California press for permission to reprint the essay by Brian Henderson, the University of New Mexico Press for permission to reprint the essay by Richard Hutson, and Continuum Press for permission to reprint the essay by Douglas Pye.

From Art Eckstein: Thanks to Michael Maas of Rice University for many stimulating conversations about the films of John Ford in general and *The Searchers* in particular. Thanks as well to Jeannie Rutenburg of the University of Maryland, who has been so patient.

From Peter Lehman: Thanks to Bill Luhr for igniting the spark of enthusiasm for the *Searchers* in me more than thirty years ago and for fanning the flames ever since; to Art Eckstein for initiating this project and inviting me to join him; and to countless students over the years who have put up with my obsession with this film in good nature and have made so many original observations about it. No acknowledgments of mine are ever complete without expressing my deep gratitude to Melanie Magisos for putting up with so many obsessions and for helping me to clarify and articulate my ideas about them.

PREFACE
A Film That Fits a Lot of Descriptions

Peter Lehman

In September of 2001, the Museum of Contemporary Art in Los Angeles created a special event around a video installation piece by Douglas Gordon titled "The 5 Year Drive-By." Held in 29 Palms in the California desert, approximately a three-hour drive from Los Angeles, the installation was described by MOCA as a projection of *The Searchers* slowed to a speed that would require five years to see the entire film, five years being the commonly assumed time that Ethan and Marty search for Debbie in the film.[1] Leaving from Tempe, I had a five-hour drive to contemplate the five-year screening of the film about the five-year search. The evening began with a dinner and the installation piece, followed by a trip to a local drive-in theater for a 35mm screening of *The Searchers,* rounded out by a return to the installation for a cash bar.

When we got to the event we were all rather surprised to see no evidence of the installation in sight. Luckily, the prospect of drinks and dinner prevented any massive disappointment. We were considering this prospect when an announcement was made that this was a good time to visit the installation. Unbeknownst to all of us, it had been set up some little walking distance from the dinner site, though it had not been visible. So we went and looked and were greeted by a drive in–theater type movie screen with what appeared to be a static image of John Wayne as Ethan Edwards from the scene where he finally meets Chief Scar. Wayne, so charismatically arresting under any circumstances, here seemed fetishized beyond belief. Indeed in the manner originally theorized by Laura Mulvey, here was the display of a body literally stopping the narrative dead in its tracks. But it wasn't the body of a beautiful, eroticized woman that supplied the visual pleasure but, rather, that of a middle-aged man that held the crowd in rapt attention. We watched the seemingly motionless image (a frame advances almost imperceptibly approximately every twenty minutes). As we watched, the daylight gave way to twilight and finally utter darkness. Ethan advanced perhaps a frame during this dramatic shift in lighting.

Douglas Gordon then spoke about growing up in Scotland in a home where he watched movies regularly with his parents. Like many boys, he loved John Wayne westerns but he remembers *The Searchers* being an exception; it didn't have the pace and action he enjoyed in the others and when he complained of this to his parents, they told him he would understand it when he was older. From that very first viewing, something in the film, however, attracted him enough to begin a never-ending set of returns to it, watching it repeatedly throughout his life. What did he learn from these repeated viewings? That the film was so dense with meaning that the only way it could be understood was by slowing down the projection rate to that equaling the film's diegetic time. If the search lasted five years, it would take five years of contemplation to unpack its meanings. The setting of the installation was of great importance to Douglas, as was the time of day. When we first approached the screen, the image was nearly lost against the dazzling background of the western desert, reminiscent of the desert in *The Searchers*. As it grew darker, the screen image and the setting were almost in balance but then, gradually, darkness enveloped the desert and the bright, crisp, larger-than-life image on the screen was all we could see, overwhelming everything else.

What does all this have to do with a scholarly volume of essays about *The Searchers*? I think both the nature of the installation and Gordon's remarks about his personal history of obsession with the film explain how this project came into being as well as tell us much about the essays we have included. *The Searchers* has obsessed many filmmakers, critics, and scholars in a manner unusual even for those with a passionate love of cinema. There is a difference between loving a film and being obsessed with it and like Gordon Douglas both Art Eckstein and I have had lifelong obsessions with this film. Yet co-editing this volume was not intended as cathartic therapy and will in all likelihood intensify rather than alleviate our obsessions with the film; it already has for me.

Douglas's conceit about the projection time is, of course, so outrageous as to need no comment. But the installation offers an absurd (in the best sense of the word) and brilliant insight into the film, aside from acknowledging obsession. In his famous formulation, Roland Barthes claimed that once read (or viewed) the classical text is used up; by the time

Preface

We join Martha and Debbie watching Ethan ride away.

the narrative is over everything has been explained. As with all such rhetorical claims, this is overstated but it points to a general truth that applies to Hollywood films—actions and character motivations are knowable and meanings tend to be clear and fixed by the time the film is over. Yet I have always felt that in *The Searchers* what happens and why is so ambiguous that all the repeated viewings in the world won't fully clarify it. If I watched the full five-year projection version, it still wouldn't be clear. And the same is true of the unusually dense narrative structures, visual motifs, stylistic features, etc. To say that it would take five years to understand all these elements of the film in one sense doesn't even go far enough—*The Searchers* is one of those rare films that reveals something new every viewing.

With most films, the more we see them the more clear they become for us and repeated viewings, however pleasurable, confirm our essential understanding of the film. My experience with *The Searchers* is nearly the opposite; the more I see it, study it, read about it, and edit essays on it, the less sure I am about anything.

Editing this anthology has brought all this to life in that there have been some wonderful e-mails from contributors acknowledging that they are always amazed to discover new dimensions to the film. And there are wonderfully collegial exchanges between Art Eckstein and myself that show that even we as editors can't always agree upon some very fundamental

Preface

aspects of the film, including the length of time the search lasts. The essays that follow represent a range of work, including a few reprints of important past contributions to understanding the film and many new essays that open up entire new areas of inquiry about the film, or reexamine and/or challenge past analyses. Until Kathryn Kalinak no one has concentrated on the function of music in the film; until Gaylyn Studlar no one has focused on the importance of the character of Martha in the film; until William Luhr few have put the film within the context of John Wayne as a star willing to portray darkly troubled characters; until James Brooks no one has focused on the historical reality of complicated kinship systems that characterized the racially diverse Southwest that supplies the film's setting; until Art Eckstein no one had explored the structural relationship between incest (too close) and miscegenation (too far); until Martin M. Winkler no one had explicated the relation between Homeric narrative and the film; until my work begun in the seventies no one had fully explored the epistemological issues raised in and by the film; and, shockingly, until Tom Colonnese no Native American voices have even been part of published, scholarly research on the film.

A similar sense of opening up new ground characterized the reprinted essays when they appeared initially, and their contributions remain fresh and important today. Brian Henderson put race relationships in *The Searchers*, a film set in nineteenth-century Texas, within the context of America's troubled racial relationships in the fifties, and it has rightfully been studied from that perspective ever since. Douglas Pye turns to that vexing problem in his essay on the complexity of race within the western genre traditions that Ford necessarily inherits and engages in the film, arguing that Ford's struggle to transcend the racial straitjacket imposed by the genre sometimes gives way to outright self-contradiction and even incoherence. Although many critics characteristically acknowledge the importance of the Monument Valley setting in *The Searchers* as well as in other Ford westerns, until Richard Hutson's essay no one fully engaged that setting in the manner that critics typically devote to analyzing narrative and more obviously symbolic and thematic material in the film. Taken together, the reprints and the new essays offer a myriad of enlightening perspectives on *The Searchers*.

This volume really has two endings that come in the form of two quite different types of responses. We have saved Tom Colonnese's essay for last because he is less interested in making yet another scholarly contribution toward interpreting *The Searchers* (Colonnese is not a film

Preface

scholar) but, rather, in articulating a Native American response to the film and the attention it has received. This marks a significant beginning in what we hope will become a much larger dialogue about race in the film involving Native American voices. David Grimsted, drawing upon his vast repertoire of knowledge about *The Searchers*, John Ford's films, the western genre, and American history gives a response to many of the issues raised in the anthology.

I want to engage in a bit of formalism myself and return to the beginning of this essay—Douglas Gordon's installation piece on the film. Grimsted rightly notes that critical judgments change over time and that during the decade that *The Searchers* was made, critics considered *The Informer* (1935)Ford's masterpiece. He is also right that few would agree today. As such, the only way to understand the mania for *The Searchers*, characterized on perhaps the grandest scale yet by Douglas, is to understand it generationally. The film has indeed obsessed the "film school" generation of filmmakers and scholars who came of age in the seventies. I for one believe it is a masterpiece and one of the greatest films ever made but that does not mean that I believe it will or should continue to obsess filmmakers and scholars, nor top ten lists nor anything else for all time. As such, Douglas's installation as well as this book are indeed evidence of a *Searchers* phenomenon. As hinted at above, I read Douglas's installation as revealing a probably unintended dimension of his and our love of the film (at least he didn't mention it)—a fascination that borders on fetishism, in several senses of the word. The film itself has become a fetish object of sorts as has the astonishing charismatic image of John Wayne/Ethan Edwards which lies at its center. Gordon could have chosen to start his projection anyplace in the film and it is not coincidence in my opinion that he chose, of all the possible images from *The Searchers*, a powerful one of Wayne, alone in the frame.

Grimsted also wisely cautions about the extent of the film's ambiguity and suggests that various readings should be tested to see which evidence and logic support best. Yet what has always amazed me about *The Searchers*, and what editing this volume has even underscored more for me, is how logical scholars and careful researchers have amassed evidence for a startling range of interpretations. In the early drafts and final versions of the essays printed here, I have read assertions that the search lasts seven years, not five; that Ethan never intends to kill Debbie; and that Debbie in fact may not have been taken by Scar as a wife. And all the assertions are supported by careful observation of the film. When Laurie refers to the

Preface

number of letters Marty has written her in five years, she may be referring not to the total time of the search, but to the time since Marty and Ethan had last returned to the Jorgensen homestead; when Ethan draws his gun at the sight of Debbie, it is Marty who presumes he intends to kill her and blocks Ethan's line of fire; and when Marty and Ethan see Debbie in Scar's tent they presume she is one his wives but he may merely be keeping her until she arrives at the proper age for marriage.

Ford's last two great westerns, *The Searchers* and *The Man Who Shot Liberty Valance* (1962) both deal centrally with epistemology, both for the characters within the film and the spectators of the film. Many of the characters in both films think they know what is going on or what has happened in the past, when in fact they don't. Similarly, the spectators of both films are at times in a similar position. And in both films, these epistemological issues are given formal expression in the narrative structure via, for example, flashbacks. In that sense, one can say both films are alike. But there is a profound difference. After the flashback within the flashback in *The Man Who Shot Liberty Valance*, the spectators of the film, along with a few characters in the film, share full and complete knowledge of what happened and why. There is no such comparable flashback or moment, or even series of moments, in *The Searchers*.

At one point in the film, the Reverend Captain Clayton tells Ethan, "You fit a lot of descriptions." (Look who's talking, a reverend of God and a captain of irregular soldiers.) What is true of Ethan (and Clayton) is true of the film itself and we don't have to choose one among them. That would lessen the film's richness. It is indeed very true that we should test and throw out descriptions that really don't fit, and that we are capable, intellectually, of deciding which descriptions those are. But we are still left with an awful lot that do fit, and the following essays give eloquent testimony to many of those descriptions.

NOTES

1. I am indebted to Susan Hunt for bringing this event to my attention. She and Michael Hart drove from L.A., and Melanie Magisos and I drove from Tempe. I suppose a bunch of *Searchers* obsessives meeting in the desert for an event of this nature already had their minds made up that a good time was to be had. And it was. As for the likelihood of something like this coming along again, "That'll be the day."

THE
SEARCHERS

Introduction: Main Critical Issues in *The Searchers*

Arthur M. Eckstein

When John Ford's film *The Searchers* was first released, some reviewers thought it just another Ford western.[1] *The Searchers* remains controversial today: the prestigious *Sight and Sound* poll of film critics worldwide ranks it fifth among the all-time greatest films ever made—and yet it stands a lowly ninety-sixth among great films in the American Film Institute listing.[2] The following book consists of essays about, or provoked by, *The Searchers,* and most of the essays (though not all) support the idea that the film should have a high reputation. This introduction provides the reader with the basic facts about the film, and indicates briefly the major issues it raises. I will also offer, however, some original contributions to research and scholarship on the movie.

The Searchers was made in the spring and summer of 1955, edited in the fall of 1955, and released in May 1956. Its director was John Ford, one of Hollywood's most famous filmmakers. In a directorial career stretching back to 1917, he made more than 130 films and won six Academy Awards (more than any won by a director in Hollywood history). But *The Searchers* came out of a period of severe personal and professional trauma for Ford: old age was catching up with him and his career itself was in jeopardy. It was his first western in five years—his return to the genre he loved most. The result was a western with a difference.[3]

The movie is based on Alan LeMay's novel, published in 1954, and the novel itself is loosely based on a true incident of Texas history: the story of Cynthia Ann Parker, who was kidnapped by Comanches at the age of nine when the rest of her family was massacred, eventually married her Comanche captor Peta Nocona (Wandering Wolf), and was not recaptured until many years later.[4] All critics agree that *The Searchers* is visually magnificent. The

1

bleak desert landscapes of Monument Valley, shot in wide screen and spectacular color—the tremendous spires and bluffs and buttes against the vast desert sky—have never looked more awesome. In terms of one's experience of *The Searchers* it is important to stress the intense visual pleasure that Ford created; as the great director Alfred Hitchcock said about Ford, the essence of any Ford movie, especially the Monument Valley westerns, was visual gratification—simple, clear, eloquent images.[5] And yet—this visual beauty is undermined by a terribly grim and dark story.[6] At the center of the film is the character Ethan Edwards (played by John Wayne), and Ethan Edwards is one of the most sinister yet compelling figures in all American cinema. *The Searchers* is the story of how Edwards spends seven years looking for his niece Debbie, captured by Comanches at the age of nine when the rest of the family was destroyed.[7] But the shock is that in the end Ethan is searching for Debbie not to rescue her but to *kill* her, because as the years go by and she has grown into a teenager, she has inevitably been "defiled" (sexually, and sexually-racially) by the Indians. In the movie, it gradually becomes apparent that all the "positives" traditionally associated with John Wayne as a heroic icon of American westerns have instead become weird negatives: stoicism and staunch endurance have become stony lack of all human feeling; skill with a six-shooter and a rifle have become out-of-control violence; the Indian fighter who protects and saves "white civilization" has instead become the destroyer of families. As Harry Carey, Jr., says of the first scene he played with Wayne in the film, "When I looked up at him in rehearsal, it was into the meanest, coldest eyes I have ever seen. . . . Eyes like an angry snake." Carey, who had known Wayne for many years, was shocked.[8]

This is not to say that *The Searchers* is totally revolutionary or subversive. Rather, it is profoundly ambivalent about the traditions of heroic frontier narrative. This ambivalence and complexity are what give the film much of its enduring fascination.

Westerns have been described as in essence "a white triumphalist genre,"[9] and there are important elements in *The Searchers* which certainly fit that traditionalist bill. Thus at the end of the film, the white female captive Debbie (played by Natalie Wood) is finally found among the Indians, is indeed rescued from the traditional "fate worse than death," and returns voluntarily to the white world. Moreover, the Indian who dared to violate her sexual and racial purity—the Comanche war chief Scar (Henry Brandon)—is killed. So, too, is the Comanche girl Look (Beulah Archuletta) who attempts to marry Martin Pauley (Jeffrey Hunter), one of the men searching for Debbie; Look thereby succumbs to the traditional

Introduction

fate of the nonwhite partner in interracial relationships in films of the 1950s. Martin is now free to marry his 100 percent white girlfriend Laurie Jorgensen (Vera Miles)—who is herself a virulent racist. This is a traditional "happy ending," and fully in line with the antimiscegenation stance of the Motion Picture Production Code as it stood in the summer of 1955, when *The Searchers* was filmed.[10]

And the actor playing the protagonist Ethan Edwards is, after all, John Wayne. Wayne's sheer forcefulness on the screen, along with his stature as the hero of innumerable other westerns, make it extremely difficult for audiences even today to disengage from Ethan: they simply do not expect John Wayne to be evil. Moreover, there are many moments in the film when the image of Ethan/Wayne riding his great horse across the vast desert landscape, or rising tall in the saddle to survey the terrain, evokes an almost instinctively positive cultural response—and there is no doubt that John Ford intentionally filmed Wayne that way.[11] The same is true of certain images of the Texas Rangers as a group, notably a low angle "heroic" shot of them mounting their horses, filmed against the night sky, just before their final violent assault on Chief Scar's camp. These scenes show that Ford found it very hard to resist the traditional call of traditionally heroic visual images.

The above considerations have led some recent commentators on *The Searchers* to charge that Ford and his film are in fact totally complicit in Ethan Edwards's violence and racism.[12] If that were true, *The Searchers* would not be worth writing about—nor would it stand so high in the estimate of many film critics. Once more, it is the film's complexities and profound ambiguities that make it a classic.

Ford himself called *The Searchers* "a psychological epic," an epic centered on the psychology of Ethan Edwards.[13] That statement is not surprising, coming from the person who was the key figure (with *Stagecoach* in 1939) in the creation of the "serious, adult" western as a genre.[14] And Ford's words about *The Searchers* as a psychological study are borne out by the film's melancholy theme song, which foregrounds Ethan as a problem from the film's first moments ("What makes a man to wander? . . . What makes a man ride away from home?")—and whose lyrics Ford personally supervised.[15]

It should in fact be obvious that however "heroic" Ethan Edwards occasionally looks in the finished film, he is not at all a traditional western hero. This is a film where John Wayne shoots people in the back (and robs them), disrupts funerals (and weddings), views all religion with open cynicism and sarcasm, and continually desecrates the bodies of the dead (gleefully shooting out the eyes of dead Comanches, or scalping them). Toward Indians he is a motivated only by brutal racism; toward whites outside his immediate family he is cold, suspicious, and often gratuitously insulting. It is implied that Ethan Edwards has been a successful outlaw before the film's story begins. In short, he is a man to whom traditional social constraints mean nothing.

What is worse about Ethan is that this grim, solitary, forbidding figure is a terrible danger *within* his immediate family as well. At the beginning of the film, when he returns to the family homestead in Texas after serving for the South in the Civil War and then fighting as a mercenary for the Emperor Maximilian in Mexico (and then following the life of an outlaw), it becomes apparent that he is in love with Martha, the wife of his brother Aaron (who owns the homestead), and that Martha is equally in love with him—despite her marriage to Aaron and her three children by him. Ethan's return home is therefore highly destabilizing to the family's life, especially because it is obvious that Ethan is in every way a far more powerful man than Aaron. The early scenes of *The Searchers*, with Ethan's unwelcome homecoming, are filled with disturbing tension (especially between the two brothers), barely suppressed eroticism (between Ethan and Martha), and barely controlled anger all around. And Ethan remains a threat to his family throughout the film: as we have said, after the Comanche raid wipes out everyone else, Ethan will spend the rest of the movie searching for his niece Debbie—Martha's daughter, his last surviving blood relative—not, finally, to rescue her but in order to kill her.

In short, even though Ethan Edwards is played by the American icon John Wayne, he can never be regarded as a traditional and "clean" western hero. Indeed, part of the power of the film comes from the startling fact that John Wayne is playing a very disturbed character: *The Searchers* would simply not have its great power if any other actor was in place of Wayne as Ethan. And we have John Ford's own word that he intended Wayne's character to be profoundly problematic.[16]

Ethan Edwards in fact fits here into the wider context of the "dark" or "psychological" western that had become a major Hollywood style by the mid-1950s. Many westerns in this period foregrounded heroes with deep psychological problems. These "dark" or "psychological" westerns began with Raoul Walsh's pioneering *Pursued* (1947)—starring Robert Mitchum in a classic Freudian story set in Monument Valley. Among the most famous of them are the five films starring James Stewart made by director Anthony

Introduction

Mann, starting with 1950s *Winchester '73* (in which Stewart kills his own brother) and ending with the Oedipal *Man from Laramie* (1955). Other important films in this genre include Arthur Penn's Oedipal *The Left-Handed Gun* (1957, starring Paul Newman), Delmer Daves's *Jubal* (1956) and *3:10 to Yuma* (1957, both starring Glenn Ford) as well as the grotesque *The Hanging Tree* (1959, starring Gary Cooper), Anthony Mann's *Man of the West* (1958, also starring Cooper), and Marlon Brando's Oedipal *One-Eyed Jacks* (1960). These "dark westerns" reflect the great impact which psychiatry was having among the Hollywood elite; and perhaps they also reflect the impact of the "disturbed" heroes of post–World War II urban "film noir."[17] John Ford always followed his own instincts as a filmmaker, but clearly he was open to this style of western: indeed, his *Rio Grande* (1950), with John Wayne as a rigid and lonely army colonel destructively torn between his family and what he perceives as his duty, is an early example of it. In this sense, *The Searchers* can be seen as the greatest of "the dark westerns"—the most magnificent cinematography, the bleakest story. Part of John Ford's brilliance and daring here lies in his ability to convince John Wayne to participate at all in a film as disturbed as this one—and to coax out of Wayne one of his most powerful performances.[18]

How Ford establishes the true (but hidden) relationship between Ethan and Martha is an instructive lesson in Ford's technique as a director. As we noted above, Ford first made his career in silent films, starting as a director in 1917; in fact, more than half of his 138 films are silents. This experience had an impact: he despised the use of dialogue to explain situations or plot developments to the audience (thinking it crude and cumbersome); he believed that *motion pictures* should propel the story forward; he believed that the visual image (combined with and reinforced by emotional music) was the absolute essence of film.[19] So, in *The Searchers,* one wordless scene between Ethan and Martha reveals to the viewer the whole sad story of their repressed love—the repressed love that is the engine behind the entire film.

The scene occurs when the local posse of Texas Rangers, led by Reverend Captain Samuel Johnson Clayton (Ward Bond), comes to the Edwards homestead to collect deputies to go after cattle thieves. (Who these thieves are is still unknown—but they will turn out to be Comanches, who are cleverly luring fighting men away from the local homesteads in order to attack the homesteads themselves). Everyone has left the Edwards house to mount up. Bond—the leader of the white community, both minister of the Gospel and captain of the community defense force—stays behind for a moment, drinking a cup of coffee. He hears the two youngest Edwards children catching their older sister Lucy secretly kissing Brad Jorgensen, the son of their nearest neighbor ("Brad and Lucy, Lucy and Brad!!"); Bond smiles, and kicks the door shut. But immediately after the comic illicit romance comes the tragic one. After an exterior shot of the door closing, Ford cuts to an interior long shot of Bond standing at the head of the Edwards dinner table. Something catches his eye offscreen right. Ford cuts to what he sees (i.e., shows it to us)—and it turns out to be a very private moment: sad Martha removing Ethan's grey Confederate army greatcoat from a wooden chest to give to him for the pursuit of the robbers, but taking time to stroke it tenderly, lovingly, her head down.[20] Ford then cuts back to Bond, who (having witnessed what the audience has just been permitted to see) stares ahead, his face expressionless. Now Ethan (Wayne) enters from the back of the frame and goes to meet his sister-in-law as she brings him his grey caped greatcoat. She hands it to him, and he chastely kisses her on the forehead (her eyes are closed); there is a moment of awkward mutual hesitation, and she reaches up helplessly toward him—then stops. Ethan turns abruptly to leave; Martha follows him to the doorway, and stands looking after him. During all this action Ward Bond has stood in the front of the frame, but slightly to one side and with his eyes averted. After Ethan and Martha reluctantly part, Bond looks down into his coffee cup with a frown, and swirls the coffee around; then he turns and goes out the door, walking silently around Martha as he exits.[21]

In this good-bye scene of Ethan and Martha, disapprovingly witnessed by Reverend Captain Clayton—the scene that is the key to the film—there is no dialogue, no spoken words: only photographed moving images with deeply melancholy music playing quietly and slowly in the background. All the audience needs to know (and to feel) about the music is that it is very sad. But this music, sometimes called "Martha's Theme," is the authentic Civil War ballad "Lorena." Now, Ford was an expert on nineteenth-century American popular music, sought to make it an integral part of the mood of his westerns, and chose the music for *The Searchers* with special care. Therefore we should assume that Ford knew the specific meaning of this song "Lorena": it is a famous lament for a love that is impossible to consummate, because it is a love that is socially forbidden.[22] Even more importantly, we now know that nothing like "the Good-bye scene of Ethan and Martha" existed in the shooting script for *The Searchers*, written by Ford's screenwriter Frank Nugent: Nugent's script contains only scattered and unclear hints concerning Ethan and Martha. Ford evidently

Introduction

changed this on the set, late in production, personally reconstructing the early part of the movie by bringing Ethan and Martha together into one traumatic moment. He did it in order to emphasize more firmly to the audience the illicit and dangerous relationship between Ethan and Martha, and he changed the shooting script in order to do it.[23]

Ethan then leaves with the posse: Martha and young Debbie are shown looking after him as he rides off. While he is away, Comanches under their war chief Scar come down on the Edwards homestead: they burn it to the ground, kill Aaron and Aaron's son Ben, rape and kill Martha, and kidnap Lucy (who is later raped and killed) and her younger sister Debbie. And Ethan—an outsider to Edwards family life, and excluded for good reasons—will now spend the rest of the movie searching for Martha's surviving daughter Debbie among the Comanches.

The wordless moment between Ethan and Martha thus provides *The Searchers* with the crucial explanation for Ethan's obsessive search for Debbie: she is the child of the woman he illicitly loves. Ford certainly assumed that most viewers would understand the implications of this scene. You could tell that Ethan and Martha had a deep but illicit love, he said, "from the way she picked up his cape, and I think you could tell from Ward Bond's expression and from his exit.... I think it's very plain to anyone with any intelligence." Ford also said that he had berated actor Walter Coy, who played Ethan's brother Aaron, for not understanding the deadly threat that Ethan's and Martha's love posed to Aaron and his marriage.[24]

Except that Ethan is searching for the child of the woman he loves in order to kill her. Here we have reached the tangled, dark heart of *The Searchers*. Why does Ethan want to murder Debbie?

One important answer is that John Ford's depiction of Ethan in his terrible search is a direct attack on white racism. Most "psychological westerns" of the 1950s did not tackle this issue, being satisfied with exploring deep tensions within families instead; *The Searchers* is the outstanding exception here, for it simultaneously does both. What Ethan fears and hates is that as Debbie grows into an adolescent, she will become sexually available to her Comanche captors, and thus will become doubly "polluted"— both sexually and racially; so she must be destroyed. In fact when she is found, Debbie has apparently become one of the wives of Chief Scar himself. Ethan's fear and hatred is of interracial sexuality, and particularly of "dark men" with white women. This fear and hatred of miscegenation, this obsession with white "purity," is one of the great forces driving Ethan along his destructive path.[25]

Ethan and Martha's relationship: the truth.

Ford's attack on white racism would have had a striking contemporary relevance in 1955–56. Of course, miscegenation between whites and Indians, which so fearsomely obsesses Ethan in 1868, was no longer a central issue for American society. But an attack on white racism in the mid-1950s could only have one deep subject: the relationships between whites and blacks. Yet the depiction of African Americans on the screen—let alone in the context of miscegenation—was in the 1950s almost impossible. The social situation under which *The Searchers* was filmed is shown by the fact that in 1955 the Motion Picture Production Code still officially frowned on any depiction of miscegenation.[26]

In this sense, it is not accidental that the script of *The Searchers* was conceived and written by Frank Nugent, in close collaboration with Ford, in the autumn and winter of 1954–55—that is, in the months after the U.S. Supreme Court ruling in *Brown v. Board of Education*. That ruling seemed to indicate that white and black children would soon be mixing together from early in their lives, at school—with who knew what consequences? Nor does it seem accidental either that *The Searchers* premiered nationwide during the first months of the Montgomery bus boycott that

Introduction

raised Dr. Martin Luther King to national prominence, and just two months after the issuing of "The Southern Manifesto" of 1956—a declaration by almost all southern U.S. congressmen and senators pledging their undying opposition to racial integration. But of course the film's response to the race question is the opposite of the southern officials; it comes in the form of the portrait of a psychologically disturbed racial fanatic: Ethan.[27] And this makes a great deal of sense, because John Ford always viewed himself politically as a traditional New Deal liberal, and thought of himself as a "liberal" on race as well.[28] The deep racial meaning of *The Searchers* has certainly not been lost on African American commentators on the film: it is, as one bluntly says, a film about a race war. It is permissible, then, to see *The Searchers* as one of the many American responses to (and expressions of) the crucial post-*Brown* American dialogue on race.[29]

Objections have recently been raised that this sort of analysis, with Comanche-white relations a stand-in for black-white relations, once more annihilates the Native Americans, by taking the Comanches not as themselves but as "empty signifiers": Native Americans are denied their own existence and become mere symbols of somebody else. Other American films of the mid-1950s dealt with "racial problems"—for instance, *Sayonara* (dir.: Joshua Logan, 1957), with its American soldiers in post–World War II occupied Japan in sometimes tragic romances with Japanese women—yet no film critic has suggested that the Japanese are "stand-ins" for African Americans.[30] It is certainly true that critics need to pay Comanches the respect of treating *The Searchers*' Comanches *as* Native Americans—or rather, as white representations of Native Americans. But that does not mean that the film cannot have a broader meaning. First, it is perfectly possible that the "Japanese war-bride films" of the 1950s were *themselves* attempting to approach, indirectly, an even more painful miscegenetic problem than the one they depicted. And on the other hand, those films are set in the real present, and deal with a real issue of the present, caused by the real U.S. occupation of Japan. *The Searchers*, however, is set in the past, a mythic past. Its "pastness" differentiates it sharply from other "racial problem" films of the mid-1950s, such as *Sayonara*—though we might now see how *The Searchers* finds a context among them. But precisely because *The Searchers* is set in the past, it can easily be seen as an allegory, and hence (again) it is not an accident that important critics, both white and African American, have seen this very powerful film that way.[31]

One might also canvass the idea that there is a relationship between *The Searchers* and another American trauma and concern of the 1950s:

the growing fear of "brainwashing" of Americans by the enemies of American society. Disturbing knowledge of and depictions of communist techniques of psychological manipulation were first brought to American consciousness by such books as George Orwell's novel *Nineteen Eighty-Four* (1948) and Czeslaw Milosz's memoir *The Captive Mind* (1953)—but these were in European contexts. American anxiety was intensified—and, equally importantly, racialized—by the shocking discovery that numbers of American prisoners of war had cooperated with their North Korean and Chinese captors during the Korean War (1950–53) and that a group of American prisoners actually preferred to stay in Communist Asia rather than return to the United States after the war. By the mid-1950s the most feared of mind manipulators thus had become nonwhites. This racialized anxiety about "brainwashing" found widespread expression in American films, most famously in Don Siegel's *Invasion of the Body-Snatchers*, released the same year as *The Searchers* (1956: the villains who inject their minds into ordinary people are nonhuman), and in John Frankenheimer's *The Manchurian Candidate* (1962: the villains are Asians). It found expression in westerns too, for instance in *The Charge at Feather River* (dir.: Gordon Douglas, 1953), where one of two white women held captive by the Cheyenne does not want to be rescued and returned to white society because she has fallen in love with her Indian captor. So we can stress that Ethan's fear that captured Debbie has become (internally) a Comanche fits into a contemporary cultural pattern—and, disturbingly, it is one of the reasons he wants to destroy her. This concern also drives Ethan's hatred and loathing of the female captives "rescued" by the U.S. Army in the winter sequence in the middle of the film: "They ain't white—not anymore. They're *Comanch*," he sneers. It is one of the most disturbing scenes in the film.[32]

In this respect, one must also remember that central elements in *The Searchers* also derive from the long-standing and specifically American literary tradition of the white "captivity narrative." *The Searchers* draws on many elements in that literary tradition, starting with the white captive being female, the desire of her relatives to find and rescue her, and her eventual rescue. The captivity narrative itself was a response to the historical experience of white captivity among Native Americans on the expanding frontier (the first example of the tradition comes from the ex-captive Mary Rowlandson, writing in the 1690s). What is striking is how quickly the tradition became characterized by anxiety caused by white captives' surprisingly easy "conversion" to Indian ways. This suggested the validity and

Introduction

strength of the Native Americans' culture—and, conversely and unacceptably, that there was something lacking in white culture.[33]

In combination, these three factors—the contemporary racial anxieties aroused by the bringing forward of white-black relations as a central issue in American society after 1954, the racialized anxiety deriving from contemporary experience of communist (and especially Asian) "mind-control," and the traditional representation of white fears concerning the impact of Indian captivity upon (surprisingly fragile) white identity—all will have worked together to provide Ethan's grim search for Debbie with a very powerful cultural meaning to the original audience. *The Searchers* thus cannot be fully understood and its meaning appreciated without placing it within this broader context of mid-1950s American cultural concerns.

Having said all this, however, none of the film's contemporary resonances should make us forget that *The Searchers* is primarily a movie about (literally) cowboys and Indians, and thus it comes out of a specific Hollywood film tradition as well. We have already seen the impact of Hollywood culture in the way that *The Searchers* appears to participate in the 1950s Hollywood phenomenon of the "dark" or "psychological" western. John Ford was in fact America's foremost director of westerns: he had been making them since 1917, and would continue to make them for almost a decade after 1956. And within the narrower frame of the western film itself, part of *The Searchers*' complexity and ambiguity derives from the fact that while the film is a powerful attack on white racism, it also marks no turning point in Ford's depiction of Native Americans.

While the whites in *The Searchers* are primitive racists, the Comanches in *The Searchers* are ferocious and frightening figures. They cannot be compared, for instance, to Cochise's morally upright Apaches in their idyllic valley in Delmer Daves's *Broken Arrow* (1950), a film which, six years before *The Searchers,* had already marked a breakthrough in the modern Hollywood depiction of Indians. There is an important line of cultural influence from Daves's film down through the peaceful, idyllic Cheyenne of Arthur Penn's *Little Big Man* (1970), and then on to the romanticized "hippie"-like Sioux (originally intended to be Comanches) in Kevin Costner's award-winning *Dances With Wolves* (1990). But Ford's 1956 Comanches are neither moral paragons nor proto-hippies. They are, above all, grim killers.[34]

It is true that in *The Searchers,* Ford does allow the Comanche point of view to be briefly expressed, in a few words by Scar revealing that whites had killed both his sons. Such was Ford's own tradition. Although in

Stagecoach (1939) the Apaches are deprived of words, and are either silent or yelling, mere violent attackers out of the landscape, Ford had begun allowing Indians to give their view of things by means of brief speeches already in the late forties. This is especially true of *Fort Apache* (1948): John Wayne himself even supports the Indian point of view in that film via a speech of his own, as does Pedro Armendarez as he translates Cochise's long and impassioned and convincing Spanish. We are given a much briefer scene in *She Wore A Yellow Ribbon* (1949)—and there is reversion to the *Stagecoach* depictions in *Rio Grande* (1950). At least Scar in *The Searchers* speaks. It is true also that in *The Searchers* we often see the Comanches living in family groups, men along with women and children and babies—and there is at least one sequence where the hideous impact of white violence on such family encampments is shockingly shown. Finally, it is true that Debbie, when she is finally found, has clearly been well treated. Yet in the end Ford's Comanches in *The Searchers* are—like the whites in the film—primarily tough and brutal and violent; and we know that this presentation of *both* sides as savages was a conscious artistic decision on Ford's part.[35] Even in Ford's late *Cheyenne Autumn*, which offers his most extensive depiction of Indians as mere victims of white aggression and greed, Native American society is not idealized as it is in the Delmer Daves tradition of westerns.[36]

Where *The Searchers* does mark a turning point in Ford is not in his depiction of Native Americans but in his depiction of *whites*. Ford had never idealized white frontier society, as one can see in the powerful portrayals of greed and hypocrisy as far back as *Three Bad Men* (1926) and *Stagecoach* (1939). Yet the white societies of those films had always contained a majority of basically good people. From *The Searchers* onward, however, the reverse is the case: Ford's white frontier society, though it may contain an occasional good person, is primarily ignorant, greedy, hypocritical—and grotesquely racist. This is true not only in *The Searchers* but in *Sergeant Rutledge* (1960: a pioneering movie about black U.S. Cavalry regiments on the frontier, in fact *Glory* thirty years ahead of its time), in *Two Rode Together* (1961: in many ways a remake of *The Searchers*), as well as—very powerfully—in *Cheyenne Autumn*.

Moreover, in *The Searchers* we have for the first time in Ford an unflinching look specifically at white violence as it is inflicted on the Indians. This comes through most shockingly in the scene at the ruins of Scar's winter camp, where it is clear that the U.S. Cavalry has perpetrated a horrendous massacre of men, women, and children: the first time any-

Introduction

thing like this had ever appeared on an American screen. We see it also in Ethan's shooting Comanches in the back and shooting the eyes out of Indian dead, his maniacal slaughter of buffalo, his riding over an Indian woman holding a baby during the final Ranger attack on the Comanche encampment, his scalping of Scar, above all in his desire to murder the Indianized Debbie. The theme of white violence and hideous brutality, based often on sheer racism, appears in stronger and stronger doses in Ford's films, starting with *The Searchers*. And much of what Ford depicted in the period 1956–64 was based on real historical incident. Yet once the scale of white violence and brutality in the conquest of the West begins to be depicted on the screen, then the traditional tale of the western as a story of heroic endeavor and adventure becomes untellable—untellable, especially, to a predominantly white audience that is paying money to see it. One reason *The Searchers* is a milestone movie is because it was in *The Searchers* that Ford, who had earlier done so much to create the film genre of the western, here began to kill it.[37]

So now we have a better idea of what specific elements in *The Searchers* make up its particularly pessimistic emotional atmosphere. Ford did not take up the idealized pro-Indian tradition of Delmer Daves, and he left his Comanches as savages, while he simultaneously bitterly criticized the racial obsessions and violence of the whites, and simultaneously placed at the center of the film one of the most disturbed figures of the "dark" or "psychological" western. No wonder that the world of *The Searchers,* filmed against a stunning but unremittingly bleak landscape, feels so grim and brutal.

This brings us back to the obsessive fears of whites in *The Searchers* concerning miscegenation. That explosive topic recurs again and again in the film—even in its subsidiary characters and incidents. Thus even Scar, the ferocious Comanche war chief, is the product of miscegenation. Henry Brandon's striking blue eyes were precisely the reason why Ford hired the actor to play Scar in the first place, and the implication was clear to people on the set: Scar himself must be half white, the son of a white captive woman.[38] Meanwhile, Martin Pauley (Jeffrey Hunter), the companion of Ethan Edwards during the years of the search for Debbie, is a young man who is part Indian (one-eighth Cherokee, perhaps more), and very dark-complected—though he has become the adopted son of Martha and Aaron. In the film, it was Ethan who long ago had found Martin and saved his life, when his parents were killed by Comanches (led, it turns out, by Scar); yet throughout the first half of *The Searchers* Ethan consistently rejects Martin precisely because he has learned that Martin himself is "tainted" with Indian blood. "Fella could mistake *you* for a half-breed!" Ethan scowls forbiddingly on first meeting the adult Martin; "Don't call me 'Uncle Ethan'—I *ain't* your uncle!"; "Come on, blanket-head!" But in Alan LeMay's original novel, Martin was fully white. So this is a major change instituted by Ford and Nugent—and as the film progresses, the miscegenated Marty grows ever stronger both morally and even physically, so that by the end of *The Searchers* he is a far more attractive and dependable figure (even though the product of miscegenation) than Ethan can ever be. The idea of a highly sympathetic "half-breed" Marty appears to be an element in the film consciously added by Ford and Nugent with the intention of highlighting Ethan's bitter racism even more.[39]

Martin, in turn, will eventually marry a white girl, Laurie Jorgensen, who seems one of the few normal people in the movie—until, that is, she suddenly turns out to be as racist as Ethan himself. In response to Marty going out one last time to try to bring Debbie home alive, she cries: "Fetch *what* home? The leavings of Comanche bucks, sold time and again to the highest bidder, with savage brats of her own? Do you know what Ethan will do if he has a chance?—He'll put a bullet in her brain! I tell you, Martha would want it that way!" These words, echoing a vicious speech by Ethan against Debbie just a few scenes before, are spoken by a woman wearing a pure white wedding dress, to the man she loves—who is himself part Indian. The self-contradiction here in Laurie's anti-Indian racism—as well as the content of her own sexual fantasies about Debbie's captivity—is striking. It reveals that Ethan's most perverse and destructive racist feelings are not aberrations within his society; on the contrary: they are *representative* of his society, just more overt.[40] Meanwhile, Laurie's brother Brad has charged into Scar's camp early in the film, in a suicidal attempt to take vengeance for the fate of his girlfriend Lucy Edwards, *not* when he learns that she has been killed by the Comanches, but when he learns that she was raped first ("Did they . . . ? Was she . . . ?"). This was a concern of Brad's mother, too.[41] And Martin himself at one point marries a Comanche girl (by mistake), in what is presented as a highly comic incident—the converse of Debbie's "tragedy"—at least to Ethan.[42] Finally, in Ford's finished version of the film, we see Ethan find Martha's blood-soaked ripped-open blue dress amid the smoking ruins of the Edwards household. It is an awful sign, to the audience and to Ethan, of what has happened to Martha—that she was raped by Comanches before being killed. This scene, too, with its terrible implications, we now know was not

Introduction

in Frank Nugent's shooting script, but was added later on location by Ford himself, to emphasize the sexual focus of the film.[43]

The neuroticism here is underlined by the fact that when Debbie is finally found, she has become the luminously beautiful Natalie Wood. And Debbie, who at nine was very sensitive and intelligent, is shown still to be very sensitive and intelligent at fifteen (she is concerned, for instance, with the searchers' safety). That is, she has not been driven crazy by her captivity, or catatonic. Nor—despite the sexual fantasies of Laurie Jorgensen—has she been turned into some sort of degraded Comanche whore. On the contrary: Debbie is not only beautiful and intelligent but also clean (not true of most people in this movie), and she is elegantly dressed, a sort of Comanche princess. And *this* is the person, clearly well treated by the Comanches, Ethan wants to kill. If only because Debbie when she is found among the Indians conforms so perfectly to the traditional Hollywood stereotype of "the valuable woman," the film makes it clear that Ethan is crazy.[44]

In fact, Ethan's conduct is *so* crazy that some commentators push his motivation even beyond his obsessive racism, and offer an even more disturbing explanation for it. Remember that the title song placed Ethan's motivations at the center of the film right from the beginning. But the words of the song have to do with Ethan's relations with his family ("What makes a man ride away from home?")—not his relations with Indians. Now: soon after Ethan's unwelcome and destabilizing homecoming, Scar comes and kills Ethan's brother and the brother's son; he rapes and kills Martha; he kidnaps the female children for himself. In other words, Scar with his violence and his sexuality annihilates the family. But in doing so, these commentators say, he is only beating the violent, sexually frustrated and deeply embittered Ethan to the psychological punch. It is *Ethan* who hates Aaron (and vice versa); it is *Ethan* who wants to possess the women of the family, of whom he has been deprived. Scar can thus be seen as Ethan's dark alter ego. He symbolizes the terrifying desires that must be suppressed if society is to survive—but which in Ethan are barely suppressed.[45]

The identification of Ethan with Scar is a pretty startling concept. But in the "psychological" westerns of the 1950s, the identification of the protagonist with an evil double who symbolized the protagonist's own dark side was not unusual.[46] In *The Searchers* this identification is most evident in the sequence where Ethan and Marty visit Scar's camp in the New Mexico desert. First, Ethan and Scar, two similarly physically imposing men, stand face to face, chest to chest, and mimic each other. And when Ethan remarks that Scar speaks good English ("Somebody teach you?" he pointedly asks—a reference to Debbie), so Scar responds that Ethan speaks good Comanche ("Somebody teach you?" he pointedly asks—and there is a fascinating implication about Ethan's own sexual history in that remark). Then, a moment before the adolescent Debbie appears for the first time and is revealed to Ethan to be Scar's wife, Ford's camera focuses in on the medal from the Emperor Maximilian once given to Ethan, then given by Ethan to nine-year-old Debbie—and which is now worn proudly on *Scar's* chest. That is: in this scene where he is revealed to Ethan as married to Debbie, Scar has literally *become* Ethan, wearing his symbols. Similarly, the film's shooting script by Frank Nugent indicates that the adolescent Debbie is supposed to look exactly like Martha—and Ethan knows and comments on it.[47] Thus at the heart of *The Searchers*, "the Indian Other has done what may not be done, and may not even be admitted to be desired." No wonder Ethan hates Indians, and especially Scar: they symbolize his own unacceptable emotions and desires. Scar is Ethan's scar.[48]

One simple fact demonstrates what Ford and his screenwriter Frank Nugent have done here with Ethan and Scar (and Debbie and Martha): in Alan LeMay's novel on which the film is based, Scar is not married to Debbie. She is merely his adopted daughter, and she truly thinks of him as her father. Naturally, they never have sexual relations. The sexual relationship between Scar and Debbie was invented by Ford and Nugent for the film.[49]

Readers of this volume will see that James F. Brooks in his essay suggests that even in the movie we actually do not know for certain that Debbie is Scar's wife. In the confrontation between Ethan and Scar, Ethan's crucial question about the women in Scar's tepee, "Are they all his wives?" is never answered, so an interesting ambiguity on this exists. But I also note that in the film no relationship between Debbie and Scar other than sexual is ever suggested to the audience, and so the audience therefore naturally will assume it exists. More importantly for the psychological reconstruction of Ethan offered above, we know for certain that *Ethan* believes the relationship between Debbie and Scar is sexual: "She's been living with a buck!" he shouts at Marty after he tries to kill her—"She's nothing but a . . . " If there is an ambiguity here that Ethan did not bother to investigate fully, this only strengthens the case that Scar is fulfilling Ethan's own fantasies.[50]

So at this point we are discussing not merely racism but an important element in racism's *origin:* the projection of unacceptable desires and emotions onto the Other, followed by hatred (and punishment) of that Other. *The Searchers* is a complex movie, but Ford in fact presented this idea with graphic simplicity in two films that bracket *The Searchers* chrono-

Introduction

Scar as Ethan's id (wearing Ethan's medal).

logically. Both in *The Sun Shines Bright* (1953) and in *Sergeant Rutledge* (1960), Ford depicted black men who are falsely accused of raping white women and are then almost lynched, only to have it revealed that the real rapists are white—and are among their chief accusers.

John Wayne himself unintentionally revealed this fundamental psychological aspect of the film in a classic Freudian slip during an interview in 1974. In discussing Ethan, Wayne declared: "He did what he had to do. The Indians fucked his wife." But what could Wayne have been thinking of? In the film the central problem within the Edwards family is—precisely—that Martha is *not* Ethan's wife. Or was Wayne thinking perhaps of Debbie, who looks exactly like Martha? In another interview, Wayne actually presented a fantasy of Ethan and Debbie living together on the Edwards ranch, in a loving relationship, after the end of the film. No doubt Wayne meant this innocently; even so, what he was fantasizing was Ethan living in satisfaction for the rest of his life with Martha-like Debbie—his mission (and his desires) finally fulfilled.[51]

Deep confusion about kinship relations, such as Wayne's above, is another mark of *The Searchers;* like obsessive fear of miscegenation, it

Arthur M. Eckstein

Scar and Ethan confront each other.

appears throughout the movie. Is the adopted, part-Indian Marty a member of the Edwards family, or not? (When Martin claims that Debbie is his sister, Ethan savagely responds, "She's your *nothin*!"). Is the "polluted" Debbie part of the Edwards family, or not? (After seeing Debbie as the wife of Scar, Ethan disowns her in his will, on the grounds that he has no blood kin, and leaves all the Edwards property to . . . part- Indian Marty). Racist Laurie Jorgensen is in love with a man who is not only part Indian but who is dressed in her dead brother's clothes, clothes Laurie gave to him. Is Martin married to the Comanche girl Look (he is, under Comanche law), or not? Is Debbie married to Scar, or not? At the end of the movie, is the rescued Debbie going to be adopted by the Jorgensens? (It looks that way.) Such confusion about kinship relations in *The Searchers* is in fact an accurate reflection of the high flexibility of such relations on the historical, culturally fluid American frontier.[52] But it also means that *The Searchers* is obsessed, from a whole variety of perspectives, with questions of family.[53]

This is all the more remarkable because in a real sense *The Searchers* was made *by* a family. John Ford (over sixty at the time he directed *The Searchers*), was the director; his son Patrick Ford (whom *he* would later dis-

Introduction

own in his will) was the associate producer. Ford's brother-in-law Wingate Smith was the assistant director; Ford's son-in-law Ken Curtis played the country bumpkin who almost marries Laurie Jorgensen (a comic version, clearly, of the tragic "false marriage" of Aaron and Martha, just as the marriage of Marty and Look is a comic version of the tragic marriage of Scar and Debbie). Dorothy Jordan (Martha) was the wife of Merian C. Cooper, an old friend of Ford's who was also producer of the film. Mrs. Jorgensen (Olive Carey) and her son Brad (Harry Carey, Jr.) really were biological mother and son. Ford had known Olive Carey since he was nineteen and she was eighteen, and Harry Carey, Jr., grew up calling Ford "Uncle Jack." Lt. Greenhill—who in the film owes his command solely to his father Colonel Greenhill—was played by Patrick Wayne, the son of John Wayne (obviously there is an inside joke here); in one scene, Wayne actually calls him "son" (ditto). And Debbie as a nine-year-old was played by Lana Wood, the younger sister of Natalie Wood who played Debbie as a teenager.[54]

Among this family, as the film was being made, there was little tension. Ford was famous for being a terrible tyrant as a director, not taking artistic advice from anyone, and bullying his actors; but on *The Searchers*, though Ford was often his tyrannical self, the set (we are told) was a happy one. Participants were also impressed with a special sense of seriousness during the filming: not only Ford's but Wayne's (who rarely stepped out of the Ethan character). Perhaps it was the nature of the story—or perhaps it was because people knew that Ford's career was on the line.[55]

The climactic moment of *The Searchers* comes when Ethan, having searched for Debbie for seven years, and having fought in the final Ranger assault on Scar's camp (and having savagely scalped Scar), pursues the terrified teenage Debbie into a canyon: she is certain that her uncle is going to kill her, and the film has been constructed so that the audience fears this as well. But at the very last moment, as she cringes from Ethan in fear, he lifts her up with both his hands—echoing a paternal gesture made by him early in the film—and then sweeps her into his arms, saying softly, "Let's go home, Debbie." In this scene, the background music becomes "Martha's Theme" (i.e., "Lorena"). Ethan will not kill Debbie, but rather he will return her to white civilization, in the form of the Jorgensen household.

Why does Ethan not kill Debbie? For an hour and a half the audience has been led to believe that he will, and at least half of the tension in the film derives from that terrible expectation.[56] And during Ethan and Marty's visit to Scar's desert camp a few scenes (or rather, months) earlier, the audience has already seen Ethan *try* to kill Debbie with his pistol ("to

19

put a bullet in her brain," as Laurie Jorgensen approvingly says)—only a Comanche arrow, shot into Ethan's shoulder, prevents it and saves her life. Ethan's action in sparing Debbie is thus as complex a mystery as his original obsession to murder her—and of course we are never directly told what is going on. Ford did not work that way: as with the scenes at the beginning of the film involving Ethan's relationship with Martha, the audience is expected to think for itself.[57]

Some early critics of *The Searchers* dismissed the sparing of Debbie as simply a happy ending tacked on for the sake of what was, after all, only a western—that is, a children's movie.[58] But whatever else *The Searchers* is, it is not a movie for children—not with its central themes being racism, illicit sexual desire that threatens the family, and miscegenation.[59] A better explanation is based on the appearance of "Martha's Theme" in the scene where Ethan spares Debbie—which seems to indicate that when the crisis comes, Debbie is just too much like Martha for Ethan to kill.[60] Indeed, in the shooting script it was precisely at this point, with Debbie on the ground and Ethan pointing his drawn revolver directly at her (and the camera looking down his pistol right at her), that Ethan was to say to her that she looks exactly like Martha. Ford cut this line from the film, however, and completely redid the scene, leaving the audience on its own.[61] And Ethan is such a frightening figure in the movie, his feelings about his (rightful) exclusion from the family so complex, that many commentators find the explanation that Debbie looks like Martha to be too simple by itself. They suggest in addition that with his scalping of Scar (who had been killed by Marty), Ethan has finally purged his soul of the demons of sexual jealousy, guilt, self-hatred, racism, and revenge that have ruled him since he first appeared on the screen. In this reading of the film, it is the destruction of the symbol of Ethan's darkest wishes—Ethan's mutilation of the dead Scar, symbol of his own disfigured psyche—that finally frees Ethan to accept Debbie. He no longer has to kill her as a scapegoat for his own unacceptable "polluted" feelings—because Scar has served that purpose.[62]

Some people will think this is reading too much dark psychology into Ethan. But the heroes of the 1950s "psychological" westerns often had such classic inner conflicts, and the use of Frank Nugent's shooting script allows us to see how deeply and consciously Ford and Nugent, and then Ford by himself, worked to make Ethan's psyche more and more sinister. This is the subject to which we now turn. The fact is that the Ethan figure of Alan LeMay's novel (there called Amos Edwards) exhibited little of the neurotic,

Introduction

antisocial behavior of the man in the film. Much more was added in Nugent's script (supervised by Ford), but we now know that the full version of the hate-filled, obsessive Ethan Edwards of *The Searchers* was created only during the filming of the movie itself, through crucial artistic decisions made by Ford. Those decisions went in only one direction—which suggests that commentators have not been reading anything dark into Ethan that John Ford did not wish them to see.

Thus in Alan LeMay's novel (which Ford and Nugent read closely), Amos Edwards is indeed secretly in love with Martha; but the simpler and nobler man of the novel never lets slip any sign of this, and the simpler Martha of the novel neither knows of it nor reciprocates it. Amos therefore does not constitute a deadly threat to the family, as Ethan does.[63] Again, in the novel the Ethan figure is no outlaw (unlike Ford's Ethan), and he is idealistic about the eventual coming of civilization to the frontier; it is *he* in fact who gives the optimistic speech on this theme which in the film is given by the motherly Mrs. Jorgensen, and which even then—taken word for word from the novel—Ford feels compelled to gently satirize as too optimistic ("She used to be a school-teacher, you know"). How different Ford's film would be, how different our impression of *Ethan* would be, if—as in the novel—he gave that optimistic speech. But the embittered, homeless Ethan of the film does not care about civilization: the violent frontier is his natural environment.[64] Even more centrally, Amos in the novel never wants to kill Debbie; he just wants to rescue her. Yet the most famous and disturbing aspect of the film is that Ethan *does* want to kill Debbie, and in the sequence in Scar's desert camp we actually see him try. Ford and Nugent invented this—just as they invented the sexual relationship between Debbie and Scar, which does not exist in the novel.[65] Finally, in the novel Amos Edwards dies a martyr to the traditional heroic code: he refuses to shoot a Comanche woman in the back (she might or might not be Debbie)—and she then turns and shoots *him*. The sinister Ethan of the movie—who does not hesitate to shoot either whites or Indians in the back, and who howls with laughter when Martin physically abuses Look—is of course far removed from any such chivalry.[66]

Or *was* the Ethan of the movie really so removed from such chivalry? Evidence from Frank Nugent's shooting script here brings an important insight into Ford's method of work in darkening Ethan's character. It turns out that in the shooting script for the movie, and apparently even in *The Searchers'* filmed rough cut, there was a sequence in which Ethan spoke out on behalf of defenseless women—on behalf even of defenseless

Comanche women. And John Ford decided to cut this sequence from the finished film.

The sequence portrayed a confrontation between Ethan and a cavalry commander who clearly is supposed to be George Armstrong Custer. His men have just perpetrated the massacre of the Comanche winter encampment found by Ethan and Marty—with men, women, and children all slaughtered (a scene that remained in the movie and which is still shocking today). The commander looks like Custer and wears Custer's famous fancy uniform. He is holding forth to newspapermen from the East about the bravery of his regiment—with himself in the lead—in the "battle" that has just taken place. Ethan enters and sourly interrupts him, remarking that next time he might try attacking where the *men* are, instead of the women and children. Ethan then suggests that if any female white captives have been killed in the fighting (which turns out to be the case), they were killed by the cavalry, not by the Comanches—because the soldiers had been shooting indiscriminately into the camp. Custer, furious, orders Ethan from the room. What follows is the famous scene between a grim Ethan and the pitiful white female captives who have somehow survived the attack.[67]

The confrontation between Ethan and Custer must have originally attracted Ford because Custer was a man whom Ford despised. Ford's film *Fort Apache* (1948) was the very first Hollywood attack on Custer's image, and Ford's production notes for *The Searchers* describe Custer as "Inept . . . arrogant . . . a phony . . . a glory-hunter."[68] The notes also show that Ford intended the winter sequence to represent the historical massacre of Cheyennes which Custer perpetrated at "the battle of the Washita" in western Oklahoma in November 1868: in Nugent's script, Custer even "misidentifies" the Comanches as Cheyennes.[69] The terrible events at the Washita would be filmed fourteen years after *The Searchers* by Arthur Penn in *Little Big Man* (1970), and it is this massacre which is threatened in the last winter scenes of *Dances With Wolves* (1990)—but we can now see that Ford got there first. He was an expert on the real history of the American West.[70]

The confrontation between Ethan and Custer must have appeared in *The Searchers*' filmed rough cut, because we actually have a publicity photo of this scene.[71] But it has disappeared from the finished version of the film. Its removal could not have been a decision made, for instance, by the management at Warner Brothers: the whole reason why Ford had formed his own independent production company with Merian Cooper in 1947— Argosy Pictures—was to ensure that he always had complete artistic control over his films; Warner Brothers merely provided postproduction facil-

Introduction

ities and acted as the distributor of Ford's finished product, in return for a hefty share of the profits. In creating his own independent production company, Ford was in fact typical of those serious-minded directors (John Huston, Frank Capra, William Wyler) who, upon returning from World War II (like Ford), refused to submit their artistry anymore to the studio system and its control of projects from above by bosses.[72] Frank Nugent himself testifies that throughout the period he worked for Ford and Argosy Pictures, Ford always had total control of the rough cut.[73] Thus it was John Ford himself, during the process of final editing, who decided to eliminate the Custer sequence from *The Searchers*.

Why did he do it? To give up the sequence must have been difficult (Ethan meets Custer). But if the confrontation between Ethan and Custer remained in the film, Ethan would become a much more conventional figure. It is one of the main conventions of Hollywood westerns that the hero does his best to defend women; Ethan's replacement of this convention by his desire to murder Debbie is one reason he appears so disturbed (and disturbing). Yet in the scene with Custer, Ethan speaks out strongly for the protection of women (even, in this case, Comanche women), expounds the traditional heroic code that it is the role of a man to engage in combat with other armed men, never women, and expresses contempt for those men (such as Custer) who do not follow the code. And this explains why the Custer sequence had to go. If it had been left in the film, the audience of *The Searchers* would have had a clear clue that Ethan, whatever his internal demons, could never kill Debbie—because that would be a terrible violation of his heroic code. The result would have been to make Ethan's internal demons much less important to the film. Ford knew, either intellectually or instinctively, that the Custer scene—whatever satisfaction it gave him—was therefore "wrong."

Conversely, the elimination of Ethan's lecture to Custer on proper manly behavior, the elimination of his assertion of the heroic code, makes Ethan a significantly darker character than he was in the final shooting script. The Ethan of the finished film never asserts the traditional heroic code, because he never follows it. He is a character perfectly capable of killing his niece, because he has no limits. And thus his internal demons remain central to the film. Ford wanted it that way, and edited the film to make sure it played that way.[74]

And here is another example of the same process. In the finished version of *The Searchers*, the winter sequence in the fort ends with a famous dolly-in to a close-up of Ethan's deeply shadowed, unshaven, and embittered face as he stares with hatred at the pitiful white women whom the cavalry has managed to recover from the Comanches (he has just said, "They ain't white—not anymore"). The imagery here is very powerful, and as Martin Winkler has noted, it is the image of a traditional western *villain*—not a hero.[75] What makes this observation even more intriguing is that in Frank Nugent's shooting script there is not the slightest indication for such a camera shot, nor is there space for it. Rather, in the script the sequence at the fort ends with Ethan expressing what seems sincere concern about Debbie's fate ("Time's running out"), and he sincerely thanks an army officer for providing what may be an important clue to her whereabouts (New Mexico).[76] Ford eliminated that part of the script entirely (the cost is that in the finished film the searchers appear to wander off to New Mexico by accident); he cut the sequence short instead, with the dramatic dolly-in to Ethan's dark, villainous and terrifying face—a shot that came out of his own imagination. It was a crucial artistic decision, for the resulting images imply to the audience that when Ethan finds Debbie he is indeed going to murder her because "she ain't white." These extraordinary images also imply that Ethan is close to insane.

The same holds true with even more intensity in the scene where, during the final Ranger assault on Scar's village, Ethan is shown scalping Scar. Ethan charges his great black horse right into Scar's tepee, finds Scar dead, dismounts, and then—in a close-up—lifts Scar's head up, pulls out a knife, and begins (with discordant music in the background) to mutilate him; the camera turns away only at the very last moment. A second later we see Ethan, remounted on his horse, emerging from the tepee with Scar's bloody scalp held in one hand, his eyes glazed. Debbie sees him too, and, filled with terror, runs away.

Ethan's scalping of Scar and then his charging around holding the bloody scalp is one of the most shocking sequences in *The Searchers*. It has caused much comment, because it is unheard of for a white heroic figure to engage in scalping, let alone ride around in triumph holding the scalp. Instead, scalping is traditionally associated with the most primitive savages—white or Indian. John Ford's own attitude toward whites who engage in scalping is made plain in *Cheyenne Autumn* (1964); when two repulsive white thugs enter a Dodge City saloon carrying Cheyenne scalps they have taken, even Wyatt Earp—portrayed in this film as a total cynic—is so appalled that he orders them thrown out of the saloon as men unfit for human company.[77] Thus it is not surprising that some critics have seen in Ethan's act of mutilating a corpse his final descent into madness:[78] the dis-

Introduction

cordant music tells the whole story. What *is* surprising is that Ford prevailed upon John Wayne—an actor much concerned with his image on screen—to do this scene at all.[79]

And this scene, too, was not in the script. In the shooting script that Nugent wrote and that Ford took out to Monument Valley, Ethan does *not* scalp Scar; the idea never occurs to him. All he does is find Scar dead in the tepee, and then he rides off looking for Debbie.[80] This means that Ford personally and spontaneously added to the film the idea of the horrific scene of Ethan scalping Scar and then riding around with the bloody scalp. He made the addition while on location in Arizona, and it bears all his most personal hallmarks: it is powerful images, actions, and (discordant) music—not words.[81]

Since scalping was a terrible transgression of the heroic code, and given Ford's contemptuous portrayal of whites who engage in it, the director's decision to add this act to Ethan's character shows his wish to create an Ethan who is problematic in the extreme. The madness which the act implies is strengthened, of course, by the audience's "knowledge" that Ethan is determined to follow up this horror with an even greater one—the murder of Debbie. And once Ethan's scalping of Scar and then his riding around with the bloody scalp shows the audience exactly what Ethan is capable of, their anxiety over Debbie's fate becomes even more intense. It also makes Ethan's ultimate sparing of Debbie's life even more mysterious—a miracle. No wonder that Ethan's final act of mercy has provoked so much psychological speculation.

There is one last great scene in *The Searchers,* and one last mystery which the film poses. *The Searchers* ends in another sequence without dialogue: merely moving images, with music in bittersweet tones in the background. Ethan returns Debbie to the Jorgensen homestead: she rides huddled against his chest, still dressed in her Comanche clothes. As we look from inside the dark Jorgensen house out through the doorway into the desert—an intentional echo of *The Searchers'* very first scene at the Edwards house, two hours (and seven years) ago—Debbie is taken from Ethan by Mr. and Mrs. Jorgensen, and enters the house (walking past the camera); then Laurie and Martin follow, their future together assured; and Ethan is left alone, standing in the doorway. He turns and directly faces the camera, a dark silhouette against the bright desert behind him. He briefly grips his right arm, as if wounded and in pain; then, instead of entering the house with all the others, he turns and walks out into the desert wind and dust. The dark door quickly closes on him.

This has become one of the most famous ending scenes in Hollywood history. Why does Ford not have Ethan enter the house—that is, come home—with all the other characters in the film?

One could of course argue that with his mission accomplished, with the Comanches defeated, with Debbie safely returned to white society, Ethan—in the tradition of the western hero—is now simply going on to other adventures. The parallel would be with the famous ending of George Stevens's *Shane* (1953), a consciously mythic ending made just three years before, where the godlike blond hero dressed in white buckskins (Alan Ladd) rides off on his white horse into the mountains as a child calls out to him, begging him to stay. Another parallel, in this line of thinking, would be the ending of every episode of the popular television western series *The Lone Ranger*.[82] But such an "optimistic" interpretation seems out of line with the deeply pessimistic tone of *The Searchers*. And the sinister, embittered Ethan Edwards—who is visually dark, almost always wears dark clothing and a black hat and rides a black horse—is anything but a traditional blond western hero. In fact, unlike Shane, Ethan does not even get to kill the "villain" (which is the ultimate sign of the hero in westerns); it is Martin (the secondary character) who kills Scar—all Ethan does is mutilate the corpse.[83] Moreover, while Shane has saved the settler community from dangerous gunmen in his movie, the only person Ethan has saved the community from in *The Searchers* is himself. No wonder that no one invites Ethan into the household at the end of *The Searchers*, and that when he walks away, no one calls him back.

And that, surely, is his tragedy: excluded from society and family at the beginning of the film, so too he is excluded at the end. Even in the "psychological" westerns of this period, we are usually given a relatively happy or at least hopeful ending, but once more *The Searchers* is different.[84] The ending scene of *The Searchers* retains a tragic edge; the refrain of the theme song, heard wistfully over the film's final extraordinary images, indicates that Ethan is still a severely disturbed person: "A man may search his heart and soul, go searchin' way out there, / His peace of mind he knows he'll find, but where, O Lord, Lord where? / Ride away."

Moreover, the question of why Ethan fails to enter the house with everyone else becomes all the more central to the meaning of *The Searchers* once we take into account the *other* ending of the film: that is, the ending in Frank Nugent's script, the ending that Ford originally took out to Monument Valley. In the shooting script's ending, Ethan *does* join everyone

Introduction

Final doorway shot: Ethan, excluded from home, holding his wounded arm.

else in entering the house; in fact, carrying Debbie and with a beatific smile on his face, he leads everyone in.[85]

The shooting script's ending of *The Searchers*—an ending in which a protective and almost motherly Ethan leads everyone home—shows that at some point during location work in Monument Valley, John Ford made the extraordinary decision to reverse that ending, and to film instead the far darker ending which we now have. "Our" ending of *The Searchers*, in other words, comes from Ford's conscious, last-minute decision to separate Ethan sharply from all others: he violated the script in order to do it. Ford's decision here brings to a culmination all his other decisions (first made in conjunction with Frank Nugent, then made by himself while actually filming) which bring into question Ethan's conduct and Ethan's character. We now know that Ford, in the very last moment of the movie, intentionally excluded Ethan from home.

Strictly speaking, we cannot know why Ford changed the original ending of the film so radically. One possible reason is that Ford is administering the final punishment to Ethan for his savage racism (which included rejection of family). After all, the Comanche-raised Debbie does enter the house (still wearing her Comanche clothes), as does the part-Indian Marty (now with his white wife-to-be). Ford excludes only Ethan, the man obsessed with racial purity. In other words, it is Fordian social criticism that forbids Ethan from entering the house. If so, of course, then Ethan is a true scapegoat, since Laurie's vicious outburst against Debbie has shown that Ethan's entire society is racist, and that Ethan is not really a mysterious aberration within it. Thus Brian Henderson suggests that for white audiences, "Our racial prejudice and our guilt are placed on his shoulders, then he is criticized, excluded, lampooned. . . . He is excluded for our sins." And that is why the ending of *The Searchers* is so moving to white audiences.[86]

Some commentators seek to shift the focus even deeper, and point precisely to Ethan's rejection of his family. They see Ethan not only as a punished exemplar of society's racism but in addition—and even more importantly—as a now-punished, previously terrifying threat to that family, a threat he has been, in one form or another, since the first moment of the movie. It is true that Ethan has not murdered Debbie, an act which would have plunged him totally into the abyss; but civilization still requires that he be shut out.[87] It would be too simple to believe that his last-minute sparing of Debbie has suddenly and completely redeemed him, cleansing him of all his previous sinister impulses. That *would* be a happy ending, and indeed *was* the happy original ending in Frank Nugent's shooting script. But Ford (we now know) consciously rejected this ending: evidently he was too much of a pessimist, or too sophisticated an artist, for it. So in the final version of *The Searchers* Ethan at the end still has not come fully to terms with the interior demons that have driven him throughout the picture: it was forces expressive of those demons that had destroyed Aaron and Martha, destroyed Ben and Lucy, that threatened Debbie, and he is still "tainted" by them.[88] As Martin Winkler puts it: in a reversal of the situation of Oedipus, who was guilty in deed but innocent in intention, Ethan is guilty of intention though innocent (at the very last moment) of deed, and thus he is by no means absolved of guilt—as his continuing status as a social outcast attests.[89]

Ethan's loneliness, exclusion, and perhaps (unconscious) sense of guilt at the end of *The Searchers* are dramatized in the sad gesture he makes as he is left by himself at the open doorway. This gesture—Ethan's sudden gripping of his right arm as if in pain—has itself become a very famous image. On the surface, it might refer simply to a physical wound: at Scar's

Introduction

camp in the New Mexico desert Ethan had been badly hit by a Comanche arrow (in the left shoulder, though he's shown bandaged on the right as well). But the way John Wayne told the story, the gesture actually originated during the filming of the (revised) ending as a spontaneous physical act by Wayne, done to honor the actor Harry Carey, Sr., who had often used a similar gesture in his silent films. It acknowledged Olive Carey, the actor's widow, who—as motherly Mrs. Jorgensen—had just come through the doorway and past the camera. Olive Carey burst into tears when Wayne did it.[90] But though the gesture may have originated spontaneously with Wayne in homage to Carey, it was John Ford who of course decided to keep the gesture in the film. Harry Carey, Sr., had been one of Ford's own chief mentors during the early part of the director's career.[91] But more was involved here than mere sentiment. The gesture even as Harry Carey, Sr., used it signified loss and sadness.[92] In Ethan's case he had received the arrow wound at a very significant moment: when he was about to kill Debbie at Scar's camp (the Comanche arrow saved her life). Moreover, at a crucial moment earlier in the narrative of *The Searchers* (though, as these things so often happen because of production scheduling, actually filmed later than the film's "final" scene), we see Ethan make exactly the same gesture. It occurs when he comments to Martin that he is hoping that Debbie will be killed by the Comanches when the Rangers launch their final raid into Scar's camp ("That's what I'm counting on," he says grimly; "I know you are," responds Martin bitterly), and Ethan then tries to veto Martin's attempt to go into the camp in secret to get Debbie out alive: "I say NO!" decrees Ethan, holding his right arm as if in pain. Luckily, he is overruled.

Of course, visual images in movies, and especially in complicated and subtle films such as *The Searchers,* are notoriously overdetermined. But it should now be clear that whatever the origins of Ethan's gesture as performed in the last scene, Ford's decision to keep the gesture, and also to *reuse* that gesture at an earlier dramatic moment, has transformed it into a symbol—a symbol of Ethan's desire to see Debbie destroyed. That is why he cannot enter the house that symbolized civilization and home. In an interview with Peter Bogdanovich, John Ford himself described *The Searchers* as "the tragedy of a loner . . . [who] could never really be a part of the family;" and he assented to the idea that this was the meaning of the door closing on Ethan.[93] So at the end of the film, we see Ethan as he was at the beginning: alone, lonely, driven, and deeply wounded. This is not reading too much into the film. Ford intended us to see it.

Arthur M. Eckstein

"I say 'No.'" Ethan, holding his wounded arm as if in pain, condemns Debbie to die in the final Ranger attack.

We have seen that *The Searchers,* while visually containing its full share of traditional "heroic" frontier images, is simultaneously subversive of the western genre in many ways; and it is most subversive here. The Euro-American "imperial narrative" of the nineteenth century, of which the American western film is an important form, tells a specific story: the transition from preexisting barbarism and disorder, through conquest, to the imposition of order. Literary critics argue that at the deepest level— odd though this sounds—the imperial story structure therefore partakes of the story structure of comedy (from initial disorder to happy ending).[94] But in *The Searchers,* while the sociopolitical disorder existing at the start of the film has by its end been suppressed by the conquest of the Comanches and the destruction of Scar, Ethan Edwards's personal disorder—which is the heart of the film and is its focus—still remains, right to the last camera shot. Ford, by depicting this, thereby raises doubts about the entire western project: not, perhaps, about its ultimate aim of imposing order and "civilization" (he is not *that* subversive), but about the high human costs involved, and the brutal methods used.[95] No ending in a west-

Introduction

ern (even in the "dark" westerns of the 1950s) is as somber as the ending of *The Searchers*. Ford has filmed, as he himself says, a tragedy.

"*Ford* has filmed a tragedy." Every production of a large-scale film is by necessity a collaborative effort: such films cannot be made by one person, however brilliant, working alone.[96] So in what sense is *The Searchers* John Ford's film (as the title of our volume declares)? In what sense is Ford—the director—the "author" of *The Searchers*? The information collected above on the stages through which the story told in the release print version of *The Searchers* developed over time allows us to answer this question much more decisively than can usually be done for large-scale Hollywood films. And this is particularly important because *The Searchers*, while controversial, is seen by numerous major critics as an outstanding achievement of post–World War II American culture. Hence Garry Wills in his study of John Wayne as a cultural icon gives *The Searchers* an entire chapter—the only film to receive a chapter of Wills's book all to itself.[97]

The Searchers is clearly the product of many talents: this includes the original novelist Alan LeMay, the cast of actors in the film, and the film's veteran production crew. One can point to the acting of John Wayne, Jeffrey Hunter, and Dorothy Jordan (Martha) on the one hand, and to the stunning color cinematography of Winton Hoch, himself already the winner of three Academy Awards for cinematography, on the other—and go right down to the stunt men who performed the many dangerous riding stunts.[98] Moreover, the shooting script that Frank Nugent wrote (with Ford's collaboration) certainly forms the basic outline of the narrative that is told in the eventual film. One might also note the contribution of Patrick Ford, the director's son: as associate producer, he organized a complex but highly efficient shooting schedule that made the principal filming in Monument Valley in the summer of 1955 go extremely smoothly despite the 115-degree heat.[99]

Yet having said all this, what is remarkable about *The Searchers* is how much of the final artistic vision is John Ford's alone. Thus it was Ford who cut from the film those scripted scenes at the fort where Ethan appeared relatively noble compared to Custer and seemed sincerely concerned about Debbie's fate, and it was Ford who added instead the now famous dolly-in to a close-up of Ethan's sinister, shadowed, hate-filled face. It was Ford who added the shocking scene where Ethan scalps Scar (and it was Ford who persuaded John Wayne to do it)—whereas he cut the dialogue that originally explained why Ethan at the last moment does not murder

Debbie, leaving this unexpected act of mercy on his part far more mysterious. It was Ford, too, who added the scene—shocking in its own way—in which Ethan and Martha, in saying goodbye to each other, make the danger of their incestuous adultery very clear. And Ford alone made the crucial decision to reverse the "happy ending" that originally existed in Nugent's script, in which Ethan rejoins the human community—substituting instead the ending that has become famous, in which the much harsher Ethan of the final version of the film is excluded from home.[100]

Most of the radical transformations Ford worked on Nugent's shooting script seem actually to have occurred *ad hoc* out on location in Monument Valley: so when we view *The Searchers* we are looking at the results of a true high-wire act by Ford. But it is *Ford's* high-wire act. He did the major script cutting and rearranging, was responsible for the final editing of the film, added crucially important material of his own and filmed it immediately on the spot, and reversed the original happy ending he had taken out on location. The fact is that none of the most famous and most moving scenes in *The Searchers* are in Nugent's script. Even the famous opening and closing shots in the final version of the movie, a point-of-view from inside a dark house with a door opening suddenly on the great desert and then—two hours later—finally closing on it, were Ford's own invention; these shots are the *opposite* of the point of view in Nugent's script, which in both cases was from the desert looking toward the house.[101] It is further striking how many of those famous and moving scenes of *The Searchers* are in fact examples of "silent" cinema: images and actions with only music to accompany them. John Ford, after all, had started in Hollywood in 1914; in his crucial interventions in Nugent's script, he depended on his oldest techniques.

There have always been stories about how Ford savagely refused to take any advice while directing a movie—not at any time. Even the greatest Hollywood stars found this out—while Frank Nugent himself downgraded the importance of the screenwriter for any Ford film, because in the end the film was Ford's vision and no one else's.[102] We are not dealing here with mere eccentricity—though Ford was an alcoholic, and apparently subject to periodic very severe depression.[103] Rather, we are dealing with Ford's fierce confidence in his view of how a film should unfold. By 1956 that confidence, that obstinacy, was backed by almost forty years as a director—and by six Academy Awards (the last in 1952). Moreover, the whole point of starting his personal production company Argosy Pictures (which made *The Searchers*) was to ensure his total artistic control over his

Introduction

product. What we can now say in the case of *The Searchers*, thanks especially to a comparison of Frank Nugent's shooting script with the release print we actually see on the screen, is that in this film John Ford came as close as any one person can, in what is by necessity a group project, to imposing that total artistic control. We can say with real conviction, then, that he is the "author" of *The Searchers*.

This introduction to *The Searchers* ends with a short account of the growth of the film's reputation, and the possible reasons behind that growth.

As noted at the beginning of this essay, *The Searchers* received only mixed reviews when it opened in May 1956. Some critics recognized that it was unusual ("John Wayne actually acts!" said one); but others thought it a rather standard John Ford horse opera.[104] The movie did well at the box office, and made money, though not spectacularly.[105] And *The Searchers* was ignored at Academy Awards time (even Winton Hoch's magnificent cinematography was passed by)—as has been the usual fate of westerns over the decades.[106] In the immediately succeeding years, serious film critics such as Lindsay Anderson and Pauline Kael issued unenthusiastic or even dismissive reviews.[107] We now know, from the memoirs especially of John Wayne's wife Pilar Pallete Wayne, how bitterly disappointed Ford was at the mixed reception which *The Searchers* originally received: he had thought of it as a master work, and thought seriously of retiring after having made it. Instead, he gritted his teeth and went on to make movies for another ten years.[108]

The reputation of *The Searchers* has certainly grown higher over time— and until recently was very high indeed. Why and how the prestige of a film grows and declines over time is a mysterious process, and surely much must depend upon the real qualities inherent in the finished film itself. I think that for most viewers, *The Searchers* has at least two crucially important qualities: its sheer, breathtaking visual beauty (the pleasure of looking at it) and a grim story of great human drama. But one other key factor in the future high reputation of *The Searchers* can already be found in a letter that a friend wrote to Ford in May 1956: older children who saw the movie were absolutely riveted to their seats.[109] Among those older children who saw *The Searchers* when it first opened was an entire future generation of film directors and critics—and they saw *The Searchers* as it was meant to be seen, on the enormous wide screens that had just come into use in movie theaters, not as it is mostly seen now, on a small television screen (videotape or DVD). Among this group of future Hollywood leaders who say they were transfixed by *The Searchers* when they first saw it in 1956 are Steven Spielberg, Martin

Scorsese, George Lucas, Paul Schrader, John Milius, and Danny Peary. Because Ford had not made a western in the previous five years, *The Searchers* was for most of this group their first experience with one of his western films; and with stunning visual images combined with a terrifying family tragedy, it is clear that *The Searchers* showed them the power that movie-making could achieve.[110] The story is that the young Steven Spielberg made a version of *The Searchers* in his backyard in suburban Phoenix in the late 1950s—with a background of bed sheets painted to look like Monument Valley.[111]

By 1980 or so, this generation of filmmakers and critics—the so-called Baby Boomers (born in the years just after World War II)—were already becoming the dominant force in Hollywood. Scorsese, Lucas, Schrader, and Milius had already directed famous films which quite consciously incorporated *The Searchers*' most famous scenes or basic themes and transferred them to new environments: *Dillinger* (Milius), *Taxi Driver* (Scorsese), *Star Wars* (Lucas; Spielberg produced), *Hardcore* (Schrader).[112] The statements of these important young directors, producers, and writers about *The Searchers* now became the benchmarks by which people judged Ford's picture, and those statements were effusive:

—"The best American movie—and its protagonist, Ethan Edwards, is the one classic character in American films" (Milius—who, like John Wayne, named one of his children Ethan).

—"I make sure to see *The Searchers* at least once a year; there are movies that are better acted or better written but *The Searchers* plays the fullest artistic hand—the best American film" (Schrader).

—"Ford's uses of emotions, the actors' changes of expression, are so subtle, so magnificent! I see it once or even twice a year" (Scorsese).

—"*The Searchers* has so many superlatives going for it: it's John Wayne's best performance; it's a study in dramatic framing and composition; it contains the single most harrowing moment in any film I've ever seen." (Spielberg)[113]

The impact of all this is clearly shown in the rise to prominence of *The Searchers* in the worldwide poll of professional film critics undertaken by the prestigious British film journal *Sight and Sound* every ten years, which asks critics to list in order of preference the ten greatest films ever made. In 1962 *The Searchers* is missing from the list; this is understandable, given the film's original lukewarm reception. Nor does *The Searchers* appear in the *Sight and Sound* critics poll in 1972. This, too, is not surprising—because

Introduction

by the early 1970s John Ford's reputation had reached a low point with established critics; he was viewed as old-fashioned, sentimental, and ultimately both socially and cinematically (artistically) conservative and non-experimental.[114] Yet already by then attention was being drawn to the film: Joseph McBride and John Wilmington had published the first major study of the psychology of *The Searchers* in *Sight and Sound* (autumn 1971).

Then, as the older generation of critics passed from the scene, the situation began to change. In the 1982 poll, a full twenty-five years after it was made, *The Searchers* appeared for the first time on the critics' list of ten greatest films—tied for tenth place. And then in 1992 it rocketed to its current status: a spectacular fifth place in the critics' list of ten greatest films.[115] Moreover, strong critical acclaim is matched by true popularity.[116] When the American Film Institute held a special showing of *The Searchers* at the Kennedy Center in Washington, D.C., in 1996 to celebrate the fortieth anniversary of the premiering of the film, the auditorium was packed; and the same was true when *The Searchers* was shown at the Warner Brothers Retrospective in Washington in 1997. And in the blockbuster *Star Wars II: Attack of the Clones* (2002), director George Lucas *again* pays a long *hommage* to *The Searchers:* Anakin Skywalker's attempt at night to save his mother in the barbarian encampment in the desert follows—literally scene for scene and shot for shot—Martin Pauley's attempt at night to save Debbie from Scar's camp at the climax of Ford's film. Anakin fails to save his mother, of course—it is the traumatic event in his life—and the following scene of her burial is an homage to the burial scene of the Edwards family in *The Searchers:* the same morning light, the same single figure (Martin, in *The Searchers*) on his knees.

Yet in the new American Film Institute Poll of the opinions of prominent Americans (1998), *The Searchers* sinks to the bottom of the top 100 greatest films—96th. That is a far cry from fifth place. The American Film Institute poll and its sample polling population has been bitterly criticized;[117] and the reasons for the failure of *The Searchers* to reach a higher ranking than 96th are unclear.[118] This situation reminds us that the reputations of films are fluid and changeable—and that the reputation of *The Searchers,* from 1956 onward, has always been controversial. So here at the end we confront our readers with crucial questions:

—Has a great movie (and a great director) been rescued by professional film critics and the "Baby Boomer" generation of Hollywood titans from the unjust snobbery of 1956 toward westerns?

—Or has the reputation of *The Searchers* gradually become overblown via the influence of film school–educated directors such as Scorsese and Spielberg, when in reality Ford's film is just a good "dark western," but one of many that were being made in Hollywood in the 1950s?

—Or, to go to the opposite pole, should *The Searchers* really be seen as a film which, despite some overpraised subtleties, is basically just an example of an objectionable "white conquest" genre that has now died away—and an example in which the depiction of relations between the genders is particularly disturbing, with women the constant victims of violence?[119]

I think that most people in cultural studies who still believe that movies or any other works of art can be inherently "great" likely also will agree that *The Searchers* is a great film. Others, who believe that "great works" are established merely by society dogma and ideological convenience, will probably only cringe at any assertion of inherent greatness.[120] The majority of contributors to this volume (though not all of them) do think that *The Searchers,* despite its faults, attempts to deal in an important way with the deepest of social and personal issues. And the very high evaluation of *The Searchers* by the current generation of major Hollywood directors—those who know best how large-scale films are actually made and how difficult it is to make them—speaks for itself. Yet what, exactly, do we mean by the term "great"? Analytically, greatness should involve high formal complexity, internal coherence, deep originality, and historical, social, and critical significance.[121] Emotionally (and even spiritually) "greatness" comes down to how successfully any work of art, including a film, can evoke powerful and long-lasting feelings in large numbers of human beings. If these criteria still seem vague, debatable, and prone to subjectivism,—if, in short, they are the stuff the humanities are made of—they still get us closer to communicating successfully what is the greatness we see in *The Searchers.*

In this introductory essay, I have sought to present many of the basic questions about the deep plot and meaning of what has been John Ford's most honored film. But the only valid answer to the final set of questions posed just above is: see *The Searchers*—and decide for yourself on its quality. I personally do not think you will be disappointed.

Introduction

NOTES

1. Mediocre initial reviews: *Time*, June 25, 1956, 58–59; *Sight and Sound* (autumn 1956): 94–95. Contrast *Newsweek*, May 21, 1956, 116–17.

2. On the very high status of *The Searchers* in the *Sight and Sound* critics poll, see the decade-by-decade summary of the poll in Roger Ebert, *Ebert's Video Companion* (Kansas City: Andrews and McMeel, 1996), 927. On the relatively low status in the American Film Institute poll of "The 100 Best American Films" (a poll of fifteen hundred prominent Americans, including but not limited to Hollywood), see *New York Times*, June 17, 1998, 1.

3. On the crisis in John Ford's career in 1953–55, see Davis, *John Ford: Hollywood's Old Master*, 260–70; Eyman, *Print the Legend*, 424–41. Ford, the child of Irish immigrants (real name: John Martin Feeny), first came to Hollywood from Maine in 1914; he worked first as a cameraman and then as an assistant director before directing his first film in 1917.

4. On Cynthia Ann Parker, the best collection of evidence is in Hacker, *Cynthia Ann Parker*. In one of his last interviews Ford was explicit that *The Searchers* was based on this story; see Swindell, "Yes, John Ford Knew a Thing or Two," 146–47.

5. On Hitchcock's emphasis on Ford's creation of visual pleasure, see Hitchcock in Studlar and Bernstein, *John Ford Made Westerns*, 291.

6. On the complex place of the fierce landscapes of Monument Valley within the emotional meaning of *The Searchers*, see the essay by Richard Hutson in this volume.

7. Does the search in *The Searchers* take five years or seven years? It is two years from the initial Comanche raid on the Edwards family to the searchers' "first return" to the Jorgensens ("I've been hangin' around this god-forsaken windscow for two long years!" says Laurie to Martin). At the searchers' "second return" to the Jorgensens, just before the climax of the film, Martin protests Laurie's impending wedding to Charlie McCorry: "But I wrote you!" She bitterly responds: "Two letters in five years!" We see Laurie receive only one letter from Martin; it comes after "the first return." If she is referring to two letters during the entire time of the search, then the search is five years; but if she is referring only to the period after the first return, then the search takes fully seven years. Gallagher opts for seven years: *John Ford: The Man and His Films*, 325. So do I. But readers should not be surprised to find scholars in this volume referring to the search as five years.

8. See Carey, *Company of Heroes*, 170–71.

9. See Maltby, "A Better Sense of History," 36.

10. On the usual fate of the nonwhite partner in miscegenetic romances in films of the 1950s, see Michael Walker, "The Westerns of Delmer Daves," in *The Book of Westerns*, ed. Cameron and Pye, 127–28. On the strictures of the Motional Picture Production Code, see Walker, "The Westerns of Delmer Daves," 127. On the correct spelling of Martin's name (often misspelled in criticism as "Pawley"), see Nugent, "The Searchers," 2.

11. On this, see Pye, "Double Vision," 229, reprinted in this volume. On Wayne's extraordinary place in American culture, and the reasons behind it, see esp. Wills, *John Wayne's America*.

Arthur M. Eckstein

12. Roth, "Yes, My Darling Daughter," 67–68; Aleis, "A Race Divided," 185–86; Whissel, "Racialized Spectacle," 53–58; and "Double Vision," the 1996 essay by Pye, reprinted in this volume. Also Dempsey, "John Ford: A Reassessment," 9–10.

13. For Ford's description of *The Searchers*, see Jean Mitry, "Interview with John Ford," in *Interviews with Film Directors*, ed. Andrew Sarris (New York: Avon, 1969), 197.

14. On the importance of *Stagecoach* in the development of the western as a serious American art form, see Eyman, *Print the Legend*, 192–208.

15. See the article on Ford and the music of *The Searchers* by Kathryn Kalinak in this volume. Earlier: Gallagher, *John Ford: The Man and His Films*, 331n (but without presenting any evidence).

16. On Wayne as symbol in *The Searchers*, see Luhr's essay in this volume.

17. Good introductions to the "dark western" as an important postwar genre: Douglas Pye, "The Collapse of Fantasy: Masculinity in the Westerns of Anthony Mann," in *The Book of Westerns*, ed. Cameron and Pye, 167–73; Jonathan Bignell, "Method Westerns: *The Left-Handed Gun* and *One-Eyed Jacks*," in *The Book of Westerns*, ed. Cameron and Pye, 99–110, as well as Walker, "The Westerns of Delmer Daves."

18. Wayne was always concerned about the "image" he projected on the screen, which makes his involvement in *The Searchers* surprising; but Ford, who had "discovered" Wayne and introduced him into the film business in the late 1920s, always seems to have had a psychological hold on the actor. On these points, see Wills, *John Wayne's America*, 288, 300 (on Wayne's concern for his "image"), and 67–77 (on Wayne's often masochistic relationship with Ford).

19. For discussion, see esp. Davis, *John Ford: Hollywood's Old Master*, 3–15, and note the quotes from Ford himself in Sinclair, *John Ford: A Biography*, 17, 101.

20. Martha here recapitulates a tender, loving gesture of simultaneous attachment and loss that can be found in many other Ford films, including *Rio Grande* (1950), stretching back as far as *Straight Shooting* (1917); on *Straight Shooting*, see the photograph in Gallagher, *John Ford: The Man and His Films*, 21.

21. For a detailed analysis of this scene and how carefully Ford as a director has constructed it, see Lehman, "There's No Way of Knowing," 123–27.

22. On Ford's use of "Lorena" in the good-bye scene of Ethan and Martha, see Eckstein, "Darkening Ethan," 4–5. "Lorena" originated in the unconsummated affair between its composer, the Rev. H. D. L. Webster, and Martha Blocksom (1850s), a love relationship that was broken off when Martha's brother-in-law forbade it. See Ernest K. Emurian, *The Sweetheart of the Civil War: The True Story of the Song "Lorena"* (Natick, Mass.: W. A. Wilde, 1962), 10–15. On Ford's expertise in nineteenth-century American popular music, see Nugent—the screenwriter for *The Searchers*—in Anderson, *About John Ford*, 244, cf. 242. Ford later used "Lorena" in the final scene of *The Horse Soldiers* (1959), to underline the forced separation of a northern officer (John Wayne) from his southern love (Constance Towers).

23. For full discussion of the complex relationship between Nugent's shooting script and Ford's finished version of *The Searchers* (the release print), see Eckstein, "Darkening Ethan." Nugent's shooting script should always play a role in an analysis of *The Searchers*, because it casts a powerful light on how the film we now see was (in stages) constructed and transformed. On the relationship between Ethan and Martha,

Introduction

compare Nugent, "*The Searchers,*" 6, 10–11, with the much more dramatic vision in Ford's release print.

24. Ford's comments on the good-bye scene: in Bogdanovich, *John Ford*, 91. Ford's admonishment to actor Walter Coy (Aaron): see Kennedy, "Burt Kennedy Interviews John Ford."

25. On issues of white female "purity" in *The Searchers,* see the essays by Studlar and Pye in this volume.

26. See Walker, "The Westerns of Delmer Daves," 127.

27. The groundbreaking discussion relating *The Searchers* to the growing post-*Brown* American racial crisis of the 1950s is Henderson, "*The Searchers:* An American Dilemma," reprinted in this volume. On Native Americans in general as substitutes for African American issues in westerns of the 1950s, see Lenihan, *Showdown,* 23–81.

28. On Ford as a New Deal liberal, see the essay by David Grimsted in this volume. Ford's American patriotism was deep and real: he was seriously wounded at Midway in 1942, and he retired a rear admiral in the U.S. Navy Reserve. Yet he was also a fierce opponent of Hollywood's postwar blacklist of communist and extreme left-wing artists (see now Eyman, *Print the Legend,* 374–88)—not because he agreed with them, but because he loathed political repression. In fact, Ford's decision in 1955 to employ actress Pippa Scott in *The Searchers*—as the tragic Lucy Edwards—was an act of courage and defiance: her uncle Adrian Scott's communist connections had led the entire Scott family to be blacklisted from film ever since 1948; her father had committed suicide. See the profile of Pippa Scott (now a human rights activist) in *People,* April 19, 1999, 93–96.

29. See Crouch, "Bull Feeny Plays the Blues," 278. After *The Searchers* Ford would repeatedly examine the problem of white racism: *Sergeant Rutledge* (1960); *Two Rode Together* (1961); *Donovan's Reef* (1963); *Cheyenne Autumn* (1964).

30. See Neale, "Vanishing American," esp. 9–10.

31. Other westerns from 1956 that deal directly with white fears of miscegenation include *The Last Hunt* (dir.: Richard Brooks), with Robert Taylor condemned as a vicious racist, and *The Halliday Brand* (dir.: Joseph H. Lewis), with Ward Bond condemned as a vicious racist.

32. On the impact of fears of brainwashing in American films of the early Cold War, see Whitfield, *The Culture of the Cold War,* esp. chapters 1 and 6.

33. On white cultural anxiety, see esp. Axtell, "The White Indians." The American literary tradition of the "captivity narrative" from which *The Searchers* derives: see Kolodny, "Among the Indians." On the historical background of actual captivity in the Texas borderlands, see the essay by Brooks in this volume.

34. On the development of the pro-Indian depictions in Hollywood films that begin with Daves's *Broken Arrow,* see Walker, "The Westerns of Delmer Daves," 124–29. There was an earlier cycle of pro-Indian depictions in 1920s silent westerns, a tradition soon forgotten: on this, see Angela Aleis, "Native Americans: The Surprising Silents," *Cineaste* 21 (1995).

35. John Ford, Interoffice Memo, January 29, 1955; Patrick Ford (associate producer), Interoffice Memo, February 1, 1955. Box 6, folder 21, John Ford Archive, Lilly Library, Indiana University, Bloomington.

36. On the lack of evolution over time in Ford's depiction of Native Americans, see Aleis, "A Race Divided," 167–86. In *Cheyenne Autumn,* the Cheyenne community

is bitterly divided among itself, and the older men (themselves deeply divided) cannot control the younger; see the comments of Place, *Western Films of John Ford*, 220–22. Compare the idealized consensual community of the Sioux depicted in *Dances With Wolves*.

37. See Nolley, "The Representation of Conquest," 80–81, esp. 88. Historical incidents: the white massacre of Scar's winter encampment is based on one of General George Custer's search-and-destroy operations in 1868; the white destruction of the Cheyenne in *Cheyenne Autumn* is based on a real events of 1878.

38. See now Henry Brandon's interview in McBride, *Searching for John Ford*, 565. It is historical fact that the great Comanche war chief Quanah Parker, the last Comanche leader to submit to white conquest, was the son of Cynthia Ann Parker and her Comanche captor Wandering Wolf, and had striking blue eyes: see William Neeley, *The Last Comanche Chief: The Life and Times of Quanah Parker* (New York: John Wiley, 1995), 174–75. Ford had the blue-eyed Brandon play Quanah Parker himself, five years after *The Searchers*, in *Two Rode Together* (1961).

39. Both Ethan's hostility to Marty on racial grounds, and the film's development of a strong and sympathetic but miscegenated Marty to contrast with the bitter, racist Ethan, are emphasized in Henderson's essay in this volume.

40. See Lehman, "There's No Way of Knowing"; see also the essay by Pye in this volume.

41. "Ethan, if the girls are . . . dead, don't let the boys waste their lives in vengeance"—a plea to which Ethan gives no answer.

42. On the mostly comic episode of Martin and the Comanche girl called Look, which has brought heavy criticism from modern commentators, see Lehman, "Texas 1868/America 1956"; and for a possible Comanche perspective on the "marriage" of Marty and Look, see Brooks's essay in this volume.

43. The scene with Martha's ripped-open dress missing from Nugent's script (missing, too, are Ethan's cries, "Martha! Martha!" as he runs to the ruins of the house): compare the finished film with Nugent's shooting script (32–33) with the comments of Eckstein, "Darkening Ethan," 16–17.

44. Debbie well treated: noted by Gallagher, *John Ford: The Man and His Films*, 335n. The historical Cynthia Ann Parker was similarly well treated by her Comanche husband; see Hacker, *Cynthia Ann Parker*, 17–19. Debbie as conforming totally to the traditional Hollywood stereotypes of what constitutes female "value" is rightly stressed by Maltby, "A Better Sense of History," 34.

45. On Scar as Ethan's double, representing his own terrible desires—which has become the standard interpretation of the film—see in chronological order McBride and Wilmington, "The Prisoner of the Desert," and Place, *Western Films of John Ford*, 164, 170, 173 (pioneering); McBride and Wilmington, *John Ford*, 152, cf. 159; Stowell, *John Ford*, 136–37; Maltby, "A Better Sense of History," 44.

46. See, for instance, James Stewart and the villainous Stephen McNally in *Winchester '73* (1950)—where hero and villain are literally brothers; James Stewart and the villainous Arthur Kennedy—a man with a similar outlaw past—in *Bend of the River* (1952; dir.: Anthony Mann); Gary Cooper and the villainous, black-clad Burt Lancaster in *Vera Cruz* (1954; dir.: Robert Aldrich); Gary Cooper and the villainous Lee J. Cobb in *Man of the West* (1958).

Introduction

47. Nugent, "The Searchers," 140.
48. The quote is from Maltby, "A Better Sense of History,"44. On the significance of Ethan's medal appearing on Scar's chest at the moment when Scar is revealed to Ethan as married to Debbie, see Eckstein, "After the Rescue," 35.
49. See LeMay, *The Searchers*, 134–35. Ford was perfectly aware that there was no sexual relationship between Scar and Debbie in the novel, since words from these specific pages of the novel appear both in the shooting script and then in the finished film. For discussion, see Eckstein, "Darkening Ethan," 7 and n. 28.
50. According to Henry Brandon, Ford—at least when he started production on *The Searchers*—did assume that the relationship between Scar and Debbie was sexual; see McBride, *Searching for John Ford*, 566.
51. On Wayne's amazing remark about Ethan's "wife," see Roberts and Olsen, *John Wayne, American*, On Wayne's fantasy about Ethan and Debbie ("and that little girl would grow to love him"), see Macklin, "I Come Ready," 30–31.
52. See the essay by Brooks in this volume.
53. On the intrafamily questions raised by *The Searchers* (including the issue of incest in multiple directions), see also the essay by Eckstein, p. 97.
54. Lana Wood later made a career of exploiting the sexuality associated with Debbie, appearing in a nude photographic layout wearing only an Indian headdress in the April 1971 issue of *Playboy*, and appearing in a film with strongly *Searchers*-like themes and directly borrowed images in 1977 (*Greyeagle;* dir.: Charles Pierce)—but with nude scenes. Wood has also indicated in interviews that even as a nine-year-old she felt awed attraction (not fear) toward Henry Brandon's Scar when he first appears to Debbie during the attack on the Edwards ranch. All this, I think, shows the dark emotional power which the story in Ford's film generates. For more on this, see Eckstein, "After the Rescue," esp. 38–46.
55. For description of what life was like on the set of *The Searchers*, see Carey, *Company of Heroes*, 165–74.
56. Half the tension, because the audience is constantly faced with *two* simultaneous questions: will the searchers ever find Debbie? but (and here is the conflict and the contradiction) what will Ethan do if the searchers *do* find Debbie?
57. Letting the audience think for itself: see Ford's own remarks on *The Searchers* in the interview in Bogdanovich, *John Ford*, 90–91, and the essay by Lehman in this volume. It is one of the secrets to the film's enduring interest.
58. So Robert Ardrey in Kenneth Macgowan, *Behind the Screen* (New York: 1962): 248.
59. See the comments of Lehman, "Texas 1868/America 1956," 396.
60. See Stowell, *John Ford*, 136.
61. For Ethan's statement, see Nugent, "The Searchers," 140 (not known to Stowell, who had the insight without it).
62. See Place, *Western Films of John Ford*, 170, 171; Stowell, *John Ford*, 136; cf. Corliss, *Talking Pictures*, 331–32 (part of an essay on Frank Nugent—though without benefit of *The Searchers* script), and Winkler, "Tragic Features," 201.
63. The Ethan figure in LeMay's novel secretly in love with Martha but a love not ever expressed or reciprocated: LeMay, *The Searchers*, 33. The difference between the novel and the film is noted briefly by Card, "*The Searchers* by Alan LeMay and

John Ford" (without knowledge of the intervening script) and more thoroughly by Eckstein, "Darkening Ethan," 3–24.

64. The optimistic speech given by the Ethan figure: LeMay, *The Searchers*, 33. Difference with Ford's film noted by Card, "*The Searchers* by Alan LeMay and John Ford," 6; cf. Eckstein, "Darkening Ethan," 6.

65. Amos Edwards's goal only rescue: LeMay, *The Searchers*, 81–83, 219. The difference rightly noted by Card, "*The Searchers* by Alan LeMay and John Ford," 7; cf. Eckstein, "Darkening Ethan," 6–7. Wills, *John Wayne's America*, 251, 253, argues that Ford and Nugent labored to create in Ethan a character *more* sympathetic than Amos in the novel—but just given Ethan's main intention in the film, this is clearly totally mistaken.

66. The martyrlike death of Amos in the novel: LeMay, *The Searchers*, 264–65.

67. The scene between Ethan and Custer: Nugent, "The Searchers," 90–92.

68. Memo, February 15, 1955, box 6, folder 21, John Ford Archive, Lilly Library, Indiana University. On the incompetent Custer-like commander in Ford's *Fort Apache* (played by Henry Fonda), see Hutton, *The Custer Reader*, 506.

69. Memo, February 15, 1955, box 6, folder 21, John Ford Archive, Lilly Library, Indiana University, Bloomington; cf. Eckstein, "Darkening Ethan," 21n. 44, and now Edward Buscumbe, *The Searchers* (London: British Film Institute, 2000), 52 and n. 57.

70. See Frank Nugent's comments in Anderson, *About John Ford*, 242–44.

71. The photograph can be found in Hutton, *The Custer Reader*, 558.

72. On the founding of Argosy Pictures and its artistic purpose, see Davis, *John Ford: Hollywood's Old Master*, 194–96. Ford's action as typical of important directors in the postwar period: Eyman, *Print the Legend*, 308.

73. See Nugent in Anderson, *About John Ford*, 244.

74. Cf. Eckstein, "Darkening Ethan," 9–11.

75. See the comments of Winkler in his essay in this volume. Cf. Winkler, "Tragic Features," and Wills, *John Wayne's America*, 259.

76. See Nugent, "The Searchers," 93–94; cf. Eckstein, "Darkening Ethan," 11–12. There are many pages in the shooting script on which Nugent does suggest camera shots (e.g., 1, 30, 32, 140, 142)—but not here.

77. On scalping in westerns, and John Ford's attitude toward whites who do it, see the essay by Winkler in this volume.

78. Most recently, Whissel, "Racialized Spectacle," 56, and Flanagan, "John Ford's West," 73.

79. Luhr, in his essay in this volume, points out that Wayne had played a number of psychologically disturbed characters in the recent past, and would do so again in the immediate future (notably the self-centered and obsessive protagonist of Ford's *The Wings of Eagles*, filmed the year after *The Searchers*).

80. Nugent, "The Searchers," 139; cf. Eckstein, "Darkening Ethan," 12–13.

81. That the addition was filmed on location is shown by the fact that Ethan's riding out of Scar's tepee holding the bloody scalp was filmed in Monument Valley itself. The actual scalping scene in the tepee, however—an interior—was filmed a month later, back on a Hollywood soundstage. Principal location filming of *The Searchers* took place in June and July 1955; soundstage interiors followed in August:

Introduction

see Dan Ford, *Pappy*, 271. Note that the scalping scene in Scar's tent, the scene with Ethan and the white captives at the fort, and the "Good-bye scene of Ethan and Martha" are all interiors; hence they were the last parts of the film actually done—at a point in production, that is, when Ford's dark view of Ethan had become (on location in Arizona) fully developed.

82. For the parallel with the ending of *Shane*, see Lehman, "Texas 1868/America 1956," 395.

83. Indeed, for all of Ethan's vaunted frontier expertise, he is never directly instrumental in tracking down the missing Debbie, either. That is done *twice* by the softly crazy old man Mose Harper (Hank Worden, a Ford regular), who—like everyone else but Ethan—enters the house at the end of the film.

84. Relatively happy or at least hopeful endings in 1950s "psychological" westerns: see Anthony Mann's *Bend of the River* (1952), *The Naked Spur* (1954), and *The Man from Laramie* (1955)—all starring James Stewart—in all of which the hero gives at least promise of settling down with the heroine; so, too, Delmer Daves's *3:10 to Yuma* (1957), where the hero's marriage (barely) survives very severe strains; and Ford's own *Rio Grande* (1950), where a similar situation prevails.

85. Nugent, "The Searchers," 142; cf. Eckstein, "Darkening Ethan," 15.

86. See Henderson's essay in this volume; cf. also Danny Peary, *Cult Movies*, 313.

87. See esp. Stowell, *John Ford*, 136.

88. See esp. Place, *Western Films of John Ford*, 170, 173.

89. Winkler, "Tragic Features," 201. Ethan may not be the only social outcast here. Despite Mrs. Jorgensen's motherly welcome, Debbie is returning to a white society where even Mrs. Jorgensen's own daughter thinks Debbie ineradicably "soiled," both sexually and racially. The historical Cynthia Ann Parker, having been "rescued" from the Comanches, was in fact treated with such condescension and suspicion by her white relatives that soon she tried to escape *back* to the Comanches, and eventually she committed suicide; see Hacker, *Cynthia Ann Parker*, 31–34. Ford knew this shocking story: he put it on the screen in *Two Rode Together* (1961). On the highly ambiguous situation of the "returned" or "rescued" woman, see Eckstein, "After the Rescue," and Maltby, "A Better Sense of History," 44.

90. See Carey, *Company of Heroes*, 173–74; Roberts and Olsen, *John Wayne*, 420–21.

91. See Gallagher, *John Ford: The Man and His Films*, 17–25, and Davis, *John Ford: Hollywood's Old Master*, 38–44.

92. See Gallager, *John Ford*, 23.

93. Bogdanovich, *John Ford*, 91–92.

94. On the general structure of Euro-American nineteenth-century "imperial" or "conquest" narratives, see Robert H. MacDonald, *The Language of Empire: Literature and Myth, 1880–1914* (Manchester, Engl.: Manchester University Press, 1994): 26–27. On the way the generic plot of narratives of imperial conquest are "comic" in form (from initial disorder, to order and a happy ending), see White, *Metahistory*, 7–11.

95. On this point, see Grimsted's essay in this volume.

96. On large-scale Hollywood filmmaking as inevitably involving the contributions of many talented people of all kinds, even in the films of great directors,—i.e., the question of personal "auteurism" in Hollywood—see, for example, Thomas Shatz, *The Genius of the System: Hollywood Filmmaking in the Studio Era* (New York: Pantheon, 1988).

97. *John Wayne's America,* chapter 20.

98. Winton C. Hoch had worked with Ford many times, and had already won the Academy Award for Color Cinematography for *Joan of Arc* (1948), *She Wore A Yellow Ribbon* (1949), and *The Quiet Man* (1952). On the dangerous riding stunts required in the filming of *The Searchers,* see Roberson's memoir, *The Fall Guy,* 156–72.

99. On Patrick Ford's contribution here, see Dan Ford, *Pappy,* 271.

100. See Eckstein, "Darkening Ethan," 17–18. Ford's habit of independence from the script is demonstrated by the fact that—in contrast to most film directors—he refused to use storyboards, on which the scenes of a script's story are laid out in succession pictorially in sketches; instead he simply carried around the entire movie in his head. See Gallagher, *John Ford: The Man and His Films,* 464.

101. Compare what we now see on screen with Nugent, "The Searchers," 1 and 142. The Nugent opening was actually filmed (its beginning can be seen in the excellent Nick Redman documentary included in the latest videotape edition of *The Searchers* released by Warner Bros.)—then discarded by Ford.

102. Actors: note the disastrous quarrel between Ford and Henry Fonda during the filming of *Mr. Roberts* (1954), when Fonda offered advice on a role he had performed six hundred times on Broadway—a quarrel that ended their long friendship; see Dan Ford, *Pappy,* 265–69. Nugent's general rule about Ford movies: see his comments in Anderson, *About John Ford,* 244; cf. Gallagher, *John Ford: The Man and His Films,* 464–66.

103. See most recently McBride, *Searching for John Ford.*

104. The quote is from the positive review in *Newsweek,* May 21, 1956, 116–17; for mediocre or negative reviews, see note 1 to this essay.

105. It was the eleventh largest grossing film of 1956; see Davis, *John Ford: Hollywood's Old Master,* 279.

106. In the seventy years of Academy Awards history, a western has won the Oscar for best picture only three times—and two of those times are relatively recent (*Dances With Wolves,* 1990; *Unforgiven,* 1993; the other was *Cimarron* 1930). None of Ford's six Academy Awards was for a western.

107. Anderson, who wrote the original negative review of *The Searchers* in *Sight and Sound,* restated his critique in great detail in 1981 in *About John Ford,* 152–60. On Pauline Kael, see her repeated negative capsule reviews of *The Searchers* in the *New Yorker,* starting in 1966; and as the reputation of the film grew, Kael's capsule reviews became ever more bitter; see the *New Yorker,* June 29, 1996, 14.

108. See Wayne, *John Wayne: My Life with the Duke,* 117; in agreement, Dan Ford, *Pappy,* 274. Cf. Davis, *John Ford: Hollywood's Old Master,* 278.

109. See Davis, *John Ford: Hollywood's Old Master,* 279. To repeat, *The Searchers,* of course, was *not* a film for children.

110. See esp. the comments of Danny Peary, *Cult Movies,* 310, speaking of his own experience.

Introduction

111. McBride, *Searching for John Ford,* 570.

112. See McBride, *Searching for John Ford,* 570–71; Buscumbe, *The Searchers,* 68. Note that Paul Schrader wrote the screenplay for *Taxi Driver* (1976) while John Milius was executive producer of Schrader's *Hardcore* (1979). Milius provides part of the voice-over in the Nick Redmond documentary on the filming of *The Searchers* in the new Warner Bros. videotape edition. In the original *Star Wars* (1977), George Lucas has Luke Skywalker discover the destruction of his foster parents' home in scenes that—shot for shot—pay homage to Martin Pauley's horror at the destruction of his foster family in *The Searchers.* Spielberg says he whiled away his time during the filming of *Close Encounters of the Third Kind* (1981) by seeing *The Searchers* twice. Another example is Michael Cimino's *The Deer Hunter* (1978—Academy Award, Best Picture), which transferred *The Searchers* and its disturbed hero to Vietnam.

113. The quotes are from Byron, "*The Searchers:* Cult Movie of the New Hollywood," 45–48.

114. See Dempsey, "John Ford: A Reassessment"; Greenspun, "John Ford, 1895–1973," 333–36 (protesting). Ford was a supporter of the civil rights movement—but also of American involvement in Vietnam.

115. On the reception of *The Searchers* until 1997, see Harry Old Meadow, "Tracking *The Searchers:* A Survey of the Film's Critical Reception," *Continuum* 11 (1997): 132–62.

116. Ibid.

117. See Paul Weinrib in the *New York Times,* July 26, 1998, 29; or *Variety,* July 29, 1998, 3.

118. The AFI poll sometimes seems to privilege more recent films over older ones: thus *Dances With Wolves* (1990), *Goodfellas* (1990), and even the crime comedies *Pulp Fiction* (1994) and *Fargo* (1996) are all ranked somewhat above *The Searchers.* In addition, Ford is generally slighted in the poll, with only three films in the "top 100," and none in the "top 20." This is odd for someone who won the Academy Award six times.

119. For *The Searchers* as merely yet another objectionable "white conquest" narrative, see the articles in note 12 to this essay; cf. the essay by Pye in this volume. On gender relations in *The Searchers,* see the essay by Studlar in this volume.

120. For an extreme example of such a position see Ivo Kamps, "Materialist Shakespeare: An Introduction," in *Materialist Shakespeare,* ed. Ivo Kamps (London: Verso, 1995), 12: "Sweeping studies of Shakespeare's critical and cultural reception have demonstrated the socially constructed character of the Shakespeare phenomenon and canon."

121. For a classic statement of this view, see Erich Auerbach, *Mimesis: The Representation of Reality in Western Literature* (Princeton: Princeton University Press, 1954), chapter 1 ("Odysseus' Scar")—which deals with representations of homecoming.

The Searchers:
An American Dilemma

Brian Henderson

In a 1979 article, Stuart Byron surveys the influence of John Ford's film *The Searchers* (1956) on several young directors and screenwriters.[1] He concludes:

> In one way or another, the film relates to Paul Schrader, John Milius, Martin Scorsese, Steven Spielberg, George Lucas, and Michael Cimino; to *Hardcore, Taxi Driver, Close Encounters of the Third Kind, Dillinger, Mean Streets, Big Wednesday, The Deer Hunter, The Wind and the Lion, Ulzana's Raid,* and *Star Wars*. . . . When one film obsesses so much talent, it won't do just to call it a cult movie. *The Searchers* is the Super-Cult movie of the New Hollywood.

The filmmakers Byron discusses do not hesitate to confirm his argument. Milius: "The best American movie—and its protagonist, Ethan Edwards, is the one classic character in films. I've named my own son Ethan after him. I've seen it 60 times." Schrader: "I make sure I see *The Searchers* at least once a year. God knows that there are movies that are better acted or better written, but *The Searchers* plays the fullest artistic hand. . . . Scorsese and I agree that *The Searchers* is the best American film, a fact that must have influenced *Taxi Driver*." Scorsese: "The dialogue is like poetry! And the changes of expressions are so subtle, so magnificent! I see it once or twice a year." Spielberg: "*The Searchers* has so many superlatives going for it. It's John Wayne's best performance. . . . It's a study in dramatic framing and composition. It contains the single most harrowing moment in any film I've ever seen. It is high on my twenty-five-favorite film list." Spielberg says he has seen the film a dozen times, including twice on location with *Close Encounters of the Third Kind*.

Byron argues that four recent films in particular have a basic story structure identical to and inspired by *The Searchers*: *Taxi Driver, Close Encounters of the Third Kind, The Deer Hunter,* and *Hard Core*. In each, "an obsessed man searches for someone—a woman, a child, a best friend—who has fallen into the clutches of an alien people. But when found, the sought one doesn't want to be rescued."

There has been a good deal of writing on *The Searchers*, as film criticism goes. In "Critics on *The Searchers*," Edward Buscombe summarizes the work of several Ford critics—John Baxter, Janice. A. Place, Andrew Sarris, Michael Wilmington, and Joseph McBride:

> Despite their sense that the film is concerned with questions of history, the critics do not in practice pay much attention to this. What is ultimately of concern is the artistry with which the film organizes the audience's responses to the characters. . . . The actual way in which the critics deal with questions of character in the film . . . lead[s] us all the time towards articulating what it is the characters are like, what motivates them, how they understand each other and how they are to be understood by us. . . . All these critics, then, to some extent treat the film as though it were a psychological novel.[2]

What Buscombe does not say, perhaps because it is obvious, is that critics of *The Searchers* have been notably focused on one character in particular, Ethan Edwards. Indeed, preoccupation with Ethan and his motives has been a constant of commentary on the film since it first appeared. Lindsay Anderson, who did not like the film, was as centered on the character of Ethan as those later critics who esteem it supremely:

> *The Searchers* begins with a promise . . . yet somehow, curiously, the effect is cold. . . . Lack of intensity in all [its] echoes reminds us that it is not enough just to set Ford down among the mesas, . . . he has to have a story—or at least a theme. And the story of *The Searchers* . . . does not turn out to be a good one for him. In the first place there is too much of it. The pictures Ford has himself produced in the last ten years . . . have relied less and less on narrative and more and more on mood.
>
> *The Searchers* is a long and complicated story, spread over eight or nine years. Moreover, its hero, Ethan Edwards, is an unmistakable neurotic, devoured by an irrational hatred of Indians and half breeds, shadowed by some mysterious crime. His search for his little niece . . . abducted by Comanches seems . . . inspired less by love or honour than by an obsessive desire to do her to death as a contaminated creature. Now what is Ford, of all directors, to do with a hero like this?[3]

An American Dilemma

Even one of the trade magazines spoke of a "problem of motivation" in a review that appeared before the film's release:

> The box office appeal of John Wayne combined with the imprint of John Ford makes *The Searchers* a contender for the big money stakes. It's a Western in the grand manner—handsomely mounted and in the tradition of *Shane*. . . . Yet *The Searchers* is somewhat disappointing. . . . Overlong and repetitious at 119 minutes, there are subtleties in the basically simple story that are not adequately explained. . . . Wayne, the uncle of the kidnapped girl, is a complex character. His motivations, from the time he appears out of the southwest plains at his brother's ranch to his similar exit after he accomplishes his mission, are unclear. . . . Wayne is a bitter, taciturn, individual throughout and the reasons for his attitude are left to the imagination of the viewer. (*Variety*, March 14, 1956)[4]

There is not one point in these passages but several: a centering on Ethan, a centering on Ethan's motives, and finding a problem with Ethan's motives, usually followed by an attempt to solve it. We have not space to sort these out, so we treat the "preoccupation with Ethan" as a single thing.

T. S. Eliot has warned against critical fascination with a fascinating character. "Few critics have even admitted that *Hamlet* the play is the primary problem, and Hamlet the character only secondary."[5] Our analysis seeks to focus on *The Searchers* the film, not *The Searchers* the saga of Ethan Edwards. This attempt opposes the weight of prior commentary: it has never been doubted that *The Searchers* concerns the uneasy relations between the restless hero, half-civilized, half-savage, and the community he benefits.

Vladimir Propp counsels that the motivations of characters have nothing to do with the structure of narrative:

> Motivations belong to the most inconstant and unstable elements of the tale. . . . Completely identical or similar acts are motivated in the most varied ways . . . [which] has no influence on the structure of the course of action, i.e., the search as such. . . . One may observe in general that the feelings and intentions of the dramatic personas do not have an effect on the course of action in any instances at all.[6]

Propp's formulae on motivation hold good for the entire "structural analysis of the narrative" tradition—Levi-Strauss, Greimas, Todorov, Barthes. Despite his motivational complications, Ethan does function rather conventionally as the hero of *The Searchers* in structural terms. His ambiguous motives do not prevent, they do not even qualify his performance of the hero's functions in the film.[7]

But *The Searchers* itself foregrounds the problem of Ethan and his motivations though the song that begins and ends the film. The first part of the song is played over the titles, its last words overlapping the figure of Ethan as he slowly approaches his brother's house: "What makes a man to wander? What makes a man to roam? What makes a man to leave bed and board and turn his back on home? Ride away, ride away, ride away." The second part of the song is laid at the end of the film over images of the settlers entering the house and Ethan then turning away: "A man will search in his heart and soul, go searching way out there; his peace of mind he knows he'll find, but where, O Lord, Lord where? Ride away, ride away, ride away." The first part of the song poses a question that we expect the film to answer. The second part of the song also poses a question, but this time we know that the film will answer neither one. The second question is rhetorical, suggesting that Ethan will not find peace of mind and that his response to this is to ride away. (The second part of the song has another function: it tells us that Ethan *is* riding away, not just going back to feed his horse before going into the house.)

The song that frames *The Searchers* seems to parallel the poem that opens Ford's *Young Mr. Lincoln* (1940), itself a series of questions. In the *Cahiers du cinéma* reading, the main function of the poem is to pretend that its questions haven't been answered yet, whereas the film itself presumes the spectator's knowledge of Lincoln. Through this "feigned indecisiveness" the film effects a naturalization of the Lincoln myth. The function of the song in *The Searchers* is opposite to this. In *Lincoln* the audience knows the answers to the question before the film begins; in *The Searchers* the audience does not know the answers to the questions even after the film is over.

To displace Ethan from the center of *The Searchers* thus seems to oppose the film itself; but the foregrounding of Ethan and his problems may be read as a ruse of the text (though not of its makers) to deflect attention from more important and hidden matters. This analysis of *The Searchers* seeks to explore different patterns of signification and to use different methods of criticism than prior criticism of the film has done. Of course it is a "reading" of the film, but it does not have the closed or complete quality that the notion of a reading suggests; it will be enough if this analysis succeeds in displacing discussion of the film. Its point of departure is the extraordinary power of *The Searchers* as film myth on a number

An American Dilemma

of filmmakers, critics, and other viewers, a power that might also be defined by the number of intelligent viewers that the film intensely repels. The moral-psychological critics whom Buscombe discusses, who are also thoroughly "author-centered," tend to assume the film's power in a way that precludes raising it as a problem. Insofar as they consider it they attribute the film's impact on audiences to the artistry of its director. But if myth is viewed as a *collective* phenomenon then the power of a myth can only be explained by reference to the community that responds to it.

This analysis has several methodological inspirations. The first is Levi-Straussian myth analysis with its Freudian emphasis on the unconscious dimension, and its Marxist emphasis on the materialist interpretation, of collective phenomena. From Levi-Strauss we take the notion that myths (and other public narratives) have an unconscious component, formed by public conflicts rather than private ones. These are contradictions either in social life or in knowledge; they explain why listeners are stirred by myths and why myths are told again and again. When these conflicts fade in social life, the power of the myth is lessened until it "dies." The myth operates by transposing the terms of the actual conflict into other sets of terms, usually in the form of binary oppositions.[8] It is the resolution of the transposed oppositions, substituted for the real conflict, that gives the myth a palliative effect. That this effect is a kind of deception accounts for the pejorative sense of the word "mythical," even in Levi-Strauss. He refuses to budge in calling myth "inauthentic" because it operates to deflect humans from identifying and resolving their actual problems. Finally, the operation of a myth—both its construction from actual conflicts and its impact on audiences—always has to do with the time in which the myth is told, not with the time that it tells of. Thus *The Searchers* has to do with 1956, not with the 1868–73 period in which it is set.

We also draw upon the *Cahiers du cinema* analysis of Young *Mr. Lincoln*,[9] which uses Levi-Strauss, among other sources, but proceeds quite differently. Levi-Strauss overlooks the text's specific modes of unfolding and elaboration in order to study its structure. *Cahiers* does its Levi-Straussian and other analyses offstage, then devotes its analysis to reading them back into the unfolding text. Our analysis also benefits from Charles Eckert's reading of *Marked Woman*,[10] notably its casual but effective combination of Levi-Straussian method and ideological analysis and its analysis of the gangster as an overdetermined figure of displacement in many films.

The Searchers is explicitly concerned with a number of anthropological issues. On its surface it treats questions of kinship, race, marriage, and the relations between tribes. These questions also have to do with the identity, status, and responsibilities of individuals: Who is responsible for the retrieval and burial of the dead, for the search and recovery of captives, for vengeance? Who can marry whom? Which marriages are binding? Which are not?

The wealth of anthropological material in *The Searchers* is itself a problem: How to proceed? Let us begin with two parallel sets of relationships that appear to structure the film. With ethnographic accuracy, the film designates Martin Pawley as one-eighth Cherokee by descent. As a child Martin was rescued (by Ethan) from an Indian raid that killed his parents; Martha and Aaron Edwards adopted him and raised him as a member of their family. Martin's parents were white settlers like the Edwardses but as our analysis will show, he functions as an Indian in the symbolics of the film, more precisely as an Indian who has become an adopted white. Martin marries Laurie Jorgensen, who is white.

Debbie Edwards is captured by Scar and his band when she is ten. She is raised as a Comanche until she reaches puberty, then becomes Scar's wife. The parallelism is evident. White woman is adopted and raised by red society, marries a red man; (part) red man is adopted and raised by white society, marries a white woman. This textual parallel poses an exchange between red and white tribes, at best a de facto exchange since there is no alliance between them. Indeed, both intertribal transfers take place in violence or as a result of violence; and each tribe subjects the outsider to a total reconditioning, designed to obliterate the effects of previous filiation, as part of his adoption process.[11] This is an "exchange" between warring tribes, between which there can be no lawful exchange and no lawful marriage.

Still, the film's parallel adoptions and marriages constitute a de facto exchange, an implied contract with reciprocal obligations to fulfill, but the film poses this symmetry only to collapse it. Indian law and adoption, intermarriage on Indian terms, are not recognized by the white settlers or by the film that takes their part; only white law and adoption and intermarriage on white terms are recognized. The film's surface progress is toward "recovery of Debbie," but this implies, and the film hardly disguises it, progress toward the destruction of Indian law and Indian society. There can be only one law, one definition of persons and relationships. *The Searchers* presents the violent triumph of that law, annihilating everything that opposes it or that it defines as "other."

An American Dilemma

This "collapse" of the film's apparent structuring opposition is itself one of the film's principal ideological and semantic operations. It is certainly overdetermined, that is, required by a number of different systems at work in the film. Let us consider briefly the figure of Debbie. Her choice to stay with the Comanches and with Scar is overridden by Ethan and Martin. Only their methods differ: Ethan wants to shoot her, Martin wants to abduct her. But the text itself rides roughshod over Debbie by making her change her mind suddenly when Martin appears to take her away, a conspicuously unmotivated act in a film that elsewhere supplies too many motives.

The figure of Debbie functions as an object in several other senses also. In Propp, she is the object of value transferred from the good kingdom to the evil kingdom and back, over whom hero and villain fight to the death. In Levi-Straussian anthropology, she is a wife exchanged for whom no other wife can be returned—the offered Indian wife Look is repudiated; therefore she must be recovered. Debbie is equated with her sexuality, by Ethan and Laurie at least, so that "contaminated" by Scar, she can only be disposed of. All this is overdetermined by the system of sexual identity and the system of subject formation of which it is a foundation. This system has a negative dimension—how men and women may not be portrayed—as well as a positive one. It is inconceivable that a man be cast in the Debbie role or a woman in the Martin role. In classical cinema, aside from some "women's pictures," named and produced as a distinct genre, a special case, a man cannot be the object of value except briefly, for example, Dean Martin's capture in *Rio Bravo* (1959), from which, however, he delivers himself. And a woman cannot except briefly be a seeker, a searcher, cannot be put in the place of performances, of proving herself through action, as Martin is. Nor can she serve apprenticeships, which make her the subject of a becoming. She is defined and valued always in herself not for herself, that is, as an object. This means, among other things, that she cannot change her social or racial allegiance by her own choice—they are not hers to change.

Thus the system of sexual identity requires that the parallelism of adoptions/marriages collapse and that it collapse on the feminine side. What about the opposition between red and white laws? The shift from a conflict between two laws to a conflict within one law is also fundamental to the film's ideological and semantic operations. First of all, it obscures the fact that the white settlers and their government, for personal and public gain, destroyed many Indian civilizations and damaged others, subjecting the survivors to white law. The film recasts the struggle between red and white laws as a conflict within one law, an ideal Law supposed to reign over all humans. Then it recasts the Indians as criminals under this law and casts the white settlers, Rangers, and Cavalry as the law's agents, who punish the Indians for their transgressions. The film is precisely structured along this axis, beginning with horrible crimes by the Comanches, which follow no acts by whites but initiate the cycle of violence gratuitously, and proceeding through intermediate stages to their punishment by whites in the end.

This structure is ideological in the traditional sense: a distortion of history in the interests of a particular class; but it is also a psychoanalytic structure. The *Cahiers* reading of *Lincoln* elucidates: "It is in the constantly renewed relationship of this group [the white settlers] with another (the Indian), in the dualism of Ford's universe. that the inscription of the structural imperative of Law which dictates the deferment of desire and imposes exchange and alliance is realized, in violence, guided by the mediating action of the hero (often a bastard) who is placed at its intersection."[12] Scar's crimes—rape, murder, dismemberment, burning—eminently violate the law that dictates postponement of pleasure. His acts stand in for the terrifying libido that must be repressed and, if unrepressed, must be punished drastically. His crimes "stand in" for libido because, of course, libido cannot be represented. The film doubles this nonrepresentability by not showing Scar's actions or even their consequences—we see not one dead body of the murdered family. These actions and their consequences are evoked only by Ethan's grimaces and outbursts, and even he most often operates to suppress representation—"Don't let him go in there, Mose—it won't help him"; "I buried Lucy back there with her own hands; thought it best to keep it from you"; "What d'you want me to do, draw you a picture?"; "As long as you live, don't ever ask me more!" This requires the viewer to project unconscious fantasies into the film, which greatly increases the viewer's involvement in it. Put oversimply, the viewer identifies unconsciously with Scar's acts and also with the need to punish them. This process, which gives pleasure by exercising libido and ego reassurance by suppressing it, imaginatively reconstitutes the structure of the self, thereby promoting what has been "the maintenance of the subject."

In both *Lincoln* and *The Searchers* there is an early crime and a subsequent movement, the bulk of each film, toward cancelling it. "It is from this ideal Law that originated the cancellation of the criminal act in the

An American Dilemma

fiction [and] the position of the Mother as the figure of forbidden violence (pleasure)."[13] As *Cahiers* argues, Lincoln is both the figure of ideal law (taking it over from his mother and Mrs. Clay) and the agent of its inscription. This forbids his resort to physical force and thereby denies the film "the usual bisection of [Ford's] fiction and the sometimes truly epic inscription of Law thereby articulated."[14] In the case of *Lincoln*, this "produce[s] the Law as a pure prohibition of violence, whose result is a permanent indictment of the castrating effects of its discourse."[15] But the inscription of law in *The Searchers* is epic indeed—the consequence of colorful adventures by action heroes, leading to a death struggle between hero and villain and an exuberant charge on the enemy's village. The party of repression confronts the party of libido in open battle. These epic lures obscure the grim business of inscribing the law that dictates postponement of pleasure—which stands forth nakedly in *Lincoln*. (But isn't Lincoln's courtroom battle with J. Palmer Cass a kind of verbal epic?) Scar is scalped (that is, castrated), a condition his name as well as his crime has predestined him:

> It is the character of the mother that incarnates the idealized figure of ideal Law in Ford's fiction... often, as in *Young Mr. Lincoln,* the widowed mother, guardian of the deceased father's Law. It is for her that the men (the regiment) sacrifice the cause of their desire, and under her presidency that the Fordian celebration takes place: this in fact consists in a simulacrum of sexual relations from which all effective desire is banned.[16]

The mother who incarnates ideal Law in *The Searchers* is evidently Martha. She is murdered in the initial crime, but it is she whom Ethan and Martin serve, for her that they pursue Debbie, recover her, and punish Scar and his followers. That she is the figure of forbidden pleasure is also clear: first for Ethan, who loves her without hope of fulfillment; second for her husband Aaron, who toils for her and, by staying on the frontier, gives up his life—"She just wouldn't let a man quit"; and, after her death, for Ethan and Martin, who devote their energies to her cause for five years, like Lincoln taking over his mother's function by looking after her children. But from this point there is a division in Ideal Law. When Debbie refuses to leave Scar, Ethan seeks to impose the law of postponing pleasure by shooting her. Laurie invokes the authority of Martha for this policy: "You know what Ethan will do if he has a chance? He'll put a bullet in her brain—and I tell you Martha would want it!" But Martin is also acting for Martha when he does all that he can to protect Debbie, from Ethan as well as from Scar. This confusion at the heart of ideal Law is one of the most disturbing aspects of *The Searchers;* it reverberates in every corner of the film.

The undoing of Debbie's adoption and marriage and of the Indian law that sanctions them turns us back to Martin's adoption and marriage and to the white law that sanctions them and prescribes their terms. Martin's adoption and marriage are the "relation left over" when the originally posed symmetry collapses, hence they are of particular interest. Martin's adoption is treated on the surface of the film as a long-accomplished fact, but beneath the surface the nature, meaning, and consequences of his adoption are far from settled. Even on its surface, the film uses the character of Ethan to question what has long been settled, notably the matter of Martin's "Indian blood" and his kinship status as an adopted Edwards (white). (It is only one duplicity of a frequently duplicitous film that Ethan is punished for his disturbing the social order by exclusion from the community, though this in some way is duplicitous also.) As in *Young Mr. Lincoln,* the unconscious material lies partly on the surface of the film but arranged so as to be partly unreadable. This makes analysis considerably more difficult than simply identifying unconscious structures. The surface of *The Searchers* is broken again and again by the edges of contradictions that lie at deeper levels. This implies, which is true, that the surface of the film is contradictory, even incoherent, in a different way. It is Ford's skill as a filmmaker that covers over and disguises these breaks again and again, indeed that makes a flowing filmic text out of them.

    We first see Martin riding a horse bareback and sliding off in front of the Edwardses' open side door; he is late for dinner. The wilderness outside the door, Max Steiner's exuberant theme, Martin's high spirits, his effortless transition from exterior to interior—these signify an ideal boyhood spent in oneness with nature. The film will soon shatter this idyll ruthlessly by taking away all of Martin's adopted family, except his hostile uncle, making him an orphan again. But it shatters the idyll even sooner by initiating another signification set: Martin's skin is quite dark and he wears a loose, colored shirt buttoned at the neck, giving him the appearance of an Indian. It is Indians who ride bareback and, in American mythology, it is only Indians who are completely at one with the environment. Martin steps tentatively into the room. The surface question—he is late for dinner, will he be scolded?—covers another question: he is an Indian, will he be welcome at the table? Much of the textual problematic revolving around Martin is posed in this scene, though in disguised form.

An American Dilemma

Marty as an Indian.

As it happens, Martin does have cause to worry on this particular evening, for his Uncle Ethan has returned. Martin is introduced and takes his seat sheepishly. Ethan looks at him suspiciously and says, "A fella could mistake you for a half-breed." Martin says that he is on-eighth Cherokee, the rest English and Welsh. Martha recalls that it was Ethan who found Martin after Indians killed his parents; to which Ethan replies, "It just happened to be me—no need to make more of it." Ethan just glares at Martin following this remark; Martha deflects his anger by saying, "More coffee, Ethan?" Then the dinner scene simply ends, in the way that Ford sometimes ends a scene, with no dramatic rounding out, no ellipsis marks. There is a cut to Martin sitting on the steps of the porch with the family dog, half turned toward the door, as though Ethan's hostility has expelled him from the family group. After a scene with the adults inside, Aaron joins Martha in the bedroom and closes the door while Ethan sits on the porch with the dog, as Martin did earlier.

In the morning, they ride after Jorgensen's cattle. When Martin calls Ethan "Uncle," Ethan says that he is not his uncle, and not to call him

Ethan stares at Indian-like Marty

grandpa nor Methuselah neither, since he can whup him to a frazzle. What should Martin call him? "Name's Ethan." The game of names between Ethan and Martin is another textual duplicity. "I'm *not* your uncle" means that Martin is not kin to the Edwards children, to whom Ethan is uncle, but the rest of Ethan's discourse turns this into a point of personal bravado and frontier democracy.

The events following Scar's raid on the Edwards homestead reveal Ethan's deep knowledge of Comanche ways, of horses, of the wilderness. He rests his horse before riding to the rescue, so he rides by Martin who has ridden his horse to death.[17] This and other incidents show that, despite Ethan's hostility, Martin has a great deal to learn from him. Other scenes show that Ethan is a good guide and teacher during Martin's five-year apprenticeship. He lets Martin see and know only what he can handle—he does not let him see Martha's body or, later, Lucy's, does not mention that he found Lucy dead, etc. Ethan also holds Martin back, hoisting him by the collar like a schoolboy, to prevent his following Brad in a suicidal attack into the Comanche camp when Martin and Brad are told of Lucy's rape and death.

An American Dilemma

Ethan's hostility to Martin begins at the Edwards dinner table but is rather restrained there. On the trail it bursts forth in a string of insults and epithets: "Come on, blankethead," (twice); "What does a quarter-blood Cherokee know about the Comanche trick of sleepin' with his best pony tied right by his side?" When Martin says he thinks they're being followed (he's right), Ethan says, "That's just the Injun in you."

A large number of textual features have to do with Martin's kinship. Many of his wrangles with Ethan have to do with whether or not he is Debbie's "brother" or otherwise her kin, so as to justify his searching for her year after year. As noted, these discussions may also be read as treating Martin's status as an adopted white. The kinship question is treated by the text at several different levels and often these levels are mixed or fused.

When the Comanches attack the pursuit party, Marty almost faints after his first shot. Mose Harper takes his rifle, Martin revives and starts firing with his handgun. This is "the young man's initiation in battle"—Anthony Perkins did this same bit in *Friendly Persuasion* the same year (1956). Below the surface, the issue is Martin's firing on his blood kinsmen. The film is quite attentive to where Martin's loyalties lie at this moment of decision. A parallel issue is raised when Martin inadvertently acquires a Comanche wife. He cannot send her back because Ethan says it will bring her tribe down on them; but Martin's misery at her being there, his kicking her away when she lies down beside him, makes clear where his loyalties lie. Ethan's calling her "Mrs. Pawley," and baiting Martin about her, link up with his other jibes about Martin as an Indian.

The kinship issue is discussed explicitly when Ethan and Martin return to the Jorgensen ranch after about a year of searching. Ethan wants Martin to stay behind, apparently because he plans to shoot Debbie now that she is a woman and defiled by the Comanches. The next morning Ethan rides off alone; with reluctant help from Laurie, Martin follows in order to stop Ethan from harming Debbie. In the bunkhouse the night before, Ethan and Martin have this discussion:

E: Jorgensen's been running my cattle with his own.

M: *Your* cattle? You mean *Debbie's* cattle.

E: He's agreed to take you on and split the increase in my herd while I'm gone. I'm pushing on tomorrow.

M: Well, I sure ain't gonna stay here. I started out looking for Debbie. I intend to keep on.

E: Why?

M: Why? . . . Well, because she's my—

E: She's your *nothin'*. She's no kin to you at all.

M: Well, I always *thought* she was—the way her folks took me in, they raised me—

E: That don't make you no kin.

M: All right, maybe it don't. Bu I intend to keep on lookin' anyway.

E: How? You got any horses, or money to buy them? You ain't even got money for cartridges. Jorgensen's offering you a good living here. Martin, there's something I want you to know—

M: Yeah, I know what you want me to know—that I got no kin, I got no money, no horses; all I got here is a bunch of dead man's clothes to wear. Well, you told me that already, so shut your mouth.

Later when they inspect recovered captives at the headquarters of a cavalry regiment, the officer asks them, "Who is this girl to you?" Martin says, "She's my—," and Ethan cuts him off: "—my niece." When they arrive at Scar's camp still later in the film, and are invited into Scar's tent, Ethan tells Martin to wait outside. Martin pushes strongly past him, saying, "Not likely." Ethan's remark may mean: I'll handle this business best without you; or: You're too young for this; but it also includes: This is a family matter and you're not part of the family. Martin's stern response is thus an assertion of kinship to Debbie (as well as an assertion of his developed maturity).

When in the next scene Martin confronts Debbie by the desert creek, he appeals to their shared childhood to break through to her; but he is also seeking from her, as the sole survivor of the family, validation of his own claims to kinship by adoption:

M: Debbie—

D: Unt-mea. (She points away.)

M: Debbie, don't you remember? I'm *Martin*. I'm Martin, your brother. Remember? Debbie, remember back. Do you remember how I used to let you ride my horse, and tell you stories? Don't you remember me, Debbie?

D: I remember—from always. At first, I prayed to you: Come and get me, take me home. . . . You didn't come.

An American Dilemma

M: But I've come now, Debbie.
D: These are my people. Unt-mea. Go. Go, Martin. Please.
E: Stand aside, Martin. (He takes his pistol from his holster.)
M: (turning to face Ethan, and shielding Debbie with his body and outstretched arms): No, you don't, Ethan. Ethan, *no, you don't!*
E: Stand aside.

What is going on in this scene is both obvious and subtle, overt and hidden. The adopted white and the adopted red confront each other and declare their kinship to each other. Martin seeks Debbie's return to white society, but he does not regard her marriage to Scar as any sort of disgrace. As one who is himself adopted, he cannot fault her loyalty to her new tribe; but as an adopted white, indeed as her brother, he must try to bring her back by any means. It is interesting also that just following this scene which affirms the kinship of Martin and Debbie, Ethan (now badly wounded by a Comanche arrow) formally disowns his kinship to Debbie:

M: (reading): "I, Ethan Edwards, being of sound mind,[18] and without any blood kin, do hereby be—
E: "Bequeath." It means leave.
M: "Bequeath all my property of any kind to Martin Pawley." What d'you mean, you don't have any blood kin? *Debbie's* your blood kin!
E: Not no more she ain't.
M: Well, you can *keep* your will. (Throws it back.) I don't want any of your property. And don't think I've forgotten what you were fixin' to do her. What kind of a man are you, anyway—?
E: She's been living with a buck! She's nothin' but a—
M: Shut your dirty mouth. I hope you die.
E: That'll be the day.

Martin persists in asserting and acting on his kinship bond to Debbie despite all obstacles. One of these obstacles is Laurie, the white woman he will marry. She reluctantly helps him to continue the search when Ethan resolutely rides off without him after their first return to the Jorgensens. On their second return, they interrupt her wedding to Charlie McCorry and then prepare to join the Rangers and the Cavalry in an attack upon Scar:

L: Marty, you're not going—not this time.
M: Are you crazy?
L: It's too late. She's a woman grown now.
M: I've got to fetch her home.
L: Fetch *what* home? The leavings of a Comanche buck, sold time and again to the highest bidder? With savage brats of her own?
M: Laurie, shut your mouth.
L: You know what Ethan'll do if he has a chance—he'll put a bullet in her brain. And I tell you Martha would want it.
M: Only if I'm dead.

In front of Scar's camp, the Reverend Captain Clayton gives the order to the Rangers to go in at sunup. Martin alone remains concerned about Debbie. He says, "Just a *minute,* Reverend—we go chargin' in and they'll kill her and you know it." Ethan: "That's what I'm counting on." Martin: "I know you are." Clayton: "Son, there's more at stake here than your sister." Ethan agrees, and tells Martin that a scalp they saw on Scar's lance (displayed by Debbie) belonged to Martin's mother. This gives Martin pause; then he says, "But that doesn't change anything. That changes nothing!" He proposes to sneak into the village to save Debbie before the attack and does so, disguising himself as an Indian—with blanket and no shirt, but with a white man's gun and holster under his blanket. Ethan opposes this, but Clayton agrees. Martin finds Debbie sleeping in Scar's tent and wakes her, saying, "Debbie, it's your brother Marty. I'm going to get you out of here." She wakes disoriented, and screams; he puts his hand over her mouth. Then she says, "Yes, Marty. Oh, yes, Marty!" Scar, on watch outside and alerted by Debbie's scream, enters the tepee—and Martin shoots him. The Ranger attack then begins, with Ethan riding wildly at its head, shooting in every direction. Ethan enters Scar's tepee, finds the dead Scar and scalps him, then rides after Debbie, separating her from Martin. Martin tries to pull Ethan from his horse, but cannot: he is knocked down instead. As Ethan rides after Debbie, Martin chases on foot, his hand on his gun, shouting, "No, Ethan, no!" He is clearly ready to kill Ethan in order to save Debbie. But Ethan does not shoot Debbie; instead he picks her up in his arms and takes her home.

The Laurie-Martin relationship deserves a note. Whether or not Martin is kin to the Edwards family has no bearing on his marrying Laurie: but the unconscious content of the kinship point, that he is a red man

An American Dilemma

adopted by white society, does bear upon it. Even on the surface of the text, if Martin is a "half-breed," a "blankethead," if Ethan is discomforted merely by sitting at the family table with him, then a fortiori he should be opposed to Martin's marrying a white woman. Yet neither Ethan nor anyone else in the film even hints at this. In the bunkhouse scene at Ethan and Martin's first return to the Jorgensens, Ethan notes Laurie's attraction to Martin with amusement as she kisses Martin good night. Also, in urging Martin to stay on at the Jorgensen ranch, he apparently accepts the inevitable match between Laurie and Martin. When the searchers return the second time and Laurie appears in a white wedding dress Ethan says to Martin with an ironic smile, "It looks like you two have a lot to talk about." He looks on the fistfight over Laurie between Martin and Charlie McCorry with good-natured neutrality.

Martin is the evident favorite of Laurie from the beginning and, it seems, of Laurie's mother also. Her father seems not to care, with perhaps a preference for Charlie, for whatever reason. The film is well under way before we see Laurie at all. She is seen in long shot at the funeral, barely coming into medium shot in a frame with several other things happening also. She says a silent good-bye to Martin, who seems awkward until he turns from her and mounts his horse.

When Martin returns for one day a year later, Laurie calls his name with loving irritability and kisses him—both of which he responds to as though barely awake. Laurie's mother asks him if he remembers her name, and he says, "Sure I do, her name's Laurie—but I darned near forgot just how pretty she was." The next morning, after more kissing, he suggests that they go steady; she replies with exasperation that they've been going steady "since we were three," and it's about time he found out about it. But her claim to an early closeness could not be proved by Martin's behavior. Upon the searchers' second return, Martin offers to go away so that Laurie can marry Charlie—to which Laurie replies, "If you do, Martin Pawley, I'll just die." (Never was the breakup of a wedding done so inertly.) Laurie tries hard to prevent Martin from going to the final attack on Scar. She wants him to remain with her now—but he goes anyway, abandoning her yet again. Despite her threats not to wait for him, Laurie does wait each time, and she joins him in the film's final tableau as they walk together into the house.

In the sexual relationship with Laurie, Martin is almost totally passive. The idea of the relationship seems to be hers, as does each step that furthers it or reinforces it. Of course this reversal of traditional roles is one of the running gags of the film. It is carried even to a bathtub scene in which the male is the object of voyeurism and horseplay and comically asserts his outraged modesty. Martin at no time displays physical desire for Laurie or a desire to marry her nor does he at any time hurry to get back to her. Martin is the love object whom Laurie chooses and seeks out. She conspicuously desires him, a desire that is presented as physical, indeed as violent, with hard kisses, pushes that knock down furniture, and a constantly agitated voice, alternating between a quaver and a screech.

The running argument between Ethan and Martin concerns in part the issue of kinship by adoption. In context this is strictly a family matter—Martin is not a blood kin of the Edwards family and, therefore, to Ethan; he has no reason to continue to search for Debbie. But altered slightly—kinship reckoned by blood *only* versus kinship reckoned by adoption also—it is also an anthropological issue, having to do with the relations between races and societies. In tracing "the Martin complex" through the film we have also traced the line of a textual duplicity. Martin functions now as part Indian, now as pure white, while in the unconscious symbolics of the film he functions as pure Indian. This "duplicity" is merely the effect of unconscious structures breaking the surface of the film at several points. It is now time to address those structures and to relate them to the dilemma of this film's power on audiences. If Martin functions as an Indian, is *The Searchers* readable as a myth about the adoption and integration of Indians in white society? Does this account for its power?

Of course, adoption is an ideological notion, a "savage" thinking of social problems and relations on the model of the family and family relations—precisely the sort of logic one finds in myths. In fact, there are historical grounds for considering the integration of Indians into white American society under the rubric of "adoption," at least in that in American history the detribalization of Indians was a conscious policy:

> Meanwhile, Congress proceeded to attempt Indian detribalization. In March of 1871, the treaty system of dealing with the Indians was ended by congressional enactment. The intent of the legislation was clear: Grant and Congress wanted the Indian civilized and Christianized. Since the tribal system was in the way, it would be circumvented. The Indian was supposed to finally become a full participant in American society, but he was to do it as an individual, not as a member of a tribe.[19]

But this does not make integration of Indians into American society, including intermarriage, an issue that requires unconscious treatment or

An American Dilemma

that stirs audiences profoundly. It may have been an issue in 1869, but it was hardly one in 1956. Indeed, there were very few antimiscegenation statutes regarding Indians at any time:

> Of the various laws which penalized illicit miscegenation, none applied to Indians, and only North Carolina's (and Virginia's, for a very brief period) prohibited intermarriage. On the contrary, several colonists were willing to allow, even advocate, intermarriage with the Indians—an unheard of proposition concerning Negroes. . . . It is suggestive, too, that Virginia's statutory definition of mulattoes extended the taint of Negro ancestry through three generations and of Indian ancestry through only one.[20]

Winthrop Jordan demonstrates Thomas Jefferson's praise of the Indian and his denigration of blacks, and argues that Jefferson's views, while extreme, are emblematic of American views generally.[21] Jefferson believed that in altered circumstances Indians would become whitemen, a transformation he thought the Negro could never accomplish. He hoped for the cultural and physical amalgamation of Indians and white Americans. "In truth the ultimate point of rest and happiness for them is to let our settlements and theirs meet and blend together, to intermix, and become one people." Such amalgamation and identification were precisely what Jefferson most abhorred with the Negro.

Will Rogers, who was a close friend of Ford and starred in three films made by him in the 1930s, and who had more Indian blood than Martin in *The Searchers,* expressed the positive view white Americans have had of the Indian, at least in modern times: "My ancestors didn't come over on the Mayflower, but they met the boat. . . . My father was one-eighth Cherokee Indian, and my mother was a quarter-blood Cherokee. I never got far enough in arithmetic to figure out just how much 'Injun' that makes me, but there's nothing of which I am more proud than my Cherokee blood."[22] The emotional impact of *The Searchers* can therefore hardly come from the issue of the kinship status and marriageability of an Indian in white society in 1956. This issue cannot be the locus of that unconscious conflict in knowledge or social life that activates every effective myth and fixes the attention of its listeners, according to Levi-Strauss. It becomes explicable only if we substitute black for red and read a film about red-white relations in 1868–73 as a film about black-white relations in 1956.

What does the opposition "kinship by blood *versus* kinship by adoption" have to do with the situation of blacks in the United States in 1956? Of course, blacks were detribalized with utmost violence by the acts that took them into slavery. As servants of plantations their own social organization was forcibly structured in relation to white society; but the questions we have considered under the rubric of "adoption" perhaps arose only with the first freed slaves and runaways. As late as 1857, the Supreme Court ruled in the Dred Scott case that Negro slaves and their descendants were not citizens of the United States or of the individual states and that prohibiting slavery deprived persons of their property without due process of law under the Fifth Amendment. In 1863 the Emancipation Proclamation freed slaves in areas in rebellion against the United States (nowhere else, e.g., Maryland). Amendments to the Constitution in 1865, 1868, and 1870 finally conferred citizenship on blacks ("all persons born or naturalized in the United States"), guaranteed their rights against the individual states, and guaranteed them the right to vote ("regardless of race, color, or previous condition of servitude").

On May 17, 1954, the Supreme Court announced *Brown v. Board of Education of Topeka*, its most important decision of modern times, some say the most important in its history. *Brown* held that in public education the doctrine of separate but equal was inherently unequal and therefore violated the black students' right to "equal protection of the laws" under the Fourteenth Amendment of the Constitution. Because it foresaw difficulties in desegregating schools kept apart for decades and (though it did not say so) anticipated resistance to its decision, the Court postponed its implementation for one year, while it considered briefs and oral arguments on the point.

May 1954–May 1955 saw heated debate regarding *Brown* throughout the country, including many defiant statements against it in the South: "I shall use every legal means at my command to continue segregated schools in Virginia"; "[The South] will not abide by or obey this legislative decision by a political court"; the Court's decision reduced the Constitution to "a scrap of paper"; any effort to integrate the South "will lead to great strife and turmoil." The State of Florida's brief on enforcement cited a poll showing that three-fourths of the white leaders of the state disagreed with the *Brown* decision, that 30 percent disagreed "violently," and that only 13 percent of peace officers said they would enforce state attendance laws at racially mixed schools.[23] The later "Southern Manifesto" by senators and congressmen from eleven southern states dismissed the Court's use of "naked judicial power" to legislate, and pledged its signers to use all lawful means to reverse the decision and to prevent the use of force in its implementation.[24]

An American Dilemma

Resistance to school desegregation was far more fierce and lasted far longer than resistance to the ending of other segregation practices during this period:

> Desegregation progressed at a relatively rapid rate in a relatively peaceable manner in most areas—from the restaurants of Washington to the buses of Montgomery to the ball-parks of the Texas League. One area alone was excepted: the schools. Streetcars and eating places and amusement parks were, after all, settings for transients with shared proximity for a limited time; schools were something else. There the contact would last for six or eight hours daily; it was from interaction with one another as much as attention devoted to lesson-books or lectures that schoolchildren derived the essence of their education. And so it was the schoolhouse that became the arena for the South's fiercest resistance to the desegregation order of the Supreme Court.[25]

Fear of intermarriage between black and white was one ground of opposition to *Brown*, explicit and implicit. Several states mention it in their briefs and cross-examinations before the Supreme Court.[26] Miscegenation was not cited more often as a likely consequence of *Brown* because in 1955 fully twenty-nine states (a majority) had statutes forbidding blacks and whites to marry. These laws were struck down as unconstitutional only in 1967.

It was in the midst of the *Brown* upheaval that the writing of the shooting script for *The Searchers* and other preparations for filming. The novel by Alan LeMay was published in 1954. Merian C. Cooper bought it that year for filming by John Ford with John Wayne as star, under a production company just formed by C. V. Whitney. According to *Motion Picture Herald*, the shooting of *The Searchers* took place between June 25 and August 27, 1955. (It was released on May 26, 1956.) I have not been able to determine exactly when Frank Nugent wrote the shooting script, but it was almost surely between early or mid-1954 and the first half of 1955, the period that coincides with the initial *Brown* uproar.

We cannot do here a detailed analysis of Nugent's adaptation of LeMay's novel; but several of the features of the film with which we have been most concerned were added by Nugent. In the novel Martin is 100 percent white, hence there is no conflict between Martin and Ethan about race;[27] but Ethan does try twice to shoot Debbie and Martin attempts to stop him. Martin does not enter Scar's village alone: he charges with the Rangers in the final battle and finds Debbie gone. Ethan is killed in the battle while running down an Indian girl he thinks is Debbie; she is not

67

Debbie, she pulls a gun from a horse and shoots him. Debbie, who has not been Scar's (or anyone's) wife or mistress, but is described as a dusky Indian maiden, has escaped to the desert. Martin trails her there and starts to make love to her on the last page. Laurie has married Charlie McCorry much earlier.

There were two great issues involved in *Brown:* the substantive question of desegregating public schools and changing the relations between black and white races, and the constitutional question of securing obedience to federal law. To certain Americans perhaps not enthusiastic about desegregation, *Brown* and the open declarations of defiance to it precipitated the most serious constitutional crisis since the Civil War and Reconstruction. In discussions at the time it was said again and again that decisions of the Supreme Court were "the law of the land" or "part of the law of the land." But whether one started from the desire for justice between the races or started from the need for compliance to law, one came logically to the same problem: How to achieve desegregation and what its consequence, near and far, were likely to be. If one began with law as an abstract principle one was perhaps more likely to approach the problem backward and in an unconscious way. This is pervasively so in a realm of "savage thought" like the construction of fictions. It is an even more complicated process in a case such as *The Searchers* where a structure preexisting the *Brown* situation is adapted under its (unconscious) pressure. This is what Levi-Strauss calls the bricolage principle: myth makes its structures out of the diverse materials at hand.

We have described the opposition between kinship by blood and kinship by adoption as a kind of mythic fulcrum—it carries both the family dispute of the story and (covertly) the social dispute of great concern to its audience. But how are we to understand the film's elaboration and treatment of the social issue, that is, of *Brown* and its consequences?

At first glance, the film's treatment seems quite clear once the conversion from story issue to social issue is made. The running argument of Ethan and Martin, as noted above, treats the issue explicitly. Martin asserts kinship by adoption by acting in all respects as though Debbie was literally his blood kin. He insists on participating in every stage of the search for her and, finally, on risking his life to save her. His devotion to her transcends other obligations and filiations; he defends her against Indians (Scar) and whites (Ethan, and the attacking Cavalry), and leaves Laurie (twice)—and even verbally attacks her—to secure Debbie's safety.

An American Dilemma

Ethan asserts Martin's lack of kinship to Debbie (and to himself) both as a general point of principle (the interview with the Cavalry officer) and as a means of directly dissuading Martin from continuing to participate in the search (the scene in the bunkhouse at the end of the first search). Ethan's insistence on literal blood lines in determining kinship, its privileges and its obligations, is historically the position of the segregationist and white supremacist. And of course Ethan returns to his brother's ranch from having fought on the southern side in the Civil War; he still wears his Confederate coat and carries his Confederate sabre. These features mark Ethan as a white southerner, displaced out west.[28] This identification of Ethan as a white southerner occurs partly on the surface of the film but is simultaneously rendered unreadable in various ways. For one thing, Ethan lacks a southern accent, which would give the game away every time he spoke of race or looked at Martin askance. Also, John Wayne was associated by audiences with westerners, not southerners; the references to the Civil War, and even to his wearing a Confederate uniform, are taken as character points, not political ones ("I take one oath at a time, Reverend"). There is no mention of the actual issues of the Civil War or, at any time, of blacks. Also, except for the dinner table scene and the ride out after the lost cattle at the beginning, Ethan's anti-Indian attitudes are motivated by the plot—"He is bitter about Martha"; hence there is no reason to see them as the film's displacement of antiblack attitudes.

There is another signification set clustered around Ethan: that of outlawism. His not accepting the surrender of his side in a war that has been over for years makes him at least a figurative outlaw. He boasts that he still has his sabre—"Didn't turn it into no ploughshare neither." (That sabre, though the mediation of a green lieutenant, later slices the ass of the Reverend Captain Clayton, symbol of religious and civil authority in the film.) Ethan was missing for three years between the end of the Civil War and 1868, when the film opens; there are hints that he was an outlaw during this time. "You fit a lot of descriptions," says Clayton. He shows up at his brother's homestead with a bagful of freshly minted $20 pieces, about the origin of which he is vague. Ethan does shoot Futterman and his two men in the back, making no attempt to take them alive; and he takes back his gold pieces, which he had given Futterman in exchange for information. This episode gets Ethan and Martin into actual trouble with the law; Clayton takes Ethan's gun (there is a moment when it appears that Ethan might resist with that gun), and orders him to Austin to answer questions.

The Cavalry enters with news of Scar, Ethan's gun is returned, and the film drops the matter. Throughout the film, though, Ethan violates the religious and social law of his people by desecrating dead Indians, by scalping his enemies, by attempting to murder his kin for marrying a Comanche, etc.

Racism was always immoral and undemocratic but *Brown* made some of its most fundamental institutions illegal. Thus *The Searchers* specifically conjoins the figure of the white southerner with the figure of the outlaw. (In the novel, Ethan came right home after the Civil War and had no bagful of money or other indicia of the outlaw, and he is no more anti-Indian than Martin or any of the other main characters.) After *Brown,* opposing the possibility of kinship by adoption, affirming kinship by blood only, places one outside the law. Thus Ethan's exclusion from the community at the end of the film is overdetermined by its unconscious structure.

Martin in effect wins the argument with Ethan by saving Debbie and by returning home to marry Laurie and settle in the community. Ethan returns home only to move on again. He is self-excluded from the community but, as Propp shows, this is functionally similar to forcible exclusion, just as self-dispatch and dispatch by another are equivalent functions. Note that the figure of the white southerner often functions as a scapegoat on the race question. Our racial prejudice and our guilt for it are placed on his shoulders, then he is criticized, excluded, or lampooned, mythically purging us of them. Thus, in *The Searchers,* Ethan is excluded for our sins; that is why we find it so moving.

The film's ending thus enacts Martin's position; the adopted one marries and enters the community as an adult male. He enjoys the full rights of kinship. But it is not so simple as this, for a number of reasons. First, Martin and Ethan debate several issues, not just this one, and the film treats the issue of kinship and race in many ways besides their arguments. Secondly, what we have called "Martin's victory" is already implicit in *Brown:* if the film merely affirmed the nonwhite's entry into white society and opposed those who oppose that entry, then it might not have as great a power on audiences as it has. At least it would not bear on the issue of greatest concern once *Brown* is a fait accompli: What will the consequences of desegregation be?

The film is concerned not only with the fact of adoption, the right to adoption under the new law of the land, but with the nature and scope of adoption, its rights and obligations. Are the adopted ones equal in rights and obligations to those who have always belonged to the society? Martin wins the argument with Ethan, but what is the price of that victory?

An American Dilemma

The film does not deal with the adoption itself, the finding of Martin by Ethan, the growing up years, etc.—those matters in the forefront of discussion and awareness in the debate over *Brown*. Rather, it looks to the other end of the adoption spectrum, that which is implied in adoption but not immediately palpable to the senses or to the imagination: What will happen when the adopted one grows up and enters white society as an adult? Thus in *The Searchers* Martin's adoption is a fait accompli. The film focuses on the consequences: on the status, rights, duties, and responsibilities of the adopted one when grown.

Although it is a myth about nonwhites by and for whites, *The Searchers* may also be read as a manual for nonwhites adopted by white society, telling them what they may expect and what is expected of them. In our analysis of "the Martin complex" in the film, we saw that Martin exhibits unwavering loyalty to the white community. He kills Indian men, spurns Indian wives, defends his sister not just against Indians but against other whites, including the most formidable white man of all. He devotes five years to find her, then risks his life to kill the villain and save her. Martin's passivity in regard to Laurie is also exemplary. The nonwhite can show no aggressiveness toward a white love object; if Martin is the example, he can hardly show or feel desire at all. Martin postpones pleasure in the Freudian sense. Laurie offers herself and the pleasures of peaceful life at home again and again, but he refuses until his mission is done. This may be read diachronically (à la Propp) that Martin cannot marry Laurie or enter society as an adult until he has proven himself as fully white, indeed as whiter than white, by the incredible number of performances he accomplishes. Or it may be read synchronically à la Levi-Strauss and Lacan: Martin immediately enjoys full white citizenship and kinship (and even wins Laurie) but this creates a *debt,* according to this film an enormous debt, that he must discharge in exchange for this gift. The debt for the nonwhite is evidently far greater than for whites. On the opposite end of the spectrum from Martin, the good Indian (nigger), there is Scar, the bad Indian (nigger). Scar precisely cannot postpone pleasure—he rapes, murders, dismembers, burns; and he is punished in the most brutal way: death, scalping, destruction of his society. The annihilating punishment that Scar receives is also a warning to adopted nonwhites of what awaits their transgressions. Correlated with Scar's crimes is the fact that he remains with his tribe, with his people, whereas Martin renounces any tribal tie, loyalty, or memory; this is the precondition of adoption.

Our reading is nonreductive—the Indian-white ideological theme remains. There is in fact a kind of double displacement operating in the film at almost every moment, whereby literal events of the text may be read in the Indian-white register and then in the black-white register. But if our concern is the power of a myth, then it is the black-white discourse that must interest us. Power selects a myth: the myth does not create it. Black-white relations were such in 1956, and arguably now as well, that the issues *The Searchers* treats could not be treated directly. This hiddenness is the mark of conflicts of great power, and the continuing power of *The Searchers* confirms audience contact with conflicts of great importance to itself but not understood by it.

As the Reverend Jesse Jackson said recently, "Racism is the curse of the American soul." As long as this remains true, *The Searchers* is likely to retain its power.

NOTES

1. Byron, "*The Searchers:* Cult Movie of the New Hollywood," 45–48.
2. Edward Buscombe, "Critics on *The Searchers*," *Screen Education* (winter 1975–76): 50.
3. Qtd. in Pye, "*The Searchers* and Teaching the Industry," in ibid., 45.
4. Qtd. in Ibid., 43.
5. T. S. Eliot, *Selected Essays* (New York: Harcourt, 1950): 12.
6. Vladimir Propp, *The Morphology of the Folktale* (Austin: University of Texas Press, 1963), 75–78.
7. There is a Proppian problem in the film's doubled hero: it is Martin, not Ethan, who kills Scar, recovers Debbie, and marries Laurie, though arguably Martin does the first two as Ethan's helper.
8. Levi-Strauss's binarism, his postulate that all myths (and kinship and totemistic structures) are built out of sets of binary oppositions, which he seems to ground in the structure of the brain itself, has been much attacked. The consensus now seems to be that binarism fits some situations well but as a universal principle of the formations of culture it is untenable.
9. "John Ford's *Young Mr. Lincoln:* A Collective Text by the Editors of *Cahiers du cinema*," trans. Helene Lackner and Diana Matias, *Screen* (autumn 1972).
10. Charles Eckart, "The Anatomy of a Proletarian Film: Warner's *Marked Woman*," *Film Quarterly* (winter 1973–74): 10.
11. But note that Debbie remembers her white childhood and language "from always," whereas Martin is a total amnesiac about his childhood, which, though among whites, stands in metaphorically for his Indian ancestry. Similarly, it is Ethan later who "speaks good Comanch": Martin speaks it hardly at all despite five years traveling among the tribes.
12. "John Ford's *Young Mr. Lincoln:* A Collective Text by the Editors of *Cahiers du cinema*," trans. Helene Lackner and Diana Matias, *Screen* (autumn 1972): 40.
13. Ibid., 42.

14. Ibid.
15. Ibid., 42–43.
16. Ibid., 40.
17. We might pause at this figure of a cowboy lugging a saddle across the plains as two riders hurry by. Is this the same Martin who yesterday rode bareback and dressed and looked like an Indian boy? A day later he is grown up and looks like a white cowboy, a prime instance of the text's duplicity, gaining all the associations of boyhood, Indian, and nature boy in one scene, and of young manhood and white cowboy in the next. Moreover, the character has grown up in a day; we have now seen him, or we think we have, as a boy in the warmth of home and then a grown man on his own on the trail the next afternoon.
18. Surely this is one of the film's little jokes.
19. Dwight W. Weaver, *The Red and the Black* (Chicago: Rand-McNally, 1976), 146.
20. Winthrop D. Jordan, *White Over Black: American Attitudes Toward the Negro, 1550–1812* (Baltimore: Penguin, 1969), 163.
21. Ibid.
22. Bryan W. Sterling, ed., *The Will Rogers Scrapbook* (New York: Grosset and Dunlap, 1976), 11.
23. Richard Kluger, *Simple Justice* (New York: Knopf, 1976), 700–747.
24. By 1970 much of the South was in substantial technical compliance with *Brown* (though the extent of actual educational desegregation varied greatly because of the growth of "white" private schools in some regions). In 1971 the Court somewhat redefined the *Brown* standard of equal education, centralizing the concept of racial balance within individual schools, and the focus of enforcement and resistance shifted to the North.
25. Kluger, *Simple Justice*, 751.
26. Ibid., 6, 28, 672, 751, passim.
27. In addition to the meanings we have traced, this change is simply good screenwriting: it introduces a dramatic conflict between the two principal characters that heightens and transforms the significance of their external adventures.
28. In fact, the north-central Texas region in which *The Searchers* is set was settled mainly by southerners before and after the Civil War. Aaron speaks of a neighbor's having been driven from this land and gone back to chopping cotton. See Richard Maxwell Brown, *Strain of Violence* (New York: Oxford University Press, 1975), 236–99.

John Wayne and The Searchers

William Luhr

Most serious discussions of *The Searchers* have positioned it within John Ford's career, within Hollywood history, or within American culture. Although these discussions generally acknowledge both John Wayne's star status and Ford's long-term use of him in his films, they tend to subsume his contribution to *The Searchers* under that of Ford. This essay examines what Wayne's performance and star image brought to the making and marketing of the film, as well as ways in which changes in his image inflected the film's subsequent reception.

When *The Searchers* appeared in 1956, it was advertised as a "John Wayne" western in theatrical trailers, print ads, and the contemporaneous half hour, promotional television show about its making. Wayne's career and star status were then at their peak; he was seven years into the remarkable twenty-six-year period during which, with one exception, he appeared in distributors' listings of the ten most popular film stars (and among the top four for nineteen of those years).[1] His star image involved a particular kind of postwar American masculinity, one defined by the challenges of the World War II military, still fresh in popular memory, as well as by the mythic status of the frontier American West.

The generation that fought World War II evidenced widespread anxiety about the erosion of individuality and masculine vitality in the postwar era. Many felt that, in the aftermath of a globally empowering victory, they were losing control of their lives. One manifestation of this was their growing concern over their ability to control their own children, the rebellious teenagers of the 1950s; another was the pervasive image of doomed, impotent, and demoralized men in many *films noir*. A highly publicized masculine fear involved losing individuating potency and becoming simply a "number," an "organization man," a corporate "man in a gray-flannel suit."[2]

Although wartime military life had stressed regimentation and submission to authority, it also signified to many a masculine proving ground, a valorizing test by fire. Wayne's contemporary military roles in films such as *Flying Tigers* (1942), *Back to Bataan* (1945), *They Were Expendable* (1945), *Sands of Iwo Jima* (1949), *Operation Pacific* (1951), and *Flying Leathernecks* (1951) presented him as heroic despite his wearing a uniform like others around him and his submission to regimentation. A popular joke in postwar military life, indicating the appeal of his persona, was to refer to John Wayne movies as "training films."[3] Wayne's military image, then, bespoke contemporary heroism despite regimentation to this generation. At precisely the same time, however, his western persona worked in the opposite way. It presented him as a man alone in an idealized past, totally unregimented, self-sufficient, and self-determining. This persona coped not with an oppressive, depersonalizing social structure, as many in the 1950s saw their era, but instead with an unformed social system open to grand possibilities for the righteous and the strong. He was perceived as a man among men in the days when "men were men." Both of Wayne's personae spoke resonantly to the anxieties of 1950s masculinity.

Wayne was consolidating his image as THE western star when the western itself occupied its cultural peak. When Gary Cooper was unable to attend the 1953 "Oscar" ceremony to receive his Best Actor award for the western *High Noon* (1952), Wayne, considered a western star of comparable stature, was selected to accept it for him. Extraordinarily popular in Hollywood, the western also dominated primetime television throughout the late 1950s. The 1959 season opened with twenty-seven westerns in prime time, constituting nearly one-fourth of prime-time programming. In January 1959, eight of the top ten rated programs were westerns.[4] In fact, when *The Searchers* was in preparation, Wayne declined the lead role in *Gunsmoke* (whose twenty-year run made it the most successful western series in television history), but famously introduced its premiere episode on September 10, 1955, as a way of lending his western star status to James Arness. Arness, a friend of Wayne's, had played supporting roles in Wayne vehicles such as *Big Jim McLain* (1952), *Hondo* (1953), *Island in the Sky* (1953), and *The Sea Chase* (1955).

The Searchers did not attain the legendary status it now holds until nearly two decades after its release, until the beginning of academic film studies and the entrance into Hollywood filmmaking of the first genera-

John Wayne and *The Searchers*

tion of directors trained in film schools. Many of these directors, such as George Lucas, Martin Scorcese, and John Milius have made explicit homages to *The Searchers* in their own films and, in interviews, have spoken reverently of it as well as of Wayne's performance in it.[5]

Curiously, however, this rise in the film's reputation occurred when the reception context for Wayne's star image was also changing. In the 1950s the masculinity he represented was attuned to mainstream culture, respected by young and old alike; by the 1970s, however, the growing youth culture considered his brand of postwar masculinity reactionary. A popular bumper sticker of the time read "John Wayne for Secretary of Defense." Jokingly invoking Wayne's screen image as a man of decisive violence, the bumper sticker also linked him with the government then embroiled in the unpopular Vietnam War. Wayne himself was vocal in his support of that government and that war. Many in the younger generation of the 1970s not only protested the actions of that government but also viewed Wayne's masculinity as detrimental to national ideals. Ron Kovic's *Born on the Fourth of July* (1976) chronicles the transformation of his young, idealistic patriotism into an embittered critique of dominant American ideology after his paralysis as a result of a devastating wound sustained in Vietnam. In the book, he recalled idolizing Wayne as a youth but summarized his subsequent sense of betrayal when he said, "I gave my dead dick for John Wayne."[6]

The complexities of *The Searchers* thus provided space for young, anti-establishment cinephiles of the 1970s both to condemn the older Wayne and his image while simultaneously valuing the film and his work in it. Wayne's remarkable performance in the film both engaged the western persona he had developed prior to that time and simultaneously undermined it. Audiences of the 1950s seem to have perceived Wayne's performance in *The Searchers* as little more than a darker variation on his established persona; some later audiences, however, attuned to changes in Wayne's image, have seen that same performance as profoundly undercutting and critiquing that persona.

The film's opening and closing scenes present Wayne's imposing and iconic bodily presence against a western desert landscape. By 1956, that presence itself had developed monumental associations. Deborah Thomas has written that "Wayne's body is often seen by other characters as bearing the marks of the statuesque/monumental: tall, hard, unyielding and representative of various institutional codes."[7] By 1956, Wayne's association for more than a decade with both wartime valor and mythic western potency had combined to suggest in his image a repository of national ideals. Twenty years later, however, those ideals were being criticized as reactionary, and Wayne's monumentality as ossified, out-of-date. The cultural pervasion of Wayne's image combined with post-1970s critiques of it have inclined many in recent decades to approach his work from a reductive and often dismissive perspective, rather than from one that accounts for the complexities of its evolution within changing eras.

Characters in some films conflate Wayne's roles with national institutions. One in *Sands of Iwo Jima*, for example, complains that Wayne's Stryker has "probably got the regulations tattooed on his chest"—implicitly saying that Stryker IS the institution (here, the U.S. Marines). Thomas cites this dialogue (75), but also points out that "Wayne's perceived monumentality in terms of its physical attributes—its frozen intractable qualities— . . . seems to provide a screen against his softer, more vulnerable traits" (76). In *The Searchers*, his stolid presence masks a profoundly ruptured and complex interior. The very monumentality of his physical presence and the rigidification of his post-1960s image may have contributed to the oft-cited presumption that he had a limited range as an actor. No film more than *The Searchers*, however, demonstrates his ability to develop a complex interior that contradicts what appears on the surface. Although the opening and closing of the film present him as stolidly resembling the unchanging and unchangeable buttes of Monument Valley that frame him,[8] his performance in the body of the film develops a profoundly complicated character.

Wayne had developed a number of behavioral strategies for his western persona even before its appearance in *Stagecoach* in 1939. In films in which he employs this persona, he often uses his body to project contradictory signals. While his height, bulk, and breadth suggest dominance and physical power, he frequently postures himself in a relaxed, restful manner, as if comfortable in his physical power and reluctant to display or employ it.[9] His laconic speech patterns, his economical, graceful movements, and his muted, even shy facial expressions reinforce this reticence. In this use of his body he resembled some western stars of his era such as Gary Cooper and differed radically from urban action stars like James Cagney or John Garfield, whose bodily posturing, facial expressions, and vocal patterns often radiated tension and provocation. Prior to eruptions of violence, Wayne's persona would often become extremely quiet and restrained, like a panther ready to pounce. Wayne drew upon this mode of presentation throughout the 1940s and 1950s in westerns like *Stage-*

John Wayne and *The Searchers*

coach, Tall in the Saddle (1944), *Angel and the Badman* (1947), and *Hondo* as well as in non-western films such as *The Quiet Man* (1952) and *The High and the Mighty* (1954).

Wayne did not always rely upon this persona during this period. He employed different, more aggressive and kinetic, performance strategies in films like *Flying Tigers, Pittsburgh* (1942), *Reap the Wild Wind* (1942), *War of the Wildcats* (1943), *Tycoon* (1947), and *Red River* (1948). In these films, he often plays maniacally driven and ambitious men in positions of command. Rather than presenting himself in a physically muted and bashful manner, he frequently appears highly stressed, intimidating, and loud. He often behaves harshly and intrusively, barking out rapid-fire commands at subordinates. In these roles he engages a model of aggressive, dominating masculinity commonly seen in films of the 1930s and 1940s. Examples include Pat O'Brien in *Ceiling Zero* (1936) or *Torrid Zone* (1940), Cary Grant in *Only Angels Have Wings* (1939) or *His Girl Friday* (1940), and Clark Gable in *China Seas* (1935) and *Boom Town* (1940). By 1956, however, Wayne's restrained persona had come to dominate his westerns. He seemed no longer to need to establish his authority through action; his physical presence did it all for him. Ford introduced Wayne's character Ringo with a dynamic dolly-in shot in *Stagecoach*—Ringo brandishes his rifle, yells "hold it," and dramatically stops the stagecoach. Seventeen years later in *The Searchers*, however, Ford introduces Ethan Edwards (Wayne's character) by simply having him dismount from his horse, say nothing, and do little more than stand there. And it is more than enough.

The opening and closing shots of *The Searchers*, then, invoke Wayne's persona as a strong, silent man of the West. However, much in his performance during the rest of the film undercuts it. At times, his actions recall some of the abrasive behavioral strategies employed in films cited in the preceding paragraph, but there is a major difference. In those films he played a man with a mission evident to all, often in command of others and impelled to dominate and drive them to his will; in *The Searchers*, he is a man alone. His behavioral abrasions more bespeak an underlying and repressed psychological torment than a clearly focused mission. Where Wayne's established western persona commonly developed a tension between his imposing physical presence and reticent manner, here he does not. He often stands and moves in a manner that bespeaks neither reticence nor shyness but, rather, intrusiveness and menace. Where his established persona often appeared relaxed and at ease, even in stressful situations, here he looks tense, troubled, often seething with rage. Where his established persona interacted comfortably with his physical surroundings and moved casually among them, here he appears profoundly uncomfortable with his surroundings and often lurches through them. Given the monumental associations that his screen image carried by this time, the film's recurring images of him troubled and losing control give his presence a disturbing, almost epochal, dimension, like a volcano about to erupt.

A few examples will suffice. The film opens with the unexplained return of Ethan Edwards to his brother Aaron's Texas homestead after an absence of roughly seven years. On the following day, Aaron, his wife Martha, and their son Ben are slaughtered by a Comanche war band led by Chief Scar, who also abducts their two daughters, Lucy and Debbie. During the funeral for Aaron's family, Ethan abrasively interrupts the service by abruptly yelling "Put an amen to it! There's no time for praying! Amen!" and, livid with vengeful fury, stalks off to hunt the Comanches. Then, in a highly unusual shot, we see the distressed mourners when, abruptly, Ethan's head and torso lurches across the frame, left to right, too close to the camera and moving too quickly even to be clearly seen. Wayne's intrusion into the shot creates a visual abrasion to parallel the narrative abrasion his character's actions have caused. In fact, his character commonly violates social decorum, as at the funeral. Earlier, while dining with his brother's family, he is introduced to their adoptive son Martin Pauley, who approaches him genially. Refusing to make a reciprocal gesture of greeting, he glares at Martin for an uncomfortably long period of time. Finally, and probably referring to Martin's darkly tanned skin and jet black hair, Ethan says, "Fella could mistake you for a half-breed." Aaron's family is stunned at, and tries to smooth over, this behavior. Significantly, Ethan's abrasive and explicitly racist remark occurs before and not after Indians slaughter Aaron's family, making his unsettling behavior more deep-rooted than simply a response to the massacre. Later, while Ethan is being introduced to Chief Scar, he abruptly cuts the introduction short by stalking up to Scar at a menacingly close distance. Glaring at the man, Ethan insultingly says, "Scar, huh, plain to see how you got your name," causing the chief to instinctively raise his hand to cover his scarred face. In all of these scenes, Wayne forgoes his traditional reticent manner and uses his body and voice to create a disturbing and intimidating presence, either by yelling and stalking out of the funeral, abruptly barging across the frame in disquietingly close camera range, eschewing traditional social niceties, or provocatively menacing other characters. Such actions not only present

John Wayne and *The Searchers*

Ethan in an ugly manner but also show Wayne's persona in an unsympathetic light, something many star actors scrupulously avoid.

One might argue that Wayne was not the creative force behind these scenes but simply played the character as scripted by Frank Nugent and as directed by John Ford. Ford would obviously have blocked out the scenes, choreographed the movement within them and determined the placement of the camera, as in the shot in which Wayne lurches across the frame unusually close to the camera. This is true, but it doesn't tell the whole story. When a star actor deviates substantially from a persona he has successfully crafted over time as, for example, when Kevin Costner accepted second billing and played a sadistic villain in *3,000 Miles to Graceland* (2001), there is generally a significant reason for it. With Costner, one might presume that, by taking on a character that severely deviated from his star image at that time, he was attempting to demonstrate a broader acting range than previously seen and possibly reverse the career decline he had experienced in the late 1990s. Wayne, however, was at the height of his career in 1956, a time when many actors are reluctant to tinker with the formula that has made them successful. Furthermore, Wayne had begun producing movies in 1947 and by the mid-1950s was known for exercising considerable control over his films and performances. Star actors are often highly selective about the roles they choose and commonly have those they select rewritten to protect and enhance their image. Many demand script and even director approval, flattering lighting and camera angles, a happy and heroic ending, a desirable costar; many will also refuse to do things they consider erosive of their image, such as weeping, displaying their bodies in unattractive ways, or engaging in cowardly or sleazy behavior. George Raft is notorious for bad career decisions along this line, purportedly turning down such career-making hits as *High Sierra* (1941), *The Sea Wolf* (1941), *The Maltese Falcon* (1942), and *Double Indemnity* (1944) because of the moral failings of the central characters.[10]

In *The Searchers*, both Wayne's character and performance deviate substantially from his established persona. Unlike the majority of western heroes he had portrayed to this time, Ethan has no successful romantic interest and does not get to face down and kill the enemy he spends the entire film stalking. Instead, Ethan scalps Scar after Martin kills him. Ethan also mutilates another Indian's corpse by shooting out its eyes, prepares to murder his own niece in cold blood, shoots men in the back, and demonstrates unregenerate racism by slaughtering buffalo to promote racial extinction. By the codes of the 1950s western, Ethan is as much a villain as a hero. And Wayne's performance, as discussed above, also deviates substantially from, even undercuts, his established screen presence.

Wayne was quite aware of the linkage among role choice, image, and performance. Both he and Howard Hawks claimed that they made *Rio Bravo* (1959) three years later to provide a riposte to the success of *High Noon* (1952). They felt that Gary Cooper's anxiety-ridden and help-seeking sheriff in that film undermined the individuality and independence of its western hero.[11] Wayne's sheriff in *Rio Bravo* does not plead for help; he even declines it when it is offered, but vanquishes the bad guys anyway. But, curiously, Wayne's portrayal of Ethan Edwards in *The Searchers* provides a far more trenchant critique of the western tradition than *High Noon*.

The Searchers begins with an event common in western lore—Indians massacre a white family and the central character seeks retribution for this savage act. The film's opening initially seems to present whites as agents of civilization in the wilderness and Indians as murderous, raping savages. But then things get strange. We learn that the presumably savage chief committed the massacre in retaliation for the killing of his own family by whites. We see the U.S. Cavalry, frequently agents of salvation in westerns of the classical era, responsible for the slaughter of Indian women and children; and we see the central white character commit the "savage" act of scalping a dead Indian. We also see rampant racism within white culture.

Unlike many classical westerns, this is not a film that glorifies the westward expansion of white culture or the traditional western hero. Instead, it critiques it all in disturbing ways. Wayne and Hawks disliked *High Noon* because they considered its hero and his town weak, not heroically self-sufficient. But Gary Cooper's Will Kane was not savagely racist, murderous, genocidal, mutilating, and possibly adulterous.

Arthur M. Eckstein has carefully traced and documented the systematic darkening of the character of Ethan Edwards, from its origins in Alan LeMay's novel, to Frank Nugent's script, to Ford's film.[12] He cites instances at each stage of the creative process of the deletion from the character of traditionally heroic attributes. This is not an isolated film in its era. Both *High Noon* and *The Searchers* point to a darkening of the western itself in the 1950s. The popular image of the traditional western, never entirely accurate, had been one of a morality fable in which the admirable hero triumphs over the evil bad guys, thus paving the way for the transformation of the "Wild West" into the "civilized" modern era. Many westerns of the 1950s, however, feature profoundly troubled, often tormented central characters. Many established western stars, well into middle age at the time, played roles of a different timbre than they had in their youth. By the 1950s, the cathartic violence to which the genre traditionally builds was frequently associated with the hero's deeply troubled and bruised psyche. Gary Cooper plays much of *High Noon* as a deeply anxious, fearful, and betrayed man. In the westerns that James Stewart made with Anthony Mann (such as *Bend of the River*, 1952, and *The Man From Laramie*, 1955), he often played men capable of almost psychotic violent impulses. Kirk Douglas played similarly tormented characters in films like *Man Without a Star* (1955) and *Gunfight at the O.K. Corral* (1957). Some of this darkening within the genre may have roots in the influence of *film noir* in the 1940s, with brooding, unheroic westerns like *The Ox-Bow Incident* (1943) and *Pursued* (1947). It also had parallels on television. In the mid- and late 1950s, television westerns were advertised as "adult westerns," implying that the genre had entered a mature phase. This addressed an identity problem for the genre, which appeared to be disassociating itself from its earlier image of dime novel fantasies suitable mainly for young boys by asserting its capacity to engage a complex range of mature experience.

Wayne could have demanded such things as a softening of Ethan's abrasiveness, a romantic partner for him, as well as a traditional happy ending. The reasons he did not reside in Wayne's career-long loyalty to John Ford and his trust of Ford's judgment. Their previous film together, *The Quiet Man*, had been a spectacular success. Furthermore, he had received critical accolades for a number of earlier and successful deviations from his star image—he had played an embittered man much older than himself in *Red River* and, soon after, another old man in *She Wore a Yellow Ribbon*. His characters in *Sands of Iwo Jima* and *Rio Grande* (1950) carry psychic scars from deeply ruptured domestic pasts. These films appeared when Wayne himself entered middle age, at precisely the time that his period of greatest popularity began. They quite possibly indicated to Wayne that a dark side to his characters, instead of detracting from his star image, might very well add depth to his performances.

Such a dark side was certainly evident in *The Conqueror* (1956), which was released immediately before *The Searchers*. In it, Wayne plays Temujin, a tribal Mongol warlord who eventually becomes Genghis Khan. Deviating considerably from traditional leading man behavior, Wayne's savage character is nakedly imperial, often murderous, and even kidnaps and rapes his leading lady (Susan Hayward). The mid- to late 1950s was perhaps the time in which Wayne was the most experimental in his choice of leading roles. In *The Conqueror* he is made up to look Asian, with altered eyes, darkened skin, a black wig, and medieval Mongolian wardrobe. At the other end of the behavioral spectrum, two years later Wayne made *The Barbarian and the Geisha* (1958). Here he plays a nineteenth-century American ambassador to Japan, garbed in formal diplomatic attire, including top hat.

An established star's image can work considerably to mute specific actions in an individual film. Alfred Hitchcock used Cary Grant's image as a counterweight to his role in *Suspicion* (1941). The actions of Grant's character, until the very end, seem to justify his wife's suspicions that he plans to murder her. Only at the end does he prove her suspicions false. Hitchcock has spoken of the tension between Grant's leading man image and his character's disturbing actions. During postproduction, in fact, an RKO producer deleted scenes implying Grant's guilt, shortening the film to fifty-five minutes. The studio head, however, had the scenes put back in. The standard wisdom by which he justified this was simple; Cary Grant could not be a murderer. Consequently, Hitchcock felt no need to include scenes softening the character.[13] Hitchcock employed a related strategy in *Vertigo* (1958) in which James Stewart's wholesome star image works to partially repress the fact that he plays one of the most troubling and disturbing characters in American film. The abrasions of Wayne's performance in *The Searchers* quite possibly worked in a similar way. This may account for the fact that sympathetic 1950s audiences did not seem to have considered Ethan a significantly different character for Wayne (though some assuredly did). However, the very ugliness of the character and of Wayne's performance may have been strikingly evident to 1970s cinephiles not disposed to see Wayne in an heroic light, and caused them to admire (even love) the film.

In *The Searchers,* Wayne's performance less resembles those of Gary Cooper in westerns than those of James Cagney in his 1950s westerns like *Run for Cover* (1955). Like Cagney's, Wayne's body and face are tense, not relaxed; his movements and physical interactions with other actors are intrusive, spatially abrasive, not recessive; his vocal patterns are not laconic and measured but often loud, harsh, and provocative. Rather than appearing to avoid violence and social abrasion, his gestures and posturing provoke them. He also plays some scenes with wholesale emotional abandon, much more characteristic in the 1950s of "Method" actors like Marlon Brando, Paul Newman, Rod Steiger, or James Dean, or for actors associated with urban action films, like Cagney or Kirk Douglas, than for actors like Wayne. When Ethan reveals to Brad, Lucy's boyfriend, that the Indians

John Wayne and *The Searchers*

had killed Lucy, Brad asks if she had been raped. Ethan explodes, snarls, "Whaddaya want me to do—draw you a picture?!" and warns him never to ask him about it again. In the scene, Wayne contorts his face and shouts with near hysterical and misdirected turmoil, manifesting Ethan's fury at the event and at having to recall what he learned of it. He yells, registers inner horror at what he himself has learned, and directs insensitive rage at the traumatized Brad for making him relive it. This is very different from Wayne's acting in *Stagecoach,* when his character Ringo is asked about the fate of his brother and he quietly replies, "He was murdered." Wayne's character's mission in that film is revenge also, but his way of revealing the precipitating injustice is contained, stoic, non-abrasive. However horrible Ringo's loss, Wayne's acting style gives the impression that Ringo has come to terms with it, will deal with it as he has to, but will not take out his fury on others. Furthermore, Ethan in *The Searchers* has no scenes of romantic involvement that foreground a shy gentility. The absence of such scenes reinforces the brittle nature of his performance. He is not a character with a future, only one coming to terms with a troubled past. The end of the film leaves him with nowhere to go.

Particularly in Ford's films, Wayne's roles seemed to be detaching from romantic involvements since the late 1940s. He has none in *Fort Apache* (1948) but looks benignly on at the romantic entanglements of younger characters. He has none in *Three Godfathers* (1949) and, in *She Wore a Yellow Ribbon,* he plays a widower, once again leaving romance to the young. In *Rio Grande* his character comes to terms with a deeply troubled marriage. *The Quiet Man,* centrally about courtship and marriage, is an exception, as are roles in some films by other directors at this time, but by the 1960s Wayne's characters either have no romantic scenes or deal very quickly, almost with embarrassment, with the few that occur.

This detachment from romantic scenes is very possibly a factor of age. In his scores of films in the 1930s and 1940s, Wayne very commonly played characters with strong romantic involvements; at times he even played a sexual aggressor. But though it would have been easy to include some romantic scenes for Ethan in *The Searchers* (as in other Wayne films of the time), the fact that there are none, and no mention of romance in Ethan's past, only adds to the character's brittleness and isolation.

Ethan's tensions are reflected in Wayne's presentation of his body. Like Chief Scar, Ethan bears both physical and psychic scars. An important scene demonstrating this comes near the end of the film after he has been wounded by an arrow. Scenes in which Wayne's characters received

William Luhr

Age and isolation: Ethan, helpless, realizes what is going to happen to his family.

serious wounds were not unusual in earlier films. In *Angel and the Badman*, for example, his character is severely wounded and near death for a significant portion of the film. But in that film, even when his character is comatose, he looks healthy, strong; his body is firm. He is physically wounded, but not really otherwise affected. He might be on the verge of fainting, but he smiles, flirts, and even faces down menacing outlaws. In the above-mentioned scene in *The Searchers,* however, Wayne's character's chest is heavily bandaged and he sits, exhausted, on a rock. His body is bent; his mood melancholic. His torso shows its age—still strong, but no longer the hard-muscled body of a young man. The skin is loose, flabby in places. This scene comes at a point in the narrative when Ethan has written his will leaving all to Marty, who has angrily rejected it. Thematically it is a profound low point for his character, and it all shows on Wayne's aging, wounded, and melancholic body.

Wayne's age is further stressed in juxtaposition with Marty's and Scar's bodies. Both roles are played by younger men who are often shirtless, revealing strong, youthful torsos. At one point, Ethan recoils when Marty

John Wayne and *The Searchers*

What kind of man are you, anyway?

calls him "Uncle" and says he's not his uncle, or Methuselah either, adding that he could easily whip Marty. In reacting so abrasively, Ethan stresses their age difference by denying it. Wayne seldom went shirtless in his films, even when young. (That may result, however, from the fact that, until the 1980s, it was not the fashion for male action stars to display their bodies. Action stars of the classical Hollywood era, such as Gary Cooper, Clark Gable, James Cagney, and Errol Flynn, only infrequently displayed their bodies, and did not develop the sculpted, body builder look of more recent stars like Arnold Schwarzenegger or Jean-Claude Van Damme.) Here, Wayne's display of his aging and scarred body and, as the film progresses, noticeably graying hair, particularly in contrast with the younger actors, all stress his age.

Deborah Thomas describes Wayne's toughness as "not a matter of hard muscularity (as one expects in an action hero), but of endurance, of taking punishment and going on" (79). As with the detachment from romance of Wayne's middle-aged roles, so also the manifestations of toughness changed in his career, shifting from dynamic athleticism to stolid endurance. In his films of the 1930s and early 1940s, he is lean, muscular, and very active.

His characters often engage in a great deal of action-hero activity, such as jumping on and off of horses, fighting simultaneously with numerous villains, or the legendary stunt in *Stagecoach* in which his character jumps from the stagecoach and leaps from racing horse to racing horse in order to control the runaway vehicle. That stunt, as Wayne readily acknowledged, was performed by legendary stuntman Yakima Canutt, with whom Wayne had a close friendship and to whom he owed a great debt for his action performances. In his early films, then, Wayne's characters manifested their toughness through action. As he entered middle age, however, stolid endurance became more and more central as the sign of his power.

Bodily injury and debility would become increasingly important to Wayne's performances after *The Searchers*. Significantly, in an earlier western, *Red River*, the first time he played a character older than himself (and the film that Ford claimed showed him that Wayne could act[14]), his character suffers a debilitating wound. In *The Wings of Eagles* (1957), a non-western that Wayne made with Ford immediately after *The Searchers*, he plays a strong, active young man who becomes paralyzed. Much of his performance foregrounds agonizing attempts to recover the use of his barely functioning legs. Wayne ended both *El Dorado* (1967) and *Rio Lobo* (1970) literally on crutches. In *The Cowboys* (1971) he actually dies. His character in his final western, *The Shootist* (1976), spends the entire film confronting the fact that his body is riddled with terminal cancer. In that film, Wayne's performance physically emphasizes attempts to simultaneously compensate for and conceal the agonies of the disease. Wayne's wounded body in *The Searchers* presages this future.

Wayne shows his age (nearly fifty) in *The Searchers*, whereas in other films of the period, such as *Big Jim McLain, The Quiet Man, Hondo, Trouble Along the Way* (1953), *Legend of the Lost* (1957), or *The Wings of Eagles*, he generally played younger characters. Nearly a decade after *The Searchers*, he had to interrupt production on *The Sons of Katie Elder* (1965) for highly publicized cancer surgery. When he returned to the shooting of the film, he cooperated with publicity stressing his renewed vitality and his performance of some of his own stunts. By the time of his Oscar-winning performance in *True Grit* (1969), however, his performances acknowledged his age. In that film, he played a one-eyed, "fat old man," as his character describes himself. Where his heroic roles in his pre-1960 films seemed a natural outgrowth of his imposing physical presence, his roles in the last decade of his life, after his discovery of cancer, stressed his heroism not as consonant with but in spite of his aging body. At the end of *True Grit*, when told that he is too old and fat to attempt to take his horse over a fence, he retorts, with swagger, "Come see a fat old man some time" and jumps the fence. The film closes on a freeze frame of him galloping toward the fence. For the younger Wayne, such an action would have appeared natural and understated; here it is a defiant one dramatizing the spirit of an old man rebelling against the limitations of his age.

The western was aging also; twenty years after *The Searchers*, the genre was moribund—infrequent in films and virtually invisible on television. Wayne's embittered performance in *The Searchers* provides a point of transition between his shyer and younger persona and the entirely hard-bitten performances Clint Eastwood would give a decade later when the western itself had entered a different phase.

Dennis Bingham has called Eastwood "a postmodern John Wayne,"[15] implying that, as Wayne's western persona was attuned to the post–World War II era, so Eastwood's was attuned to the post-1960s era. The last star to dominate the western before, and during, its decline in the 1970s and 1980s, Eastwood's persona was built upon his "Man with No Name" character in three Italian made, Sergio Leone directed westerns of the 1960s: *A Fistful of Dollars* (1964; U.S. release 1967), *For a Few Dollars More* (1965; U.S. release 1967), and *The Good, the Bad, and the Ugly* (1966; U.S. release 1968). In these films, Eastwood plays a profoundly violent, barely vocal, amoral and virtually post-Apocalyptic character. He mixes traditional western clothing styles and dresses in a gaucho style flat hat and a Mexican style poncho that, in long shots, at times makes him resemble a shrouded figure of death. The character is virtually devoid of the heroic and altruistic components of the traditional western hero. The optimism for the future, for the American historical project, standard in the western from its origins and eroding in the 1950s, is absent from these films and from this character. Eastwood was in his early thirties when he made these films, the same age at which Wayne made *Stagecoach*, but where Wayne's persona darkened and became more embittered over time, Eastwood's began dark. Each persona reflected the dominant and shifting tones of the western genre in their times. Eastwood's characters seem born middle-aged and cynical; they seldom radiate the youthful optimism evident in many of Wayne's roles of the 1930s and 1940s.

The western in the pre–World War II era allowed for the optimism and buoyant athleticism of figures like Tom Mix, Buck Jones, and the young Wayne. It even allowed for the hybrid phenomenon of "singing cowboys" such as Gene Autry and, later, Roy Rogers. Wayne himself played such a character, "Singing Sandy," in *Riders of Destiny* (1933). Although singing cowboys continued through the 1950s on television (both Autry and Rogers had popular television series), any traces of one had long disappeared from Wayne's characters by that time. Furthermore, the seriousness of television's "adult western" image was not compatible with the playfulness of singing cowboys, and "adult" programs like *Gunsmoke, The Life and Legend of Wyatt Earp,* and *Cheyenne* were marketed as being different in kind from the Rogers and Autry shows. There is, however, an odd manifestation of a singing cowboy in *The Searchers* in the preposterously yokelish character of Charlie McCorry, who serenades Laurie.[16] His very ridiculousness seems like a satirical comment on the type. By the 1960s, the generic playfulness that allowed for such characters in earlier times had largely disappeared (outside of satire and parody), and the notion of a singing cowboy is virtually inconceivable in Eastwood's signature westerns, though, curiously and atypically, he did portray a version of one in the musical *Paint Your Wagon* (1966).

As with Wayne a generation earlier, Eastwood's star image was built upon two very different personae. One was a contemporary agent of the state, not the military as with Wayne, but "Dirty Harry," a heroic but embittered San Francisco police detective. The second Eastwood persona was the Man with No Name from a mythic, savage western past. Although, as noted above, Eastwood was a relatively young man when he made the Leone westerns, the growing bitterness of the western in the 1950s seems distilled and crystallized in his flinty, violent character. It seems to have been all the western had left. And thus Eastwood's Man with No Name is a lineal descendant of Wayne's Ethan Edwards.

Now, nearly half a century after *The Searchers,* Wayne's star image has also entered a different phase. On Christmas Day 2001, the Turner Broadcasting System cable channel played continuous John Wayne films from 8:00 A.M. until 5:00 A.M. the next morning. More than twenty years after his death in 1979, the reception context for his work and image has changed again. The generational divisions of the Vietnam War have subsided and Wayne is now presented as holiday family entertainment. And when *The Searchers* is shown on television, it, as in the 1950s, is largely promoted as another John Wayne movie.

This essay is dedicated to Bob and Carole Banka. They know why.

John Wayne and *The Searchers*

NOTES

Thanks to Arthur M. Eckstein and Peter Lehman for their helpful revision suggestions for this essay, and added thanks to Peter for thirty years of insightful and enthusiastic conversation about *The Searchers*.

1. Wills cites these ratings from the Quigley poll of film distributors in the *International Motion Picture Almanac* (New York: Quigley, 1992, 50–51) as part of his convincing argument for the uniqueness of Wayne's popularity in his singularly perceptive book, *John Wayne's America*, 12.
2. There is an enormous body of commentary dealing with cultural shifts and anxieties about depersonalization in 1950s culture. Some useful texts are Elaine Tyler May, *Homeward Bound: American Families in the Cold War Era*, revised and updated edition (New York: Basic Books, 1999); Larry May, ed., *Recasting America*; C. Wright Mills, *White Collar: The American Middle Classes* (New York: Oxford University Press, 1956); David Riesman, *The Lonely Crowd: A Study of the Changing American Character* (New Haven: Yale University Press, 1950); and William H. Whyte, *The Organization Man* (New York: Simon and Schuster, 1956).
3. I have heard this anecdotally from a number of people who served in the military during this era, including Jack Kravitz, U.S. Army Specialist 6th Class, who served at Field Station Berlin, U.S. Army Security Station, from 1966–69; Robert Banka, MD, Commander, U.S. Naval Medical Corps, who served in the 1970s and 1980s; and James Elvin, who served in the U.S. Air Force in the 1950s.
4. J. Fred McDonald, *Television and the Red Menace* (New York: Praeger, 1985), 130.
5. See, for example, Buscombe, *The Searchers*, 66–68.
6. Ron Kovic, *Born on the Fourth of July* (New York: McGraw-Hill, 1976), 98. Kovic's response is quoted and contextualized in Wills's *John Wayne's America*.
7. Thomas, "John Wayne's Body."
8. See Hutson's essay in this volume for a discussion of the imagery of the harsh stone monoliths of Monument Valley in *The Searchers*.
9. Wills discusses Wayne's *contrapposto* posturing as well as his overall bodily presentation in *John Wayne's America*, 18–19 and elsewhere. He devotes chapter 3 to Wayne's debt to legendary stuntman and stunt director Yakima Canutt. On p. 59 Wills quotes Wayne describing how, early in his career, he studied and imitated Canutt's physical movements and speech patterns, particularly Canutt's tendency to lower his voice and slow his tempo when angry.
10. Billy Wilder recounts Raft's refusal to appear in *Double Indemnity* in Ivan Moffat, "On the Fourth Floor of Paramount: Interview with Billy Wilder," *The World of Raymond Chandler*, Miriam Gross, ed. (New York: A and W, 1978), 48–49. Other instances of Raft's role choices are discussed in Rudy Behlmer, "'The Stuff That Dreams are Made Of': *The Maltese Falcon*," 114–15, and William Luhr, "*The Maltese Falcon*, The Detective Genre, and *Film Noir*," 5, both in *The Maltese Falcon: John Huston, Director*, ed. William Luhr (New Brunswick, N.J.: Rutgers University Press, 1995).
11. Todd McCarthy, *Howard Hawks: The Grey Fox of Hollywood* (New York: Grove Press, 1997), 548–49.

12. Eckstein, "Darkening Ethan," 3–24.
13. See Francois Truffaut, *Hitchcock* (New York: Simon and Schuster, 1985), 43 and 142.
14. Gallagher, *John Ford: The Man and His Films*, 256.
15. Dennis Bingham, *Acting Male: Masculinities in the Films of James Stewart, Jack Nicholson, and Clint Eastwood* (New Brunswick, N.J.: Rutgers University Press, 1994), 173.
16. See Martin Pumphrey, "Why Do Cowboys Wear Hats in the Bath? Style Politics for the Older Man," in *The Book of Westerns*, ed. Cameron and Pye, 56.

Sermons in Stone:
Monument Valley in *The Searchers*

Richard Hutson

The Searchers begins with a place and date on a black screen: "Texas 1868." A hole opens in the center of the screen, a door opening to a view of the buttes and spires of Monument Valley. A woman, in silhouette, steps through the rectangular frame and looks outward into the valley, into what could be either a magnificent liberation or a dire threat. The interior from which she steps is black, conforming to the silhouette and starkly contrasting with the massive expanse and gorgeous color of Monument Valley.

This elementary contrast introduces the viewer to the drama of human action set within a landscape that appears to serve as its theatrical background. But the contrast between the human and the landscape is so sharp that we might wonder how or if the two can have any relationship to each other than mere juxtaposition. As the viewer follows the gaze of the woman, a rider appears. He is moving through a corridor framed by twin buttes, which themselves suggest another threshold or door. But this exterior framing seems only a futile gesture toward drawing a boundary, toward drawing lines that can never be enclosed. The landscape beyond remains sublimely open. Is this a natural expanse hostile or indifferent to the dark enclosure of the building, or is it an echo of this family interior? Can this landscape be assimilated to this interior, or must they remain two different worlds in stark contrast, "two modes . . . significantly juxtaposed to provide . . . a silhouetting effect"?[1]

The Searchers is not the first narrative that John Ford set against the backdrop of Monument Valley, but in this instance the human drama seems too close to the buttes and the desert. The valley encroaches upon the human activity—or rather, human enterprise has extended too far into a land that cannot support it. Unlike Ford's classic *Stagecoach* (1939), where

Monument Valley is a desolate and hostile environment to be passed through, *The Searchers* involves people who are inhabitants of the valley itself, striving to make it their home, living, as Mrs. Jorgensen says, "way out on a limb." We are invited to admire the missionary purpose of these settlers as they do culture's work against the unassimilated otherness of the landscape. But the buttes and spires of the valley are not merely alien; in their melancholy impassivity and majesty, they suggest haunting affinities with human purposes, as if they also express a missionary resolve. Perhaps we can say that the landscape projects the human drama as a silhouetting effect of its presence. But it is also true that Monument Valley is itself a silhouette produced by the human narrative. The film is rich with stark contrasts and suggestive affinities, contrasts of characters both moving and immobile. Even the landscape can become mobile at times, as it, too, contributes to this most basic of the film's dialectics of silhouette and action.

As Hegel noted, "the world of spirit and the world of nature continue to have this distinction, that the latter moves only in a recurring cycle, while the former certainly makes progress."[2] But Ford's sense of the relation between culture and nature complicates, and even reverses, Hegel's distinction. For John Ford, it is the human drama that moves, or explains its movement, by invoking the circular. A number of film scholars have noted the formal circularity of *The Searchers,* with the door opening from black onto the desert at the beginning and closing back to black at the end. And as a captivity narrative, the film has an obvious circularity about it, with its clear sequence of departures and returns. "We'll find her," Ethan assures himself and Marty, "just as sure as the turning of the Earth." If the human narrative is ordered by the circular, the natural turnings of the Earth take on an open-ended linearity in the film. And the strong visual presence of Monument Valley imposes a sense of temporality, an antihuman version of "progress."

The science of geology offers a linear, chronological account of the formation and development of Monument Valley and suggests the narrative meaning of the landscape. As viewers, we do not need to know all of the details about these geological matters; even without the aid of scientific knowledge, we can surmise that the buttes are the remnants of eons of wearing away (actually, around 25 million years), wearing away by the relentless and "irresistible forces of wind and water," by the erosions and volcanic actions of "upheaval, faulting, and tearing," all of the primeval incidents of "geologic phenomena."[3] The buttes and spires and cliffs may be accounted for in a cosmic narrative about massive ellipses, rifts, unrecoverable traumas and desolations, standing now, according to Richard Klinck, as "tombstones, monuments to past furies that swept through the Valley."[4]

According to Roger Callois, "Stones posses a kind of *gravitas*, something ultimate and unchanging, something that will never perish or has already done so."[5] As the expression of the paradox of nature's forces, of an indestructibility within massive destruction, of immutability within mutability, the buttes of Monument Valley are inherently a mystery. As geological formations they are both fragile, not particularly resistant to erosion, and an expression of nature's resolve, its will to survive. Thus they become the objects "of prolonged reverie, meditation," because we can never know whether they are a sign of life or a sign of death. Perhaps they serve as "pure sign."[6] They inevitably present a mood as a framework for human activity, but they cannot offer any specific communication to the human community.

Because the buttes represent the presence of the past as unburied but also unknowable, we can never be quite sure whether action and setting oppose each other, mimic each other, or supplement each other's frailties and strengths. In the scene where Ethan and Marty return to the Jorgensen ranch for the first time for a temporary pause in their quest to find Debbie, the two men ride up to a white Gothic-style house standing against one of the imposing buttes of the valley. The house is itself a monument to Christian militancy, a sign of culture and domestication confronting the equally monumental butte.[7] The origins of this architectural style are as lost in the mists of western past as the origins of the buttes are lost in the mists of geological history. Here are two monuments confronting each other, each challenging the other, as it were. But we might also posit this juxtaposition in a different manner. Perhaps when the Jorgensens built their fragile outpost of western culture and civilization, they sought the butte for protection from the more active and hostile features of the natural environment. The scene suggests a contrast, a confrontation between two modes of monumentality. But we may read the juxtaposition as contestatory, mimetic, or indicative of a deep, unfathomable kinship, a reciprocity between two modes of memory, human and inhuman, trying to bridge the gap between one monument and another.

In any case, the *gravitas* of the valley comments on the human activities and narratives that take place within its mise-en-scène, offering some kind of access to the tragic, the pathological, and the ridiculous aspects of the human drama. For example, even the misunderstandings of adolescent love must be evaluated in terms of resoluteness. Marty's comic innocence,

Tombstones: the vast desert of *The Searchers*.

his inability to understand when a courtship or marriage is taking place (either in the white world or the Indian world), is made ominous by reference to other unfathomable "marriages" that have never taken place—between Ethan and Martha, between Ethan and Scar, between the white and red inhabitants of the land. Most significantly, the solemnity of the monuments underscores the issue of human will. In their irresoluteness, Marty and Laurie could easily lose each other, perhaps for the same reasons that Ethan and Martha lost each other earlier.

For critics such as Jane Tompkins, masculinity is achieved through identification with the western landscape, especially desert and rocks. "The rhetoric of the landscape works in favor of the particular masculine ideal Westerns enforce,"[8] so that landscape becomes "a kind of gender allegory where the land plays a series of roles."[9] Identification with the landscape substitutes for identification with the human community or for marriage to a woman. It is reasonable to understand Ethan's madness as an exaggerated commitment to the fantasy of male power and autonomy imagistically linked to the geology of the valley. But the question remains: What can such identification mean?

Monument Valley in *The Searchers*

The Jorgensens house: a home in the wilderness.

In Ford's vision, the buttes of Monument Valley are linked to madness not because they represent a testing ground for male achievement but because they are expressions of the pathos and pathology of resolution. Ford tends to see women as being just as resolute as men, so landscape here cannot be reduced, as it could be in the books of Louis L'Amour or the films of Budd Boetticher, to gender identification, to the necessary trials of masculinity. In Ford's vision of the West, both nature and human beings must cling to their "symptoms" for their very survival. The pathological is the very sign of the authentic. Like the monuments of the valley, Ethan is resolutely committed to the dead, madly (and therefore sublimely) clinging to the unrecoverable. Right to the end of the film, we do not know whether Ethan will rescue Debbie from the Comanches or kill her. If purity of heart is to will one thing, Ethan's resolve to hunt Debbie becomes torn somewhere along the way. We could say that his resolution has always been, like the meaning of Monument Valley, unreadable. Is his dedication to the hunt actually loyalty to the dead Martha, even as he can express his everlasting loyalty ("one oath at a time") to the defeated and dead nation of the Confederacy?

Ethan is a ruin, and he takes his nourishment from ruin. His quest for Debbie becomes the support of his being, supplemented by his virulent racist hatred—and the profound exasperations of his many defeats. His madness, his unalterable resolve, is his primal hold on human motivation and thus becomes the monument of human intentionality as a memorial. His madness is a sign that his will is intact, even as it is severely thwarted.

In the opening scene of the film, Martha and Aaron Edwards and their children move out of the interior of the house to stare into the valley. Their slow movement and placement on the porch, as George M. Wilson notes, "has an odd, unrealistic, ceremonial character. It is as if they were executing a pattern in a peculiar, solemn dance."[10] They see a rider emerging from the desert dust, out of the depths of the valley, from between the monuments, and identify him with a question: "Ethan?" The return of "the prodigal brother" draws out the ceremonial or dancelike movement of the family. All ritual, Slovoj Zizek suggests, is "an affair of obedience to the dead . . . letter,"[11] the dead letter of memory, the substratum of loyalty to beloved human beings (especially dead ones), to one's own sense of family or tribe. In John Ford's films as in nobody else's, human behavior strongly tends toward pattern, ritual, ceremony as homage to the dead—as the monumentalization of memory. Like old Mose Harper ("Is that old goat still creakin' around? Whyn't somebody bury 'im?" Ethan asks), Ethan is a remainder, a remnant, a ghost left over from trauma.

To Ford, all authentic human behavior seems a form of ritual memory, and civilization itself is a monument, a memorial to and of the past, obedience to the dead letter of past human narratives. Memory may be only a fragment, but this reduced version of the past is all that we have, and John Ford's characters hold on to memory as if their very survival depends upon it. Human behavior is memory as fallen knowledge, which keeps us always on the verge of recovering, if not a totality, at least something that can substitute for a totality.[12] The attempt to recover not the totality but at least *something* (that can substitute for the totality) is possible because our fallen knowledge always refers to a massive reserve of unconscious knowledge, just as the buttes of Monument Valley always refer to an unfallen earth. Likewise, the unconscious to which human behavior refers is collected in the external environment of Monument Valley. We could say that human behavior and Monument Valley need the verification and support of each other because each serves as the necessary unconsciousness or heterology of the other. Whereas each seems to demand the

Monument Valley in *The Searchers*

satisfaction of its enigmas within its own mode, each can use the other to gather up its mysteries and eloquent silences.

Just as Monument Valley is an unrecoverable geological narrative, the human drama that takes place before our eyes is mysterious, resistant to any archaeological efforts. A whole series of questions to Ethan go unanswered, as if he is a leftover whose whole story we will never be able to reconstruct. In two excellent essays on *The Searchers,* Peter Lehman has made abundantly clear the pattern of confusions about Ethan and his relationships with others. In general, Lehman notes, "the film abounds in oddly indeterminable character relationships and actions,"[13] and is created out of "a pattern of narrative elision," leading him to characterize it quite aptly as "an absentee narrative."[14] Scenes, conversations, events, motives—all become baffling to the viewer for lack of essential information.

Tag Gallagher has emphasized that the depiction of the various characters illustrates "universal solipsism." "Everyone inhabits a private world," and communication is nearly impossible between "such myriad solitudes."[15] The viewer is presented with a narrative mixing of the most primitive and basic plot, the resolute hunt for a missing captive, with a barrage of exasperating undecidables and silences. Although there is a strong focus on Ethan's resolute quest for his kidnapped niece, that narrative clarity is saturated by an opacity that works mainly by hints and inferences. The viewer is forced to speculate about a number of unanswered questions in order to close at least a few of the many frustrating gaps in knowledge. John Ford and his scriptwriter, Frank S. Nugent, have represented what Paul Ricoeur refers to as fundamental narrative wisdom; "One makes a plot with what one knows, and a plot is by nature 'mutilated knowledge.'"[16] Likewise, Monument Valley is a composition in mutilation, in fallenness and fragmentation, just as Ford's most memorable human beings are also mutilated figures, ruins, unable to communicate.

But much as the narrative forces us to accept its terms even as it tempts us to reach for more understanding, Monument Valley tempts us to fill up the spaces between the buttes with our imagination even as their beauty depends upon our accepting them in their haunting and mysterious incompletions and mutilations, in their references and gestures, in their provocative relationships to each other and to the human characters. For John Ford, human characters are to be found in ritual patterns of behavior, in plots and in natural settings that always have already been mutilated. Human actions and their settings always are belated, ruins and memorials to ruin.

Richard Hutson

Marshall Brown suggests that the "silhouetting of coup de theatre [what I am calling human narrative or action] against tableau [or landscape] is a juxtaposition of two kinds of temporality. On the one hand, the coup de theatre radically separates 'before' from 'after' and thus establishes the forward- moving, linear temporality of dramatic action. The static, colorful tableau, on the other hand, tends to develop symbolic resonances."[17] Although *The Searchers* provides us with a narrative of human action within a spatial setting, it is appropriate to see the foreground of human action and the background of Monument Valley as "two kinds of temporality," and thus as two different kinds of narrative.

The narrative of *The Searchers* is always a double narrative. The juxtaposition of the two modes of being, of temporality, of narrative, leads to the inference that there must have been a primordial sundering of these two modes, and each mode indicates something of the effects of this split. In the foreground of the human action, time can always be mentioned or alluded to as a conscious theme of human activity ("The war ended three years ago"; "Ya, yust this time a year ago"; "Ethan rode on an hour ago"; "I've been hangin' around this god-forsaken windscow for two long years"). In the much longer geological temporality of Monument Valley, time seems to be suppressed by or gathered within the spatiality of a static, colorful tableau. Monument Valley, in *The Searchers,* is a highly theatrical exterior, as if nature had decided to call attention to itself in its spectacular theatricality. Monument Valley came to be John Ford's signature setting because it served as landscape pure and simple, the archetypal West, landscape as frame, landscape in general rather than as a particular locality where actual westward expansion took place. In fact, like the landscapes that have preoccupied American painters, such as the Rocky Mountains or the Sierras, Monument Valley would *never* have tempted white settlers into thinking that it could be developed for civilization. This land is outside of civilized assimilation, heavily marked by its inutility; hence its theatricality, its openness to symbolic resonances. In its unassimilable ruggedness, it can therefore always stand for the generalized or mythologized harshness of the American frontier experience. It is always a challenge to the ordinary activities or instrumentalities of human work. In this respect, it is the land as opposition to humanity's purposes. From its past, the United States inherited the master narrative of humanity engaged in an epic, ennobling struggle against the inhospitality of a rugged land, the wilderness. So, too, for *The Searchers:* here the diachrony of the human activities appears in profile against the most desolate and unassimilable synchrony of the valley

Monument Valley in *The Searchers*

Fierce landscapes.

setting, By 1956 the United States had reached the limits of its traditional commitment to Manifest Destiny. If destiny might still be buried within human resolve, it was no longer manifest in its implications.

In its serenity and indifference, Monument Valley does not enter into an explicit struggle with the human settlers, and the settlers make very few references to their setting. Environment is assumed, the way it is in most human behavior. Lars Jorgensen may gesture despairingly at "this country," indicating an inhospitable land that thwarts human endeavor, or Mrs. Jorgensen may say, "Someday this country's gonna be a fine good place to be." But setting is primarily a tacit reference point. Besides, it is white humanity that enters into the arena of struggle, encroaching upon a land already claimed by a culture that the white settlers do not recognize.

Thus the valley can never be merely a background for settlement or the efforts to constitute an ordinary life. It may be that there is a clear impulse to turn attention inside, to the interior of hearth and home and to the rituals of everyday life, shutting out the bleak background. For John Ford, this impulse is expressed as ritual, the attempt to ward off the encroachment from the outside and monumentalize behavior, to construct a sense of tradition. But *The Searchers* is about the *interruption* of these rituals. Rituals are perpetually disrupted in the narrative, just as something disrupts the blackness of the screen before the door opens in the center. The pattern of interruption continues throughout the narrative as searches, ceremonies, conversations, and thoughts are interfered with definitively, undermining any hope of clarity.

What we see throughout the film are attempts to suppress information, to keep knowledge hidden. At first Martha is the most active suppressor, especially of questions from the children. When Ben, for instance, asks Ethan where he has been for the last three years, his mother shuts him up before he can get an answer; when Reverend Captain Clayton asks Ethan if he is wanted for a crime, Martha interrupts in an attempt to distract the two. But a number of other characters try to conceal knowledge and foreclose explanation. When Ethan begins to tell Marty something crucial about the past, Marty interrupts him, and we never find out what this information might be. Ethan withholds knowledge about his discovery of Lucy's body from Brad and Marty, then reveals the truth to them under pressure later, causing Brad to burst into suicidal action. Toward the end, Ethan offers information to Marty about Marty's mother—namely, that her scalp was one of those displayed on Scar's lance when they were in Scar's camp. His belated revelation is intended to lead the Texas Rangers to exterminate Scar and his people (including Debbie). In fact, the dialectic of suppression and belated disclosure goes on throughout the narrative, as does the pattern of interruption, which has the same effect as suppressing questions and information. (It is clear that the information in question is in fact very destructive.) Ethan, as has often been noted, is always interrupting the ceremonial activities of families and communities, the ceremonial activities so dear to Ford both on film and in his real life. Even though Ethan's return to his brother's homestead might be considered a completion of the family, it is also the interruption that opens the narrative itself; it may even be that Ethan's return has brought with it the Comanche attack. Most famously, Ethan early in the film interrupts the most sacred of Ford ceremonies, a burial—in this case, the burial of his own family—in order to get on with his vengeance, while Ethan and Marty late in the film interrupt the other most sacred of Ford ceremonies, the community dance, when their arrival at the Jorgensens stops the wedding of Laurie and Charlie.

As Lehman demonstrates, this continuing loss of information, this suppression of or interference with explanation, contributes to the funda-

Monument Valley in *The Searchers*

mental obscurity of the narrative. These suppressions, withholdings, and interruptions hollow out serious gaps, definitive laconisms, in the action. In effect, the inexplicable holes in the story find their echo in the vast holes or laconisms in the landscape, which the various buttes call our attention to. We may feel that in some utopian act of recovery, the total meaning of the human drama may be brought into the light. But these acts of recovery are always going to be incomplete; they can only bring fragments of the original totality back, much as the recovery of Debbie only yields a metonymic-mnemonic remnant of the Edwards family. Debbie will be able to serve the human community in the same manner as the buttes of the valley serve as metonymic-mnemonic remnants of an unfallen, original landscape. But the real heroism of human action lies in the recovery of the remnant, the memorial, which, like that of the unfallen world of nature, can only be present to us as profoundly corroded with the massive and sublime ellipses of earthly existence, within and outside of human action. Civilization corrodes and destroys knowledge, which makes necessary a supplement of the external world as its other. What I am suggesting is that an echo of this absentee narrative is to be found in the theoretical or presumed narrative of the geological landscape, that the ellipses of the human narrative need the supplement of a narrative otherness. But all that this sublime external narrative can do is echo, rather than complete, the ellipses in the human narrative. All the human narrative and the cosmic narrative of the valley can do is what the buttes can do—serve as monuments, memorials, to a relationship of affinity that has been lost forever. In John Ford's world, all we can have of the past is the legend, a monument to heroic action, sacrifice, and death (which—he knows—is only part of the story).

Ford's and Nugent's story is itself a memorial to perhaps the most primordial national narrative of the New World—the forward, heroic march of humanity, conquering and appropriating even the most desolate wasteland, refusing to remain on this side of the frontier. The human narrative of *The Searchers,* like Monument Valley, condenses in its monumentality all that is left of a spirit still loyal to the traditions of Western civilization in general and of the United States in particular. Both human narrative, the coup de theatre, and cosmic narrative, the tableau, may trail off into an irrecoverable, absolute past, a past without origin. But the doubleness of the narrative modes presented the post–World War II United States with one of its most compelling spectacles. For Ford, however, narrative as memorial, as mourning and loyalty, is the surest way of possessing the United States—of *re*possessing it. Like Monument Valley, human memory, as embodied in narrative, represents an immense loss even as it refuses to lose all. For the 1950s, Ford believed that the greatest service he could render was to depict the legend of U.S. history. For him, such a legend was a precious contribution, resonating with the immensity of loss even as it resonated with the intolerance, tragedy, brutality, and loyalties of a nation's history.

The impassive rocks of the valley may be serene, but the valley does strike back against the settlers in the figures of the Indians. Monument Valley is presented as an inhospitable land, both in its passivity and in its violent human activity. In fact, none of the white settlers seems able to distinguish the Indians from the harsh landscape. Lars tells Ethan that it was not Ethan who killed his son Brad during the search for Lucy and Debbie, it was "this land"—referring to the bleak inhospitality of the setting. (It was the Comanches who killed Brad.) Aaron Edwards mentions early on that many of the settlers have given up trying to settle this land, and have returned to the places they had left. The land is harshly unresponsive to human effort, even without the Indian threat. But something within it also actively strikes back. There is not only a natural other, there is also a cultural other that appears to be unassimilable. The white settlers seem unable to understand either the violence or the hospitality of the native Americans. The Indian attack at the beginning that destroys Ethan's family is utterly unanticipated. And Marty will discover that he is married to the Comanche girl Look without ever understanding how, or even that it has happened. The white culture has great difficulty in comprehending or accommodating the alien culture that is at home in the valley landscapes. Whereas the wives, Martha Edwards and Mrs. Jorgensen, keep holding on to the possibility of a secure settlement in this land, the men seem to have their doubts. Even Mrs. Jorgensen acknowledges that it may take a hundred years and "our bones in the ground" before the land can pass for domesticated or settled territory.

The white inhabitants cannot ignore this unresponsive outside, because their deepest intention is to transform it into the inside of a cultural closure. The narrative strongly suggests that the deeply desired correspondence between people and landscape is still only a desire, a projection into a distant future, a fantasy; the elementary experience here for whites is the discrepancy between humanity and landscape. Or, rather, the desired correspondence may already be accomplished, but as a reciprocity of great violence between the white settlers and the marauding Comanches—who themselves are responding to white attacks that left Scar

Monument Valley in *The Searchers*

with two dead sons and which created a grouping of white settlers on what must originally have been *Comancheria*. The haunting correspondences that Ford presents visually and inferentially between the conflicting cultures and the modes of humanity and landscape are violent or unconscious.

In fact, the native Americans tend to be seen as the animation of an otherwise indifferent landscape. In what Joseph McBride and Michael Wilmington refer to as "one of the most astonishing tours de force in *The Searchers,* the procession of the horsemen between the parallel lines of Indians,"[18] the Indians seem to emerge from the earth and out of the buttes of the valley, as if they were an activated extension of the buttes. Like the buttes, their visual procession is a profiling. If the whites' activities can be silhouetted by the buttes, the buttes also are silhouettes, now extended in their hostility by Chief Scar's Comanche warriors, who appear to peel off the rocky depths of the buttes and march in processions that echo the formations of the earth and rock.

Monument Valley has never been assimilated or appropriated by human activity. Just as the stone monuments on a grave mark the narrative of an individual life, Monument Valley will serve Ford to memorialize western settlement as the essential narrative of national foundation. Such a narrative is no longer literally possible. After all, Frederick Jackson Turner announced in 1893 that the frontier had disappeared and that we would have to construct a political life from then on without the aid of the frontier experience. Monument Valley is thus a kind of completion of the myth of frontier expansion, a monument to a narrative that now can only be idealized, the ghostly aftermath of the classic frontier encounter between the interiorizing projects of human endeavor and a resisting exterior landscape. And the landscape can also satisfy the particular need for a narrative that is a monument to the legend of U.S. expansionist will. Through the monument and the legend, that which is lost returns to the light of day and manifests its presence before the eyes of the living.

As John Brinkerhof Jackson has suggested, a "traditional monument . . . is an object which is supposed to remind us of something important. That is to say it exists to put people in mind of some obligation that they have incurred. . . . [I]t is venerated not as a work of art or as an antique, but as an echo from the remote past suddenly become present and actual."[19] Ford's narrative is a monument to such a past. In Monument Valley, nature manifests itself as unassimilable, limitless temporality. Human effort shatters against the impassive fixation and immobility of the monument and returns to an archaic mode, the hunt for a captive. Ford intended to remind us that our history vastly precedes political covenants and constitutions. As Jackson claims, "a society which sees itself as having slowly evolved, beginning with the very first settlements in its own environment, is more likely to celebrate its legendary, half-forgotten origins in the landscape."[20] The film reverts to this primitive tale and insists upon its vast symbolic resonances. But, of course, what makes *The Searchers* a film of the 1950s is Ford's insistence, thanks to Monument Valley, that his narrative is the legend of the West, not the experience of the West. The classic Cold War era, with its sense not merely that the frontier was gone but that the frontier was, perhaps, always a myth, also was marked by a strong belief that these myths were necessary to hold on to a national purpose with some semblance of coherence and relationship to a national past. The postwar era invented, as it were, a tradition of the United States, and no one had a more acute or complex sense than did Ford of the necessity for myths, for legends.

Such self-conscious inventions carried with them the strong possibility of disavowal ("We know that it's myth, but even so"). In fact, we can always ask if these magnificent buttes and spires are repositories of our his-

Ethan contemplates Scar's final encampment.

Monument Valley in The Searchers

tory's meaning, a meaning that can be recovered for the present, or whether they are merely stony substances with no meaning whatsoever. Do they invoke too much meaning or rather the loss of meaning? The same question can be asked of the human narrative in its clarity, opacity, and ambivalence. Ethan possesses meaning, thoughtfulness, contempt, hatred, madness. But what is his meaning? What does Ethan want? Ford's plot, with its disturbed and unattractive hero and its theatricalized landscape, carries an immediate disavowal: This narrative of white endeavor could never have taken place, but even so.

The conjunction of this landscape and this narrative of human activities and relationships illustrates the mutual need for two different temporalities, two different realms. With their combined significances, they construct a powerful and profound "even so," which for Ford would have to serve as the ground of a moral imperative.

The self-contained buttes and monuments present a model of carrying on with a sense of destiny in the recognition of irrecoverable loss. They and their human inhabitants form a community of national cultural memory that could serve both as inspiration and critique.

NOTES

I would like to thank Kathleen Moran for her helpful discussions with me on this essay.

1. Marshall Brown, "The Logic of Realism: A Hegelian Approach," *PMLA* 96 (March 1981): 231.

2. *Hegel's Logic,* trans. William Wallace (Oxford: Oxford University Press, 1975), 291.

3. Richard E. Klink, *Land of Room Enough and Time Enough* (Salt Lake City: Gibbs M. Smith, 1984), 3.

4. Ibid.

5. Roger Callois, *The Writing of Stones,* trans. Barbara Bray (Charlottesville: University of Virginia Press, 1985), 2.

6. Ibid.

7. The architectural style of the Jorgensens' house is the simplified Gothic style that was recommended to Christians in the middle of the nineteenth century as a witness to their religious faith. See Alan Gowans, *Images of American Living* (New York: Harper and Row, 1964), 309–15.

8. Tompkins, *West of Everything,* 77.

9. Ibid.

10. George M. Wilson, *Narration in Light* (Baltimore: Johns Hopkins University Press, 1986), 141.

11. Slovoj Zizek, *The Sublime Object of Ideology* (London: Verso, 1989), 43.

12. In one of the most moving moments of Ford's earlier film *She Wore a Yellow Ribbon* (1948), also shot in Monument Valley, the cavalrymen of C Troop present a watch to their commander, the elderly Captain Brittles (John Wayne) upon his retirement. The watch is inscribed, "Lest We Forget." And it is a sign both of Brittles' fragility and determination that he has to take out his glasses in public to be able to read the inscription. We are not told of the many individual acts of kindness and competence that the single phrase on the watch, "Lest We Forget," must substitute for— must remain the monument, the remnant and the sign for. And the narrator at the end of the film declares explicitly that all these acts have been forgotten, and exist now only as "a cold page in the history-books"; yet, the narrator concludes, the completed United States (including the most inhospitable parts of the West, symbolized by Monument Valley) is also a monument to those acts.

13. Lehman, "Texas 1868/America 1956," 391.
14. Lehman, "There's No Way of Knowing," 95.
15. Gallagher, *John Ford: The Man and His Films*, 327.
16. Paul Ricoeur, *Time and Narrative*, vol. 1, trans. Kathleen McLaughlin and David Pellauer (Chicago: University of Chicago Press, 1984), 170.
17. Brown, "The Logic of Realism," 231.
18. McBride and Wilmington, *John Ford*, 154.
19. John Brinkerhoff Jackson, *The Necessity for Ruins* (Amherst: University of Massachusetts Press, 1980), 91.
20. Ibid.

"Typically American":
Music for *The Searchers*

Kathryn Kalinak

Imagine hearing these lyrics, the original first verse to Stan Jones's title song "The Searchers," as the credits for John Ford's film of the same name begin:

> The horizon's like a woman
> With her arms flung open wide
> And a man that's tryin' to fill his heart
> Ain't got no place to hide.
> Ride away—Ride away—Ride away.[1]

It is the second verse of this song that found its way into the film and, with its unanswered and unanswerable set of questions, catapulted a Hollywood genre film into metaphysical dimensions.

> What makes a man to wander
> What makes a man to roam
> What makes a man leave bed and board
> And turn his back on home.
> Ride away—Ride away—Ride away.

In all likelihood, it was Ford who made the change.

Although no other Ford western has generated as much critical attention as *The Searchers*, and though many critics acknowledge the importance of music to the film's overall meaning (and at least two have addressed the score in some depth)[2], a systematic and full-scale analysis of the music has yet to be written. A number of questions are central to such an analysis. I'll begin with Ford himself. If indeed it is Ford's hand at work in changes to the lyrics of the song "The Searchers," what part did Ford play in the creation of the musical score of this or any other of his films? Next, how do songs work as part of a musical score and how do songs operate in a Ford western? The score for *The Searchers* was produced at a time when the film score in Hollywood was under tremendous pressure to update its sound. What is the impact of the collision between Stan Jones's fifties-inflected theme song and Max Steiner's classically inflected film score? And finally, what is the relationship between the film and contemporary social developments? How does music enter into that relationship? In a film so consciously attuned to matters of race and gender, how does the score, and particularly its songs, contribute to the process through which such ideologically fraught concepts are constructed? This article is an attempt to chart the territory in which such questions might be answered.

John Ford once claimed he preferred "good music" to "bad dialogue" but his antipathy for the inverse was legendary.[3] He growled at Peter Bogdanovich in their famous interview: "I hate music in pictures—a little bit now and then, at the end or at the start."[4] His comment provides a provocative point of entry into a discussion of Ford's participation in the musical scores for his films for, like so many other statements made by Ford, this one obscures as much as it elucidates. It is difficult to authenticate authorship, musical or otherwise, in a studio system known for its resistance to recognizing individual achievement (not to mention spotty production records, unreliable bookkeeping, and the vagaries and vanities of human memory). Yet what is known about Ford's relationship to music would hardly support the disdain he voiced to Bogdanovich. Ford took an active role in the creation of the musical scores for his films.

To begin with, Ford was deeply knowledgeable about music and exploited it on and off the set. His employment of Danny Borzage, who entertained cast and crew with accordion on Ford's sets (and who played "Bringing in the Sheaves" whenever Ford arrived on one), suggests to what extent Ford depended upon music during production. Ford also owned an impressive record collection encompassing a variety of musical styles, eras, and idioms. The backbone of the collection are ethnic and folk recordings: Irish, Scottish, and Welsh ballads; Mexican folk song; Latin dance music; Hawaiian and Tahitian music; and American hymnody, spirituals, and popular song, including parlor ballads by Stephen Foster. But Ford also owned numerous recordings of nineteenth-century European art music

Music for *The Searchers*

(with a strong Russian component), original cast recordings of Broadway shows, and opera highlights. Among the artists represented in his collection are Paul Robeson, Burl Ives, Bing Crosby, Xavier Cugat, Billy Eckstine, and the Sons of the Pioneers.[5] Typically, Ford would put records from his collection on the "victrola," using them as the background score for scripting sessions.[6] In fact, these recordings may have provided a kind of temp track: at an early stage of production, particular musical material became associated with specific scenes and Ford had enough power over the production to preserve those connections in the film score.

In the case of *The Searchers*, there is strong evidence to suggest that the final cut of the music was presided over by Ford. Steiner was apparently miffed to discover, at a sneak preview, that his score had been edited. A letter from C. V. Whitney to Steiner addresses his concerns. "I can assure you that the end result is typically American. This, I am sure, is what Mr. Ford wanted to achieve, and I feel he has done it. For my part, I understand your criticisms. I am satisfied, however, that the mood of reality in the picture is furthered by Mr. Ford's cuts."[7] It sounds as if Ford deleted some of Steiner's nondiegetic cues. The result privileged more of the American source music and gave the film a leaner sound than Steiner had originally created. Ford was in control here, and he exercised that control in matters large and small throughout production. Ford's collaborators, such as *The Searchers'* screenwriter Frank Nugent, had learned to put up with this.[8] But Steiner was clearly irritated.

A second mark of Ford's influence can be read from the film scores themselves which encompass a variety of different styles, idioms, and composers and move back and forth between the heavily post-romantic studio-era scoring of a film such as *The Searchers* to a sparsely scored and almost totally source-dependent film such as *Stagecoach* (1939). The recurrence of particular leitmotifs (such as Alfred Newman's theme for Ann Rutledge in *Young Mr. Lincoln* (1939) resurfacing in Cyril J. Mockridge's score for *The Man Who Shot Liberty Valance* (1962) three decades later or "The Trail to Mexico"[9] employed as leitmotif for the stagecoach in a variety of films with different composers), the repetition of specific source music ("The Cuckoo Waltz" in Newman's *Young Mr. Lincoln* and Mockridge's *My Darling Clementine* (1940); "Jubilo" in Steiner's *The Searchers*, David Buttolph's *The Horse Soldiers* (1959), and Howard Jackson's *Sergeant Rutledge* (1960); and "Lorena" in *The Searchers* and *The Horse Soldiers*), and the omnipresence of hymns (especially "Shall We Gather at the River") all strongly suggest the hand of Ford.

Kathryn Kalinak

Ford's participation in the scripting process of *The Searchers* was "very intense," as Arthur Eckstein has convincingly argued,[10] and production records indicate a similar involvement with the music. When "Ethan" was still "Amos" (the original name from Alan LeMay's novel) and casting had barely begun, Ford was already including musical selections in his story notes to screenwriter Frank Nugent and producer Patrick Ford. For the wedding sequence, for instance, Ford suggested "Blue Bonnet" and "The Yellow Rose of Texas," a personal favorite of Ford's with "The Bonnie Blue Flag" pencilled in (an addition or a correction?)[11] Neither "The Bonnie Blue Flag" nor "Blue Bonnet" was used in the wedding sequence (they were replaced by the song "Jubilo"), but "The Bonnie Blue Flag" did find its way into the film, where it appears prominently in the film's famous opening sequence. "The Yellow Rose of Texas" can be heard exactly where Ford intended it—as the assembled wedding guests await Laurie's arrival. Studio publicity even cited Ford's participation, crediting him with the choice of "The Yellow Rose of Texas" for a "nostalgic square dance scene," noting that Ford "picked the sentimental ditty from a dozen other favorites in his musical collection of Americana."[12] Of course, "The Yellow Rose of Texas" is hardly the "sentimental ditty" that Warners Publicity dubbed it. Perhaps Warners was thinking of the Mitch Miller version widely circulating in 1955 which sanitized the lyrics. The "Yellow Rose" of the original refers to a mulatta woman of supposedly great sexual attractiveness.[13] Given the origins of the song in the nexus of race and sexuality, its appearance in a film obsessed with miscegenation is a complicated allusion to say the least and one to which I will return later in this essay.

The theme song for the film, "The Searchers," similarly bears the mark of Ford. Max Steiner, one of the architects of the classical film score, and Hollywood's most prolific composer, wrote the score and supervised the film's music, while Stan Jones, a sometime member of Ford's stock company, wrote the song. With a hit song on country-western charts ("Ghost Riders in the Sky"), Jones enjoyed parallel careers in Hollywood as an actor and songwriter. He knew Ford in both capacities, having worked with him on *Wagon Master* (1950) and *Rio Grande* (1950). (He would also work on *The Horse Soldiers*.) Jones composed eight verses of the song "The Searchers."[14] That those song lyrics found their way to the film's director (instead of, say, to Steiner, the film's composer) is highly atypical of the studio system's assembly line mode of production. But that these lyrics, in their entirety, found their way to Ford is not. Ford took an active interest in the musical scores of his films and he knew Stan Jones. Did Ford ask

Music for *The Searchers*

about Jones's progress? Did Jones run the lyrics by the old man? The key here is that the lyrics are in the director's files and not in the music files.

All of the verses to "The Searchers" in Ford's files were recorded by the Sons of the Pioneers[15] but someone chose verses two and seven to be used in the film, neither the expedient nor (without the benefit of hindsight) the particularly appropriate choice. I'm putting my money on Ford.[16] After all, it is just like Ford to avoid the obvious. The original first verse with its clear allusions to Martha and last verse with its conventional ending (and more allusions, it seems, to Martha) may have been too pointed. Ford chose instead not to "spell it out" for the audience. Here is the full set of lyrics, which reveal the talent, and the insight into the film, of the person who chose to use only verses two and seven—that is, John Ford himself.

"The Searchers" by Stan Jones

Chorus: Ride away—Ride away—Ride away.

The horizon's like a woman
With her arms flung open wide
And a man that's tryin' to fill his heart
Ain't got no place to hide.

What makes a man to wander
What makes a man to roam
What makes a man leave bed and board
And turn his back on home.

Now a man will search for fortune
Of silver and of gold
The silver he finds in his hair
While a weary heart grows old.

Some men search for injuns
Or hump-backed buffalo
And even when they found them
They move on lonesome slow.

Kathryn Kalinak

> The rustling of the dry brown leaves
> Along the frosty ground
> Whispers soft of autumn time
> But a wanderer fears that sound.
>
> The snow is deep and oh so white
> The winds they howl and mourn
> Fire cooks a man his meat
> But his lonely heart won't warm.
>
> A man will search his heart and soul
> Go searching way out there
> His peace o' mind, he knows he'll find
> But where Oh Lord, Lord where.
>
> Me I go on searchin'
> For where there ain't no hate
> For a tender love I'm dreamin' of
> A'fore it gets too late

Song has always been a distinguishing feature of Ford's films, particularly the westerns. I'd like to summarize here an argument I've made elsewhere regarding the function of song in Ford, and expand it with *The Searchers*.[17] The classical Hollywood film score depended to a large extent upon music's expressivity, its ability to tap into cultural associations in order to harness meaning and control emotional response. Song functions as a kind of aural shorthand in this process, reliably summoning up these associations that are often, though not always, encoded through lyrics. When we hear "Jeanie With the Light Brown Hair," for instance, as Hatfield's leitmotif in *Stagecoach*, we do not actually have to hear the lyrics for thoughts of the antebellum South to be summoned up. Foster's ballad creates a mood of sadness and loss which focuses on Hatfield and through song the audience is made to understand and sympathize with this man. Ford was well aware of the power of music; this is why he concerned himself so closely with its use. As early as 1928, Ford spoke of the need to explore "sound as well as sight images" and throughout his career consciously attended to the

Music for *The Searchers*

expressive power contained in music.[18] Song is among the classical Hollywood film score's most dependable methods for controlling audience response and Ford's films avail themselves of this power.

Consider the title song, "The Searchers." Its lyrics not only structure the narrative to follow but set up an important thematic connection between Ethan and Scar duly noted in much of the criticism on the film and on which the film's meaning depends: "What makes a man to wander, What makes a man to roam, What makes a man leave bed and board, And turn his back on home?" Ethan is established as a wanderer and the reason why he wanders is established as the central question of the film. One immediately thinks of Ethan's own translation of Nawyecka Comanche: "Sorta like round about: man says he's going one place, means to go t'other." LeMay, in the source novel, translates "Nawyecky" as "Them As Never Gets Where They're Going."[19] I favor James Brooks's translation of the Comanche term in this volume—"wanderer"—because it highlights similarities between Ethan and Scar: both are wanderers—Scar by tribal association, Ethan by nature and by circumstance.[20] (Even Chris the dog links them. He barks at only two people: Ethan and Scar.) Wandering, a central connection between the two adversaries, sustained throughout the film in a variety of ways, is initially posited by the music. (Is this one of the reasons why Ford chose the second verse with its focus on wandering to open the film?)

The seventh verse of the song (and, in fact, the only other verse of the original eight that we hear), is sung at the end of the film. If we were waiting for an answer to the questions the song initially posed, we would be disappointed—for the last verse offers only more questions: when will the searching end and "Where, Oh Lord, Lord where?" Stan Jones's original final verse, though containing some ambiguity, provides more closure. The searcher charts his course for true love, "A 'fore it gets too late," a creaky device to end the song and the quest that structures it. The ending of the film would certainly have been altered if this original eighth verse had been used. The discarded first and last verses overtly shape the search around a woman and a man's desire for her, telegraphing a pedestrian message about true love conquering all. Succeeding verses map out this quest through a variety of pursuits and in different geographic locations and climates. Without the frame of verses one and eight, however, the song is dramatically changed from a rather prosaic search for romantic love to a metaphysical search for what can never be found. It must have been Ford's decision. His notorious work habit of "collaborating" with other production personnel, whether they liked it or not (and which clearly alienated Steiner), the song lyrics' paper trail (which leads to Ford), and his penchant for avoiding the obvious (for example, Ethan's decision to save Debbie instead of murder her, deliberately mystified by Ford who deleted key lines of Ethan's dialogue) all point to Ford.[21]

The representation of women in Ford westerns, often dismissed in the past, has been a subject of some interest recently. Both Gaylyn Studlar and Peter Lehman in this volume address the position of women in *The Searchers*. Music provides ballast for both their arguments. Lehman reminds us that narratively women are contained in the film, limited in the expression of their desires and restricted in their actions: "Men search and women wait at home."[22] Song figures importantly here, from the lyrics of "The Searchers" which structure the film exclusively around men as narrative agents ("What makes a *man* to wander, What makes a *man* to roam") to the period music which objectifies women as objects of desire ("Lorena," "The Yellow Rose of Texas"). Studlar, situating her discussion in the larger context of the history of the western, both literary and filmic, makes a fascinating point about the construction of the wilderness and women's relationship to it. While the genre is characterized by a "fundamental ontology [which] depends upon constructing the West as a site of masculine retreat,"[23] Ford's westerns complicate that gender division. The wilderness is associated with the feminine in *The Searchers:* Martha, who "wouldn't let a man quit" a life on the frontier; Mrs. Jorgensen, who gives the film's most impassioned speech about the wilderness and life "way out on a limb"; Laurie, who voices the anger and frustrations of living on the edge of civilization; and Look, who represents the possibility of living at peace with the wilderness (if only the cavalry would leave her alone). The music supports this connection in subtle ways: it is Martha, whose presence is instilled in the leitmotif which represents the family on the frontier; it is Look's leitmotif which forms the aural backdrop for the reading of Martin Pauley's letter which describes his life searching on the frontier, and it is a woman who literally becomes the frontier in Stan Jones's original lyrics ("The horizon's like a woman, With her arms flung open wide"). That this woman can be read as Martha herself may even figure into the film: in the farewell scene between Ethan and Martha, Martha raises her arms("flung open wide"?) as if to embrace Ethan but stops and her arms fall helplessly to her side.

Let me now turn and examine how the music works in detail in a few crucial scenes. The score for *The Searchers* begins with a mighty cym-

Music for *The Searchers*

bal crash and a dramatic Max Steiner cue. But only moments into what is heralded as a classically inflected Romantic film score, the quiet, melancholic, and folksy song "The Searchers" displaces the symphonic Steiner sound. It is the first verse of "The Searchers," with its strumming guitar accompaniment and the voices of the Sons of the Pioneers (featuring *Searchers* player and former Pioneer Ken Darby), that functions as a Main Title against which the credits appear. When the song reappears in the film it crosses the diegesis from the conscious recognition of song to the less conscious perception of the musical score. Here, it enters the terrain of Max Steiner, who needs a bit of an introduction.

Max Steiner had scored three films for Ford in the mid-thirties: *The Lost Patrol* (1934) was the first, and the second was the film for which both men won their first Academy Award: *The Informer* (1935). Ford and Steiner had worked closely together on *The Informer*, choosing the Irish ballads that can be heard in the film. Additionally, Steiner composed the score's major leitmotif in preproduction so Ford could film actor Victor MacLaglen in perfect synchronization to it. Working in advance of a rough cut was an unusual practice for Steiner and not one he repeated with other directors. ("I never read a script; I run a mile when I see one."[24]) Steiner and Ford parted company after one last film, *Mary of Scotland* (1936), though not through any deliberate action on either man's part; Steiner left RKO, where Ford had been working, for Warner Brothers in 1937 and it was not until 1955 that the two men's paths converged again.

Warner Brothers distributed *The Searchers* but it was not the Warner Brothers' connection that brought Ford and Steiner together again. (*The Searchers* was produced by C. V. Whitney Pictures, an independent production company with a distribution deal with Warner Brothers.) In fact, by the fifties Steiner was finding himself passed by in favor of younger composers with more contemporary scoring styles and he left Warner Brothers in 1953 when his decades-old contract was not renewed. He moved into the more speculative world of music publishing, continuing to freelance as a composer. While the Warner Brothers Publicity machine still described Steiner as "big league," he, clearly, was not playing in the majors anymore.[25] Exactly how Steiner came to score *The Searchers* is not documented, but Steiner archivist James D'Arc suggests that it was "a kind gesture from old friend and *Searchers* producer Merian C. Cooper." Cooper was the producer of the film that helped to launch Steiner's Hollywood career over twenty years earlier, *King Kong* (1933).[26] If this was the case, it was an easy enough favor to extend: Steiner had scored a number of prominent westerns in his career, including *Dodge City* (1939), *The Oklahoma Kid* (1939), *Virginia City* (1940), *Santa Fe Trail* (1941), *They Died With Their Boots On* (1941), *The Treasure of the Sierra Madre* (1948), and a film many critics have cited as a precursor to *The Searchers, Pursued* (1949).

Even after Ford's interventions, *The Searchers* remains among the most classical of all of Ford's film scores, along with Steiner's score for *The Informer*, those by Alfred Newman for Ford's Twentieth-Century Fox productions (especially *Young Mr. Lincoln* and *How Green Was My Valley* [1941]), and Victor Young's for *The Quiet Man* (1952). As such the score for *The Searchers* represents a distinctly different approach to musical accompaniment from earlier westerns such as *Stagecoach* and *My Darling Clementine* both of which used a leaner approach (less scoring and smaller musical ensembles) and depended more upon source material. The score for *The Searchers* also reflects another musical trend, however: the monothematic score, often based in the styles and idioms of popular music, was beginning to infiltrate and even dominate the scoring scene.

Theme songs had been a phenomenon in Hollywood since the twenties when movie studios bought music publishing houses for the purpose of marketing sheet music generated by their films. As studios saw the mechanical reproduction of music replacing actual performance in American homes, they began investing in the recording industry, buying record labels as they had previously purchased publishing houses. Theme music, often arranged as song, could be simultaneously released as sheet music and on record. (Some notable examples include Tara's Theme recast as "My Own True Love" from *Gone With the Wind* [1938], "Laura" from *Laura* [1940], and "The Third Man Theme" from *The Third Man* [1949].) But before the fifties, theme songs remained largely the by-product of a film score. In the case of *Laura,* for instance, lyrics were hastily added to David Raksin's signature tune to accommodate public interest.

Occasionally, selections from motion pictures scores, or soundtracks as they were called, were produced, often composed of selections from numerous films. Such a recording was released in September of 1956 to capitalize on the box-office success of *The Searchers*. Although the album featured a scene from *The Searchers* on the cover, selections from *Gone With the Wind, Charge of the Light Brigade* (1936), *Four Wives* (1939), and *A Stolen Life* (1946) formed the bulk of the recording; little of the music from *The Searchers* found its way onto the record itself. In fact, the only musical selection from the film was titled "Indian Idyll," an adaptation of the cue, "News of Debbie."[27]

Music for *The Searchers*

The phenomenal success of "Do Not Forsake Me, Oh My Darlin'" from *High Noon* (1952) proved a turning point in the role of popular music on the soundtrack, alerting Hollywood to the vast potential revenue that could be harnessed through tie-in recording sales. The suddenly old-fashioned romanticism of classical Hollywood film scoring relinquished its place to more contemporary musical idioms. Theme songs began to monopolize the soundtrack.[28] Sometimes plopped onto the beginning or ending of a film (a practice that continues to this day), sometimes endlessly recycled in every situation cued for musical accompaniment, theme songs became de rigeur in Hollywood of the fifties. One need only hear a film like *Comanche* (dir.: George Sherman, 1956) in content if not ambition related to *The Searchers* (both are captivity narratives), to experience fully how wincingly inappropriate a theme score can be.[29] Steiner's score for *The Searchers*, featuring a song by a celebrated country-western composer and yet steeped in the most classical of Hollywood's scoring principles, provides an interesting flashpoint between the two institutional practices, reflected in the film's opening moments: Steiner's cymbal crash and symphonic cue is suddenly followed by juxtaposed Jones's quiet and folksy theme song. For *The Searchers*, Steiner would develop, adapt, and weave Jones's title song into the classical Hollywood film score. To do so, Steiner would recast Jones's song as a leitmotif and unleash the full resources of the symphony orchestra in its deployment.

The classical film score exploited leitmotifs to channel meaning through the score quickly and dependably. Certain musical passages, often melodies, associated with particular characters, geographic locations, historic time periods, or even abstract ideas, helped to anchor meaning as well as control audience response. The power of a leitmotif to affect filmic meaning is aptly demonstrated in Ethan's homecoming through Steiner's treatment of Jones's song. Through its lyrics, its performance in the main title, and its initial placement in the diegetic portion of the film (as Ethan appears against the horizon), "The Searchers" becomes associated with Ethan. In the opening sequence of the film, that connection is reinforced and developed through the music. For instance, when Ethan and his brother Aaron first meet, we hear the opening phrase of the song arranged for strings, with cellos deep in their register carrying the melody. The silent, but attendant lyrics of that musical phrase, "What makes a man to wander," hang over this awkward meeting, suggesting something sad is in the background here, something that has transpired between the brothers, sending Ethan "to wander." The instrumentation, particularly the cellos, further suggests a melancholic dimension to their meeting. (Steiner, in fact, marked it "triste" [sad] in his original sketches.)[30] The musical cue continues as Ethan approaches his sister-in-law Martha and kisses her politely on the forehead, implicating her in Ethan's wanderings. Later, when Aaron remarks that Ethan's money looks "fresh minted" (and thus implying that it has been stolen), this same musical phrase (and its silent lyrics), can be heard, tying criminality into Ethan's past.

Motivic material from Jones's song resurfaces in the film as a leitmotif for Ethan. Its attendant, unvoiced lyrics provide an interesting commentary on Ethan's motivations. For instance, moments before the posse finds the grave of a Comanche killed in the murder raid on the Edwards ranch, we hear the orchestra play the musical phrase accompanying "where, oh Lord, Lord where" in a slow and "tired" reiteration. Here the music literally voices the men's frustrations in their futile search for the girls. (The score opens up moments later when Ethan majestically guides his great horse down a steep descent.) When Brad dies, the orchestra plays the music accompanying the refrain, "Ride away, ride away, ride away," a commentary on Brad's fate and a reminder that the search will continue. Nothing will stop Ethan. And the music accompanying the opening questions, "What makes a man to wander, What makes a man to roam" can be heard in several key sequences reminding us of Ethan's initial motivation for the search: "heavier and more ominous"[31] with a fuller orchestral deployment as Ethan initially joins the search and the posse rides off after Ethan ignores Mrs. Jorgensen's pleas to protect Marty and Brad; in a subdued string version when a wounded Ethan is nursed by Martin; in an ominous arrangement when Ethan and Martin view white scalps on Scar's lance; with strident instrumentation during the final attack on the Indian village (Steiner marked the moment in the score when Ethan scalps Scar "as loud and shrill as possible"[32]); and, strident again, as Ethan tracks a terrified Debbie moments before he rescues her.

There is information to suggest that, at an early stage of production, Jones's song was intended to be reprised, vocally, by members of the cast including John Wayne, Ward Bond, Jeffrey Hunter, and Harry Carey, Jr. This was, in fact, explicitly promised in a studio press release as the production was under way in June 1955.[33] Such a scene would certainly have been in keeping with the design of many of Ford's other westerns where the performance of song is privileged as a telling mark of character. Think of Chihuahua (Linda Darnell) singing "Ten Thousand Cattle," in *My Darling Clementine* or William Kearney, the "Abilene Kid" (Harry Carey,

Music for *The Searchers*

Jr.) singing "The Streets of Loredo" as a lullaby to the newborn baby in *3 Godfathers* (1948), or the stationmaster's Apache wife, Yakeema (Elvira Rios), singing "Al pensar en ti" in *Stagecoach*.

Song, in Ford westerns, can also serve a more global function, forging community by linking characters through the act of song (and sometimes dance). "Drill, Ye Terriers, Drill" in *The Iron Horse* (1924), "She Wore A Yellow Ribbon" in the film of the same name, "The Cuckoo Waltz" in *My Darling Clementine*, "I'll Take You Home Again, Kathleen" in *Rio Grande*, and the deleted "Ten Thousand Cattle" from *Stagecoach*[34] all work in this way. That, at least initially, Ford was thinking along these lines for *The Searchers* is intriguing, particularly given the cast members involved. It looks as if, at some point, there was going to be a reprise of "The Searchers" by these men, bonding them in some way in their search for Debbie and Lucy. Stan Jones composed eight verses for the song; it makes sense that at least some of them were meant to be dispersed throughout the film.

The Searchers' dependence upon leitmotifs extends beyond the use of its title song, however. Another song to appear in *The Searchers* is "Lorena," which functions instrumentally as a theme for Ethan's brother's family, including—and specifically—Martha. This song is not original to Steiner, nor was it the first time he used it in a film score. "Lorena" is a Civil War–era song (first published in Chicago in 1857) that became a favorite with Confederate soldiers. Steiner first used "Lorena" in *Gone With the Wind* where an instrumental version can be heard as a waltz beneath a conversation between Scarlett O'Hara and Captain Rhett Butler at the Ladies Hospital Committee bazaar and ball in Atlanta. It seems highly likely that Steiner got his inspiration from the Margaret Mitchell novel where "Lorena" figures prominently at the Atlanta ball and serves as a marker for lost love and tragedy. Scarlett, buried at the back of the hall behind a concession stand, hears the orchestra break into "the sweet melancholy" of "Lorena": "What a beautiful waltz. She extended her hands slightly, closed her eyes and swayed with the sad haunting rhythm. There was something about the tragic melody and Lorena's lost love that mingled with her own excitement and brought a lump into her throat."[35] Using period music as a major leitmotif is a scoring practice atypical of Steiner, who, especially in a film filled with period music, liked to compose his own leitmotifs. But it is entirely typical of Ford, who gravitated toward source music.

While the lyrics of "Lorena" are not used in *The Searchers*, they certainly would have been known by Steiner and Ford and would have been

First page of "Lorena."

available to members of the audience who recognized the tune. Lorena's lost love is a forbidden one: "We loved each other, then, Lorena, More than we ever dared to tell." Later, the speaker confesses: "A duty, stern and pressing, broke, The tie which linked my soul with thee." The use of "Lorena," especially in the opening moments of *The Searchers,* underscores not only the unspoken love between Ethan and Martha but telegraphs its forbid-

Music for *The Searchers*

den nature and tragic outcome. As noted by Arthur Eckstein, the original version written by Reverend Webster, was based on his own failed romance with a woman named Martha who was forbidden by her brother to continue the relationship. In the autobiographical story on which the song is based, the love is not adulterous per se, but in the song, there is a clear implication that this is the case.[36] Thus "Lorena," while functioning generally as a leitmotif for the Edwards family hearth and home, specifically refers to Martha.

Narrative placement of "Lorena" in the opening of the film similarly points to Martha. We first hear this leitmotif, a distillation of the song's melody, as the film begins and at the very moment when Martha opens the door at the Edwards ranch, revealing Ethan's arrival. The melancholic loss, encapsulated in the song's lyrics, is emphasized by the largely string instrumentation of this cue, its strumming guitar accompaniment bridging nicely from the lonely guitar of the Main Title. The initial performance of the "Lorena" leitmotif is followed by a lengthy quote from another source, "The Bonnie Blue Flag," a patriotic Confederate anthem, obviously meant to suggest Ethan's Confederate past and (like his relationship with Martha), another lost cause. The music establishes Ethan's status as defeated, specifically as a conquered Confederate soldier. Gradually, the "Lorena" leitmotif begins to focus around Martha: it can be heard immediately after Ethan kisses her in greeting and later when he kisses her good-bye. Interestingly, we hear "Lorena" when Ethan presents Debbie with his war medal. The connection between Martha and Debbie, initially posited here in the music, will return importantly later in the film. A nostalgic parlor arrangement with harpsichord and strings accompanies Ethan's fraught glance at Aaron's entrance into the bedroom he shares with Martha, Martha's furtive fondling of Ethan's coat, and the famous good-bye kiss between Ethan and Martha. (In fact, the good-bye scene is the only scene in the film where the full song is heard and is not interrupted.)

Steiner described the quality he wanted in the opening scenes to orchestrator Murray Cutter as "real old fashioned,"[37] and he specifically asked for a harpsichord with violins and violas for the good-byes. The parlor arrangement is revealing. Parlor arrangements were a common form of musical marketing in the nineteenth century, directed at women who comprised a significant portion of amateur musicians who played in the home. Parlor arrangements capitalized on a limited number of instruments (piano/harpsichord and string instruments such as the violin) typically found in an upper-middle-class parlor. With its connotations of upward mobility, eastern refinement, and female performance, the parlor arrangement, and especially its use of the harpsichord, alludes to a past that the film does not refer to, and points directly to Martha. Interestingly, when "Lorena" is heard in a later Ford work, it is also used as a leitmotif for a female character. In *The Horse Soldiers*, "Lorena" serves as an aural marker for the southern belle, Miss Hannah Hunter (Constance Towers).

"Lorena" returns, at various points in the film, to flesh out the unspoken motivation and emotional content of several key sequences: Ethan's discovery of Martha's body (where it can be heard in the minor); the disbanding of the posse and the continued search by Ethan, Martin, and Brad; the first glimpse of a grown-up Debbie as she descends a cliff toward Martin (cut short by the intrusion of harsh brass and percussion as Ethan spots her); Martin's embrace of Debbie when he rescues her in Scar's tepee; and Debbie's return to the Jorgensen ranch at the end of the film (displaced by a final reiteration of the song, "The Searchers," now and only for the second time with lyrics).

Two instances merit more in-depth analysis. The first is when the posse realizes that they have fallen for a Comanche trick to lure them away from their now unprotected homesteads: Ethan's glance, toward offscreen, over the back of his horse, indicates his realization that his family is as good as dead.[38] The use of "Lorena" as accompaniment here, performed low in the violin's register and cast into the minor, anchors Ethan's close-up specifically around Martha and foreshadows her fate. This is soon confirmed when, upon his arrival at the site of the massacre, he calls out her name and searches for her body.

"Lorena" also performs a similar function at one of the film's most critical and ambiguous moments: when Ethan decides to rescue Debbie instead of kill her. That it is Debbie's physical resemblance to her mother that precipitates Ethan's sudden turnaround is clearly indicated in earlier versions of the script (and elsewhere) where Ethan looks at Debbie and "says softly, 'You sure favor your mother.'"[39] In typical Fordian fashion, Ford deleted the dialogue from the final shooting script,(and replaced it with "Let's go home, Debbie"), obfuscating or, at the very least, confusing Ethan's motives. Or perhaps Ford was simply being pragmatic. Since the actor playing Debbie, Natalie Wood, bears no physical resemblance to the actor playing her mother, Dorothy Jordan, Ford may have felt that the original dialogue strained credulity. For whatever reason, a key moment (perhaps *the* key moment) in the film remains unexplained. Peter Lehman reminds us that much of the film works in this way. Without explicit dia-

Music for *The Searchers*

logue cues, the "audience is left to choose on the basis of highly ambiguous scenes, expressions, and gestures."[40] And, of course, the music. It is "Lorena" which accompanies Ethan's lifting of a tense and terrified Debbie into the air. Based on the song's original lyrics, its narrative placement, and a telling musical arrangement of it, I have argued that "Lorena" functions as a specific aural marker for Martha. Thus, I would argue that hearing "Lorena" at this moment in the film brings us back to the figure of Martha, who returns to the scene and supplies Ethan's motivation. The extent of that motivation, however, remains ambiguous: does Ethan save Debbie because she looks like her mother or because a respect for the memory of Martha prevents Ethan from harming Debbie? Steiner, however, was thinking otherwise. He titled the cue "Reunion of Ethan and Debbie,"[41] obviously referring to the earlier scene between them (a scene which Ford is clearly reenacting here) and prioritizing the connection between Ethan and Debbie in Ethan's motivations. Here music seems complicit with Ford's penchant for mystification and offers ambiguity at just the moment we desire certainty.

The classical film score is identifiable not only by its dependence on leitmotifs but, on a structural level, by its intricate interconnectedness between music and narrative action, a characteristic epitomized by Steiner's tendency to respond to the slightest narrative provocation with music. Steiner's habit is noticeably toned down from earlier scores (*The Informer* provides a hyper-explicit case in point) but there are enough examples left in *The Searchers* to mark the score as vintage Steiner: among them, Scar's short leitmotif played *sforzando* and *tremolo* whenever his name is mentioned (in fact, descending *tremolo* is a Steiner trademark for Indians); the musical cue which simulates dripping water in the cave sequence where Marty and a wounded Ethan seek cover; *tremolo* strings upon Aaron's discovery that Ethan's money is "fresh minted"; falling cadences to accompany the tragic story of Martin Pauley's origins; a cymbal crash to represent Brad Jorgensen's death; a musical stinger (a *sforzando* chord) to punctuate the comic business between Ethan and the Reverend Captain Clayton during the Indian attack on the posse; and even mickey mousing as Martin makes his first entrance, leaping off a horse, or later, more sinisterly, when a harp glissando mimics the flight of birds moments before an Indian attack. There are no moments in *The Searchers* quite as intrusive as the one Ford describes to Bogdanovich in his condemnation of bombastic film scores ("I hate to see a man alone in the desert, dying of thirst, with the Philadelphia Orchestra behind him"[42]). Nonetheless, even after he toned down the score (much to Steiner's displeasure), Ford appears to have disliked the score intensely.[43]

Music brings meaning to film in a variety of ways. I'd like to return to song and continue an exploration of its meaning for *The Searchers* where it is the interruption of song that has much to tell us. Tag Gallagher, in his biography of Ford, describes *The Searchers* as "an atypical Ford movie in its concentration on a solitary hero rather than a social group."[44] But it seems to me that *The Searchers* is very insistently about social bonds as well as the lack of them and in this way embodies the typical Fordian preoccupation with the function of community on the frontier. I read the film as recording the struggle and perhaps even the failure of community facing the overwhelming odds of hostile Indians and inhospitable terrain. It is interesting the way that defeat hovers over the film, from the personal (at the beginning of the film it is revealed that the Edwardses' neighbors, the Todds and the Jamisons, have given up and left the land; the Edwards themselves are massacred and their ranch destroyed) to the public (the disintegrated nations that haunt the film: the Confederacy, the independent republic of Texas, the Spanish New World, the Comanche nation). It is the vulnerability of the American nation on the edge of the western frontier that is chronicled in *The Searchers* and it is interrupted song that marks that tenuousness as insistently as the narrative itself does.

Surely there are few more inhospitable places on the American frontier to settle than Monument Valley, John Ford's stand-in for north-central Texas in 1868. Mrs. Jorgensen describes it as living "way out on a limb," but life among the buttes seems even more precarious than that. This was not the first film (nor the last) that Ford shot in Monument Valley. But as Richard Hutson observes, in his essay in this volume, unlike *Stagecoach*, where Monument Valley is a place to be "passed through," *The Searchers* poses the Valley as home:[45] "[Like] the landscapes that have preoccupied U.S. painters, such as the Rocky Mountains or the Sierras, Monument Valley would never have tempted the [nineteenth-century] white settlers into thinking that it could be developed for civilization. This land is outside of civilized assimilation, heavily marked by its inutility."[46] White settlers pay a heavy price for their insistence (and for their disavowal and destruction of another, prior culture that has made its peace with the land). In this environment, hostility emanates from two fronts: the landscape itself and the Comanches who live in it. And, as many critics have noted, the film often conflates the two, spectacularly, in the stunning sequence in which Comanches appear on a ridge above the posse, as if produced by the

Music for *The Searchers*

very rocks beneath their feet, and more subtly, when Lars Jorgensen says to Ethan that it was "this country killed my boy," when, in fact, it was the Comanches.

Community has been so whittled down in and by this environment that it seems to be made up of only two families—the Edwards and the Jorgensens. The insularity of this community is so complete that when the marriageable offspring from one family seek a mate, they look no farther than each other. (Witness Lucy Edwards and Brad Jorgensen or Laurie Jorgensen and Martin Pauley, or, more intriguingly, Ethan and Martha in which family members turn inward). In this world with such a tenuous hold on civilization altogether, the rituals that have always been an important social mechanism on Ford's frontier take on added weight and importance. More than a ceremonial glue to bind the community together, rituals in *The Searchers* are a bulwark against the chaos and malevolence of the surroundings.

Hence there is no surer sign of the community's fragility in *The Searchers* than the interruption of its rituals. Peter Lehman has argued persuasively for the structural importance of interruption in *The Searchers*,[47] but interruption is at its most dramatic when human voices raised in song are silenced. In one of the most arresting moments in a film filled with arresting moments, Ethan interrupts the singing of "Shall We Gather At the River" at the funeral of Martha, Aaron, and their son, Ben, to begin his pursuit of vengeance. The disruption constituted by his interference with the ritual of the funeral and its attendant singing is heightened by the choice of song: "Shall We Gather at the River" at its most appropriate.

A Methodist hymn, "Shall We Gather at the River," is framed upon a Calvinist notion of predestination: those who have already been marked as chosen in this life gather to cross the River Jordan to the afterlife and "sit at the right hand of God." The hymn's determinism and overarching sense of fatalism (only those who will be judged worthy by God are allowed to cross and be judged by Him) serve *The Searchers* well, especially at the Edwards funeral with its discomforting sense that these deaths were somehow fated once Ethan arrived on the scene. Vengeance transplants grief and possibly reconciliation, both of which are interrupted as is the ceremony itself when the search for the survivors commences. The mourners go their separate ways. The film's own discomfort at this moment is reflected in the music. Ethan announces—"Put an amen to it. There's no more time for praying. Amen!"—and interrupts the song. But the score provides a final symphonic reiteration of the hymn that Ethan suspends, putting its own "Amen" to the ruptured ritual (with church bells, no less, giving it that distinctive Steiner touch).

"Shall We Gather at the River" returns two more times, both at the aborted wedding between Laurie and Charlie McCorry. It is first heard, rather inappropriately (and somewhat ominously given that we last heard it at a funeral) as the processional for Charlie and the Reverend Captain Clayton. They await a Laurie who never enters, having been waylaid by the entrance of Ethan and Marty, and the music stops. After Marty and Charlie duke it out for Laurie's hand, a lone fiddler begins "Shall We Gather" once again, presumably to inaugurate Laurie's walk down the aisle. But this time the hymn is literally interrupted by Charlie who proclaims, "There ain't going to be a wedding." And that's the end of that.

Interrupted music abounds in *The Searchers,* both diegetic and nondiegetic. The castanets dance performed by a sultry Latina in the New Mexican saloon is interrupted not once but twice by Martin Pauley, whose sexual naivete (or disinterest?) blinds him to her intentions, and thus not only her music but any possibility of a tryst between them is forestalled.[48] The "Skip to My Lou" number sung by Charlie McCorry is shortened; we hear only a single verse of a song characterized by the multiplicity of its verses. (A copy of all twelve verses are in Ford's production notes.[49]) Even a fiddle finds itself in danger in *The Searchers.* During the fistfight between Charlie and Marty, the instrument has to be "rescued" by the Reverend Captain Clayton from sure destruction.

Then there are the nondiegetic interruptions: the theme song interrupted by a cymbal crash when the posse finds the seventh Comanche grave, and later by "Lorena" when Ethan tracks Debbie to the mouth of a cave. And, if one considers the lyrics of the title song and the questions with which it frames the text—"What makes a man to wander," What makes a man to roam?"—the film itself becomes a kind of long, unanswered question. The only two diegetic songs which are not interrupted are "The Yellow Rose of Texas" and "Jubilo," both performed at the aborted wedding of Laurie and Charlie, which brings me to the representation of race in the film and the ways in which music participates in its construction.

Music, of course, is never innocent and never has been. Like any product of culture, it bears a dynamic relationship to the ideology of that culture and is, in fact, part of the process through which ideology circulates. Music's relationship to social discourse is not always immediate or obvious, however, giving rise to the notion that music has special status as an art form, free from the intervention of historical forces. But music, and,

Music for *The Searchers*

in *The Searchers*, especially song, carries ideological impact, connecting to and reinforcing key issues in American cultural mythology: the frontier, Manifest Destiny, and the simultaneous and mutually dependent development of the American nation and the American character. Music also opens up avenues for reading the film in terms of particular issues circulating in fifties America, especially the nascent civil rights movement.

Central to America's cultural mythology is the process of defining a nation. Useful here is Annette Hamilton's concept of the "national imaginary": "the means by which contemporary social orders are able to produce not merely images of themselves but images of themselves against others."[50] National identity is established by a process of elimination, crucial to which is the Other against which national identity can be carved out. In America, the Other is the Indian whose prior claim to the wilderness must be disenfranchised.[51] Music has an important part in this project, especially in film, embodying this Otherness aurally through the exploitation of ideologically loaded musical signifiers for what lies outside civilization, rationality, and even humanity.

Race is, in fact, the starting point of *The Searchers*, musically speaking. Although most listeners remember the title song as opening the film, it is actually a Steiner cue, a romantic rendering of stereotypical "Indian" music that begins *The Searchers*. Steiner described this brief cue as "an Indian *Tosca*":[52] a prominent tom-tom rhythm played on the timpani under a melodic design which features descending intervals. Here Steiner taps into powerful musical stereotypes for the representation of Indians: the tom-tom rhythm (four equal notes with the accent on the first) and a descending melodic contour (repeated descending intervals, often thirds or fourths). This musical language, lying outside the conventional rhythms, harmonies, and melodic patterns of western art music, was a powerful indicator of Otherness, and trailed with it connotations of the primitive, the exotic, and the savage.

Musical stereotypes for the representation of western Europe's Others—Turks, Chinese, and Arabs, in particular—developing concurrently with western imperialism and exploding on the musical scene in the nineteenth century, provided the model from which "Indian" music derived: unusual, repetitive rhythms; modal melodies; short, descending motifs; a tendency to veer away from conventional major and minor tonalities toward chromaticism; and a reliance upon unusual instrumentation, especially involving percussion. As Michael Pisani has documented, such musical stereotypes were ready at hand for composers and performers in the nineteenth century looking for ways to accompany Indians on the stage and in wild west entertainments such as outdoor extravaganzas and pageants.[53] Extant music from *Buffalo Bill's Wild West*, for instance, includes clear examples of these stereotypes, in compositions such as "On the Warpath" and "The Passing of the Red Man."

Pisani argues, as does Claudia Gorbman, that actual examples of Native American song, captured and preserved through ethnographic transcription and recording, had far less impact on the musical representation of Indians than did popular culture.[54] In fact, Pisani makes a strong case that even serious art composers in this and other countries borrowed their model for the musical rendering of Indians from these popular sources (such as Dvorak for his *New World Symphony*). Not surprisingly, these stereotypes found their way into film.[55] Gorbman points out that "stock Indian music" was fully developed by the 1910s, verifiable by even a cursory glimpse into any of the several important musical encyclopedias of the era.[56] Not surprisingly, cliches for Indianness made the transition to sound where they provided the foundation for the representation of Indians in the classical western, and hence to *The Searchers* where tom-tom rhythms, modal melodies, striking instrumentations, and unusual harmonies are in abundant display whenever Indians are on the screen (and sometimes when they are not).

And yet, I am willing to acknowledge that *The Searchers'* representation of the Indians is more complicated than it seems on first hearing. Charles Ramirez Berg has recently argued that Ford's insistence on multiculturalism in his westerns—in particular, his focus on the margins of American society, its immigrants and outcasts instead of its WASP mainstream—counterbalances the undeniable stereotyping in Ford and provides a more "nuanced" approach to ethnicity than does much classical Hollywood cinema.[57] Music can be a part of this argument. Clearly, *The Searchers* falls into racist stereotypes through its deployment of conventional musical clichés. But the sheer amount of music devoted to Indians, including important leitmotifs (however stereotypical they may be) for two Indian characters, and the structural placement of that music opens up space for a more nuanced reading.

Musically speaking, it is the Indians who are allied with the frontier in *The Searchers*, an interesting development from earlier Ford westerns. In *Stagecoach*, for example, music accompanying the awe-inspiring vistas of Monument Valley is derived from the American folk idiom with simple rhythms, lean texture, and familiar melody. This land is marked as

Music for *The Searchers*

white. Indians belong on the reservation; they are intruders on the landscape of Monument Valley, terrorizing the rightful heirs to the frontier, the white settlers. Indian music intrudes on the score as well. Written in a completely different idiom from the music which accompanies the stagecoach and its inhabitants, the music accompanying Indian presence (or scenes displaying their handiwork) is menacing, depending on some of the most recognizable musical clichés for Indian savagery: tom-tom rhythms, use of the exotic intervals of the fourth and fifth, and descending contours. (The famous pan to Indians waiting to ambush the stagecoach could serve as an example here.) When Indian music is heard in Monument Valley, we know there is trouble.

In *The Searchers*, the frontier belongs to the Indians, musically speaking—a reminder that this harsh land is theirs and white settlers are the encroachers. Thus it is "Indian" music that opens the film and provides most of the aural accompaniment to scenes of the wilderness; even when Indians are not on screen, we can hear cues for their presence. "Indian" music, for instance, is heard during the scene following the departure of the posse, as the group descends into Monument Valley. Whereas in *Stagecoach*, Indian music seems out of place in Monument Valley, in *The Searchers*, it seems literally to emanate from it. I agree here with Hutson that whites are out of place in Monument Valley.[58] Music dramatically underscores their intrusion on the wilderness.

In *The Searchers* we are given one brief glimpse into the culture of Mexico, when Ethan and Marty enter New Mexico Territory tracking Scar. In *Stagecoach* and *My Darling Clementine*, it is the Hispanic and native American cultures which blend and sometimes conflate. But in *The Searchers* (as in *3 Godfathers*), it is the Hispanic and Anglo cultures which do so: Ethan and Marty's dress (they have adopted articles of Mexican clothing—the sombrero, a new red-checked shirt for Ethan, worn not tucked in and belted); their language (they both speak Spanish, Ethan fluently, Marty more haltingly), and even in their eating customs (Marty devours frijoles). In a cantina, marked as Other by its crude architecture and Mexican handiwork on display, Ethan and Marty meet a man, Emilio Fernandez y Figueroa, who claims to be able to take them to Scar and does. In the scene in which Figueroa brings Ethan and Marty to Scar's encampment, the Mexican culture functions as a buffer between the Indians and the settlers, a point of mediation between them. The conversation with Scar takes place in a mix of Spanish, "American," and Comanche. Importantly, however, the music belongs to the Indians, beginning with the prominent tom-tom rhythm that can be heard at the beginning of the lengthy cue, once more indicating that this "medicine country" of sand dunes and stone monoliths is theirs. "Indian" music even accompanies the climactic scene in which Debbie appears in Scar's tepee and, following a reprise of "Lorena," the standoff between Marty and Ethan when Ethan attempts to kill Debbie.

Additionally, two Indian characters in *The Searchers* have leitmotifs: Scar and Look. Scar's leitmotif is little more than a musical cliché for savagery (a series of descending chromatic intervals) heard whenever his name is mentioned. But Look's leitmotif is a more complicated and also more ambivalent. The cue Steiner titled "News of Debbie" is the second longest cue in the film (3:07). Although the title of the cue is focused on Debbie and the cue itself accompanies the reading of Martin Pauley's letter to Laurie, it is Look, Martin Pauley's Indian wife, who commands the soundtrack, not the white characters around whom, ostensibly, the narrative is organized. Look's leitmotif does incorporates many of the stereotypes of Indian music, including the tom-tom rhythm, downward contour, and modal melody. But for Look, Steiner, first, opens up the orchestral palette, using flutes and other woodwinds, and especially violins, instruments not typically associated with Indians, and second, offers us an identifiable melody for an Indian character. Look's portrayal in the film is as complicated as the music's representation of her and as ambivalent. One of the most deeply moving scenes in the film remains, as least for me, the discovery of Look's death at the hands of the cavalry. Even Ethan is touched. And yet, this is the same character at whom we are expected to laugh when Marty kicks her.

A fairly standard interpretation in the critical canon of *The Searchers* reads the film in terms of the civil rights movement of the fifties with Indians as stand-ins for African Americans. Given classic expression in Brian Henderson's piece, "*The Searchers:* An American Dilemma,"[59] this argument sees the film as repressing the actual presence of African Americans, and displacing black/white relations onto the classic western standoff between cowboys and Indians. Hence the deeply troubling issue of miscegenation gets played out in *The Searchers* between Indians and whites.[60]

Music adds, I think, an interesting layer to this argument. If what the film is holding at bay are the tensions of contemporaneous race relations in fifties America, then music may be one of the telltale markers of the ultimate impossibility of that repression. African Americans do not literally appear in *The Searchers*. But they resurface in Debbie's black-haired rag doll, Topsy (a clear reference to an African American character in *Uncle Tom's Cabin*); in the racial ambiguity of Mose Harper;[61] and in the minstrel music that forms the aural backdrop for the wedding of Laurie and Charlie: "The Yellow Rose of Texas" and "Jubilo."

"The Yellow Rose of Texas" (1858)

There's a yellow rose in Texas, that I am going to see,
No other darky knows her, no darky only me
She cried so when I left her it like to broke my heart
And if I ever find her, we nevermore will part.

She's the sweetest rose of color this darky ever knew,
Her eyes are bright as diamonds, they sparkle like the dew;
You may talk about your Dearest May, and sing of Rose Lee,
But the Yellow Rose of Texas beats the belles of Tennessee.

When the Rio Grande is flowing, the starry skies are bright,
She walks along the river in the quite [sic] summer night:
She thinks if I remember, when we parted long ago,
I promised to come back again, and not to leave her so.

Oh now I'm going to find her, for my heart is full of woe,
And we'll sing the songs togeather [sic], that we sung to long ago
We'll play the banjo gaily, and we'll sing the songs of yore,
And the Yellow Rose of Texas shall be mine forever more.

Minstrel song here needs some discussion. As I've argued elsewhere, minstrelsy found its way into the western film score where it functioned as a marker of authenticity, presented as and mistaken for folk song.[62] I think that both "The Yellow Rose of Texas" and "Jubilo" function most obviously in this way: authenticating the film's depiction of life on the frontier as they accompany the square dance which precedes the aborted wedding. But their origins on the minstrel stage mark these songs with another, older discourse that needs to be uncovered. Minstrel songs themselves trail a complex and ambivalent discourse about race that has been elided over the last century, a discourse that, when uncovered, reminds us of how central race has been to the formation of American national identity and how complicated. In *The Searchers,* minstrel song serves to highlight the film's own deeply ambivalent discourse about race, helping to push to the surface what is deeply buried in the film. And finally, "The Yellow Rose of Texas" and "Jubilo" are packed with particular meaning derived from their individual construction and history, enriching our understanding of race and its representation both in the nineteenth century, when these songs were composed, and in the twentieth century, where they continue to be heard.

Blackface minstrelsy was created to reinforce white superiority, and a song such as "The Yellow Rose of Texas" demonstrates many of the ways in which it did so. The song constructs an African American speaker (identified as a "darky" in the song's original lyrics) whose lack of education and inferior social status are signaled by the misspellings and ungrammatical constructions, typical of minstrelsy, peppering the verses (such as his description of his heartbreak as "it like to broke my heart"). (See the verse at the end of this essay.) The song's narrative chronicles the loss the speaker experiences upon separation from his lover. That the speaker's grief is meant to be comic (or at the least not taken quite seriously) is marked by the buoyancy of the music. The spirited rhythm, derived from its use of eighth notes and the intermittent use of a sixteenth, undercuts, or is at least at odds with, the supposedly tragic emotions the speaker describes.

The rose of "The Yellow Rose of Texas" is identified in the lyrics as a Texan mulatta, the *yellow* rose of Texas. Yellow, of course, is a common nineteenth-century signifier for a person of mixed race, a reading confirmed in the second verse of the song when the speaker identifies his "dearest" as "the sweetest rose of color this darky ever knew." Here we have yet another of the defining tropes of minstrelsy: the powerful and alluring sexuality of the African American female. References to this "rose's" sexual allure are oblique but unmistakable, including a provocative claim that she is superior to her white counterparts. Like many other minstrel songs, "The Yellow Rose of Texas" has become disconnected from its minstrel past and wrapped up in folklore and legend. Descriptions of "The Yellow Rose of Texas" as an authentic folk song, and sometimes even a "Negro folk song"[63] abound during the twentieth century, and reports that the song originally commemorated a notorious episode in Texas history persist well into the 1990s, despite clear historical evidence to the contrary.[64] "The Yellow Rose of Texas" was published in 1858 and performed in this country and Europe by, among others, the Christy Minstrels.[65] It was commandeered as an

Music for *The Searchers*

anthem by Confederate soldiers from Texas and later was sung by the Texas Rangers. Of course, in order for "The Yellow Rose of Texas" to function as a Confederate patriotic song, references to its minstrel origin had to be elided. It was in the 1860s that "darky" became "soldier" and "the sweetest rose of color" was changed to "the sweetest little flower," transforming the song's disturbing subtext of race, gender, and sexuality into a conventional romance. It was probably this version of "The Yellow Rose of Texas" that Ford was thinking of when he requested it for the aborted wedding, resonating the Confederate past of Texas (and of many of the male characters in the film) through the scene and perhaps even foreshadowing Charlie McCorry's own lost cause—his quest for Laurie.

The redefinition of "The Yellow Rose of Texas" from minstrel to folk song continued throughout the twentieth century when a variety of alterations and embellishments got attached to the song. During the 1930s, for instance, the art composer David Guion created a new melody for a sanitized set of lyrics as part of the centennial celebration of Texas independence. This new version became a staple of the country-western music scene (and was recorded by the Sons of the Pioneers in 1943). In August of 1955 Mitch Miller's (even more sanitized) version hit the charts. The score for *The Searchers* uses neither the original minstrel lyrics nor the Confederate version adapted during the Civil War; neither does it use the more thoroughly laundered Mitch Miller lyrics which would have been widely circulating during the film's shooting schedule in the summer and fall of 1955. The version of "The Yellow Rose of Texas" heard in *The Searchers* can be situated somewhere along the continuum from minstrel song to "folk" tune. Like the film's position on race, it is somewhere "in between."

Minstrel song was created to reinforce white superiority but it did not always function in a totalizing manner. Minstrelsy can be described as a multifaceted practice, one that contains virulent racism and sometimes ambiguity about that racism. The second minstrel song in *The Searchers* is "Jubilo," also known as "The Year of the Jubilo" and "Kingdom Comin,'" a huge hit for the Christy Minstrels in the 1860s. "Jubilo" is one of a small number of minstrel songs that demonstrate ambiguity of the form and complicate its racist intention. Composed by noted abolitionist songwriter Henry Clay Work in 1862 (complete with minstrel dialect) and transferred to the minstrel stage shortly thereafter by the Christy Minstrels, "Jubilo," was composed to further the cause of abolition. Its lyrics tell the story of a plantation taken over by its slaves, awaiting Lincoln's soldiers. (This, a year in advance of the Emancipation Proclamation.) In *The Searchers*, "Jubilo" can be heard as one of the dance tunes at the wedding. But it also becomes entwined with "The Yellow Rose of Texas," providing a kind of chorus between verses of that song.

The choice of "Jubilo," especially in juxtaposition to "The Yellow Rose of Texas," complicates an already complicated discourse on race circulating through the music. Douglas Pye, in an article reprinted in this volume, "Double Vision: Miscegenation and Point of View in *The Searchers*," argues that racism is "inherent" in the genre, making "almost any attempt to produce an anti-racist Western a paradoxical, even contradictory, enterprise. It is, in effect, impossible to escape the genre's informing White supremacist terms."[66] I think his argument is amply demonstrated by the use of minstrel music in the film where an abolitionist song ("Jubilo") comes smack up against an example of the racism more characteristic of the form ("The Yellow Rose of Texas"). *The Searchers* is struggling with the issue of race and that struggle is writ large in the musical score.

And there is something else. It is interesting to me that so much of the source music in *The Searchers* is tied up with a minor plot point: Ethan's past as a Confederate soldier. The Confederacy and its cause get tied up into the film in a variety of ways, not the least of which is through the music, even that music which is not, on the face of it, southern. "Lorena," a parlor ballad composed by a northern minister and published in Chicago, was, nonetheless, a favorite of Confederate soldiers. "The Bonnie Blue Flag," a Confederate patriotic song composed by Harry Macarthy,[67] commemorates the unofficial flag of the Confederacy, a bonnie blue flag with a single white star, used earlier by a variety of states, including the sovereign state of Texas from 1836 to 1839. Hence it was often carried by Confederate cavalry, especially those from Texas.[68] "The Yellow Rose of Texas," with changed lyrics, was adopted by Texas recruits (along with other Confederate soldiers). There's something disturbing about what these songs get attached to: the family and the chaste, unrequited love between Ethan and Martha ("Lorena"); Ethan's heroic appearance, materializing as he does from the wilderness itself ("The Bonnie Blue Flag"); communal life on the frontier ("The Yellow Rose of Texas"). There is a kind of diffused melancholy for the antebellum South circulating in *The Searchers* which the music helps to focus and crystallize into a nostalgia for a less complicated and more graceful time. I would not want to argue that *The Searchers* represents the Confederacy unproblematically. On the surface of the text, Ethan's destructive racism is condemned, and that racism is con-

Music for *The Searchers*

nected to his status as a Confederate soldier. But, in attaching the Confederacy, through its historic roots in song, to moments in the film that encapsulate heroism, family values, noble sacrifice, and community, the antebellum South cannot help but be ennobled in the process.

I am reminded here of Douglas Pye's description of the film. "The film probably goes further than any other western in dramatizing and implicating us in the neurosis of racism. But in wrestling as a Western with the ideological and psycho-sexual complex that underlies attitudes to race, it is working *within* almost intractable traditions of representation."[69] Music in *The Searchers* is also working within the culture of fifties America. It is asking a lot to expect a film to transcend the biases and prejudices of its day. In *The Searchers,* the music betrays the inability of the film to completely do so.

How much did Ford and Steiner know of the origins of these songs? How much did audiences of the fifties register these meanings? Much more work needs to be done on nineteenth-century popular song and particularly minstrelsy around the issues of meaning (how does the meaning of this music change over time?) and reception (how are these new and sometimes different meanings experienced by audiences across time?). But it is clear that Ford knew the abolitionist origins of "Jubilo." The song can be heard in three different Ford westerns scored by three different composers and, in two of those films, in narrative situations which clearly point to the song's original abolitionist thrust: in *The Horse Soldiers* it can be heard as Union troops pass an African American church and its congregation gathered outside; and in *Sergeant Rutledge,* it underscores a scene in which Rutledge, a black soldier, talks about freedom. Steiner himself used "Jubilo" in *Virginia City* as one of the dancehall tunes heard in the Sarazac Saloon, a stronghold of Union sympathizers, and juxtaposed it with "The Battle Cry of Freedom," a popular Union patriotic song outsold during the Civil War only by "The Battle Hymn of the Republic."

"The Yellow Rose of Texas" would have been much more present in the minds of fifties audiences than it is today and especially so in 1955 when the Mitch Miller version occupied the number one spot on Lucky Strikes Hit Parade for six weeks. (It spent fourteen weeks on the list and ended up the number five song in the country for 1955.) While the minstrel origins of "The Yellow Rose of Texas" might not have been widely known, its attachment to the Confederacy was still pronounced. The cover of the sheet music for Mitch Miller's version features a photo of Miller in a Confederate uniform. Ford was well aware of this dimension of "The

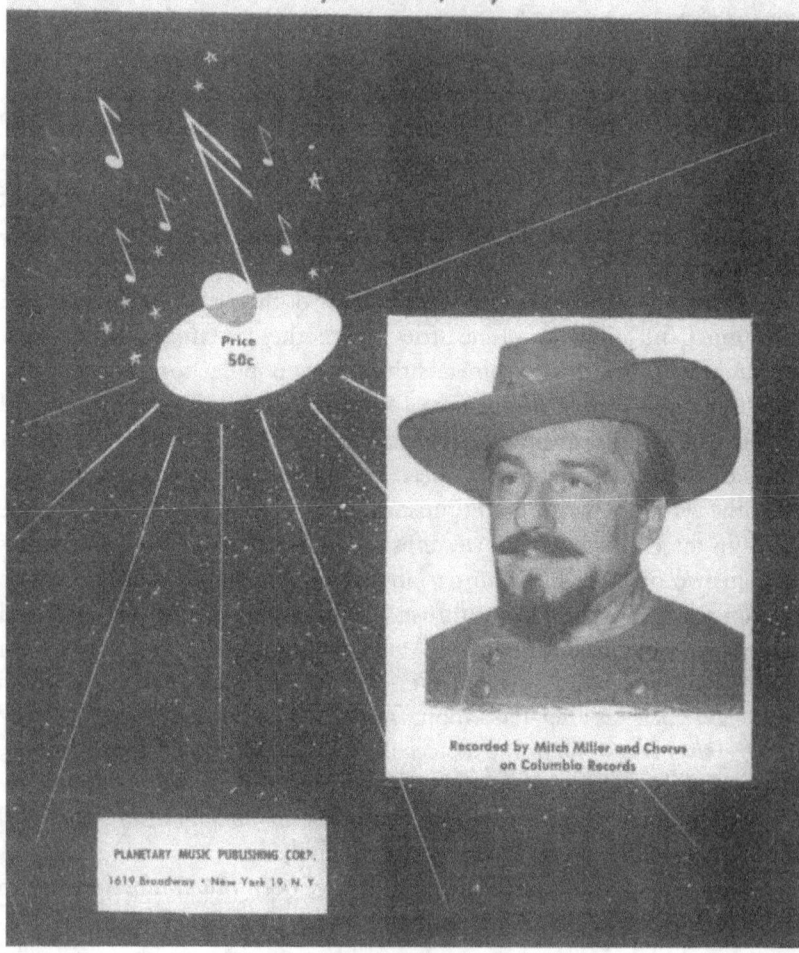

Sheet music cover of "Yellow Rose."

Music for *The Searchers*

Yellow Rose of Texas." He had originally intended to couple it with "The Bonnie Blue Flag" for the wedding scene. The "bonnie blue flag," of course, was the flag of the Confederacy, and its pairing with "Yellow Rose" strongly suggests that Ford knew that "Yellow Rose" was a Confederate anthem for Texas troops. As the song was a favorite of Ford's (and Ford himself was extremely knowledgeable about American music in general and nineteenth-century music in particular), it seems inconceivable to me that he did not also know its origins in minstrelsy. As for "Lorena," the song was still popular in the South in the fifties, suggesting that its Confederate attachments were not as elided as they are today. And its lyrics would have been more available to contemporaneous audiences as well. Steiner and Ford both knew the Confederate background of "Lorena." Steiner used it in *Gone with the Wind* to accompany a Confederate ball and it turns up in *The Horse Soldiers* where it serves as a leitmotif for a southern belle.

As spectators in the twenty-first century, we have lost some of these cultural connections and thus our understanding of the film is diminished. But these connections can be recovered. Minstrel music in *The Searchers* is a rich and deeply significant component of the film score where it functions as a displacement for what the film in particular, and the genre as a whole, did not and perhaps could not address: African Americans. Nineteenth-century popular song functions importantly, too, and its connections to the Confederacy are equally revealing. Music as a discourse has been historically resistant to analysis. Listeners and producers alike have tended to perceive music as free of the intervention of social forces. But as the score for *The Searchers* reminds us, music is never innocent; it carries with it the seeds of its culture. Ultimately, song reminds us of how central race was in American culture in the 1950s and how fraught with tension.

"A Man will search his heart and soul, Go searching way out there, His piece o' mind he knows he'll find, But where oh Lord, Lord where, Ride away, Ride away, Ride away." The film ends with a question, and one expressed musically at that. The search is not over; its terrain has simply changed from the literal to the figurative, from the wilderness to the recesses of the human mind. That this shift into the metaphysical has been signaled by the music indicates the importance of the score in the film's design. The prominence of the song in the film's final moments (and Ford's choice of these enigmatic lyrics) reminds us of exactly how central music is to the work of John Ford and to the meaning of *The Searchers*.

NOTES

Thanks here go to Arthur Eckstein, whose meticulous editing and insightful suggestions shaped this article in important ways.

1. Stan Jones, lyrics to *The Searchers,* John Ford Archive, Lilly Library, Indiana University, Bloomington.
2. See James D'Arc's 1996 introductory essay, "Max Steiner and *The Searchers,*" in the liner notes to *The Searchers: Composed and Conducted by Max Steiner* (MS 101, Film Music Archives, Brigham Young University) and Jack Smith's liner notes for the same.
3. Dan Ford, "The West of John Ford," 37.
4. Ford qtd. in Bogdanovich, *John Ford,* 99.
5. John Ford Phonograph Disk Collection, MSS 2352, Music Library, Brigham Young University.
6. Patrick Ford qtd. in James D'Arc, "What's in a Name: The John Ford Music Collection at Brigham Young University," *Cue Sheet* 5 (1988): 115.
7. C. V. Whitney to Max Steiner, December 9, 1955, Steiner Collection, Brigham Young University.
8. Thanks to Arthur Eckstein for pointing this out to me.
9. The period piece, "The Trail to Mexico," was first used in *Stagecoach* as a leitmotif for the stagecoach itself. That score has an interesting production history; it was created by a team of six composers (five of whom are credited). For an analysis of this score, see my "'The Sound of Many Voices': Music in John Ford's Westerns," in Studlar and Bernstein, *John Ford Made Westerns,* 169–92.
10. See Eckstein, "Darkening Ethan," 3–24.
11. Story notes, John Ford to Pat Ford and Frank Nugent, January 27, 1955, John Ford Archive, Lilly Library, Indiana University, Bloomington.
12. Publicity release, Warner Brothers Archive, University of Southern California. A typical example of studio ballyhoo, in this case, turns out to be surprisingly accurate.
13. Thanks go to Arthur Eckstein for encouraging me to research this song in more depth.
14. When the song was published as sheet music in 1956 by W. Witmark and Sons, four of the eight original verses were included: verses two, three, six, and eight.
15. This recording can be heard on the Brigham Young University compact disc of the score, *The Searchers: Composed and Conducted by Max Steiner,* reproduced from the original music track recordings in the Max Steiner Collection at Brigham Young University.
16. So does Gallagher who claims that Ford chose the verse which ends the film; he does not, however, cite any evidence for his claim. See Gallagher, *John Ford: The Man and His Films,* 331.
17. See my "'The Sound of Many Voices': Music in John Ford's Westerns," 169–92.
18. Ford qtd. in Gallagher, *John Ford: The Man and His Films,* 54.
19. LeMay, *The Searchers,* 104.

Music for *The Searchers*

20. Brooks, "That Don't Make You Kin!," in this volume.
21. See Eckstein, "Darkening Ethan," 14.
22. Lehman, "You Couldn't Hit It on the Nose," in this volume.
23. Studlar, "Sacred Duties, Poetic Passions: John Ford and the Issue of Femininity in the Western," in Studlar and Bernstein, *John Ford Made Westerns*, 44.
24. Max Steiner, "The Music Director," in *The Real Tinsel*, ed. Bernard Rosenberg and Harry Silverstein (London: MacMillan, 1970), 392.
25. Memo, Walter MacEwen to J. L. Warner, December 5, 1955, Warner Brothers Archive, University of Southern California.
26. James D'Arc, "Max Steiner and *The Searchers*," liner notes, "*The Searchers: Composed and Conducted by Max Steiner,*" 9.
27. See RCA Victor LPM-1287.
28. In an interesting variation of this process, Buddy Holly, unknown to the Warner Brothers or C. V. Whitney Pictures, created his own theme song, of sorts, when, struck by Ethan's signature line—"That'll be the day"—composed a hit song with that title.
29. Thanks to Arthur Eckstein for calling this film to my attention.
30. Max Steiner, pencil sketches, *The Searchers*, Warner Brothers Archive, University of Southern California.
31. Steiner, pencil sketches, *The Searchers*.
32. Ibid.
33. Publicity release, June 24, 1955, Warner Brothers Archive, University of Southern California.
34. See my "'The Sound of Many Voices': Music in John Ford's Westerns," 177–79.
35. Margaret Mitchell, *Gone With the Wind* (New York: Macmillan, 1936), 168.
36. See Eckstein, "Darkening Ethan," 23–24n. 70.
37. Steiner, pencil sketches, *The Searchers*.
38. Walker describes this moment as one of "'prospective pastness.' . . . At the moment of Wayne's/Ethan's close-up, the family may still be alive, but by the time Ethan gets there, the family *will have been* killed (or abducted). It's already too late, even though it hasn't happened yet" ("Captive Images," 223).
39. Nugent, "The Searchers," March 1956, 140. See also Synopsis, *The Searchers* (submitted to the Production Code office), Academy Of Motion Picture Arts and Sciences, Special Collections. In this later version, the words "he says," are changed to "he thinks." See Eckstein, "Darkening Ethan," 14, for a more detailed analysis.
40. Lehman, Preface to this volume, 000.
41. Steiner, cue sheet for *The Searchers*, Warner Brothers Archive, University of Southern California.
42. Ford qtd. in Bogdanovich, *John Ford*, 99.
43. See Baxter, *The Cinema of John Ford*, 26.
44. Gallagher, *John Ford: The Man and His Films*, 328.
45. Richard Hutson, "Sermons in Stone: Monument Valley in *The Searchers*," in *The Big Empty: Essays on Western Landscapes and Narrative*, ed. Leonard Engle (Albuquerque: University of New Mexico Press, 1994), reprinted in this volume.
46. Hutson, "Sermons in Stone," 196.

47. Lehman, "Texas 1868/America 1956," 387–415.

48. In the novel, this tryst does occur and its interruption and derailment in the film has important consequences for the character of Marty and the theme of miscegenation.

49. John Ford Archive, Lilly Library, Indiana University, Bloomington.

50. Annette Hamilton, "Fear and Desire: Aborigines, Asians, and the National Imaginary," *Australian Cultural History* 9 (1990): 16.

51. I use the word "Indian" here and throughout the essay to denote the construction Hollywood projected onto Native Americans. As Maltby so succinctly states it, "In the Hollywood western, there are no 'real' Indians—no Iroquis, no Lakotas, no Navajos, only Hollywood Indians." See Maltby, "A Better Sense of History," 35.

52. Steiner, pencil sketches, *The Searchers*.

53. Michael Pisani, "'I'm an Indian, Too': Creating Native American Identities in Nineteenth- and Early-Twentieth-Century Music," in *The Exotic in Western Music*, ed. Jonathan Bellman (Boston: Northeastern University Press, 1998), 218–57.

54. Gorbman, "Scoring the Indian." See also Pisani, "I'm an Indian, Too," esp. 220–33.

55. See Pisani, "I'm an Indian, Too," 231.

56. Gorbman, "Scoring the Indian," 236.

57. Berg, "The Margin as Center."

58. Hutson, "Sermons in Stone."

59. Henderson, "*The Searchers:* An American Dilemma," reprinted in this volume.

60. Neale argues that such readings, while not without merit, dismiss the obvious ways in which Indians function as Indians, relegating Native Americans and their position in fifties America to the margins of the text (if they are considered at all). Clearly there are ways in to read the film in terms of its treatment of native Americans, a question not without import in 1956. For a reading of *The Searchers* as a film about Native Americans and their position in postwar American society, see Neale, "Vanishing Americans."

61. As I read Mose Harper, he is of undetermined race. His skin tone is dark and he speaks with the cadence of stereotypical black speech.

62. See my "How the West Was Sung" in *Westerns: Films Through History*, 155–76. Much of my argument here is derived from this article.

63. See esp. Martha Anne Turner, "Emily Morgan: Yellow Rose of Texas," in *Legendary Ladies of Texas*, ed. Francis Edward Abernethy (Denton: University of North Texas Press, 1994), 28, and "Legend of the Yellow Rose" *Texas Highways* 33 (1986): 58–62.

64. The legend attached to (and eliding the minstrel origins of) "The Yellow Rose of Texas" centers around a mulatta whose sexual prowess supposedly won the Battle of San Jacinto for Texas (under the command of Sam Houston). For her part in seducing Mexican General Santa Anna and thereby delaying his preparations for battle, this woman, possibly named Emily, who may or may not have been a slave, supposedly inspired a folk song in her honor. This originary myth was largely hearsay until the late 1950s when a nineteenth-century manuscript by English traveler William Bollaert was published reporting this story as true. Whether or not it is, there appears

Music for *The Searchers*

to be no verifiable link between this woman and the genesis of the song. Recent historians have begun to debunk the myth itself. As Margaret Swett Henson persuasively argues, the legend surrounding "Emily" masks a threatening historical reality: the pervasive and largely condoned rape of women of color by white men. According to Henson, if any sexual congress did occur between General Santa Anna and "Emily," it was almost certainly not consensual, at least not on the part of "Emily," and she offers historical circumstances to substantiate her claim. For more on the genesis of "The Yellow Rose of Texas," see particularly Margaret Swett Henson, "West, Emily D.," entry in The *Handbook of Texas Online:* http://www.tsha.utexas.edu/handbook/online and "She's the Real Thing," *Texas Highways* 33 (1986): 60–61. See also Francis E. Abernethy, *Singin' Texas* (Dallas: E. Heart Press, 1983), 164–65.

65. I have read numerous sources which report that a handwritten copy of the lyrics, held in the archives of the University of Texas at Austin, dates the song to 1836 and thus predates the publication of the minstrel song by two decades. I have my doubts. The actual manuscript in question bears no date (and to my knowledge has not been authoritatively dated) and I remain unconvinced by arguments that claim it was written in 1836. For a summary of these arguments see Martha Anne Turner, *The Yellow Rose of Texas: Her Saga and Her Song* (Austin: Shoal Creek, 1976), 41–47.

66. Pye, "Miscegenation and Point of View," 229, reprinted in this volume.

67. Macarthy, famous for his "personation concerts," is often described as a "variety entertainer." I suspect he entertained on the minstrel stage.

68. The design of this Confederate flag serves as the basis for the present-day flags of the states of Virginia and South Carolina, and the melody can still be heard as the fight song for Georgia Tech.

69. Pye, "Miscegenation and Point of View," 229.

Homer's *Iliad* and John Ford's *The Searchers*

Martin M. Winkler

Scholars dealing with American history or popular culture frequently refer to "the myth of the West" but only rarely examine the European origins of this myth or its parallels to classical mythology. In this paper I turn to Greek heroic myth as an archetypal precursor of the American western film in general and of John Ford's *The Searchers* in particular. Epic poetry, the earliest form of ancient literature, best preserves the mythical concept of heroism, whose roots can be traced back to the historical Bronze Age and to prehistoric Indo-European culture. In *The Searchers*, Ford's understanding of heroism places especially the figure of Ethan Edwards and the film's ending in the cultural tradition of Homeric epic. While critics and filmmakers refer to analogies between Ford's cinema and classical epic, their comparisons as a rule are rather general.[1] I propose to demonstrate in greater detail that *The Searchers* belongs to the epic tradition of Western culture. Specifically, I will relate Ethan to Achilles, the central hero of the Homeric *Iliad*, the earliest classical work. My aim is not only to point to the unbroken continuity from archaic Europe to modern America but also to indicate a hitherto neglected way of understanding the complex protagonist of Ford's most powerful film. I begin with an outline of the heroic character of Achilles and then turn to *The Searchers*. Robert Warshow's well-known essay on the western hero will serve as my link between the *Iliad* and Ford's film.

I

The *Iliad* is a poem of war and contains explicit descriptions of violence and death in battle. As the poet states in the introduction, his theme is the wrath of Achilles, the greatest of the Greek heroes in the Trojan War. Achilles' anger is at first directed against Agamemnon, son of Atreus and supreme leader of the Greek forces. Achilles' wrath later turns against Hector, son of King Priam of Troy and greatest of the Trojan heroes, who has slain Achilles' only close friend, Patroclus, in a heroic duel.

The poet begins with an invocation of his Muse and describes the suffering and destruction which Achilles' wrath will bring upon the Greeks themselves rather than on their enemies:

> Sing, goddess, the anger of Peleus' son Achilles
> and its devastation, which put pains thousandfold upon the
>   Achaians,
> hurled in their multitudes to the house of Hades strong souls
> of heroes, but gave their bodies to be the delicate feasting
> of dogs, of all birds, and the will of Zeus was accomplished
> since that time when first there stood in division of conflict
> Atreus' son the lord of men and brilliant Achilles.[2]

His quarrel with Agamemnon causes Achilles to withdraw from fighting in the war until the death of Patroclus recalls him to the battlefield. The *Iliad* presents an increasingly savage spiral of violence in a series of duels between Greek and Trojan heroes.

The reason why Achilles is the greatest of the Greek heroes, "the best [Gk. *aristos*] of the Achaians," as the poet regularly calls him, is his prowess in battle. Achilles not only kills more Trojans than any other Greek but also kills particularly famous heroes. According to the Greek idea of heroism, the glory of the slain then attaches itself to the reputation of their killer. At his moment of glory a hero embarks on an extended killing spree, in which he proves his mettle. Being the best on the battlefield constitutes the basis of the European concept of heroism. The Greek term for this is *aristeia*—literally, "state of being the best." The ultimate reward for a hero's *aristeia* is his acquisition of "unperishing glory" (*kleos aphthiton*), which will keep his name famous beyond his death and assure him a kind of immortality. The longest and most graphic description of an *aristeia* in the *Iliad* is that of Achilles in Books 20–22, which culminates in his killing of Hector.

Rather than being an unquestioning apologia of war or a glorification of violence and martial heroism, the *Iliad* derives much of its emotional impact from its unflinching descriptions of the horrors of war. It achieves its ultimate greatness as a literary work of art and its enduring moral force and cultural importance by revealing the limits of the heroic code of *aristeia* and by both presenting and exposing the morally questionable side of violence and war. The figures of Hector and Achilles best illustrate this crucial aspect of the poem.

Before their decisive duel in Book 22, Hector is tempted to save his life by running away from Achilles, whom he knows to be the superior hero. But heroic duty and concern for his reputation have made flight impossible. Hector reflects on his foreseeable fate in an interior monologue:

> Now, since by my own recklessness I have ruined my people,
> I feel shame before the Trojans and the Trojan women with trailing
> robes, that someone who is less of a man than I will say of me:
> "Hector believed in his own strength and ruined his people."
> Thus they will speak; and as for me, it would be much better
> at that time, to go against Achilles, and slay him, and come back,
> or else be killed by him in glory in front of the city.
> (22.104–10)

The heroic code, which had elevated Hector to the level of the *aristos* among the Trojans, is about to cost him his life.[3] In the duel between Hector and Achilles any reader of the *Iliad* is emotionally on Hector's side, particularly since the interference of the goddess Athena, Achilles' protector and helper, is decidedly unfair (22.214–47 and 276–77). Hector realizes that now he must pay the price for his heroism:

> No use. Here at last the gods have summoned me deathward.
> . . . it was Athena cheating me,
> and now evil death is close to me, and no longer far away,
> and there is no way out.
> (22.297–301)

For Achilles, however, the triumph over his greatest enemy turns into a test of his humanity, a test which he initially fails. In clear violation of ancient codes of conduct and far exceeding any justifiable limits of heroic anger in war, Achilles taunts the mortally wounded Hector and threatens to leave his corpse to be devoured by dogs. Hector begs for the release of his body to his father for the sake of burial. Achilles' denial of this request points to the lack of humanity which the savagery of war can bring about in a combatant. Achilles' vicious utterance to Hector before he kills him—"I wish only that my spirit and fury would drive me / to hack your meat away and eat it raw" (22.346–47)—is intended to show that *aristeia* and the fury of war may easily lead to morally wrong behavior. This is a side of warfare readily intelligible to all readers of the *Iliad*, both ancient and modern. Achilles' refusal reveals his excessive hatred of the enemy beyond death, for in ancient belief ritual burial is a requirement for the soul to be able to enter the Underworld, its appropriate place. Achilles denies Hector's spirit peace even in the hereafter. Achilles will continue his revenge by dragging Hector's dead body behind his chariot around the city of Troy in full view of Hector's parents and widow (22.395–515) and later, in a daily ritual, around the burial mound of Patroclus (24.14–22). Moreover, Achilles cuts the throats of twelve Trojan princes over Patroclus's grave as if they were so many sacrificial animals (23.175–77). Both his mutilation of Hector's corpse and this human sacrifice represent the climax of Achilles' sacrilegious wrath. No trace of heroic glory remains. The poet had already indicated as much at the close of Book 20, when he describes Achilles embarking on his killing spree:

> As inhuman fire sweeps on in fury through the deep angles
> of a drywood mountain and sets ablaze the depth of the timber
> and the blustering wind lashes the flame along, so Achilles
> swept everywhere with his spear like something more than a
>   mortal
> harrying them as they died, and the black earth ran blood.
> Or as when a man yokes male broad-foreheaded oxen
> to crush white barley on a strong-laid threshing floor, and
>   rapidly
> the barley is stripped beneath the feet of the bellowing oxen,
> so before great-hearted Achilles the single-foot horses
> trampled alike dead men and shields, and the axle under
> the chariot was all splashed with blood and the rails which
>   encircled

the chariot, struck by flying drops from the feet of the horses,
from the running rims of the wheels. The son of Peleus was
straining
to win glory, his invincible hands spattered with bloody filth.
(20.490–503)

These lines with their similes taken both from the natural environment and from human culture are by no means the most graphic description of violence in the *Iliad*. Their function is to prepare us mentally and emotionally to follow Achilles down his path of savagery.

A particularly important aspect for Achilles as epic hero is his isolation and loneliness, the price for heroism which ancient, medieval, or modern heroes must pay for the very eminence which elevates them over their fellow warriors. Achilles' retreat from fighting with the other Greeks is the first step in his isolation. The loss of Patroclus then makes this isolation complete. Even when he returns to battle to revenge Patroclus, Achilles fights alone and apart from the ranks of the others. As we will see, only his quiet moments with Priam in Book 24 allow him to overcome this inhuman solitude and restore him to his fellow man. But even that return to the community will be no more than temporary, for Achilles himself will soon meet his death in the Trojan War, though it is outside the scope of the plot of the *Iliad*. Achilles' death is a reversal of the death of Hector. This time Achilles will be on his own, and a god, Apollo, will help the weaker hero, Paris, to kill the greater one. (A clear hint appears at 19.416–17.) Achilles will die in an isolation comparable to Hector's. Heroes live alone most of their lives, and most of them die alone.

II

A number of heroic themes which have become canonical in Western culture since the *Iliad* recur in the different genres and media of modern popular culture, particularly in the American western film. Robert Warshow's "The Westerner," one of the most perceptive essays on western heroes, illustrates some of their archetypal features.

Warshow notes about the westerner that "he can ride a horse faultlessly, keep his countenance in the face of death, and draw his gun a little faster and shoot it a little straighter than anyone he is likely to meet." This is an obvious enough point, familiar to all viewers. But we can see how far

Isolation, anger, heroic action: Ethan at the burning Edwards house.

it reaches back into the earliest stages of Western culture if we express it in Greek terms: the westerner is the *aristos,* the best. Warshow continues: "These are sharply defined acquirements, giving the figure of the Westerner an apparent moral clarity which corresponds to the clarity of his physical image against his bare landscape; initially, at any rate, the Western movie presents itself as being without mystery, its whole universe comprehended in what we see on the screen."[4] The key word in Warshow's phrase about "moral clarity" is its qualifier—"apparent." Such clarity exists only on the surface and only in superficial westerns. By contrast, western heroes are worthy of serious attention only when they are morally ambiguous or questionable. As Warshow points out, "guns constitute the visible moral center of the Western movie, suggesting continually the possibility of violence."[5] Heroes are heroes in the traditional sense of the word because they find themselves in circumstances which require them to use weapons. They are men of violence. Warshow concludes from this: "The truth is that the Westerner comes into the field of serious art only when his moral code, without ceasing to be compelling, is seen also to be imperfect. The Westerner at his best exhibits a moral ambiguity which darkens his image and saves him from absurdity; this ambiguity arises from the fact that,

Homer's *Iliad* and John Ford's *The Searchers*

whatever his justifications, he is a killer of men."[6] In serious westerns, and only in these, do we then find the "mature sense of limitation and unavoidable guilt" which surrounds the protagonists of such works. But how does such seriousness affect us, the viewers? As Warshow puts it: "Since the westerner is not a murderer but (most of the time) a man of virtue, and since he is always prepared for defeat, he retains his inner invulnerability and his story need not end with his death (and usually does not); but what we finally respond to is not his victory but his defeat."[7] Warshow's words parallel those with which classical scholar Cedric Whitman has characterized the *Iliad* as an epic from which "the heroic pattern without thought, victory without implicit defeat" is almost entirely absent.[8] The hero's defeat is most gripping to audiences or readers when it is of a moral nature rather than being merely a defeat at arms.

III

We may find such moral complexity in John Ford's conception of Ethan Edwards in *The Searchers*. The duality or ambiguity in this ostensibly heroic figure, played by the actor who more than anybody else in screen history embodies the western hero, is an intentional play with and against the expectations which audiences have brought and still bring to this kind of film. Ford presents us with a protagonist who is, on the one hand, an accomplished westerner—the *aristos* among the heroic and the common people who inhabit the film's societies, both whites and Indians—and, on the other hand, of all cinematic westerners psychologically the most serious in Warshow's sense.

Ford introduces Ethan as a warrior at his first appearance in the film. He is wearing his Civil War uniform years after the end of the war. Ethan soon explains that he does not believe in surrender. "I still got my sabre," he says, "didn't turn it into no plowshare, neither." But Ford immediately undercuts this surface heroism. After the war Ethan had continued to lead a violent life and committed a number of crimes, for he possesses a bag of "fresh-minted" dollars and is a wanted man ("You fit an awful lot of descriptions"). Nevertheless, others defer to his obvious leadership qualities and experience; nobody gives commands to Ethan until he has accepted them as being in charge. When he abdicates leadership, as to Captain Clayton, the results are predictably bad (Ethan on one of Clayton's orders: "Don't ever give me another"). Ethan is right to tell Brad and Martin, his fellow searchers: "I'm giving the orders." He knows the desert well enough to survive in it and is intimately familiar with Indian customs. He knows, for instance, that their horses cannot be stampeded at night because Indian warriors keep them tied down right beside them.

Ethan's perseverance in his search for his niece Debbie stems from his knowledge that the Indians eventually give up and can then be conquered by somebody who refuses to relinquish his pursuit. Most important, both for Ford's characterization of Ethan as western hero and for the film's emotional impact on the viewer, is the moment when Ethan sees through the diversionary tactics of Scar's raid on the settlers. Only Ethan realizes that Scar is on a murderous campaign against the whites. He also knows that it is futile to race back to try to save the lives of the settlers who had stayed at home, though these include his brother's family and the woman he loves. Ford shows the anguish arising from Ethan's understanding of Scar's strategy in a powerful medium close-up of Ethan's face, when Ethan is mechanically rubbing down his horse and staring into the distance. In his mind's eye he is witnessing the slaughter of his relatives.

A visual epitome of Ethan's heroic qualities occurs during the film's climax. When Ethan and the rangers are attacking Scar's camp on horseback, Ford inserts a brief shot of Ethan galloping at top speed and firing his revolver. The background of the image is blurred, so that Ethan appears almost to be elevated above the ground. This view of Ethan lasts for no longer than five seconds, and its significance is easily overlooked, though it is one of the most beautiful individual images in the entire film. A painting in motion, it represents a heroic-romantic apotheosis of the westerner. That Ford here gives us a visual impression of the concept of *aristeia* becomes evident from the fact that he grants only Ethan such a moment of visual glory and beauty. The image bears out Robert Warshow's observation: "A hero is one who looks like a hero."[9] Ethan has never looked more heroic than at this point, nor will he again. But the context of this shot undercuts its surface heroism. It appears in the whites' raid against the unsuspecting Indians after Clayton, with Ethan's assent, had told Martin: "We won't be able to pick and choose our targets." These words reveal the attack's real goal, not the rescue of Debbie but the extermination of the Indians, including women, children, and Debbie—a slaughter of the sort whose aftermath we have seen earlier in the film's cavalry sequence.

The darkness of Ethan's character as Ford will gradually reveal it in the film is his savagery and increasing obsession and madness. These features completely undercut Ethan's heroic qualities and make him, in Warshow's sense, morally questionable. I here limit myself to a brief sum-

Homer's *Iliad* and John Ford's *The Searchers*

Heroic vengeance: Ethan shoots the eyes out of a dead Comanche.

mary of this central aspect of the film since I have elsewhere described it in detail.[10] Ethan lives on the border of savagery and civilization; he is in fact more at home in the desert than in civilized society. Since the Indians in Ford's film represent untamed nature in opposition to civilization, it is not surprising that Ethan is like them in several ways. His fringed scabbard is like an Indian's, and he speaks the Comanches' language. He is also familiar with their religion, as his desecration of the dead Indian early in the film reveals. Most importantly, Chief Scar is no less than Ethan's alter ego.[11]

In the course of the film, up to and including Ethan's final encounter with Scar, Ford places ever-increasing emphasis on Ethan's negative side. From his obsession with causing the deaths of as many Indians as possible by killing buffalo to his comment on the mad girls at the fort ("They ain't white—not anymore"), Ethan appears less and less like a traditional hero. When the camera tracks in to a close-up of his face after he says the words just quoted, the moment reveals his soul, just as the earlier close-up of him over the back of his horse had done. But now it is that of someone obsessed by murderous hatred and rage.[12] If a hero is the one who looks like a hero, then a villain is the one who looks like a villain. At the moment here

Ethan at the Fort: "They ain't white—not anymore."

described, Ethan looks like anything but a hero. His unshaven face is partly obscured by the shadow of his dark hat and his eyes are glowering at the girls, for whom the viewer feels nothing but compassion and sorrow. If this shot were lifted from its context and shown to an audience unfamiliar with *The Searchers* but familiar with the standard iconography of westerns, no doubt all would identify Ethan as a villain, even if they recognized John Wayne.

In this way Ford makes Ethan's eventual attempt on the life of his niece dramatically convincing to the viewer, though it remains shocking. There can be no doubt that Ethan, after he has recognized her in Scar's tent, fully intends to shoot Debbie, and only Martin's interference and a timely arrow from an Indian warrior save her life. Shortly after, Martin reads Ethan's last will and testament, and Debbie's uncle now denies all ties of kinship with her. On his search Ethan had withdrawn into himself more and more; from this moment on, he is utterly removed from any human bonds. *The Searchers* thus presents a protagonist in an isolation as extreme as Achilles' had been. The death of Patroclus in the *Iliad* and the death of Martha in *The Searchers* are parallel catalysts for the murderous obsession

Homer's *Iliad* and John Ford's *The Searchers*

and inhuman isolation of Achilles and Ethan and will lead them to the extremes of human existence.

Ethan had earlier killed three men by shooting them in the back while they were running away, an action incompatible with the unwritten code of behavior for western heroes.[13] His mutilation of a buried Indian finds an even more horrifying parallel at the climax of the film when he scalps Scar. As with Achilles' abuse of Hector's corpse, this act reveals Ethan's inhumanity. In both cases the abuse of a dead enemy's body is a clear sign of isolation from society and its norms. In the American western film, scalping by whites presented as heroes never occurs. The films include scalping scenes only rarely if at all, since the act is regarded as morally repugnant and hence inappropriate for whites. As Henry Nash Smith put it in his classic study of the American west: "Leatherstocking, who always insisted that the white man and the Indian had different 'gifts,' had never condoned scalping by whites."[14] Particularly telling examples of this tradition occur in some films of the 1960s. The villain of Budd Boetticher's *Comanche Station* (1960), a former army officer court-martialed for the massacre of an entire village of peaceful Indians, rejects the hero's suspicion of being a scalphunter ("You think I'd do something like that?"), and the film reveals him to speak the truth. Although the same man has no scruples to plan the murder of a young white woman, scalping, for him, is clearly beyond the pale. It is no surprise then that the eponymous gang of whites in Sydney Pollack's *The Scalphunters* (1968) represent the scum of the earth. And a scene in *Cheyenne Autumn* (1964), Ford's last western, shows that the director's view on scalping is the same: When some rowdy cowboys throw an Indian scalp on the saloon bar in Dodge City, even an otherwise imperturbable Wyatt Earp is outraged. This traditional view of scalping reappears almost thirty years later in Walter Hill's *Geronimo: An American Legend* (1993). It also can be found in recent fiction. One of the two protagonists of Larry McMurtry's novel *Dead Man's Walk* refuses to take a Comanche scalp; so does the hero of Guy Vanderhaeghe's *The Englishman's Boy*, who also threatens to shoot any of his fellow whites if they scalp any one of the Indians he has killed.[15]

The shooting script of *The Searchers* does not include the scalping of Scar; instead, Ethan dismounts before Scar's tent and "runs to the tepee flap, whips it open and glares" at Scar's corpse. "He turns," the shooting script continues, "and his face is a mask of frustration"; then he sees Debbie.[16] The shooting script makes it evident that Ford himself added Ethan's act of scalping Scar, intending it to be a shock for the audience and an indication of Ethan's debasement. As did Achilles, Ethan hates his enemy beyond death, and through such hatred he becomes dehumanized. Taking a scalp is an even greater act of immorality than shooting people in the back. In the course of the film Ford goes to unparalleled lengths to darken the character of its "hero."[17]

It will be evident by now that the moral clarity which cinemagoers tend to expect from westerns and usually find in routine films has no place in Ford's work. Certain other aspects of its plot serve to reinforce the ambiguities in Ethan's character. Ford subverts the standard expectations with which audiences come to watch westerns and their heroes to an astonishing degree. Viewers and critics have often overlooked these turns in the plot despite their importance for the development of character and narrative. Two of them are particularly noteworthy. First, in spite of all his experience, Ethan keeps losing track of Debbie and never manages to find her on his own. Instead, others provide him with vital information. One of these is the slimy trader Futterman, who hopes to make money off Ethan. On no less than two occasions it is, ironically, Mose Harper, the film's holy fool, who puts Ethan back on the right track. Ethan may be an indefatigable searcher, but he is not a finder. We may compare the mythical archetype of divine helpers of heroes in the literary tradition, such as the goddesses Athena and Thetis as Achilles' guardians in the *Iliad*.

Secondly, and in a deliberate flouting of all viewers' expectation of what should happen at the climax of a western, Ford does not include a shootout or fight to the death between the film's two greatest warriors, Ethan and Scar. The final duel which audiences demand from their westerns never takes place, and Ethan does not even get to fight, much less kill, the man he has pursued for years. Ethan simply comes too late. Instead, it is Martin, in mythological terms an apprentice hero, to whom Ford gives the searchers' last confrontation with their enemy.[18] Ethan is denied what would have been his act of greatest heroism—in Greek terms, his *aristeia*. But Martin's moment of glory is no rite of initiation into heroic manhood, either. It is, in fact, a deliberate anticlimax, for the death of Scar is almost ridiculously accidental. A little dog sets the stage for a great war chief's death—its yappings lure Scar out of and away from his tent, into which Martin can then sneak unobserved to find Debbie again. This circumstance signals to the viewer Ford's intention to go against both audience expectation and heroic archetypes. Ford does not even show Scar's face at the moment of his death after his return; he removes all and any heroism from everybody involved in the moment. This is the most unusual refusal to conform to the conventions of his genre by a famous Hollywood director whose name more than anybody else's is associated with the western. Since *The Searchers* is a western without a showdown, the only revenge Ethan can take on Scar, and the only outlet for his anger, madness, and frustration accumulated over the years, is an act of barbarism. Ford shows us Ethan riding into Scar's tent, jumping off his horse, pulling the dead man up by the hair and thus into camera range, and drawing his knife. Although he does not show the actual scalping, Ford cuts away only at the last possible moment. For mid-1950s cinema, this is a unique instance of a director not only going to an extreme himself but also pushing his protagonist's character to the limit. But even if we do not witness the moment of scalping, Ford makes sure that we understand and feel its full impact. When he rides out of Scar's tent, Ethan, his face a rigid and blank mask, is holding the scalp in full view.[19] He has now taken his revenge on Scar, and he sees Debbie right in front of him. The search which had relentlessly driven him on for several years is now over. But Ford's film is not over yet.

IV

The two strands of my argument concerning the *Iliad* and *The Searchers* converge with their endings. The *Iliad* would not be the enduring work of art which it is if it had ended with Achilles' killing of Hector in Book 22 or with the funeral games he holds in honor of Patroclus in Book 23. The climax of the poem comes in its last book when, with divine sanction and aid, King Priam visits Achilles and begs for the release of Hector's body. Upon arriving at Achilles' hut, Priam assumes a suppliant's posture and kisses Achilles' hands, those which had killed Hector as well as many other sons of Priam's. The king invokes the bond of father-son kinship when he reminds Achilles of his distant father, "one who / is of years like mine, and on the door-sill of sorrowful old age" (24.486–87) and who, as Achilles knows, will never see his son again. Priam continues:

> Honour then the gods, Achilles, and take pity upon me
> remembering your father, yet I am still more pitiful;
> I have gone through what no other mortal on earth has gone through;
> I put my lips to the hands of the man who has killed my children.
> (24.503–6)

The poet now tells us that Priam's words "stirred in the other a passion of grieving / for his own father" (24.507–8) and that "the two remembered" (509) and wept, the one for his son, the other for his father: "The sound of their mourning moved in the house" (512). Achilles then reaches a state of emotional calm, brought about by his very sorrow:

> when great Achilles had taken full satisfaction in sorrow
> and the passion for it had gone from his mind and body, thereafter
> he rose from his chair, and took the old man by the hand, and set him
> on his feet again, in pity for the grey head and the grey beard,
> and spoke to him and addressed him in winged words: "Ah, unlucky,
> surely you have had much evil to endure in your spirit . . .
> when I am one who have killed in such numbers
> such brave sons of yours? . . . you and I will even let
> our sorrows lie still in the heart for all our grieving. . . .
> Such is the way the gods spun life for unfortunate mortals,
> that we live in unhappiness, but the gods themselves have no sorrow."
> (24.513–26)

The bond of humanity that unites Priam and Achilles is strong enough not only to bridge the gap between enemies in war but even to remove, through their awareness of man's sorrowful fate, the otherwise insurmountable obstacle that would keep the killer of another man's sons away from their father. The two parallel father-son pairs—Peleus and Achilles, Priam and Hector—point to the common humanity which the enemies share even after more than nine years of a devastating war. Achilles, who knows that he will himself die in this war, overcomes his anger. At this stage in the *Iliad*, manly pride or a sense of satisfaction in heroic deeds are no longer the issue. Achilles feels affinity with Priam's suffering. The Greek term for such compassion is *sympatheia*, hence English "sympathy." Achilles thinks of his aged father, who will never see his only child again, and in this way he finds self-knowledge and recovers his humanity.[20]

Homer's *Iliad* and John Ford's *The Searchers*

Achilles' victory over his vengeful instincts elevates him to a superhuman level; as the poet observes: "he seemed like an outright vision / of gods" to Priam (24.630–31). Achilles' greatest victory is over himself, and this victory more than his conquests in battle makes him not only the *aristos* among Greeks and Trojans but also a model of heroism in a deeper sense, both in antiquity and for all future.

Classical scholar Mark Edwards has described the importance of Book 24 of the *Iliad* in the following terms:

> The tale of Achilles' loss and his vengeance might have ended with his killing of Hector in Book 22, or with the magnificent funeral he gave his dead friend in Book 23. This is the usual conclusion of such tales, and has ended many western movies. The killing of a friend must be avenged, and the Greeks would be satisfied when this had been done. But it is the special greatness of the *Iliad* that Homer was not content with this, and in the final book he added a further episode to the completed vengeance pattern. Vengeance does not relieve Achilles' grief; only when he overcomes his fury against Hector through sympathy for old Priam, and sees his own loss as a part of universal human suffering, can he return to an acceptance of life on human terms. Then the poem ends quietly with Hector's funeral, honoring the dead hero and foreshadowing the death to come for Troy and its people and for Achilles himself.[21]

These words provide a concise summary of the significance of the ending of the *Iliad* and show that without Book 24 the poem could not have become the humane and influential work that it is.

V

The first point to be noted in any comparison between Book 24 of the *Iliad* and the ending of *The Searchers* is that Achilles' bloody frenzy has not abated after his mutilation of Hector, and neither has Ethan's after his mutilation of Scar. As soon as he sees Debbie, Ethan furiously pursues her, even knocking down Martin, who tries again to prevent him from killing her. But now comes the turning point both in the film and for Ethan's character. As Achilles did in the *Iliad,* Ethan redeems himself and regains his humanity. By the time he has caught up with Debbie, he is beyond killing. Paraphrasing a line from the *Iliad* quoted earlier, we may say that the passion for violence has gone from Ethan's mind and body. Ethan's psychological development at this stage in the film may be linked to the

Aristotelian concept of catharsis in Greek tragedy.[22] To the girl's initial disbelief in Ethan's change of heart and to the viewer's utter surprise, he takes her up in his arms: "Let's go home, Debbie." As in the scene between Achilles and Priam, the ties of kinship are stronger than the urge to kill. To attentive and emotionally involved viewers Ethan's act at this moment is understandable and believable—if nevertheless at first surprising—because Ford had incorporated several references to blood kinship into the earlier parts of the film. We may even say that, just as Achilles had come to feel for Priam's suffering, so Ethan now may have come to feel for Debbie's fate since her kidnapping. Put differently, and in the terms employed by Mark Edwards, Ethan now has overcome his fury against Scar through sympathy for Debbie. Even Achilles' gesture of raising Priam from his kneeling position finds a parallel in Ethan raising Debbie, an act which furthermore reminds the viewer that he had lifted her up after his arrival at the beginning of the film. This act is the visible acknowledgment and affirmation of kinship—on an emotional level between Achilles and Priam, literally between Ethan and Debbie.

The price which Ethan pays for this return to humanity and morality is a fate parallel to that of archaic mythological figures such as Ahasver or Moses.[23] Although he can take Debbie back to white society, Ethan cannot himself return to civilization. In the film's famous last shot, a door silently closes on Ethan, who has turned away to walk back into the desert after the others have gone inside. Ford does not show us which of the characters present in this scene actually closes the door. Instead of presenting us with a realistic and thus emotionally uninvolving explanation for the door's closing, Ford emphasizes the poetic nature of the moment. The door closes as if by its own power or, to put it differently and perhaps more appropriately, as if by a higher necessity. The very fact that nobody is keeping Ethan out, either intentionally or inadvertently, reinforces the ending's poignancy. The moment signifies that Ethan's usefulness for society has come to an end. His final gesture of hugging his right arm with his left hand before turning back into the wilderness expresses not simply his isolation but, more tellingly, his unconscious realization that society has forgotten or abandoned him. Just as he had earlier forced the spirit of the dead Indian whose eyes he had shot out to wander forever between the winds, so he is now himself condemned to a similar kind of existence. With the closing of the door *The Searchers* ends as quietly and with as great an emotional hold on its audience as the *Iliad* did. We respond to Ethan's loneliness because we feel his defeat. As already mentioned, Achilles does not die in the *Iliad*, but he will die in the Trojan War. Ethan does not die in the course of his search for Debbie or at the end of *The Searchers*, but he will have no more than a kind of living death, without kin or society: "Ride away, ride away."[24]

Careful attention to the film's final moments reveals that the closing of the door is, in fact, achieved by an artificial device. A lateral wipe created in postproduction and not the actual movement of the door completes the film.[25] What could be the reason why Ford had this wipe superimposed over the motion of the door closing, which he had filmed on the set? While certainty is impossible, we may attempt an interpretation by focusing on the one obvious difference between the wipe and the door: their speed of movement. The wipe serves to accelerate the closing of the door. To go to such lengths of manipulating an otherwise straightforward, not to say routine, shot must have been a conscious esthetic and therefore thematically significant decision. Since we know that Ford had complete artistic control over the film, this decision can only have been his.[26] It is therefore likely that Ford, seeing the footage of the closing door after the filming was completed, judged its movement to be too slow and had it sped up by way of the wipe. As a result the door now seems to close on Ethan much more abruptly than it would have done without this change. The effect on the viewer is that Ethan is almost forcefully excluded from the others. As a result, the wipe makes it impossible for viewers to linger over the highly emotional image of Ethan walking back into the wilderness; it counteracts the sympathy or pity we are beginning to feel for him in his loneliness. And this must be the ultimate reason for Ford's insertion of the wipe: it is an unsentimental—better: antisentimental—moment, one which darkens Ethan both literally and figuratively. After almost exactly two hours of screentime, during which Ethan had been present throughout, the wipe now forcefully dissociates us from him; at the same time it indicates Ford's own dissociation from Ethan as well. This is the last instance in the film in which Ford undercuts his "hero." In its alienating effect it may be compared to the ending of Alfred Hitchcock's *Vertigo* two years later, another emotionally gripping film about a man disturbed and obsessed and one which rapidly and almost forcibly removes its protagonist from the audience at his moment of final and irreversible loss. Both *Vertigo* and *The Searchers* were made at a time when characters such as their protagonists were rarely to be encountered in American cinema.[27]

The most recent attempt at a realistic explanation for the door's closing at the end of *The Searchers*—"the wind fortuitously blows shut the

Jorgensons' [*sic*] door"[28]—is an almost willful misunderstanding of this moment as well as a clear contradiction of what appears on the screen. Since the door closes from inside the house and not from outside, only a sudden draught of wind blowing through the Jorgensens' house could have closed it, but no sound of the door banging shut is to be heard on the soundtrack. Literalism of the kind just quoted only ignores the emotional impact and true nature of the film's ending.[29] David Thomson's summary is more to the point: "The ending is magnificent, lovely, definitive yet mysterious."[30]

We may, however, forgive the critic his mistake when no less an authority on Ethan than actor John Wayne has thoroughly misunderstood the film's ending. When asked by an interviewer about the future fate of Ethan, Wayne answered: "I'm sure that he went off and got on his horse and went into town and had a few belts. . . . I think that Ethan was strong enough to go out and maybe putting up . . . corrals and buying cattle and selling them . . . and gradually getting to where he'd take his hat off and go in the house. And that little girl would learn to love him and it would be a good life."[31] This is one of the most astonishing examples of an actor's lack of comprehension of an important aspect of the character he plays, the more so because Wayne's performance as Ethan ranks with the greatest acting achievements in American cinema.[32] When Ethan turns away from society, we do not see him walk over to his horse and "ride away," as the film's opening song, which is now back on the soundtrack, might make us believe; instead, we observe him walking straight back into the empty desert. A later integration of him into a peaceful community seems highly unlikely, desired neither by Ethan nor by anyone else.

VI

Ethan's return to the desert makes him comparable to Tom Doniphon in Ford's *The Man Who Shot Liberty Valance* (1962). Both Ethan and Tom are played by the same actor and represent the old violent West which has to yield to a more peaceful society. In *The Searchers* the words of Mrs. Jorgensen to Ethan and her husband express this theme most directly.[33] The barren wilderness of the desert will be turned into a fertile garden through the establishment of an agricultural and eventually urban civilization which has no use for the man of arms. Ethan and Tom are necessary to help bring about the process of civilizing the country, but they cannot themselves make the transition from savagery to civilization, joining the new society to which the future belongs. What John Baxter has said about the Fordian hero in general applies in particular to Ethan and Tom:

> Ford makes most of his heroes outsiders, chronic wanderers who accept the necessity of serving society, admire its virtues, secretly wish to be part of it but are driven by personal motives to reject its security. Occasionally a Ford film shows a man settling down, but more often the last shot is of him marching, riding or walking on, accepting with resignation his burden as scapegoat and saviour. Society needs its heroes, but when the danger is past they must be ejected lest they endanger the smooth working of the social machine. These transitional figures accept the stigma of all heroes since the beginning of society, and their characters often have mythical or biblical overtones. Expiators of society's guilt or solvers of its problems, they are also prophets and guides, mystical forerunners of mankind's next development. . . . The men played by John Wayne are especially close to Ford's ideal of self-sacrifice.[34]

Ford himself was well aware of society's need for heroes, as becomes clear from his words about his western *Fort Apache* (1948), a thinly disguised retelling of the story of George Armstrong Custer and the Little Bighorn: "It's good for the country to have heroes to look up to."[35] But as Ford also said: "To exalt man 'in depth,' this is the dramatic device I like."[36] At the time of filming *The Searchers* he restated this position in greater detail: "The situation, the tragic moment, forces men to reveal themselves, and to become aware of what they truly are. . . . The device allows me to find the exceptional in the commonplace. . . . What interests me are the consequences of a tragic moment—how the individual acts before a crucial act, or in an exceptional circumstance. That is everything."[37]

In this way even a figure as morally ambiguous as Ethan can elicit, and is meant to elicit, our sympathy. A man who had both endured and inflicted suffering, Ethan is a victim of civilization—whose taboo on his love for his sister-in-law had made Ethan an outcast from home, family, and society—just as his massacred relatives had been victims of savagery. In the *Iliad*, the poet's as well as his listeners' or readers' sympathies are with the victims of war; in *The Searchers*, Ford's and the viewers' are, too. A telling example is the scene in which Ethan and Martin come upon the scene of the cavalry's massacre of an entire Indian village. In images that recall nineteenth-century photographs from the Indian wars (if, in our mind's eye, we imagine them to be in black and white rather than in Technicolor), Ford shows us dead bodies frozen in the snow.[38] Moments

Scar's winter camp: The impact of white violence.

later the searchers will find the corpse of Look, Martin's young Indian wife, also a victim of indiscriminate slaughter.

The price exacted for the advancement of a civilization born from war, violence, and suffering is the true subject of *The Searchers*. For this reason the film represents the highest achievement by a director whom Robin Wood has rightly characterized as "the American cinema's great poet of civilization."[39] And in this regard the film is a modern descendant not only of the *Iliad* but also of the other ancient epic that examines the same theme with the same depth of compassion and understanding: Virgil's *Aeneid*. *Arma virumque cano*: "Arms and the man I sing," Virgil, the great poet of Roman civilization, begins—a timeless theme, forever new.[40]

Ford, no doubt unconsciously, took recourse to fundamental heroic archetypes in *The Searchers* and in numerous other films. This becomes evident when we compare the duality and ambiguity inherent in the Fordian and Homeric hero figures with an even older pattern. In his study of Indo-European hero mythology Jaan Puhvel makes the following point: "The warrior . . . had an ambivalent role as single champion or part of a self-centered corps or coterie, both a society's external defender and its

Homer's Iliad and John Ford's The Searchers

potential internal menace."[41] The key to the undiminished power which *The Searchers* exerts on its viewers lies in the archaic and mythical nature of its narrative. Ford and his screenwriter Frank Nugent darkened the film's central character far beyond what Alan LeMay, the author of the 1954 novel, had been able to achieve. Ford's film has taken its place among the quintessential works of American culture, an especially stark example of the tradition of the Indian captivity narrative, which novelist and critic Robert Stone has characterized as "an ongoing American epic."[42] But we may also compare Ford's Ethan and his driven, morally questionable character with another quintessentially American figure, Melville's Captain Ahab.[43] We are also reminded of another western film in which John Wayne had played a comparable character, Howard Hawks's *Red River* (1948).

Unlike LeMay's book, Ford's film has kept its emotional hold on audiences for almost half a century. Not least for its mythic-heroic qualities, both ancient and American, it is likely to continue to do so. In 2001, for example, Chuck Workman's short film *The Spirit of America*, a response to September 11 that consists entirely of clips from 110 famous films, opens and closes with the first and last shots of *The Searchers*. In its three to four minutes, Ford is represented by more films than any other director.

NOTES

1. A recent example is this observation about Ford by writer-director John Milius: "He's a storyteller like Homer. When Homer got through with a story, you had something you can read forever." The quotation is from Nick Redman, *A Turning of the Earth: John Ford, John Wayne and "The Searchers"* (1998), a documentary included in the "Special Edition" videotape issue of *The Searchers* (Warner Home Video, no. 16334). An illustrated article on the film in *Look* called it "a Homeric Odyssey" upon its release; see McBride, *Searching For John Ford*, 557. Clauss, "Mythic Paradigms in *The Searchers*," adduces several Homeric and other classical parallels to the film. I examine it in connection with Greek tragedy in Winkler, "Tragic Features in John Ford's *The Searchers*," in *Classical Myth and Culture in the Cinema*, ed. Martin Winkler (New York: Oxford University Press, 2001), 118–47, which provides a list of standard works on the film at 125–26n. 22.

2. *Iliad* 1.1–7. All quotations from the *Iliad* are according to *The Iliad of Homer*, trans. Richmond Lattimore (Chicago: University of Chicago Press, 1951), 59. For the sake of consistency and greater familiarity I have changed the spellings of some Greek names from Lattimore's, e.g. "Achilleus" and "Hektor" to the more common "Achilles" and "Hector."

3. Cf. Jasper Griffin, *Homer* (New York: Hill and Wang, 1980), 43–45. I examine this aspect of heroism in connection with the western film in greater detail in

"Homeric *kleos* and the Western Film," *Syllecta Classica* 7 (1996): 43–54. For a general comparison of classical and western heroes see my "Classical Mythology and the Western Film," *Comparative Literature Studies* 22 (1985): 516–40.

4. The quotations are from Warshow, "The Westerner," *Partisan Review* 21 (1954): 190–203. I cite from its reprint in Warshow, *The Immediate Experience*, 135–54, quotations from 139.

5. Warshow, "The Westerner," 139.

6. Ibid., 142.

7. Ibid., 143.

8. Cedric H. Whitman, *Homer and the Heroic Tradition* (Cambridge: Harvard University Press, 1958), 167, describing the *aristeia* of Diomedes in Book 5 of the *Iliad*.

9. Warshow, "The Westerner," 153.

10. "Tragic Features in John Ford's *The Searchers*," 125–32.

11. Cf., for example, "Tragic Features in John Ford's *The Searchers*," 127–28. By contrast, Martin may be seen as Ethan's good side or as the embodiment of the good qualities in himself which Ethan denies or represses. That Ethan, despite his racism toward the racially impure Martin, still feels affinity for him becomes evident in some scenes: when he encourages Martin to stay with the Jorgensens rather than to continue the search for Debbie, when he kids around with Martin while setting his trap for Futterman, when he makes Martin his heir, and when he pats Martin on the shoulder before the latter's dangerous descent into Scar's camp. These moments foreshadow Ethan's eventual overcoming of hatred and obsession, as does his reaction to finding Look's dead body.

12. Buscombe, *The Searchers*, 34, provides a good color still of this moment.

13. As late as 1976, when making his last film, John Wayne refused to have his character shoot anybody in the back: "It's unthinkable for my image." The quotation is from Wills, *John Wayne's America*, 300. Wills (*John Wayne's America*, 286), discussing Ford's *The Man Who Shot Liberty Valance* (1961) and earlier in his chapter on *The Searchers* (251–61), seems to be unaware of the implications of the ambush scene for Ethan's character since he omits to discuss it.

14. Smith, *Virgin Land*, 83.

15. Larry McMurtry, *Dead Man's Walk* (New York: Pocket Books, 1996), 163–64; Guy Vanderhaeghe, *The Englishman's Boy* (New York: Picador, 1998), 286.

16. The quotations are from p. 139 of the revised final shooting script of the film.

17. See Eckstein, "Darkening Ethan," 3–24.

18. On the presence of the apprentice-hero archetype in the American western tradition, see Smith, *Virgin Land*, 69–70.

19. A color still at Buscombe, *The Searchers*, 39, just before Ford's close-up on Ethan's face.

20. In his analysis of *The Searchers*, Wills refers to the *Iliad* several times (*John Wayne's America*, 251–61), and his chapter title, "The Fury of Ethan," is meant to point to Achilles' anger. But in his discussion of the scene between Achilles and Priam (257–58) Wills so far misrepresents the emotional power and ethical importance of their encounter as to conclude that Achilles had merely been "punishing himself, and

Homer's *Iliad* and John Ford's *The Searchers*

that is superfluous" (258). Such trivialization of Homer is the more astonishing in light of Wills's knowledge of classical literature and culture.

21. Mark W. Edwards, *Homer: Poet of the Iliad* (Baltimore: Johns Hopkins University Press, 1987), 301.

22. Details in "Tragic Features in John Ford's *The Searchers*," 120, 132–35.

23. Cf. "Tragic Features in John Ford's *The Searchers*," 141–43. My discussion there, esp. that of the ending of Sophocles' *Oedipus the King* at 142, reinforces the fact that *The Searchers* firmly belongs within the archetypal heroic (and tragic) tradition.

24. On the film's theme song, from which these words come, see Eckstein, "Darkening Ethan," 5. Ford specifically chose its lyrics; see Gallagher, *John Ford: The Man and His Films*, 331n. Buscombe, *The Searchers*, 73–74n. 64, provides the song's full text.

25. The digital videodisc edition of the film—Warner Home Video, no. 14651 (1997)—provides us with the image clarity and possibility of replay necessary to see what is really happening. When the door of the Jorgensens' house begins to close—at 1:58:31 on the DVD's timer—a fast black wipe moving left-to-right across the whole screen overtakes the door a second later and causes the impression in us that the door's movement continues. Since the wipe is a later addition, it does not completely match the movement of the door but makes for a noticeable moment of roughness.

26. Cf. Davis, *John Ford: Hollywood's Old Master*, 194–96, and Eckstein, "Darkening Ethan," 10, on Ford's independence (via Argosy Pictures, his production company).

27. In the final shot of *Vertigo*, the "hero" slightly tilts his head to the right and almost imperceptibly opens his arms. The effect is of despair, resignation, and loneliness. Cf. Robin Wood, *Hitchcock's Films Revisited* (New York: Columbia University Press, 1989), 129: "He is cured [of his vertigo], but empty, desolate. Triumph and tragedy are indistinguishably fused." A further connection between *Vertigo* and *The Searchers* lies in the fact that Vera Miles, Ford's Laurie Jorgensen, was originally set to play Hitchcock's Madeleine/Judy. In 1957 Miles played the wife who descends into a state of psychotic depression in Hitchcock's *The Wrong Man*, a foreshadowing of Madeleine's obsession with death in Hitchcock's immediately following work. In view of such psychological instability in both these films, the violent outburst of Laurie to Martin about Debbie during the wedding sequence in *The Searchers* takes on additional meaning. Just as the elegance and poise of Madeleine, expressed primarily through her clothing, is in stark contrast with her death wish, so Laurie's bridal dress, a symbol of virginal innocence and sweetness, throws into relief the unexpected viciousness of her language about Debbie ("the leavings of a Comanche buck, sold time and again to the highest bidder") and her desire for Debbie's death, which, she says, even Martha would want. On this moment cf. the comments by Crouch, "Bull Feeney Plays the Blues," 278–79.

28. Darby, *John Ford's Westerns*, 221.

29. For examples of other elementary mistakes about the closing-door scene see Baxter, *The Cinema of John Ford*, 145, and Quart and Auster, *American Film and Society*, 54: "The stirring long shot of his [Ethan's] riding away." Wills's description of the film's opening and closing shots in terms of the silent cinema's use of an opening and closing iris (Wills, *John Wayne's America*, 254–55, 260–61) is awkward in that the

rectangular doorways of the film contrast with the circular nature of an iris and in that such "irising" occurs without simultaneous camera movement. The old canard that the doors at the beginning and end of the film are one and the same seems to be indestructible; see, most egregiously, the contradictory statements at Davis, *John Ford: Hollywood's Old Master*, 276–77. Gallagher, *John Ford: The Man and His Films*, 338, also discusses the ending's realistic aspects ("as in our world, people live separately. . . .: Ethan walks away for the most commonplace of reasons"), but at least he incorporates them into its poetic nature ("in a moment, the hero disappears and only a lonely, aging man is left"). The criticism of the film's ending by Wills in *John Wayne's America* (17): ("[Ethan's] deep fires of revenge burn so fiercely through the picture that extinguishing them in the final scene looks contrived") is unconvincing and contradicted by Wills's own later statement: "The filming [of the scene] tells us we are in the realm of symbol" (260). For a more convincing analysis of the film's ending see Eckstein, "Darkening Ethan," 14–16.—The ending is one of two parts of *The Searchers* which critics regularly misunderstand and misinterpret even today; the other is the white captives scene in the film's cavalry sequence. Recently Douglas Pye, "Double Vision: Miscegenation and Point of View," 232–34; Wills, *John Wayne's America*, 258; and McBride, *Searching for John Ford*, 563, have all attributed their madness to the Indians among whom they have lived, though Ford makes it unmistakably clear that their mental state results from the horrors of the army's annihilation of the Indian village whose aftermath Ford has just shown us. On the cause of the captives' madness see my counterargument in "Tragic Features in John Ford's *The Searchers*," 130–31 and 133–34; cf. Eckstein, "Darkening Ethan," 9–11. Criticism of *The Searchers* also focuses on Debbie's abrupt change of mind about her return to white society; McBride, *Searching for John Ford*, 564, goes so far as to call it the film's "most glaring flaw." But the literary tradition of sudden changes of mind in, for example, Euripidean and Shakespearean drama makes the moment in the film perfectly comprehensible, as I argue in the paper cited above at 137–41.

30. Thomson, "Open and Shut," 31.

31. Macklin, "I Come Ready," 30–31.

32. On Wayne's performance and his understanding of Ethan cf. McBride, *Searching for John Ford*, 557–58.

33. I partially quote her speech and discuss its archetypal context in "Tragic Features in John Ford's *The Searchers*," 146.

34. Baxter, *The Cinema of John Ford*, 21; cf. 92, on the hero of Ford's *The Grapes of Wrath* (1940). See also Gallagher, *John Ford: The Man and His Films*, 336–37.

35. Qtd. in Bogdanovich, *John Ford*, 86.

36. Qtd. in Gallagher, *John Ford: The Man and His Films*, 302.

37. Qtd. in Andrew Sarris, ed. *Interviews With Film Directors* (New York: Avon, 1969), 197.

38. The documentary-like realism in this scene becomes evident if we compare it with photographs of the massacre at Wounded Knee; see photos 66–75 in Richard E. Jensen, R. Eli Paul, and John E. Carter, *Eyewitness at Wounded Knee* (Lincoln: University of Nebraska Press, 1991), 105–14. Eckstein, "Darkening Ethan," 21–22n. 44, adduces George Armstrong Custer's massacre of the Cheyennes at the Washita River, Oklahoma, in November 1868.

Homer's *Iliad* and John Ford's *The Searchers*

39. Wood, "Shall We Gather at the River?" 12. This essay also appears in John Caughie, ed., *Theories of Authorship: A Reader* (London: Routledge, 1981), 83–101, and in Studlar and Bernstein, *John Ford Made Westerns*, 23–41.

40. The significance of both the *Iliad* and *The Searchers* for modern America may be gauged by their thematic parallels to the American war in Vietnam. On the subject see Slotkin, *Regeneration through Violence*, 562–64, and *Gunfighter Nation*, 441–86 (chapter titled "Gunfighters and Green Berets," including a discussion of *The Searchers*), and esp. Jonathan Shay, *Achilles in Vietnam: Combat Trauma and the Undoing of Character* (New York: Simon and Schuster, 1995) on combat trauma; the title of his book is particularly revealing. See also Ian C. Johnston, *The Ironies of War: An Introduction to Homer's* Iliad (Lanham, Md.: University Press of America, 1988), 139–41, on connections between Vietnam films and the *Iliad*, and Erling B. Holtsmark, "The *Katabasis* Theme in Modern Cinema," in *Classical Myth and Culture in the Cinema*, 23–50, at 65–77, on the mythological theme of the descent to the underworld in westerns and war films. W. J. Hug, "Images of the Western in Selected Vietnam Films," in *Continuities in Popular Culture: The Present in the Past and the Past in the Present and Future*, ed. Ray B. Browne and Ronald J. Ambrosetti (Bowling Green, Ohio: Bowling Green University Popular Press, 1993), 176–90, discusses western overtones in Vietnam war films, while Michael Coyne, *The Crowded Prairie*, 120–41 and 206–8 (notes), examines Vietnam overtones in the western. For Martin Scorsese's *Taxi Driver* (1976) as a post-Vietnam retelling of *The Searchers* see David Boyd, "Prisoner of the Night," *Film Heritage* 12 (1976–77): 24–30, followed by Mortimer, *Hollywood's Frontier Captives*, 111–31. Boyd's title refers to McBride and Wilmington, "Prisoner of the Desert," 210–14; reprinted in McBride and Wilmington, *John Ford*, 147–63. The phrase, referring to Ethan, is a translation of the film's French title, *La prisonnière du désert*, which, however, refers to Debbie. Paul Schrader, the screenwriter of *Taxi Driver*, has affirmed that the parallels to *The Searchers* in *Taxi Driver* were intentional; see Schrader, "Letter to the Editor," *Film Heritage* 12 (1977): 44, and cf. Kevin Jackson, ed., *Schrader on Schrader* (London: Faber and Faber, 1990), 22 and 155. Concerning the sometimes strange fate of films it may be worth noting that in 1999 Scottish video artist Douglas Gordon used *The Searchers, Vertigo,* and *Taxi Driver* for video and audio installations in, respectively, Berlin, London, and New York. Peter Schjeldahl, "Eurosplash," the *New Yorker*, May 10, 1999, 90–94, provides a description at 90–91 (with illustration of *The Searchers* being projected in the Neue Nationalgalerie, Berlin) and 93.

41. Jaan Puhvel, *Comparative Mythology* (Baltimore: Johns Hopkins University Press, 1987), 242.

42. Robert Stone, "American Apostle," the *New York Review of Books*, March 26, 1998, 26. This is a review essay of Alfred Kazin's *God and the American Writer* (1997). The tradition of captivity narratives in early American literature receives extensive treatment at Slotkin, *Regeneration through Violence*, 94–179 and passim. Girgus, *Hollywood Renaissance*, 25–55, links *The Searchers* to American Puritanism and captivity narratives, but not all his observations are correct or convincing. The same may be said about Mortimer, *Hollywood's Frontier Captives*, 29–48 (on *The Searchers* and the tradition of captivity narratives, mainly following Slotkin); on the film's ending she observes (49) that it suggests "that Ethan's status as hero has remained unchallenged" in the course of the film because "the last shot mirrors the opening shot"—an untenable simplification.

43. Cf. Newton Arvin, *Herman Melville* (New York: Sloane, 1950), 170 (on Ahab's "murderous destructiveness directed outward against the Other") and esp. 175–81; the latter passage contains numerous references to ancient Greek literature, esp. epic, and myth. Cf. Greil Marcus, *The Dustbin of History* (Cambridge: Harvard University Press, 1995), 212, followed by Wills, *John Wayne's America*, 271; Girgus, *Hollywood Renaissance*, 47 (on Martin Pawley as Ishmael to Ethan's Ahab); and esp. Smith, *Virgin Land*, 76–80. As D. H. Lawrence observed in his *Studies in Classic American Literature* (1923): "The essential American soul is hard, isolate, stoic, and a killer. It has never yet melted" (qtd. in Girgus, *Hollywood Renaissance*, 43); cf. McBride, *Searching for John Ford*, 558. The observation by Girgus, *Hollywood Renaissance*, 51, on Ethan's "penchant for suffering on his search, a journey that becomes an exercise in alternating sadism and self-punishment," fits Ahab equally well. For the importance of the *Iliad* on the origins of epic American literature, including epic narratives in prose, see the extensive discussion by John P. McWilliams, Jr., *The American Epic: Transforming a Genre, 1770–1860* (Cambridge: Cambridge University Press, 1989).

What Would Martha Want?
Captivity, Purity, and Feminine Values in *The Searchers*

Gaylyn Studlar

"Whence flow the blessings that cluster around the family circle? Can they be traced to any other source than to that mother whose intelligence and purity have shed over it her mild and cheering influence?
The domestic circle, the cherished home of the affections, and the dwelling-place of every social virtue, was transplanted from Eden, and seems to be the only relic of paradise left to fallen man."
—*The Household*, vol. 1, 1868

The symbolic importance of women as primary representatives of civilization and white society is a longstanding convention of the western. In spite of generic ubiquity, the textual appearance of this convention can be accompanied by considerable ideological and narrative tensions. At their core, these tensions arise from the genre's frequent association of civilization in general—and white women in particular—with the repression of the very qualities of frontier freedom and masculine prowess that the genre is assumed to celebrate. This has led Martin Pumphrey to the view that "the genre makes an absolute and value-laden division between the masculine and feminine sphere."[1] In keeping with such commentary, Jane Tompkins claims the genre "struggles and strains to cast out everything feminine" so that the western's hard, violent heroes can leave domesticity behind and assert their masculine domination over land, self, and Other.[2] In fact, Tompkins refers to John Ford's film, *The Searchers* (1956), as being exemplary of the western's denigration of femininity in that "what women stand for—love and forgiveness in place of vengeance—is precisely what the activity [men's avenging violence] denies . . . the discourse of love and peace which women articulate is never listened to."[3]

John Ford's *The Searchers* does indeed reveal the ideological tensions in the struggle between the spheres of forgiving femininity and vengeful masculinity. The western's conventional masculine values of anarchic freedom and violent individuality are embodied by the ostensible hero, Ethan Edwards (John Wayne), and familiar cultural norms based on maintaining female sexual and racial purity dominate the frontier ethos portrayed in *The Searchers* as they do in the genre as whole. But just as John Ford's early western classic, *Stagecoach* (1939), rejects the one narrow model of civilization (the kind that creates a "Law and Order League") to embrace another, broader view of the virtues and the virtuous in an ideal society, *The Searchers* rejects narrow notions of female worth dependent on racial and sexual purity as incompatible with its ideal vision of the nation, community, family—and femininity.

Furthermore, the film embraces the unexpected goal of blurring the western's often polarized spheres of masculinity and femininity to establish a constellation of feminized values that extend across the boundaries of gender and generation. Based on Christian forgiveness, love, and tolerance, these values are brought into open conflict with racial and sexual difference constructed in binary terms. Thus, far from demonstrating Tompkins's claim that "the discourse of love and peace which women articulate is never listened to," *The Searchers*, I will argue in this essay, illustrates the triumph of "feminine" values that are ultimately "listened to" by Ethan Edwards as well as by the film's audience.

To suggest of a Fordian western an ideological move of this sort that runs contrary to norms of constructing gender in the genre is certainly not without scholarly precedent. Richard Slotkin, for example, has noted that in the military family that dominates *Fort Apache* (1948), "women's values stand equal to men's."[4] Yet Ford also has been severely criticized for his portrayals of women. Writing in 1975, Michael Dempsey dismissed Ford's female characters as "mired in stereotypes" and "simply 'waiting women' whether they are wives, mothers, daughters, or prostitutes." Dempsey goes on to describe them as "generally coy, angelic, abstractions of Holy Womanhood."[5]

Ford may well succumb to a sentimental idealization of white women, but in *The Searchers*, even more than in *Fort Apache*, the foregrounding and valorization of feminine values challenge gender norms of the western. These values—Christian, domestic, civilized—are not only

Captivity, Purity, and Feminine Values in *The Searchers*

equal to those traditionally exhibited by men in westerns—they are constructed as being clearly superior to those of an aggressively racist masculinity that is held up by the film for critical scrutiny. Furthermore, generic norms are also overturned in *The Searchers* by the expression of female-aligned values across the gender divide. Some men, notably Martin Pawley (Jeffrey Hunter), embrace values identified as feminine, even as some women, including Pawley's love interest, Laurie Jorgensen (Vera Miles), come to be aligned with masculine values.

In *The Searchers*, the symbolic linchpin of this ultimate triumph of a feminized sphere of values is Martha Edwards (Dorothy Jordan) a character killed twenty minutes into the narrative. Martha Edwards may die early in the film, but her brief appearance does not mean she is unimportant. On the contrary, as I will show, her presence—and absence—exerts an unrivaled impact on characters' actions, ideals, psychology, and social relations, especially as they relate to her daughter, Debbie, who is kidnapped by the Comanche.

Within a variation of the captivity narrative, *The Searchers* is a seminal twentieth-century fictional account of red-white relations that centralizes the meaning of nineteenth-century white womanhood at the American frontier of "Texas 1868." Unlike historical captivity narratives, *The Searchers* is not a first-person account of a woman's response to either the attack leading to captivity or to her experiences in an alien culture.[6] Instead, it is a story of the responses of emotionally vulnerable individuals and an isolated frontier community to the destruction of a family and the kidnapping of a child. As the story of the search for the child unfolds over a time span of several years (the timeline is obscured), it develops into a study of individual and community responses to the captivity of a "woman" who does not desire rescue. I will show how these responses to the captivity of Debbie Edwards inevitably embody radically different responses to Martha and to her representation of nineteenth-century ideals of womanhood in relation to "the cherished home of the affections." The opening scene of *The Searchers* depicts Ethan Edwards (John Wayne) as he returns "home" to his brother Aaron's Texas ranch after seven years occupied by wandering, apparent banditry, and military service for the Confederacy and Mexico. The very next night, Comanche raiders brutally massacre Aaron (Walter Coy), his wife, Martha (Dorothy Jordan), and their young son, Ben. Ethan finds their bodies, then sets out with neighbors and the adopted Edwards son, Martin Pawley (Jeffrey Hunter), to rescue his two nieces, who have been taken captive by the Indians. Teenage Lucy (Pippa

Scott) is soon found raped and murdered along the trail. Her fiancé, Brad Jorgensen (Harry Carey, Jr.), goes mad at the news and is killed by Comanche. Martin Pawley and Ethan Edwards continue to search for nine-year-old Debbie (Lana Wood). After a period of recuperation at the Jorgensen ranch, Ethan and Martin go off again; years later they finally locate Debbie at Scar's encampment in New Mexico. When grown-up Debbie (Natalie Wood) is finally located, she is acculturated to Comanche life and asserts that the Comanche are her "people." Debbie has attained sexual maturity and become a wife to Chief Scar (Henry Brandon), the man who led the raid on the Edwards homestead. Ethan unsuccessfully attempts to shoot Debbie. Later, in explanation of his desire to kill her and to justify his declaration that he has no living "blood kin," he remarks bitterly: "She's been living with a buck. She's nothing but a . . ." Martin Pawley cuts him off in protest. Martin ultimately kills Scar and "rescues" Debbie. At the last moment, when Ethan again appears ready to kill Debbie, he turns away from his vengeful quest and helps Martin take Debbie to her new home with the Jorgensens.

The Searchers is often cited by scholars as one of the genre's most powerful explorations of miscegenation.[7] Marty Roth has argued that the film lays bare the fact that "what is at stake in the [western] genre is female purity." According to Roth, it accomplishes this because, in foregrounding miscegenation and linking it to Indian-hating, the film must work out this theme "through the daughter" (the captive Debbie).[8] The problem of defining femininity, in both its sexual and social dimensions, is obviously at the heart of the film's exploration of race. It is also at the heart of Ford's exploration of the family as the key to the future of the nation and the most important value in his moral order. In Ford's vision of the frontier, the family is the basis of community and individual identity, whether that family is made up of Comanche, "Texicans," or, as is so often the case in his films in the 1940s and 1950s, the surrogate family unit of the military.

Preoccupied as they tend to be with family, Fordian westerns are often filled with women. Andrew Sarris has noted that even Ford's silent westerns offered a "profusion of mothers, sisters, wives and sweethearts in a supposedly rootless genre."[9] Even when relatively small in number, as in *The Searchers,* women are important to a degree that is rarely exceeded by other films of the genre.[10] Robin Wood suggests that in Ford's westerns, women are both the "pretext for civilisation . . . and the guarantee of its continuity."[11] No doubt influenced by the director's Irish heritage, women are *the* crucial element in the Fordian family. As a measure of how crucial

Captivity, Purity, and Feminine Values in *The Searchers*

women are to the notion of the family as the bedrock of civilized life, families without mothers are frequently portrayed in Ford's films as completely lacking in humanity, perverse and destructive. Such is the case with the Clantons in *My Darling Clementine* (1946), the Cleggs in *Wagon Master* (1950), and the other family of Cleggs in *Two Rode Together* (1961).

Certainly Ford's is a traditionally Eurocentric view of American womanhood, and his films never seek to reconceive the traditional gendered social roles of white women or rewrite the history of nineteenth-century social relations. It follows that women in Ford's West uphold traditional feminine values—home and family, marriage and parenthood, religion and altruistic sacrifice. I have argued elsewhere that female characters in Ford's films, such as nurse-turned-schoolmarm Clementine Carter (Cathy Downs) in *My Darling Clementine,* may seem to represent women as stereotypical agents of civilization, but Clementine and other female characters, such as Lana Martin (Claudette Colbert) and Mrs. McKlennan (Edna May Oliver) in *Drums Along the Mohawk* (1939), Mrs. Abby Allshard (Mildred Natwick) in *She Wore a Yellow Ribbon* (1948), Kathleen Yorke (Maureen O'Hara) in *Rio Grande* (1950), Mary Beecher (Constance Towers) in *Sergeant Rutledge* (1960), and Deborah Wright (Carroll Baker), *Cheyenne Autumn* (1964), often come to embody the pioneering spirit in ways that blur the genre's conventional inscription of gender difference.[12] For example, a conventional reading of *Drums Along the Mohawk* might label Mrs. McKlennan as "masculinized," but her complexity speaks to more general trends in Ford's inscription of femininity. Mrs. McKlennan emerges as the ideal of the independent American type, regardless of gender. The widow of a military man, she is plainspoken and demanding, but also generous and compassionate. She recognizes the social limitations placed on her gender (women must wait as men go to war), but her gender does not prevent her from being a prosperous and respected farmer. Nor does her age keep her from expressing herself as a sexual being (in her relationship with Adam Hartmann [Ward Bond]).

Ford's complication of female sexuality extends beyond the treatment of sexually experienced single women. It also applies to the western's traditional stereotypes of purity: the ingenue and the mother. However, Ford's westerns also show how these types can be sexually responsive, even assertive, at the same time they are respectable representatives of the family. For example, this is true of Philadelphia Thursday (Shirley Temple) in *Fort Apache* as she assertively pursues a good-looking young lieutenant. This adds considerable narrative tension to *Fort Apache,* as it will to *The*

Searchers.[13] In the latter, this kind of approach to femininity will complicate the construction of Martha Edwards as a pioneer mother as well as of Debbie Edwards

Although Ford's westerns usually construct women in relation to and corollary to men, women like Mrs. McKlennan often represent key Fordian values of courage, independence of thought, and emotional resiliency. Sometimes they assume strenuous physical challenges, as Lana Martin does in both farming and fending off Indian attack in *Drums Along the Mohawk* and Denver (Joanne Dru) does in *Wagon Master* by journeying by wagon and by foot across the wilderness. They also exemplify more traditional female virtues of altruism and "maternal" nurturing, as Mrs. Allshard does in nursing a wounded soldier through dangerous field surgery in *She Wore a Yellow Ribbon*. The scene is played for humor. The doctor has no anesthesia, just whiskey to deaden the soldier's pain during surgery. The soldier's gallantry—and Mrs. Allshard's—leads to each downing drink after drink, accompanied by ribald singing. After the surgery is finished Nathan Brittles (John Wayne) pats Mrs. Allshard on her head as she sits, bilious and half-drunk, on the edge of the wagon with a pan in her lap. Certainly, this could be read as evidence of Ford's paternalistic attitude toward women, but Brittles' gesture has to be read in the context of the film's development of the gentle friendship between the two as equals and their mutual devotion to the military as family.

Extending the departure of his female characters from generic convention, Ford's westerns also challenge the expectation that only the sexually "pure" woman, whether virginal ingenue or devoted mother can properly represent civilization. In silent films such as *The Iron Horse* (1924) and *Three Bad Men* (1926), Ford offered sympathetic representations of sexually "impure" women that, nevertheless, fall within the boundaries of generic convention. In *Three Bad Men,* Millie (Priscilla Bonner), sister of the outlaw Bull Stanley (Tom Santschi), runs away with a man who attempts to force her into prostitution, but neither her brother nor the film is judgmental; Bull's love for her is unchanged; he holds her in his arms as she dies. In *The Iron Horse* prostitutes are shown ministering tenderly to one of their own after she falls victim to an Indian attack in which the women mounted a fierce defense alongside the men of the railroad. While recognizing that society stigmatizes those who are exchanged outside of marriage, Ford's films allow these women characters to show unexpected physical courage as well as emotional depth.

Captivity, Purity, and Feminine Values in *The Searchers*

What is the source of the complexity of Ford's female characters—and their sexuality? To answer this question properly, especially with regard to *The Searchers*, we may need to remind ourselves of Andrew Sarris's remarks in another context: "Ford was demonstrating as early as 1917 that there was a distinction between what he rendered unto the genre in the currency of conventions and what he rendered unto himself in the coinage of feelings."[14] Just as this observation applies to the depiction of women in Ford's silent westerns, it also applies to Ford's sound films.

With the director's return to the western for the first time since the advent of the talkies, he demonstrated with *Stagecoach* that he was willing to defy censorship as well as convention to make a "fallen" woman his film's heroine.[15] For the first time too, he would allow such a female character to defy convention by living with her sins rather than dying for them. Even as Ford's female characters often challenge the sexually experiences/good woman, East/West, civilization/wilderness, female/male ideological divide, Ford's westerns also challenge the notion that an inferior femininity represses the greater values of frontier freedom and masculine prowess that the western is assumed to celebrate.[16]

Early in *Stagecoach,* an organization of middle-class women called the Law and Order League is shown marching a prostitute down the sidewalk to put her on the stage and out of the town of Tonto. The film presents these women as objects of comic ridicule as they scour out Dallas (Claire Trevor) as one of the "the dregs of the town." As they walk, the soundtrack accompanies them with a comically bumptious, piccolo-topped version of "Shall We Gather at the River" that suggests the absurdity of the women's self-righteous mission. However, as ridiculous as the League may appear, their social prejudice is depicted as quite serious in its ability to wound emotionally. Within earshot of Dallas, one member of the League remarks that a respectable army wife, Lucy Mallory (Louise Pratt), shouldn't lower herself by being on the same stagecoach with "that creature." A reaction shot shows Dallas attempting to retain her composure and ignore the demeaning comment aimed at her.

This situation reveals one of the key complications that Ford's westerns, including *The Searchers,* present: the contrast between characters' view of the importance of traditional female sexual purity in maintaining civilization and the film's perspective regarding what makes a woman morally admirable and socially valuable. Just as Debbie Edwards will be condemned by the frontier pioneer community for her survival among the

Comanche, Dallas continues to be subjected to the harsh moral and social judgment of the WASP mainstream along the stagecoach journey to Lordsburg. Scorned by the more respectable passengers, she still evidences altruism and compassion toward those who snub her. She will care for Lucy Mallory and her newborn baby with selfless devotion. The difficult journey proves her to be the character most aligned with traditional feminine virtues.

In Ford's West, women remain tokens of traditional patriarchal exchange between men; they exist as symbols of the private, the domestic, the familial, and the sexual. Nevertheless, even the most sexually tainted woman, like Dallas, who is economically forced into a life of socially ostracizing sexual exchange, has the potential to become the center of a family, a mother, and, therefore, a guardian of the future of the nation. The escaped convict, the Ringo Kid (John Wayne), asks her to marry him and start a family. At the end of *Stagecoach,* they are sent on their way to freedom by a drunken physician, Doc Boone (Thomas Mitchell) and Curley (George Bancroft), a generous lawman. The men save the couple from, in Doc's sarcastic words, "the blessings of civilization." Those unwelcome "blessings," as the film has shown us, are represented by the Law and Order League and an encroaching hierarchy of class imposed by an Eastern model of middle-class respectability. Ringo and Dallas are forced to escape to Mexico. There, they will sustain the true "blessings" of ideal frontier society through their family life in the wilderness, beyond the reach of the law and a social caste system that condemns them.

Just as *Stagecoach* challenges the western's narrative formula that usually condemns sexually experienced women to a troubled existence outside of the family and marriage, *Wagon Master* is also an important precursor to the complexity of *The Searchers* with regard to women.[17] In the film, Travis's (Ben Johnson) initial impression of Denver (Joanne Dru), the medicine show entertainer, is that she is a drunken frontier whore. She does appear unrefined and overtly sexual. Denver, like Mrs. McKlennan, shows how Ford's female characters can be sharp-tongued critics of male behavior as often as they are ministering angels. Knowing Travis has passed judgment on her character, she declares in defiance: "I've done nothing I need be ashamed of, no matter what you and your friends say." Is she saying she hasn't been sexually active or is Denver saying that she has, but it is nothing for which she has to be ashamed? We can't be sure, though we may suspect that, in going around the censors through a strategy of purposeful ambiguity, Ford is suggesting the latter. Defying the audience's genre-trained expectations, Denver refuses to explain herself or her past. Later, Travis will propose to

Captivity, Purity, and Feminine Values in *The Searchers*

her, but she rejects him. In the end, they will find new lives, together—as a couple—with the Mormon pioneers.

Through characters like Dallas and Denver, Ford complicates the genre's traditional valuation of woman's sexual purity and the genre's conventional view of who, among women, can best represent civilization's virtues. In *The Searchers* we see Ford push this even further in the construction of Debbie Edwards's captivity—the most socially condemned sexual exchange a white woman at the nineteenth-century frontier could experience. Debbie's survival and her retention of personal integrity (her intact sense of self) is already foreshadowed by Dallas and Denver, while Ford has long since shown his compact with a sexually experienced and competent but respectable "good" woman, so that the traditional dichotomy is simply not so sharp between feminine purity and degrading sexual experience in Ford's work.

The breakdown of this dichotomy is registered in Ford's depiction of Debbie Edwards, but also in that of Martha, the symbolic linchpin of the triumph of the feminized sphere of values. She is the heart of the family, "the cherished home of the affections" and the center of a normal, truly "civilized" emotional life in Ford's vision of the West. If we consider Ford as an ethnic filmmaker steeped in traditional family-centered Irish American values, this is not unexpected, but Martha Edwards becomes more than an object of nostalgia and sentimentality paying tribute to the cult of the mother.

Through Martha's secret, mutual attraction to her brother-in-law and his violent response to her death, it is evident too that the virtuous mother can become the emotional center of a threat to the domestic and emotional normality that she otherwise represents. Martha is properly sexual with her husband, Aaron, but she is also obviously attracted sexually to her brother-in-law, Ethan. In spite of her conscious sexual attraction to Ethan (witness her stroking of his Confederate coat as well as many other moments of interaction between them), Martha is still an icon of feminine power and virtue in Ford's system. Ethan's illicit love for Martha is twisted into his obsessionary desire to kill her killer (Scar)—and then to kill Debbie—whose captivity leads her to "consensual" sexual relations with her mother's killer.[18] Because what Ethan does in relation to Debbie, the captive, is never separable from his loss of Martha, the symbolic function of woman is not explained solely by an understanding of Ethan's aversion to Debbie's miscegenation with Scar as being rooted in his racism. Martha is the most important woman in the film, for it is through her that responses to

Debbie's captivity and her "purity" are defined, not only for Ethan but also for Martin Pawley and other characters, including Laurie Jorgensen and Mrs. Jorgensen. Finally, to understand *The Searchers* and its view of captivity and female purity, we must understand Martha's role in the film.

The opening sequence of *The Searchers* visually articulates the significance of Martha Edwards in Ford's value system. The screen is black, and then a door opens to frame, in the distance, a bleak western landscape, a desert without trees, framed by jagged peaks. This is the front door of the frontier homestead of Aaron and Martha Edwards; from inside the modest house, Martha Edwards, in silhouette, stands at the doorway, then walks outside. As she moves, the camera, placed inside the house (behind her), begins to move with her (tracking in) as she walks out onto the porch. A reverse shot shows Martha as she looks off into the distance, shading her eyes against the glare of the sun. It then reverses and returns to her original field of vision to show us what she sees: the distant figure of a man on horseback, making his way to the house. We take Martha's opening of the door at this moment and her brother-in-law's slow journey of arrival as a coincidence of timing, but we will learn it is an emotionally prescient one. Through a subsequent series of carefully orchestrated behavioral, musical, and visual cues, the film reveals that Ethan and Martha share a deep but repressed love.

This famous opening scene is worth our attention in discussing Martha's crucial role in *The Searchers*. Joseph McBride and Michael Wilmington have noted that camera movement is quite rare in Ford in that "usually his fixed framing keeps the characters subservient to the camera's viewpoint."[19] As an exception to this pattern, the opening of *The Searchers* parallels a scene in *The Sun Shine Bright* (1953) in which, as Wilmington and McBride observe, "the camera's imitation" of the hero's movement "actually immerses us in *his* (emphasis original) viewpoint."[20] Contrary to Frank Nugent's shooting script of *The Searchers,* Ford chose to align the camera and the audience's optical point of view with Martha and with the home, not with Ethan Edwards.[21] Rather than align his camera with the subjectivity of Ethan and make Martha and the house the object of his look, Ethan remains the object of Martha's and our own curious look. He is stranger, the question mark, an uncertainty literalized through the one word query, "Ethan?" that Aaron Edward hesitatingly asks of Martha as he steps up beside her to peer across the desert expanse.

Ford's visual scheme allows Martha and the house to become the "known" in contrast to Ethan as the unknown. The grounding of the film's

Captivity, Purity, and Feminine Values in *The Searchers*

opening scene in Martha's point of view and the resulting sequence of shots encourages an emotional alignment of the audience with Martha, an appealing and comforting figure suggesting the ideal pioneer woman. She is a neat, slim woman in a light blue dress and crisp white apron. She is mature, not a girl, but attractive. Martha will be joined by her family, who quietly stands on or in front of the porch to observe the approaching man (we see them from an oblique angle capturing the entire family). In a one shot, Debbie (Lana Wood) is introduced with doll in hand as she attempts to quiet their barking dog.

When Ethan reaches the house, he is formally greeted by his brother with a handshake. Facing Ethan, Martha sweeps back in a graceful retreat, a gesture that recalls something of the formality and graciousness of her Old South origins. Yet there is also something of a coy girlishness in her look at Ethan that accompanies the gesture and prefigures the revelation of the secret love she shares with her brother-in-law. Martha welcomes Ethan to the comforting domestic world that she has created, but it is a world Ethan will disturb with his racial animus and with his unsatisfied emotional needs. The sequence that follows serves to contrast Martha and Ethan as representatives of two very different moral orders, one associated with domesticity and love, the other with wandering and vengeance.

Inside the home, Martha gently oversees a scene of contented domesticity. The home is clean and orderly, the children are well mannered and happy. The first shot inside the house is of Ethan lifting Debbie above his head and then holding her in his arms. Contrary to his interactions with everyone else in the family, Ethan's relationship to Debbie is softened by Debbie's charming impulsivity and her childish spontaneity of emotion. Debbie seems the most enthusiastic about his return. At one point, she suddenly stands on her dinner chair. "Marty, here's Uncle Ethan!" she shouts to Martin Pawley as he enters the room. In what will later seem ironic, considering what he attempts to do to her, she is the only one who does not seem either in awe of him or slightly afraid of him.

In Ethan's seven years absence, Martha and Aaron have persevered at ranching and raised a family obviously started before Ethan left (Lucy is sixteen). Aaron Edwards is a rather passive presence as Martha orders her children in their chores, reacts to their concerns, and sets the domestic agenda. Aaron credits his wife with keeping their family on their own land even as other families have given up to go back to poverty in the defeated South ("chopping cotton"). Aaron's tribute to her is clearly and proudly stated: "That Martha, she just wouldn't let a man quit." In a strange way

The warm, cozy interior of the Edwards house: the world created by Martha

this too will be Ethan's story, but in a destructive rather than a constructive way. While Martha motivates Aaron in life, in death she motivates Ethan, who becomes "a critter who just won't stop comin'."

Ethan's secret love for Martha has determined his staying "beyond all reason to" before the Civil War, his long absence, and now, his unexpected return. The three children of Aaron and Martha offer good evidence of sexual compatibility between them, and Aaron and Martha appear contented and affectionate; yet it becomes evident that Martha's has feelings beyond familial affection for her brother-in-law. We have no reason to believe that Martha's sexual fidelity as a wife has been compromised by her love for her brother-in-law. On the contrary, there is an overwhelming sense that their love has been frustrated, which makes what small tokens of love shared between them in life acquire a special poignancy after her death. Those tokens gain in emotional impact because of their association, after Martha's death, with the fate of her daughters. Ethan's Confederate coat, caressed by Martha with loving attention in the privacy of her bedroom, becomes a shroud for daughter Lucy, raped and murdered by Comanches and buried by Ethan along the trail. Ethan's military medal is

Captivity, Purity, and Feminine Values in *The Searchers*

given to Debbie as a "gold necklace" in a kind of displaced display of his affection for Martha. The medal/necklace that Ethan dismisses with the phrase "Don't amount to much," comes to mean a great deal more within the context of Debbie's captivity. It becomes a war trophy Scar uses to taunt Ethan ("[Seen] this before?"), even as Debbie is displayed as a sexual war trophy when Scar selects her, of all his wives, to bring the scalp pole to show Martin and Ethan.

In contrast to Ethan's interaction with Debbie as a child, any physical demonstration of affection between Martha and Ethan is characterized by a ritualized formality. This formality can be read as the Victorian norm, but it also may be interpreted as a mask of restraint to cover deeper emotions. The formality of that behavior is duplicated almost exactly in the interaction between Martha and Martin Pawley (kissing her on the forehead, touching her shoulder, etc.). Perhaps the parallel created between Martin and Ethan in this regard is to make the wrenching, visible impact that Martha's death has on them both register more strongly to the audience. It also gives some indication of the outsider status that both share: Martin is adopted. Aaron and Martha function as his parents, yet he calls them "aunt" and "uncle." Ethan is related by blood to Aaron, but his sexual attraction to Martha, and hers to him, threatens the family.

The formality between Ethan and Martha verges on breaking down when Ethan bids Martha goodbye immediately after she has been observed cradling his coat in her arms. Echoing Martin's behavior toward Martha, Ethan kisses her on the forehead, but here Martha looks surprised—caught in the act of unmasked emotions—and rushes to the door to follow Ethan out. Outside, Martha will draw Debbie to her side, and together, they watch Ethan ride out into the desert. This is the last time we will see Martha alive.

Although her appearance in the film is brief, Martha positively defines the emotional landscape of the home as based on the Christian ideals of compassion and love. Ethan will ignore these ideals, and, in fact, he will attempt to pull Martin away from them. In spite of Ethan's resistance, these values ultimately will also "speak to him" at the very moment he is determining whether Debbie will live or die. These ideals demonstrate a holdover from the nineteenth century that clearly influenced a wide range of Ford's films.

This influence is rooted in popular nineteenth-century American notions of mourning and Christian-influenced ideas on the meaning of death. Ford's films often sentimentalize death through a strategy that suggests the sentimental, feminized culture of the nineteenth century is transplanted to his fictional nineteenth-century West. Here human beings express their deepest feelings most transparently in mourning for the dead. Scenes of mourning in Ford, such as Wyatt Earp's visit to his brother James's grave in *My Darling Clementine*, or that of Nathan Brittles to his wife and daughters' graves in *She Wore a Yellow Ribbon*, suggest the nineteenth-century view that death did not change the fact that the loved one was irreplaceable. As Karen Halttunen has noted, mourning was a Christian lesson in loving one another, for "the bonds of love that stretched across the divide of death were thus believed stronger than those ties that bound families together in life."[22] At its best, the process of mourning would hold the promise of wider benefits to society. "Mourning was regarded," says Halttunen, "as the most sacred of social feelings because the heart softened by affliction turned with greater love not only to the departed loved one, but to all living members of the family, and finally to all mankind."[23] Thus, in *My Darling Clementine*, Wyatt tells James, killed by rustlers, that he hopes that he will be able to make the country "safe for kids like you."

Ethan Edwards obviously violates the norm that Ford establishes through protagonists like Wyatt Earp or Nathan Brittles, or even Abraham Lincoln (Henry Fonda) in *Young Mr. Lincoln* (1939), in the demonstration of mourning as a genteel expression of emotional expressivity and the preparation of the bereaved for good works that extended his/her love for the departed. The famous scene in which Ethan cuts short the funeral of the Edwardses sets in motion his quest for vengeance in place of proper mourning and love rather than hate. Yet, while critics have often given almost exclusive interest to the racist response of Indian-hating Ethan Edwards to Debbie's captivity, the film gives equal weight to the response of Martin Pawley, one-eighth Cherokee, but nevertheless orphaned not just once but twice by Indian attacks. Martin's emotional losses make his compassionate response to Debbie's acculturation to her captivity seem all the more remarkable, but it is fully predictable within the patterns established in the Fordian oeuvre.

Like Ethan, Marty's attitude toward Debbie's accommodation to Comanche life is filtered through his love for Martha. However, his love is accompanied by his affiliation with the ideals of compassion and love, those "feminized" values that she, as a mother, stand for in the Fordian system. Although both Martha and Aaron have adopted Martin Pawley, it is only Martha whose behavior suggests that she loves Martin as her own child. She caresses him on the cheek as he bids her good night. He, in turn, obviously loves her. When Martin and Ethan return, too late, to the

Captivity, Purity, and Feminine Values in *The Searchers*

Edwards house after the murder raid, both will be calling for one person only—Martha (in a Ford change to Nugent's script).[24] But contrary to Ethan, the ideals Martha personifies exert an unrivaled posthumous influence over Martin's actions that is positive by the standards of feminine values. Martin's love for Martha extends to his unconditional love for Debbie—as his sister. In this, he refuses to reduce Debbie to the symbolic value of her sexuality, a sexuality on which white civilization props its "superior" racial identity. This is why, in part, the ending of the film is so much more powerful than that of the novel, where Debbie and Marty become lovers.[25] Unlike Ethan, Martin adheres to the roles established in the family. He does not threaten the family through a conflation of platonic and sexual love.

Martin's response to Martha's death is to insist on rescuing the adult Debbie and bringing her home in spite of the opposition of everyone except for Mrs. Jorgensen. Toward the end of the film, as the Texas Rangers prepare to enter Scar's village, Ethan goes so far as to try to whip up Marty's sense of revenge against Debbie. He tells him that the long, wavy scalp on Scar's lance was his birth mother's. "That don't change it. That don't change nothing," replies Martin. He insists on being allowed to go in by himself to attempt a rescue of Debbie. In contrast to Ethan, Martin's compassion and love for Debbie illustrate the proper Christian response to death in the nineteenth century. Martin demonstrates the Christian lesson in love that mourning the death of the departed one was supposed put into motion, but for Ethan, the softening of his heart does not occur until, apparently, the moment he lifts the adult Debbie in her arms and abandons his quest to kill her.

The scene in which Ethan refers to the scalp pole and tries to whip up Martin's feelings of revenge makes explicit how the story of *The Searchers* is the story, on one level, of the struggle for Martin's soul.[26] This struggle is between Ethan and Martha. In this struggle, Martha—and "feminine" values—win out, and the film makes it clear that it strongly approves of this triumph of the "feminine." Martin's actions may seem unusual for a western protagonist, but they are not unusual in Ford's westerns. As I have argued elsewhere, Ford's films again and again reaffirm the "softer" feminine values including devotion to happy domesticity, displays of romantic love and sentimental affection, and commitment to principles of forgiveness and nonviolence.[27] He attaches these to women, but also to normative masculinity through characters such as Gil Martin (Henry Fonda) in *Drums Along the Mohawk,* Nathan Brittles in *She Wore a Yellow*

Ribbon, Sandy and Travis (Harry Carey, Jr., and Ben Johnson) in *Wagon Master*—and Martin Pawley in *The Searchers,* among others. In this respect, Ethan Edwards is the remarkable exception to Ford's male heroes, who are notably communal and gentle. Thus, in Ford's westerns, men often embrace values identified as primarily feminine while some women, such as Marty's love interest, Laurie Jorgensen, are aligned with masculine values that reduce female worth to sexual and racial purity.

Blonde, attractive, middle class, *and* in love with Martin since childhood, Laurie would initially seem to represent the generic ideal, the sexually innocent, sympathetic woman who brings civilization to the frontier. But Laurie becomes the voice of patriarchal sexual norms that condemn the captive female who assimilates—culturally and sexually—into Indian society. After Martin tells her he will set out again to "fetch her home," Laurie echoes Ethan in the harshest terms: "Fetch what home? The leavings of a Comanche buck sold time and again to the highest bidder—with savage brats of her own? Do you know what Ethan will do if he has a chance? He'll put a bullet in her brain. I tell you, Martha would want him to."

This is not the first time that the implicit question, "What would Martha want?" is answered. Immediately after the massacre, at the end of the Edwards funeral, Mrs. Jorgensen (Olive Carey) recounts the emotional intertwining of her family with that of the Edwards (Lucy with Brad, Marty with Laurie). Ethan tells her to come to the point. The point is a simple one, based on Mrs. Jorgensen's answering of the question, "What would Martha want?" She says: "It's just that I know that Martha would want you to take care of her boys as well as her girls, and if the girls are dead, don't let the boys waste their lives in vengeance. Promise me, Ethan!" He ignores her and rides off. The visualization of this exchange suggests a world dangerously out of order. The burned roof of the dugout where the family's bodies were found looms asymmetrically and ominously over Ethan and Mrs. Jorgensen. The visuals and the dramatic music suggest that this is a scene of momentous danger, and, indeed, it is, for Ethan's implacable desire for revenge will dominate not only his own life for the next five years but Marty's, and will also lead to the death of Brad Jorgensen.

Articulated directly and indirectly, the question, "What would Martha want?" becomes the center of a struggle of interpretations over Debbie's captivity. This struggle of interpretations is played out most obviously between characters (Ethan vs. Marty, Laurie vs. Mrs. Jorgensen). While Laurie says directly that Martha would want a Comanche Debbie dead rather than have her sleeping with the enemy, Mrs. Jorgensen's post-

Captivity, Purity, and Feminine Values in *The Searchers*

funeral speech suggests (by tone and her hesitation before the word "dead" in reference to the girls) that she knows the girls likely will be raped, but that Martha would not care about racial and sexual purity. If the girls are raped and their purity violated, then Ethan shouldn't lead the boys (Martin, Brad) into wasting their lives in vengeance. That vengeance, as we come to learn, will go so far as to include Ethan's belief that he must kill Debbie.

As with Laurie's later speech to Marty, Mrs. Jorgensen calls upon Martha as the ultimately authority. Yet, as a mother, Mrs. Jorgensen's speech has the weight of authority (and truth) that Laurie's does not. As a mother, she knows that "that Martha would want you to take care of her boys as well as her girls." By way of contrast, Laurie's hate-filled speech reveals her desperation to keep Marty home from what she regards as a pointless search for someone now beyond the pale of white society's norms. By evoking Martha, she psychologically exploits the dead woman's importance to Marty. To say that Martha would want Debbie dead is, as Marty (and the audience) immediately knows, a misinterpretation of Martha Edwards's values.

The struggle over interpreting Debbie's captivity and Martha's wishes also occurs within the psyches of the characters, particularly within Ethan, as he struggles to come to terms with Martha's violent death and her daughter's conversion to the culture of her mother's murderers. As Mrs. Jorgensen suggests, what would it mean for those who mourn her to carry out Martha's wishes for her surviving children? For Martin Pawley, the answer is in rescuing Debbie, or at the very least, understanding, as he says, that she is "better she's alive and living with Comanches than her brains bashed out." But Ethan, even from the first time, early in the film, when he, Marty, and the Texas Rangers come upon the band of Comanche that hold Debbie and Lucy, wants to ride into their midst, to commence killing. Captain Samuel Clayton (Ward Bond) immediately recognizes that such an action will likely lead to the girls' deaths, and that Ethan knows this, and he refuses to allow this course of action for that very reason.

The traditional western as both literature and film aligns masculinity with a racially biased position that at all costs, even the cost of the woman's life, maintains that white civilization and female sexual purity must be preserved in opposition to red-savagery and female sexual degradation. "Indian-haters" like Ethan Edwards come to embody the masculinist and racist positions attributed as being central to the western's representations. This position is not unfamiliar in Ford's westerns, even though Ethan Edwards may be its most extreme example, and it is one that

Ford complicates long before the appearance of *The Searchers*. For example, in Ford's *Stagecoach*, Hatfield (John Carradine), prepares to use his last bullet to shoot Lucy Mallory (Louise Pratt) to save her from falling into the hands of the advancing Apache.[28]

Hatfield has been presented rather unsympathetically throughout the film. He is a fallen southern gentleman, and his attempt to reestablish his own connection to a lost way of life is symbolized by his exaggerated attempts to protect Lucy Mallory as an exemplar of his ideal of genteel, antebellum southern womanhood. At a stage stop dinner, he insists on moving Mrs. Mallory to a seat by the window. He says it is so she will be near a cool breeze, but far more important, obviously, is for her to be further away from the impure Dallas. His behavior is clearly motivated by his own tainted social status: he displays an unusually virulent prejudice against Dallas, an attitude that would otherwise seem out of keeping with one of his experience as a gambler, a profession almost as disreputable as the prostitute's.

Hatfield is established as a character virtually obsessed with female purity. He has joined the stage journey for the sole purpose of protecting a woman he does not know, yet Ford does not present Hatfield's decision to kill Lucy, so familiar a gesture in the western, as purely a nod to generic convention or simply a neurotic projection of his idealization of Lucy Mallory as "a great lady." It is also prepared by the narrative in the character's response to other experience: Earlier in the film, Hatfield, in a characteristic gesture of chivalry, covers the dead body of a beautiful young woman killed by Apaches at a stagecoach ferry crossing. The woman's corpse is awkwardly posed on a wooden board sticking up out of the ground, suggesting that she was raped or tortured. This scene would appear to be an articulation of objective reality and Hatfield's reaction to it, but there are hints that the woman also represents a projection of his psyche. As a beautiful young ingenue with long, fair hair she is absolutely contrary in appearance to those worn, middle-aged women who so often inhabit Ford's West.[29] She could be read as a literalization of Hatfield's idea of vulnerable white womanhood victimized by savage lusts, but the very short scene suggests the appropriateness of Hatfield's gesture toward a victim of atrocity rather than a criticism of his fear of miscegenation.

Like Hatfield, Ethan Edwards's attitudes toward female purity and miscegenation are associated with the projection of his desire for ideal white womanhood—Martha. Like Hatfield, he is a former Confederate who clings to the symbols of his past life. Martha, one might argue, holds

Captivity, Purity, and Feminine Values in *The Searchers*

pride of place among these symbols. Her soft southern accent, refined manners, and quiet resiliency suggest the ideals of southern womanhood that Hatfield sees in Lucy Mallory. In a scene very much analogous to Hatfield's covering of the woman's body, Ethan Edwards's vision is also projected into the texture of the film. This scene occurs at the fort, where Martin and Ethan go to search for Debbie among the female captives, both dead and alive, recovered by Custer's Seventh Cavalry.[30] Marty and Ethan enter a large room where the living captives are held. Two middle-aged women sit in a corner. The one who sits on the floor is obviously mentally unhinged; she is beyond uttering a sensible sound. She grabs Debbie's doll from Marty, and treats a doll as if it were her living child. Two blonde adolescent girls in gingham dresses, not far removed in age from Debbie, are incongruously smeared with warpaint; one silently clings to the other; the latter can only grin wildly, giggle, and stare at Martin Pawley. A soldier remarks that it is hard to believe the women are white. Ethan replies: "They ain't white—not anymore. They're Comanch." Ethan turns and a much-cited dolly in shot captures his grim face as he stares at the woman with the doll.

Douglas Pye argues that this scene shows that horror of miscegenation not only resides in the response of Ethan Edwards but in the film's point of view to suggest that "the neurosis [of racism] is not wholly confined to the film's characters."[31] But, unlike the scene of Hatfield covering the body in *Stagecoach*, this scene does not suggest that Ethan feels any compassion toward the women. It registers something of Ethan's mental state. We can't be sure what—associating the woman with Martha? With Debbie? With sexual violation and impurity? And the scene does show white women damaged by their experience in captivity. But it also tells us that these women are beyond Ethan's understanding. He can only label them as white or as Comanche, pure or impure, according to how their sexuality as been exchanged (among white men or among red). Other scenes, both those with Debbie and also those with Look (Beulah Archuletta), the young Comanche woman who forms an attachment to Marty, clearly demonstrate that these captives do not behave the way Comanche women do. In his rational moments, Ethan knows this. After soldiers kill Look, Ethan covers her body with a blanket in a gesture that parallel's Hatfield's at the stagecoach ferry in *Stagecoach*. He shows compassion for Look and demonstrates a moment of sorrow over the death of someone so obviously innocent, as Marty suggests, of any crimes against anyone, red or white. This is a moment that prefigures Ethan's giving up his quest to kill Debbie and is a sign that Martha's values will triumph, even in Ethan. That this moment comes before Ethan sees the women at the fort and registers a horror of miscegenation only serves to complicate the film. We can read Ethan's revulsion in response to the female captives as both justified (in terms of western convention and the fulfillment of audience expectations) and also as something the film is critiquing, as yet another example of his inability to understand the world in the compassionate way that Marty embraces.

It should be recognized, in this respect, that *The Searchers* makes distinctions between different kinds of miscegenation (Marty, adopted and loved by Martha without concern for his Cherokee origins, part-Indian Marty and Swedish American Laurie, Debbie and Scar, Lucy's gang rape and murder) but Ford's careful historical placement of his tale in "Texas 1868" holds the implication that at least one type of cross-culture miscegenation cannot be separated from the experience of women as sexual pawns in warfare. The returned captives at the fort may be traumatized by their experience of being kidnapped by the enemy in a war, but also, perhaps, by being in a twilight zone between the two cultures, neither fully of one nor the other.

In her successful accommodation to Comanche life, Debbie challenges the common definition of purity in relation to white womanhood. Unlike her mother and sister, Debbie is not raped and killed, nor is she driven mad, the demonstrated fate of some of the captive women at the fort. Just as Dallas's prostitution is portrayed as an accommodation made to survive in *Stagecoach*, Debbie's marriage to Scar is a successful accommodation to circumstance. Like Dallas's affront to traditions of white female "purity," Debbie's cultural and sexual accommodation may be an affront to the white community (one even worse than that of Dallas), but the film seems to suggest that is a sign of personal strength on Debbie's part, not impurity. Her actions, taken to survive, relegate her to the status of a whore and a racial traitor who has willingly fraternized with the savage enemy.

The contrast between Debbie's healthy assimilation in Comanche society and the rescued women recalls historical accounts of enormously different responses to captivity.[32] Ford visualizes this contrast in unmistakable, even melodramatic terms. Wilmington and McBride argue that "our first glimpse of Debbie as a woman makes it clear that . . . Miscegenation has not destroyed her identity, but deepened it."[33] Ford sets up Debbie's introduction as a grown woman (of fifteen?) to depict her as

Captivity, Purity, and Feminine Values in *The Searchers*

the virtual wish fulfillment of Marty's desires. She is obviously *worth* rescuing. A high string tremolo begins on the soundtrack as Debbie appears on the distance at the top of a huge, windswept sand hill. The hill forms an abstract backdrop as she vigorously runs down to meet Marty at a stream. Dressed in softly muted mauve velvet, she is a vision of the captive as "Indian Princess." On the soundtrack, "Martha's theme" (the Civil War tune of lost love, "Lorena,") accompanies her, lest we forget who she is, especially to Marty: she is Martha's lost daughter. In the terms that Martha established, in emotional terms, she is his "sister," just as Martha, obviously, became his "mother."[34]

If Debbie has successfully adjusted in her life with the Comanche, why does the film seem so arbitrarily to insist on her rescue—one that might seem unnecessary to secure her happiness and safety? If we return to the question, "What would Martha want?" we understand the narrative imperative that demands her rescue and that Martin effect that rescue as her "brother." The rescue is necessary to prove the superiority of Martha's values—and Ford's. Debbie must believe, like Marty, that it is not "too late" for her to be rescued and restored to her mother's realm of the loving pioneer family. Martha's values also must be powerful enough to divert Ethan from his vengeance. Ford helps convince us it is not too late through visual arguments as well as Marty's verbal ones. Although Debbie is ostensibly in a family (her Comanche one), Ford never allows us to see any affective qualities that he normally associates with happy domesticity. Through this absence, the concept of family and home associated with Martha Edwards trumps Debbie's familial—and sexual—ties to the Comanche. Like Dallas in *Stagecoach,* Debbie may accept her situation, but there is precious little proof that she is contented in it.

Nevertheless, to secure Debbie's return as Martha's daughter, the clock must be turned back. When Ethan approaches Debbie to kill her, we hear "Martha's Theme" on the soundtrack. He lifts Debbie up as he did when she was a child. When he brings her down into his arms, it is to embrace, not kill her. The combination of the music and the gesture recalling the past—in Martha's "cherished home of the affection"—offer proof that this moment is a triumph of Martha's "feminine values" over Ethan's racist, avenging masculinity.

After her rescue, Debbie is continued to be visually constructed as childlike as she sits in front of Ethan on his horse and as she enters the Jorgensen farmhouse under the protective arm of Mrs. Jorgensen. Real world complications, like a pregnancy by her Comanche husband, are held

Debbie returned: the triumph of Martha's values.

in abeyance by this visual strategy of infantalizing Debbie. If Debbie were to come home "with savage brats of her own," then Scar's children would no doubt test the limits of Christian love and tolerance.[35] Instead, the ending suggests Debbie can once again become a child to a loving mother and reclaim her place as Martha's daughter.

It is not too late for Debbie, but it is too late for Ethan. The camera resumes the location it held at the beginning of the film, and thus evokes the structuring absence of Martha Edwards; from within the Jorgensen house, the camera and the audience observe all the participants—with the exception of Ethan—enter the home to claim the promise of contented domesticity.

The white woman's sexuality may be what is "at stake" in the western's conventional war between white "civilization" and red "savagery," but as John Ford demonstrates in *The Searchers,* the claims of the genre for the meaning of female purity can be held up for scrutiny, even in a film in the classical mode. The question of woman's role within the war between races that leads to kidnapping, captivity, and miscegenation is presented in a number of Ford's other late career films including *Two Rode Together*

Captivity, Purity, and Feminine Values in *The Searchers*

(1961), *Donovan's Reef* (1963), and the director's final film, *Seven Women* (1965), but nowhere are they as powerfully presented as in *The Searchers*. As I have attempted to show, *The Searchers* works "through the daughter" in critiquing racism, but it also works centrally through the figure of Martha Edwards and more broadly through the framework of "feminized" values that are brought into open conflict with the established generic appeal of "masculine" values associated with violence and vengeance. These feminized values suggest that, by any standard, *The Searchers* interrogates conventions attached to the western's normative construction of masculinity as thoroughly as it interrogates female purity and miscegenation. By doing so, it recenters the western in unexpected territory, in "the domestic circle, the cherished home of the affections," where what the mother wants may be the most important thing of all.[36]

NOTES

Epigraph taken from Norton Juster, *A Woman's Place: Yesterday's Women in Rural America* (1979; reprint, Golden, Colo.: Fulcrum, 1996), 59–60.

1. Martin Pumphrey, "Masculinity," in Buscombe, *BFI Companion*, 181.
2. Tompkins, *West of Everything*, 127, 41, 63–64, 73, 81.
3. Ibid., 41. Buscombe says: "Clearly Tompkins did not listen to Laurie's speech, nor to any of Marty's counterarguments" (*The Searchers*, 73n. 53).
4. Slotkin, *Gunfighter Nation*, 335. Pam Cook has drawn attention to Ford's interesting treatment of gender in noting that his films "produced some significant reverberations" in their exploration of the "inherent tensions" in the western's expected depictions of women. See Cook, "Women," in Buscombe, *BFI Companion to the Western*, 240–41.
5. Dempsey, "John Ford: A Reassessment," 2, 4, 7.
6. In 1682, Mary Rowlandson's story of her experiences as a captive of Narragansetts was published; it became the most famous Puritan account of Indian capture. For this and other early captivity narratives, see Alden T. Vaughan and Edward W. Clark, *Puritans among the Indians: Accounts of Captivity and Redemption, 1676–1724* (Cambridge: Harvard University Press/Belknap Press, 1981). On captivity narratives, see also Richard VanDerBeets, *Held Captive by Indians: Selected Narratives, 1642–1836* (Knoxville: University of Tennessee Press, 1972) and Gary L. Ebersole, *Captured by Texts: Puritan to Postmodern Images of Indian Captivity* (Charlottesville: University Press of Virginia, 1995).
7. For example, Virginia Wright Wexman calls the film "Perhaps the most revealing film in the entire Western canon in terms of miscegenation." Wexman, "Star and Genre: John Wayne, the Western and the American Dream of the Family on the Land," in *Creating the Couple: Love, Marriage, and Hollywood Performance* (Princeton: Princeton University Press, 1993), 114. See also McBride and Wilmington, *John Ford*.

193

Douglas Pye remarks in "Double Vision: Miscegenation and Point of View in *The Searchers*": "The film probably goes further than any other Western in dramatising and implicating us in the neurosis of racism."

8. Roth, "Yes, My Darling Daughter," 70.

9. Sarris, *John Ford Movie Mystery*, 21.

10. Ibid.

11. Robin Wood, "*Drums Along the Mohawk*," in *The Book of Westerns*, ed. Cameron and Pye, 174.

12. See also Studlar, "Sacred Duties, Poetic Passions," in Studlar and Bernstein, *John Ford Made Westerns*.

13. For an extended discussion of Philadelphia Thursday's sexual pursuit of Lt. O'Rourke, see Studlar, "Sacred Duties, Poetic Passions," in Studlar and Bernstein, *John Ford Made Westerns*, 57–60.

14. Sarris, *John Ford Movie Mystery*, 22.

15. On the negative reaction of the Breen Office of the PCA to *Stagecoach*'s script, see Matthew Bernstein, *Walter Wanger: Hollywood Independent* (Berkeley: University of California Press, 1994), 148.

16. See Studlar, "Sacred Duties, Poetic Passions," in Studlar and Bernstein, *John Ford Made Westerns*, 50.

17. Studlar, "Sacred Duties, Poetic Passions," in Studlar and Bernstein, *John Ford Made Westerns*, 50–51.

18. We do not actually know if Scar himself killed Martha, but his responsibility is given weight in the film's visual arguments since he is the only Comanche whom we actually see in the murder raid. In a highly emotionally charged scene, he is introduced as he throws a shadow over the young Debbie as she cowers in hiding on her grandmother's grave site. We then see him in close up as he looks at Debbie, then raises his head and blows a horn (buffalo or ram) to summon his braves.

19. McBride and Wilmington quote Ford's remarks to Fred Zinneman, "You know, you could be a pretty good director if you'd stop fooling around with that boom and quit moving the camera so much. . . . I don't move the camera unless there is a very, very good reason for it" (*John Ford*, 146).

20. McBride and Wilmington, *John Ford*, 146.

21. Eckstein, "Darkening Ethan," 23n. 67.

22. Karen Halttunen, *Confidence Men and Painted Women: A Study of Middle-Class Culture in America, 1830–1879* (New Haven: Yale University Press, 1982), 130.

23. Halttunen, *Confidence Men and Painted Women*, 132.

24. For a complete account of these changes, see Eckstein, "Darkening Ethan."

25. LeMay, *The Searchers*, 272. As Eckstein has suggested to me, some lobby cards advertising the film may visually confuse the sexual relations between Debbie and Martin by emphasizing Martin's bare chest as he embraces the rescued Debbie. John Huston's *The Unforgiven* (1960) has the Native American girl raised by whites become her brother's intended wife. This film may have one of the creepiest, most incest-laced shots in classical Hollywood film: Burt Lancaster (as the brother) sits between his "sister" (Audrey Hepburn) and his younger brother (Doug McClure). He turns and embraces the lovely male ingenue, McClure, and then turns to the other

Captivity, Purity, and Feminine Values in *The Searchers*

side and kisses the equally lovely female ingenue, Hepburn. See Eckstein's discussion of this film below.

26. The novel makes this struggle more explicit, perhaps, in making the narrative that of Martin's.

27. See Studlar, "Sacred Duties, Poetic Passions," in Studlar and Bernstein, *John Ford Made Westerns*, 60–64.

28. Hatfield is killed by the Apache before he can shoot Lucy, and she, along with the other passengers, are saved by the last minute arrival of the cavalry.

29. See, for example, the women at stage stops and frontier outposts in Ford's westerns, such as Jane Darwell as Miss Florie, the station manager in *3 Godfathers* (1948), Billy Pickett's wife (Marga Daighton) in *Stagecoach*, or "Ma" (Mary Gordon) in *Fort Apache*. If Miss Florie and these other are not appendages of men, it should also be acknowledged that these women are most often older, and thus in the category of women most often desexualized in the western.

30. On the script's portrayal of Custer, see Eckstein, "Darkening Ethan," 10–12.

31. Pye, "Double Vision: Miscegenation and Point of View," below. McBride and Wilmington also note that the scene is "so disturbing that the spectator may momentarily wonder whether Ford is not succumbing to the same fear of miscegenation" (*John Ford*, 162).

32. See Joanna L. Stratton, *Pioneer Women: Voices from the Kansas Frontier* (New York: Simon and Schuster, 1981), 123–24. On the case of Cynthia Ann Parker, a nine-year-old Texas girl kidnapped by Comanches who later was returned to white society against her will, see Eckstein, "After the Rescue," 34. See also Jack C. Ramsay, *Sunshine on the Prairie: the Story of Cynthia Ann Parker* (Austin: Eakin Press, 1990).

33. McBride and Wilmington, *John Ford*, 162. On Debbie as an "assimilated body" in Comanche culture, see Joan Dagle, "Linear Patterns and Ethnic Encounters in the Ford Western," in Studlar and Bernstein, *John Ford Made Westerns*, 124–25. On the ending that "does not quite hold together," See Dagle, "Linear Patterns," 126.

34. The bathtub scene at the Jorgensen ranch reinforces the importance of categorization of family roles to Marty. Breaking in on Marty as he sits washing in the bathtub, Laurie remarks that she is unfazed by seeing men in such situations because she has brothers. Marty responds: "Well I ain't one of them."

35. In *Two Rode Together*, Guthrie McCabe (James Stewart) sees a captive teenage girl, Frieda Knudsen, with a baby and a man who is obviously her Comanche husband and decides to leave her in the camp rather than take her back to her parents. Guthrie decides it is too late for Frieda to be returned to white society.

36. Juster, *A Woman's Place*, 60.

Incest and Miscegenation in *The Searchers* (1956) and *The Unforgiven* (1959)

Arthur M. Eckstein

In 1950 Octave Mannoni provided—on the basis of his personal experience in French Madagascar—a startling psychoanalytical interpretation of racism and obsession with miscegenation within colonial elites. Mannon had been amazed to discover that despite the great mass of rumors of the rape of young white women that circulated among the French colonial elite during the native rebellion on Madagascar in 1948, he had not found a single case that was actually based on fact. How, then, to account for the ferocious fears (or rather, the ferocious fantasies) of the whites—which helped fuel a repressive military campaign that had resulted in 100,000 real native deaths? The explanation for those fantasies, Mannoni argued, lay mainly in the repressed tendencies toward sadism, rape, and/or incest within the whites themselves—"the image of the misdeed which both frightens and fascinates us, projected onto others."[1] He continued: "This mass of confused emotion, charged with savage sexuality, is an important though invisible element in the composition of color-prejudice."[2] Here Mannoni might have noted how, a full century earlier, the Great Indian Mutiny of 1857 allowed the British popular press to depict in pornographic style the sexual torture of naked white women by fierce dark-skinned men—sketches that ordinarily would never have been permitted to be published.[3] As in the case of Mannoni's Madagascar, none of *these* incidents happened either.[4]

Within this broad phenomenon of the projection of unacceptable impulses onto the native "Other," however, Mannoni was emphatic specifically about incest fears and fantasies. On that issue he wrote the following:

Arthur M. Eckstein

> I have seen people who appeared to have no racialist bias lose all rational composure when confronted with the question: but what if your daughter wanted to marry a negro, a native?
>
> The reason is that such an argument disturbs certain uneasy feelings within these people themselves—more exactly, *incestuous* feelings. And so they turn to racialism as a defense [against those feelings]. In so doing, they reveal, in their naivete, the repressed emotions upon which their racial theories are in fact based.[5]

A bold hypothesis: and though Mannoni's ideas remain highly controversial, his book *The Psychology of Colonization* is now viewed as a classic in many quarters, especially among psychoanalysts and anthropologists influenced by Jacques Lacan (with whom Mannoni later worked closely).[6] Mannoni's fundamental idea of the colonialist's projection outward of his own unacceptable impulses onto the native Other, followed by the attempt to regulate and (if necessary) punish the Other, has become a staple of analysis of nineteenth- and twentieth-century imperialist texts, including films with "imperialist" themes. And this last genre—"imperialist" film—is one into which the American western easily fits, because "white triumphalism" is the western's basic theme, and the imposition of white order upon Indian disorder is its primary mythic narrative.[7] Two recent examples will suffice to show the contemporary relevance of Mannoni's fundamental idea of colonialist projection: the 1995 study of highly conflicted European views of race and the dangers of miscegenation by Robert J. C. Young and the 1996 essay on John Ford's representation of race in the nineteenth century (especially but not exclusively focused on Indians) by Richard Maltby.[8]

The purpose of this essay, however, is to use not only Mannoni's basic idea of colonialist projection but also his more specific hypothesis about the deep connection between overt fear of miscegenation and covert fantasies of incest as a tool of analysis of the two films made by famous directors in the late 1950s from the two novels of frontier Texas by Alan LeMay: John Ford's *The Searchers* and John Huston's lesser-known *The Unforgiven*. What I hope to show is how Mannoni's basic idea, but also his specific proposition concerning the inner connection between incest and miscegenation, illuminate the dark issues addressed in these two films. Conversely, I hope to show that the complex and conflicted imagery of these two films helps to confirm Mannoni's insights regarding the psychological origins of racism and obsession with miscegenation.

The Searchers, of course, is the subject of this volume of essays, and by now needs no introduction.[9] Let us turn to the film's final stunning

Incest and Miscegenation in *The Searchers* and *The Unforgiven*

image. In the film's last scene, John Ford brings all the characters of the film in through the doorway into the house that symbolizes civilization and community—all save one, the film's protagonist, Ethan Edwards (played by John Wayne). Edwards is instead shown in deep shadow, viewed from inside the house looking outward, standing alone in the doorway, holding his arm as if in pain; then he turns from the camera and wanders out into the dust, and the door closes quickly on him, and we go to black. This has become one of the most famous endings in film history.

Ethan Edwards is thus punished and rejected. Moreover, we now know that in the original ending of the film, in the final shooting script written by Ford's screenwriter Frank Nugent, he was not: he led everybody home.[10] So why did John Ford decide in the end to punish and reject Ethan? Partly, it must be because Ethan throughout the film has been a vicious racist. White racism became an issue of increasing concern to Ford in his last decade of filmmaking, and it was a theme he returned to again and again. Condemnations strongly appear in Ford's *Sergeant Rutledge* (1960—a pioneering movie whose depiction of heroic black soldiers in the U.S. Army of the nineteenth century prefigures *Glory* by a full thirty years), in *Two Rode Together* (1961—a variant on *The Searchers*), in *Donovan's Reef* (1963—where the issue for whites is acceptance or rejection of mixed-race children), and in *Cheyenne Autumn* (1964—where whites are almost uniformly depicted as racist thugs).

In addition, by his desire to kill his niece Debbie because she has been "soiled" by having sex with Indians, Ethan Edwards is violating the institution which in John Ford's films is probably the most sacred institution of all: the nuclear family. From his initial silent films such as *Straight Shooting* (1917), right through to *Donovan's Reef* in 1963, Ford's movies insisted on the fundamental moral goodness of the family, on its all-forgiving nature, on its role as a bulwark protecting individuals from an often brutal outside world.[11] No Ford hero ever attempts to destroy a member of his family; if anything, one of the themes that Ford found most congenial was the *inclusion* (or reinclusion) of outsiders (or prodigals) within the family or the small familylike group.[12] And all this the loner Ethan Edwards is grimly bent on destroying—out of racism, and obsessive fears and horror of miscegenation. Indeed, we now know that Ford eliminated from the release print of *The Searchers* a filmed scene (an argument between Ethan and a genocidal General George Custer) in which Ethan appeared as a defender of innocent women and children (even Comanche ones)—in order to make Ethan's character appear even more dark and problematic, his intent to murder his niece Debbie because "she's been livin' with a buck" all the more real and dangerous.[13]

And perhaps, in discussing Ethan's darkness, we can go even deeper than this: because it is not just Debbie whom Ethan seems somehow driven to annihilate. The film begins with Ethan's long-delayed return home to the family homestead in Texas after the Civil War—a return that is highly disruptive to family stability because Ethan is in love with his brother's wife, and she with him. Tension, bitter hostility between the two brothers, and repressed erotic attraction dominate the early scenes of the film. The repressed eroticism is most apparent in the famous scene between Ethan and his sister-in-law where Ethan and Martha almost kiss, pulling away from each other at the last moment—a scene Ford added on his own to the original script, and which Ford said was intended by him precisely to underline the illicit relationship (i.e., incestuous adultery).[14] A little later, while Ethan is away, the war chief Scar and his Comanches come and burn down the homestead, kill Ethan's brother and the brother's son, rape and kill Martha, and abduct the female children. In other words, Scar utterly destroys the home of Ethan's brother, and takes all the women for himself (or destroys them). But in so doing, commentators have suggested, Scar is merely acting as the embittered and violent Ethan's dark alter ego: he symbolizes Ethan's own unacceptable jealousies, impulses, hatreds—and he acts as the agent of their fulfillment. Scar does what Ethan wants to do but cannot do, and cannot even admit wanting. No wonder Ethan hates Indians.[15]

Nor is even this the end of the dark tangle of emotions in *The Searchers*. I think that another crucial theme in the film—though it could only be approached very indirectly—is a repressed sexual relationship between Ethan the "searcher" and his niece, young Debbie, now a captive of Scar. Thus Ethan is deeply and frustratedly in love with Debbie's mother Martha, and in Frank Nugent's shooting script he explicitly says that the now-teenage Debbie, when finally found, looks exactly like Martha: "You sure favor your mother," he says softly—as he is about to kill her.[16] In the finished film, this line of dialogue has been cut (Ford hated explanatory dialogue). Nevertheless, in this scene, where Ethan at the last moment decides not to kill Debbie but to take her back to white society—to take her back even though, young as she is (fourteen or so), he believes she has been sleeping with Scar as Scar's wife—the background music is "Martha's Theme." Thus Ethan's sparing of Debbie is entangled in his feelings for Martha.[17]

Moreover, "Martha's Theme" is a piece of music itself very heavy with meaning. It is in reality the authentic Civil War ballad "Lorena." The song

Incest and Miscegenation in *The Searchers* and *The Unforgiven*

Debbie sees Ethan for the first time—snarling dog.

has its origin in a forbidden love affair by its author, H. D. L. Webster, and its theme is explicitly to mourn a love whose physical consummation is impossible because it is prohibited by society.[18] Now, John Ford always personally chose the folk music for his films set in the nineteenth century, and he did it with expertise and scholarly care—as Frank Nugent, the screenwriter of *The Searchers*, has emphasized.[19] And thanks to film music scholar Kay Kalinak, we also now know that Ford had total control of the music for *The Searchers*, much to the anger of composer Max Steiner.[20] This means that Ford was personally responsible for the appearance of "Lorena" at crucial moments in *The Searchers;* and since Ford was deeply knowledgeable about American popular songs of the Civil War period, he knew the damning words of "Lorena." So we can say that Debbie *is* "Lorena"—that is, a version of desired-but-not-to-be-attained Martha ("Lorena"). Ethan wants to kill her (she has given herself to another). And he wants to love her.[21]

As discussed in the introductory essay to this volume, John Wayne himself (whose performance as Ethan is the greatest of his film career) unintentionally revealed this fundamental psychological aspect of the movie in later interviews. In 1974, in discussing Ethan, Wayne declared: "He did what he had to do. The Indians fucked his wife." A wonderful Freudian slip: Martha was not—and never could be—Ethan's wife! Or was Wayne thinking of Martha-like Debbie? In 1976, Wayne actually revealed a fantasy of his in which Ethan and Debbie after the end of the film live together on the old Edwards homestead, which they rebuild: "And that little girl would learn to love him." No doubt Wayne meant this innocently; even so, the fantasy is Ethan living contentedly for the rest of his life with Debbie, who looks exactly like Martha.[22]

In explaining why Debbie is quickly taken away from Ethan in the final scene of *The Searchers* and placed under the protection of the Edwardses' surviving neighbors instead, Tag Gallagher asks, "Is Ethan to live with fourteen-year-old Debbie? Surely she is better off with the Jorgensens." Yes, indeed.[23]

In fact, it is in the great sequence in Scar's camp in the desert, where Ethan first learns in Scar's tepee (guarded by skulls) that young Debbie is living now as Scar's wife, that Ford establishes most clearly that Scar is Ethan's dark alter ego. A scene where the two big, violent, embittered men stand face-to-face and mimic each other is followed by one where Ford's camera focuses in sharply on the medal from Emperor Maximilian of Mexico, once given to Ethan and which Ethan gave to Debbie, but now worn proudly on *Scar's* chest. That is, Scar here has completely taken Ethan's place . . . but as what?

Ford himself called *The Searchers* "a psychological epic"—he knew what he had created.[24] And as discussed in the introduction to this volume, Ford and Frank Nugent—and then Ford working by himself—consciously worked to make Ethan Edwards in the film a far darker and more problematic personality than the Ethan figure in Alan LeMay's novel on which the film is based.[25] Yet Ford also chose to leave questions in *The Searchers* such as the one above without explicit and direct answer—which is part of the fascination of the film.[26] Mannoni, on the other hand, provides us here with a very blunt answer indeed. The horror that Ethan finds in Scar's camp—on the surface, the ultimate white horror of forced miscegenation with the dark man—is in fact simultaneously the fulfillment of Ethan's own unacceptable fantasies: "The savage is identified in the unconscious with a certain image of the *instincts*—of the id, in analytical terminology. And civilized man is painfully divided between the wish to 'correct' the 'errors' of the savages and the desire to *identify* himself with them in his search for some lost paradise." Debbie is Martha; Scar is Ethan's scar.[27]

Incest and Miscegenation in *The Searchers* and *The Unforgiven*

And meanwhile young Debbie herself, played by the luminously beautiful Natalie Wood (then sixteen), has become, because of the explicitly sexual nature of her relationship with Scar, an unalterably sexualized object—as psychologists tell us is always the case in our society with respect to those who have been sexually abused.[28]

Here it is Alan LeMay's original novel which is most clear about the sexual implications involved in the fantasy of "rescue" from miscegenation, and the strange connection between miscegenation and incest. At the end of LeMay's *The Searchers*, young Debbie, rescued from the threat of miscegenation, immediately gets happily into bed with her rescuer—not her uncle, as it happens, but her stepbrother Martin Pauley. She has loved him, she declares, "from always." Well, one could hardly get more explicit than that—especially in the 1950s.[29] Similarly, Debbie's gold locket is a gift from Marty in the novel, not a gift from Ethan (in the form of his war medal): but then, LeMay's *The Searchers* was always Marty's story, told from his point of view, and focused on his development as a person, not on the Ethan figure.[30] What John Ford and Frank Nugent evidently did, once John Wayne was signed for the film and would clearly be its central figure, was to transfer the psychosexual relationship existing originally between Debbie and Marty to Martha/Debbie and *Ethan*. A remnant of the original sexual relationship between Debbie and Marty would still have been visible to the audiences of the film in 1956, however: photographs in the lobby advertizing the film showed Debbie, in her Comanche clothes, leaning up and huddling against the naked, massively muscled chest of the film's Marty (Jeffrey Hunter).[31]

In Ford's *The Searchers*, of course, Debbie does *not* get right into her bed with her rescuer (leaving John Wayne's later fantasies aside). Still, it is worth noting that in the early scenes of the film, nine-year-old Debbie (played by Lana Wood, Natalie Wood's younger sister) is presented for her part as quite overtly seductive toward Ethan ("If you gave *me* a gold locket, I'd wear it *all* the time."), and the medal Ethan gives her in response to her seductive plea is clearly a token of his love for Martha. In 1971, Lana Wood posed nude for *Playboy* wearing only an Indian headdress.[32]

Moreover, in *The Searchers* Marty in a way still does get to marry his stepsister, just as in LeMay's novel. The stepsister is Laurie Jorgensen—the girl who gives Marty her dead brother's clothes to wear, in an important scene in the middle of the movie (when he is naked), and whose mother treats Marty as her own adoptive son.[33] And the situation between Marty and Laurie is made even more complex because Laurie is a racist who hates miscegenation as much as Ethan himself does, as comes through in her vicious outburst against Debbie just before the final rescue. Yet the man to whom she proclaims her ferocious disdain for Debbie because Debbie is sleeping with an Indian, the man whom she loves, is himself in the film part Indian—yet he is also dressed in her brother's clothes. That Marty would be part Indian was an element added to and emphasized in the story of *The Searchers* by Ford and Nugent, for in Alan LeMay's novel he is 100 percent white.[34]

In exploring this disturbing nexus of ideas, emotions and fantasies, and in exploring Debbie's ultimate fate in Ford's *The Searchers*, I have elsewhere employed another movie as an instrument of analysis: *Prime Cut* (dir.: Michael Ritchie, 1972). In *Prime Cut* we also have an embittered and violent middle-aged man (Lee Marvin—a favorite actor of Ford's, by the way), a man who is an outlaw and an outsider, who "rescues" a sexually abused teenage girl—played this time by the luminously beautiful Sissy Spacek (her first film role). What follows the "rescue," however, is—precisely—the immediate development of a sexualized romance between the middle-aged man and his teenage "rescuee." The connection to the half-repressed themes in *The Searchers* is obvious enough. But most interestingly, the director Michael Ritchie has revealed that the highly sexualized romance between the embittered and violent middle-aged "rescuer" and the luminous young (and soiled) "rescuee" was actually something *imposed* upon *Prime Cut* by audience-response testing. That is: this was a fantasy desired and encouraged by popular culture; it was not the story the director originally intended (and originally shot) for the film. Ritchie says he protested against the imposition of "rescue-and-romance" (or perhaps, given the differential in power between the two participants, we should really call it "rescue-and-rape"). But to no avail; this is the theme that dominates the finished version of the movie. Ethan Edwards would not have been surprised.[35]

Still, though the theme of *Prime Cut* may help to illuminate certain half-repressed tensions in *The Searchers*, Michael Ritchie also indicates that there was no conscious connection between the two movies.[36] So let us now turn to a film that *does* have a close, integral and conscious connection to *The Searchers*, as a way of further reading the dark themes outlined above.

After the success of *The Searchers*, Alan LeMay wrote a second novel dealing with white pioneer life in frontier Texas. The second novel was titled *The Unforgiven*. It was set in the same historical period as *The*

Incest and Miscegenation in *The Searchers* and *The Unforgiven*

Searchers (in fact in 1874, the same year in which *The Searchers* comes to an end), and in the same region of northwest Texas (below the Red River, east of the Caprock, in the Pease River Valley). What is most striking about LeMay's *The Unforgiven*, however, is that its plot is the conscious reverse of *The Searchers:* in *The Searchers* a white man is looking for his young niece, kidnapped by Comanches, whereas in *The Unforgiven* it is the white family that has kidnapped a young Kiowa girl and raised her as their own—until, that is, her Kiowa relatives come searching for her.

LeMay's second novel was made into a western film three years after Ford's *The Searchers* by the famous director John Huston. Huston had many fine films to his credit: *The Maltese Falcoln* (1941), *The Treasure of Sierra Madre* (1948), *The African Queen* (1951). But while Ford's film has, over the past four decades, taken its place as a central cultural artifact of post–World War II America, and has exerted a profound influence over the younger generation of Hollywood film directors, the same cannot be said for Huston's *The Unforgiven*. Huston's film is a workmanlike job, with some excellent landscape photography and a couple of well-acted scenes (notably from Lillian Gish and Joseph Wiseman); but on the whole the impression is of an overly long and rather dull and mediocre finished product. Again, John Ford thought of having *The Searchers* be his final Hollywood film, the capstone of his lengthy and distinguished career; it was clearly a work of great emotional importance to him.[37] Huston, on the other hand, later said that he did *The Unforgiven* primarily for the money—though he also hoped it would make a strong statement about racism—and that he could not bear to watch even the first reel.[38] The movie's screenwriter, Ben Maddow, later expressed similar indifference to it—even though *The Unforgiven* was Maddow's first openly credited screenwriting job since he'd fallen victim to the Hollywood blacklist seven years previously, so one would have expected it to have more importance.[39] *The Unforgiven* has also—in great contrast to Ford's *The Searchers*—been almost completely passed over by serious film critics: it does receive a substantial notice in Edward Buscombe's *BFI Companion to the Western* (1988), but more usually it is ignored, as in Richard Slotkin's *Gunfighter Nation* (1992), or in Jane Tompkins's equally important study *West of Everything: The Inner Life of Westerns* (1992), or in Jim Kitses and Gregg Rickman's important collection of essays on western films, *The Western Reader* (1998).[40]

Given the attitude taken toward *The Unforgiven* by its major creators, and the disdain shown by most critics, one might well ask: why should we

Arthur M. Eckstein

examine this movie at all? The reason, as David Ehrenstein has said, is that the simplistic plotlines and easy solutions of mediocre films can sometimes tell us as much or even more about important social-psychological issues than do the complex, subtle, and deeply thought-out works of committed artists.[41]

In the present case, though the theme of incestuous romance covered over by hatred of miscegenation—the "inner life" of *The Searchers*—is only hinted at by John Ford, in John Huston's *The Unforgiven* the approach is shockingly blunt. This difference in tone is partly because in *The Searchers* the fantasy of incestuous romance is continually thwarted and frustrated (Ethan Edwards never gets Martha, and in the end he never gets Martha-like Debbie either, despite John Wayne's daydreams)—but in *The Unforgiven* the fantasies of incestuous romance entertained by the central characters are in fact completely *fulfilled*. Moreover, in *The Unforgiven* the fulfillment of incestuous romance is—simultaneously—an act of miscegenation. That is, the violation of the traditional boundaries of prohibited sexuality—too close, too far—are in this film paradoxically *converged*. And in contrast to the ending of *The Searchers*, which is powerful but highly ambiguous and deeply melancholy, the result of the fulfillment of the incest/miscegenation fantasies in *The Unforgiven* is a simple and happy ending.

This contrast with *The Searchers* is all the more striking because *The Unforgiven* is in many ways the same movie, populated with many of the same characters. The general historical and general geographical setting is, as I have said, the same: the early 1870s northwest Texas frontier. The immediate social-economic milieu is also the same: as in *The Searchers*, we focus on two neighboring ranch-owning families whose personal relationships are closely intertwined (the Edwards and Jorgensen families in *The Searchers;* the Zachary and Rawlins families in *The Unforgiven*); there is also the same small cloud of lesser neighbors who help form the posse that plays a crucial role in each film; and in both films we are so far out on the frontier that there is not even the usual dusty western town. Most importantly, however, within the Zachary family, which equates to the Edwards family as the central site of emotional conflicts, those emotional conflicts are the same—focused, as in *The Searchers*, on concerns simultaneously about incest and miscegenation.

The dominant male figure in the Zachary family is the eldest of three brothers, Ben Zachary (played by Burt Lancaster); *the Unforgiven* was intended to be primarily about him.[42] And Ben Zachary is a figure remark-

Incest and Miscegenation in *The Searchers* and *The Unforgiven*

ably like Ethan Edwards: grim, stern, an expert frontiersman—and past normal marrying age. Following the death of his father at the hands of the Kiowas (Ethan Edwards's mother had been killed by Comanches[43]), Ben has devoted himself to making the Zachary homestead a successful ranch. He has done this partly by establishing an economic partnership with the neighboring Rawlinses, and partly by wielding a whip hand over his two weaker brothers. Ben is emotionally closed, except to two people: his elderly mother (played by Lillian Gish), and his young stepsister Rachel (played by Audrey Hepburn). In fact, the central problem for Ben Zachary is that he is deeply *in love* with his much younger stepsister—and she, in turn, is deeply in love with him. But of course the fulfillment of that love is impossible because of the social circumstances, and indeed the very existence of that love has to be denied: for just as Martha Edwards was Ethan Edwards's sister-in-law, so Rachel Zachary (though in fact a foundling) has been brought up from childhood as Ben Zachary's sister, and that makes her (like Martha) beyond reach. It would be too close to incest. This is the main reason for Ben Zachary's grimness, loneliness, and barely suppressed anger.

As is, this family situation is unresolvable: as was the case with the original family conflict in *The Searchers*, the conventions and prevailing social mores forbid the "natural" marriage which "should" take place. But as in *The Searchers*, terrible events now converge to explode the suppressed family tensions. First comes the arrival of a crazed old man named Kelsey, dressed in a Confederate coat and wielding a saber (Joseph Wiseman), who accuses Rachel of being in reality a Kiowa. Second comes the arrival of a Kiowa war chief and his men: informed about Rachel by Kelsey, they demand Rachel back, for she is the war chief's (*real*) sister, kidnapped by whites as a child. There is a face-to-face confrontation between Ben and the war chief, between Rachel's stepbrother and her real brother, alter egos: it parallels the face-to-face confrontation between Ethan and Scar, the one prevented from marrying the mother, the other really married to the daughter (who looks just like the mother). And finally comes Rachel's decision to marry the oafish and repulsive Charley Rawlins, the eldest son of their neighbors (played by Albert Salmi). This latter sudden decision by Rachel immediately follows her overt (and physically seductive) attempt to get *Ben* to marry her. It is an offer that Ben is forced to dismiss as a joke—you can't marry your sister!—but both of them know it is not a joke at all. In fact, Rachel's agreement to marry the oafish Charley is an act of teenage revenge on Ben for Ben's having rejected her. And Ben's reaction to the news of the upcoming nuptials—the nuptials that should have been *his*, but which social constraints forbid—is to get bitterly drunk.

Charley Rawlins, like Charley McCorry in *The Searchers* (whom he most resembles), like Aaron Edwards, like Scar, is the hideous "false marriage," displacing the "beautiful" and "natural" marriage, that lies at the heart of both films based on the Alan LeMay novels. But the emotional disaster of Rachel's "wrong" marriage to Charley Rawlins, which would deny her to Ben forever, is averted at the last moment—because Rachel is in fact a Kiowa. Kelsey urges the Kiowas to murder Charley (which they do); a posse is subsequently organized to hunt Kelsey down; and finally comes Kelsey's open accusation, before the grieving Rawlings family and the assembled neighbors, concerning Rachel's own "tainted" origins and nature.

Here the meaning of the title of the film (and the novel)—*The Unforgiven*—is finally revealed. Years ago, during a war with the Kiowas, Kelsey's small son had been kidnapped by them when his ranch was burned and his wife killed; the Zacharys, having found baby Rachel in a burning Kiowa camp, refused to offer her in exchange for the son. Kelsey has never forgiven them. He has spent the long intervening years searching for his son among the Indians, at the same time hounding the Zacharys from place to place with his story—always revealing what Rachel is. This is the world of *The Searchers,* of course, with Kelsey in his pain and malevolence yet another version of Ethan Edwards: Kelsey's son, like Ethan's brother, is named Aaron; Kelsey's family has suffered the same destruction which Ethan's family has, at the hands of the Indians; even Kelsey's Confederate grey coat and his cavalry saber recall Ethan's appearance as he rides out of the desert in the first scenes of Ford's film; in one of those scenes Ethan gives his saber to Aaron's son—named Ben.[44] Lillian Gish eventually kills Kelsey (she hangs him), but it is too late: the story is out once again.

Debbie, in *The Searchers,* has become an Indian; Rachel, in *The Unforgiven,* really *is* an Indian.[45] And the society of white settlers on the far Texas frontier in *The Unforgiven* is as unforgivingly racist as the society of white settlers on the far Texas frontier in *The Searchers.*[46] Thus if Rachel is an Indian, that means she is sexually untouchable: not in the way she is untouchable in the first half of the film, when for Ben to touch her would be incest (a defilement of her purity), but untouchable now in exactly the *opposite* way—because *she* is actually "dirty," and thus to touch her would *be* defilement. That is: it would be miscegenation. "Kiowa squaw!" screams Mrs. Rawlins at Rachel, grieving for her son Charley: "Dirty, filthy Kiowa

Incest and Miscegenation in *The Searchers* and *The Unforgiven*

squaw!" The actress playing Mrs. Rawlins looks and acts much like the motherly Mrs. Jorgensen in *The Searchers* (heavyset, middle-aged, and normally good-humored); but in *The Unforgiven* this Mrs. Jorgensen becomes a racist monster who actually screams "Nigger!" twice in succession, at Rachel.[47]

And yet if the racist white settlers of *The Unforgiven* have a sexual horror of miscegenation, it also seems that this sexual horror has its strange attractions. For in the nighttime scene before the Rawlins cabin where Kelsey is hanged and Rachel's identity is revealed (by far the most extended and effective dramatic scene in the film), the beautiful teenage Rachel is not only subjected to horrifying verbal and racist abuse but is also—and simultaneously—threatened with being stripped naked. The undertone of sexual prurience and violation is striking. Here the contradictions between the "dirty" Indian as forbidden yet attractive sex object and the "pure" sister as forbidden yet attractive sex object reaches an apex.

The sexually forbidden and the sexually "unclean" (or "defiled") as sexually vulnerable and hence as subtly attractive: that is the theme in this central scene in *The Unforgiven,* that is the theme in the central scenes in *Prime Cut,* and (as I have suggested) that is the underlying tension in the last section of *The Searchers* as well. It is why the young, rescued (and totally sexually defiled) semi-Indian Debbie is taken away from her uncle Ethan in the final scene of that movie. Thus in the cultural space where fantasies of incest and fantasies of miscegenation intersect, beautiful teenage Debbie and beautiful teenage Rachel share the same fate. It is a fate dictated by popular imagination.

These aspects of the fantasy underlying *The Unforgiven* become all the clearer when we examine the last third of the film, and its startling conclusion. The Rawlins family and all the other neighbors now break all ties with the Zacharys, because they have been secretly harboring "a red-hide." This ruins the Zacharys financially; even more importantly, now they will be left to defend themselves alone against the Kiowa onslaught when the Indians come to retrieve Rachel. Indeed, the Zachary family itself now splits apart over Rachel, with the middle brother (Audie Murphy—his best film role) abandoning the family in a racist fury.

But that is not the only betrayal or threat of betrayal within the Zachary family. For when the Kiowas first come to try to get Rachel back, offering many horses for her, Rachel sees her (real) brother for the first time, leading his warriors and dressed in elegant buckskins and riding a white horse, and she exclaims, "Isn't he beautiful!" Lillian Gish recoils with horror: "He isn't beautiful, he's a Kiowa!" And one can see in her face the sudden terrible suspicion that perhaps with Rachel "blood will tell" after all. That is, despite being raised white, she will be attracted instinctively back to her Kiowa heritage—and to her magnificent brother, a charismatic, powerful man (just like Scar in *The Searchers*). The question of what Rachel will do in a crisis is left hanging right to the penultimate moment of the movie.[48]

This next-to-last scene in *The Unforgiven*, between Rachel and her real Kiowa brother, is part of the grand climax of the film: the Kiowa assault on the Zachary homestead. It is one of only two conventionally exciting sequences in this very long movie (the other being the posse's pursuit of Kelsey across the desert, before he is brought back to reveal the truth about Rachel). Just as the Zachary family is riddled with repressed sexual-emotional conflicts similar to those of Ethan Edwards's family, so too the Zachary ranch house in *The Unforgiven* is exactly the ranch house from *The Searchers:* the same large house made of sod bricks, the same wooden gun ports attached to windows to "fort up" in case of Indian attack, the same buried, beloved parent (killed by Indians) off to one side. And the Kiowa assault on the Zacharys is a replica of the terrifying Comanche assault that destroys the Edwards family toward the beginning of *The Searchers:* against an isolated house with few able-bodied defenders, coming suddenly out of the desert at night, organized by a mysterious and powerfully charismatic leader (Scar in *The Searchers;* Rachel's real Kiowa brother in *The Unforgiven*). By this point in our discussion, of course, we should not be surprised at such similarities. The fact is that Alan LeMay wrote the same book, dealing with the same conflicts, twice.[49]

There are, to be sure, two major differences between the Comanche raid at the beginning of *The Searchers* and the Kiowa raid at the end of *The Unforgiven*, but even these differences only serve to underline how closely the structural elements of the two films resemble each other. First, whereas in *The Searchers* the result of the Comanche attack is not only the destruction of the Edwards family but also the abduction of the female children, in *The Unforgiven* the purpose of the Kiowa attack is to recover a girl child who has been abducted by whites years before. In this sense, it is indeed a bit like the final scenes of *The Searchers*—the attack on Scar's camp to rescue the long-ago abducted Debbie (but of course the roles here are reversed). Second, whereas in *The Searchers* Ethan Edwards is absent from the house when the Comanches attack, and the Edwards family is thus destroyed, in *The Unforgiven* the Ethan figure—Burt Lancaster's powerful, grim and sexually frustrated Ben Zachary—is present to help the defense.

Incest and Miscegenation in *The Searchers* and *The Unforgiven*

(It is the middle, weaker, less important brother who is missing—having rejected the family for racist reasons.) And Ben Zachary's presence makes all the difference in the world, exactly as Ben Edwards (Aaron's adolescent son) thinks in *The Searchers* that Ethan's presence would have made to the besieged Edwards family at the beginning of that picture. Ben Zachary shows forth all his frontier expertise and stolid determination unfazed by odds as he leads the fighting-off of Kiowa assault after Kiowa assault, and thus leads the Zachary family to survival.

In the course of the defense of the Zachary homestead, however, the elderly mother is seriously wounded, and then she dies. Her intense emotional connection to young Rachel is emphasized: Lillian Gish is given a long and moving soliloquy in which she explains to her eldest son Ben why she refused to give baby Rachel up long ago: the beautiful Indian baby was a replacement for her own stillborn white child; her breasts were aching with milk to give her. The sexual imagery here is striking, and I mention it because of what immediately follows. As soon as the elderly mother dies of her wounds, Ben Zachary proposes marriage to his sister Rachel: she happily, giddily, accepts, and that is followed by a passionate embrace. The youngest brother (an adolescent, like Rachel) looks on, grinning.

Yet how is this union to be tolerated? Rachel is not only much younger than Ben (at least twenty years: a teenager to his mature man in his mid-thirties), but she has also been raised from infancy as his full sister—which means that the marriage is heavily incestuous at least at an emotional level. But Rachel is also a Kiowa—so that the stark frontier (and the stark 1950s) prohibitions against miscegenation are also, simultaneously, being violated. In fact, when *The Unforgiven* was made in 1959, it had been only three years since the Motion Picture Production Code had officially given up its strong opposition to the depiction of miscegenation of *any* kind, and of course most white American society in the real world outside the movie theater harshly disapproved of it.[50] The audience of *The Unforgiven*, however, is clearly being called upon not merely to tolerate this simultaneously incestuous and miscegenetic love match, but to look upon it with favor—and with pleasure.

Perhaps one might partially explain this situation by accepting what one might call "the Woody Allen defense": after all, the marriage of Ben and Rachel is *not really* incest (any more than is the marriage of Woody Allen and Soon-yi Previn: he was merely in the role of her stepfather for fifteen years while she was growing up). Though Ben and Rachel have experienced each other as brother and sister, they are not actually brother and sister;

therefore marriage between them is legally permissible, and any psychological issues should not be pressed. But in *The Unforgiven* this argument cannot be pressed very far, because it was the fact that Ben and Rachel had grown up as brother and sister together, with all this implied, that forced Ben earlier in the film to reject Rachel's only half-joking proposal of marriage. If the issue was real and serious then—real enough and serious enough for Ben to destroy his life and Rachel's life over it—then it cannot simply have disappeared now.

A similar explanation of why the audience is supposed to approve of and find pleasure in the ultimate union of Ben and Rachel might be: this is *not really* miscegenation, either. After all, Audrey Hepburn is just about the most elegant Kiowa imaginable, and in reality she is of course white. She is really just a "play Kiowa." Moreover, when white people in 1950s America expressed harsh disapproval of miscegenation, they were thinking of sexual relations between whites and blacks, not between whites and Indians: romances between whites and Indians (especially between white men and Indian women, as in *The Unforgiven*) did appear on screen, and were evidently viewed as not too disturbing.[51] The fact that Rachel is not an African American is, I agree, something of a mitigating factor in the miscegenetic situation portrayed at the end of *The Unforgiven*. But just as the entire plot of the first half of the film revolves around the fact that Ben and Rachel are brother and sister, so the entire plot of the second half of the film revolves around the facts that Rachel *is* a Kiowa and that most white characters react to this with horror and disgust. That even includes one of Rachel's own stepbrothers, when he learns the truth: he rejects her, and leaves the family. In *The Searchers,* of course, the union of white and Indian was hardly viewed with calm; and Rachel in *The Unforgiven* is explicitly said to be very dark. Most importantly, only a few scenes before the passionate embrace of Ben and Rachel as they agree to marry, we have witnessed Rachel being called explicitly the terrible N-word: we get a close-up of this, with Mrs. Rawlins (who is the counterpart of Mrs. Jorgensen) screaming it at her twice. Thus the racial chasm existing between Ben and Rachel Zachary in the film is not played down for the original 1950s audience but on the contrary is repeatedly underscored and emphasized— emphasized sometimes in ways that an audience today will find both shocking and offensive. And John Huston, the film's director, is clear in his memoirs that this emphasis on the miscegenetic aspect of Ben and Rachel's romance is exactly what he intended.[52]

Incest and Miscegenation in *The Searchers* and *The Unforgiven*

So despite some mitigating factors, the relationship between Ben and Rachel really *is* incest, and—simultaneously—it really *is* miscegenation. Perhaps at one level the audience can find all this tolerable (and even pleasurable) because the romance of Ben and Rachel is also the romance between the two major stars of the film, Burt Lancaster and Audrey Hepburn—a romance which (despite everything) the audience expects. But this particular romance occurs in family circumstances combined with racial circumstances so bizarre that it is hard to accept such a simple answer as the complete one. So I would suggest that another part of the reason why the situation is tolerable (and even pleasurable) is because, as Jane Tompkins says, in westerns "what the hero experiences is what the audience experiences: what he does, they do too."[53] That is: the simultaneously incestuous and miscegenetic union of Ben and his young sister Rachel can be tolerated (and even viewed with pleasure) because it somehow fulfills a widespread but usually suppressed fantasy among the audience. It is a fantasy in which, as Mannoni saw, the spectre of miscegenation ("too far") helps cancel out the incest ("too close"). Alan LeMay was not writing ordinary historical novels: it cannot be an accident that incestuous-miscegenetic romances are at the center of both of them (Ben and his stepsister the Kiowa Rachel in *The Unforgiven;* Marty and his stepsister the Comanche-ized Debbie in *The Searchers*). LeMay was undoubted knowledgeable about the Texas frontier, but at heart he was writing—and wrote twice—a powerful, twisted family romance.

And perhaps one can go even further. Ben turns to Rachel for love and marriage as soon as his mother dies—and immediately after his mother has underlined her own emotional closeness and physical connection to Rachel. The incest fantasy here is thus perhaps not (or not only) with the sister (or daughter, since Rachel is young enough to be Ben's daughter) but with the mother: purely Oedipal. Similarly, it is not so much the young semi-Indian Debbie (young enough to be his daughter) whom Ethan really wants in *The Searchers,* but rather the woman whom Debbie has replaced and exactly resembles: the pure and motherly Martha (her mother), forbidden earlier to Ethan because Martha is his sister-in-law. In fact, Debbie is kidnapped by Scar right in front of Ethan's mother's grave. The inscription on the gravestone in front of which Scar finds nine-year-old Debbie, who looks like Martha, reads: "HERE LIES MARY JANE EDWARDS, KILLED BY COMANCHES, May 12, 1852, a good WIFE & MOTHER, in her 41st year."[54] In other words, behind the strangely alluring fantasy of incest and

213

Arthur M. Eckstein

miscegenation (forbidden and forbidden) which marks both *The Searchers* and *The Unforgiven* may also lie an Oedipal fantasy pure and simple, presented only very indirectly, but providing a dynamo of enormous emotional power. Just watch the scene where Ben and Rachel (white brother and red sister) kiss: it is electric with the frisson of the forbidden. No wonder, then, that at the end of *The Searchers,* Ethan is condemned—just like Oedipus—to wander in eternal exile.[55]

In support of the idea that with these themes of incest and miscegenation we are dealing with prevailing deep structures of popular fantasy, I would point to the plots of three other powerful and popular films.

First, *Mandingo* (dir.: Richard Fleischer, 1975): a box-office success long derided by critics as mere melodrama, it has recently been viewed with some justification as an important film about race in America because it bluntly confronts all the sexual issues at the heart of racism.[56] *Mandingo* is set on a pre–Civil War plantation in the Old South devoted to "breeding" slaves for sale—that is, it exists totally for the sake of sex. In the film, the son of the vicious white plantation owner—who himself has a slave lover—rejects his new white wife (Susan George) when he discovers that she is not a virgin; she is not a virgin because she has been sleeping with her own brother; in revenge for rejection, she takes her own black lover (Ken Norton) from among the plantation's slaves; he, in turn, while involved in this absolutely forbidden miscegenetic love affair, is also simultaneously sleeping with his sister. The end result in *Mandingo* is catastrophe for all concerned.[57] Then there is *The Lover* (dir.: Jean-Jacques Annaud, 1992), a film that enjoyed good box-office success and made the autobiographical novel by Margeurite Duras on which it is based into a U.S. bestseller. In this film, set in French Indochina in the 1930s, an extremely young adolescent French girl (played by Jane March) has a sexual affair with a rich Chinese man in his twenties (Tony Leung). Leaving aside the age difference (which would make the relationship criminal in the United States), such a miscegenetic relationship is absolutely forbidden to white women in French Indochina because it is a terrible violation of French colonialist-racist ideology, which demands "purity" for white women. The older brother of the French girl—a virulent and violent white racist—hates her and her lover because of the relationship (her unanswerable reply is that the family needs the Chinese man's money). Simultaneously, though, the relationship between the older brother and the girl verges itself on the incestuous—as does, even more explicitly, another (younger) brother's. Moreover, the film simultaneously shows the angry, racist older brother as

Incest and Miscegenation in *The Searchers* and *The Unforgiven*

the only child in the family who is closely bonded to the mother—in fact, too closely bonded.[58]

Finally, we return to Texas with *Lone Star* (dir.: John Sayles, 1996). The film is set in a contemporary Texas town near the Rio Grande border. Its hero (Chris Cooper, playing a sheriff) is in love with a Mexican American girl (Elizabeth Pena). This in itself is a violation of the racist code of the town's dominating white population, and indeed Chris Cooper thinks that his sheriff father (Kris Kristopherson) had violently forbidden the relationship years before, when he and Elizabeth Pena were teenagers in love, because, precisely, of racism—for the father is viciously and violently anti-Mexican (as well as antiblack). But it turns out that there was another, even deeper and secret reason why the sheriff father violently opposed the relationship: the girl is both Mexican American and Chris Cooper's half-sister. Yet at the end of the film, the hero and heroine, aware now of their real relationship, decide to move in together anyway, fulfilling their love in spite of everything. *Lone Star*, then, offers the same startlingly happy ending as *The Unforgiven*. And it is John Sayles's most financially successful film.

It should be clear by now that John Huston was tapping into widespread popular fantasies involving incest and miscegenation as he constructed his own film back in 1959 (and so was John Ford, back in 1955/1956). But the deep structures existing specifically between *The Searchers* and *The Unforgiven*, intimately connecting them, are shown by one final incident. The marriage-betrothal of Ben and Rachel Zachary occurs during a lull in the Kiowa assault on the Zachary homestead. The Kiowa assault soon begins again, and despite all of Ben's grim and efficient efforts, undaunted by Kiowa numbers, it eventually is very close to success. The turning point comes when Rachel's magnificent Kiowa brother breaks into the burning Zachary ranch house and confronts her—to take her home. Ever since she first saw him and was instinctively drawn to him, the audience has been in suspense as to what she would do in such a confrontation. Now we find out. Rachel hesitates before him, wide-eyed, a pistol held at her side . . . he smiles . . . and then she knowingly shoots her own brother dead. The parallel is of course with the death of Scar in *The Searchers*. In that case, the annihilation of the Comanche alter ego of Ethan Edwards leaves him free—at least momentarily—to possess his young niece (the image of his illicitly beloved sister-in-law Martha). Here in *The Unforgiven*, Rachel kills her Kiowa brother (her real brother)—which leaves her free to marry her brother.[59]

Arthur M. Eckstein

Family unity is asserted in yet another way at the end of *The Unforgiven:* Cash, the brother who has rejected Rachel for racist reasons because she is a Kiowa, returns to the Zachary homestead at the very last moment, to help fight off the Kiowas. The unified Zacharys are thus saved (or rather, save themselves), and the last scene of the films shows the surviving members of the family standing outside the burnt but still structurally intact ranch house—a fine symbol of the racial furies (both internal and external) that have now been fought off.[60] The unity of the family, however, comes at a price: presumably Ben Zachary's two younger brothers will now fully accept his marriage to their sister, the Kiowa Rachel. Ben, simultaneously committing both incest and miscegenation, will thus take his rightful place, finally and completely, as the head of the household.

A happy ending indeed. It is, of course, Ethan Edwards's fantasy of total power over the family (and, we know, it is John Wayne's fantasy version of it too), a fantasy existing from the very first uncomfortable homecoming scenes in *The Searchers*, now finally fulfilled. Perhaps no one can ever have Mother, or become Father; and in *The Searchers* even Ethan's young and "soiled" niece is soon taken away from him. But in *The Unforgiven*, the other movie made from Alan LeMay's novels, the Ethan figure actually *marries* the Debbie figure. And by doing so, he seizes total control of the family.

It is worthwhile here to emphasize once again how close Rachel and Debbie are to each other in symbolic attributes. Both are in some sense profoundly displaced personages. Both are in some sense now *semi*-Indians: Debbie, though white, has spent her formative years among the Comanches, has had a fierce and powerful Comanche husband, and is dressed *as* a Comanche; Rachel, though a Kiowa, has spent her formative years among whites, and—through the shooting of her biological brother and her expressed desire to marry her white stepbrother—has shown that she is totally willing to adapt to (surrender to) white society.[61] And both Debbie and Rachel, though both extraordinarily young, are associated intimately with the mother figures of their respective films (Debbie biologically and in appearance to Martha; Rachel because her white stepmother *makes* the connection, overtly and in strangely sexualized language, in a dramatic soliloquy). In addition, as we have noted, the rescued Debbie at the end of LeMay's novel *The Searchers* declares her emotional and sexual love for her stepbrother: which is exactly the same incestuous ending as in *The Unforgiven*.

Incest and Miscegenation in *The Searchers* and *The Unforgiven*

What I am suggesting, of course, is that more than Ethan's own suppressed fantasy (which John Wayne himself sensed) is finding fulfillment amid the development of these complicated and contradictory relationships; rather, it is a suppressed fantasy widely held within the audience itself that is finding expression here, and—in *The Unforgiven*, at least—finding a happy resolution. *The Searchers* and *The Unforgiven* are movies about obsessive hatred and fear of miscegenation, hatred and fear which the films take care to condemn: that is their overt story line, and it demonstrates the sociological importance of both films for our understanding of the post–*Brown v. Board of Education* fifties in America.[62] But considered in tandem, both these films also tend strongly to confirm Octave Mannoni's original insight into the strange psychological connection between obsessive hatred and fear of miscegenation and secret incestuous desires: because that is their *covert* story line, rising finally to the surface in Ben and Rachel Zachary's simultaneously incestuous and miscegenetic marriage. I doubt that Mannoni ever saw either *The Searchers* or *The Unforgiven* (though he lived into the 1970s); but it is unlikely that he would have been surprised either at the ferocious "colonial" racism depicted in these two films, at the deeply conflicted family relationships they also depict, or at their final resolution. "What makes a man to wander, to ride away from home?" asks the title song of *The Searchers* right at the beginning of the film, in seeking to explain Ethan.[63] Mannoni wrote: "Whatever one may think before analysis, it is himself that a man is looking for when he goes far away."[64]

NOTES

1. Mannoni, *Prospero and Caliban*, 19–22, 110–21, qtd. on 111. Published originally in Paris in 1950 with the title *Psychologie de la colonisation*.
2. Ibid.
3. See the shocking illustrations from the British popular press in W. G. Broel, *Crisis of the Raj: The Revolt of 1857 Through British Lieutenants' Eyes* (Hanover, N.H.: University Press of New England, 1986), 84ff.
4. See the comments of Thomas Metcalf, *The Aftermath of Revolt: India, 1857–1870* (Princeton: Princeton University Press, 1964), 290.
5. Mannoni, *Psychology of Colonization*, 111n. 1 (emphasis in the original).
6. For the close collaboration between Mannoni and the famous psychoanalyst Jacques Lacan in the writing of *Psychology of Colonization*, see Octave Mannoni, "The Decolonization of Myself," *Race* 7 (1966): 329. On the intellectual controversy engendered by Mannoni's book, see Maurice Bloch's introduction to the 1990 English translation of *Psychology of Colonization*, v–xix.

7. See Maltby, "A Better Sense of History," 36.

8. Young, *Colonial Desire*, esp. chapter 6 ("White Power, White Desire"); Maltby, "A Better Sense of History," esp. 44 ("The Indian Other has done what may not be done, and may not be admitted to be desired, and may not be shown"). It is not surprising that the University of Michigan Press decided to print a new issue of Mannoni in 1990—still in print in 2001.

9. For detailed discussion of the reputation and wide influence of *The Searchers*, see my introductory essay in this volume.

10. See "The Searchers" (John Ford Archive, Lilly Library, Indiana University, Bloomington), 142. For discussion of the original ending of *The Searchers*, see the introductory essay by Eckstein in this volume.

11. On this aspect of Ford's work, see esp. Lindsay Anderson, *About John Ford*, 205–8.

12. For this theme, see esp. McBride and Wilmington, *John Ford*, 62–109.

13. See Eckstein, "Darkening Ethan," 9–11. The implications of Ford's cutting of the Custer scene are also discussed in Eckstein's introductory essay in this volume.

14. Ford's comments on the scene: see his interview in Peter Bogdanovich, *John Ford*, 91. The scene added to the original shooting script by Ford, once back from primary location shooting in Monument Valley (August 1955): see Eckstein's introductory essay in this volume. In LeMay's original novel, the Ethan figure's love of Martha is also explicit; see *The Searchers*, 33. But it is never acted upon, nor reciprocated in the slightest by Martha—unlike what occurs in Ford's film.

15. For the list of commentators on this aspect of the film, see Eckstein's introductory essay in this volume.

16. Nugent, "The Searchers," 140.

17. Noted rightly by Stowell, *John Ford*, 135–36.

18. "We loved each other then, Lorena, / More than we ever dared to tell. . . . / 'If we *try*, we may forget,' / Were words of thine long years ago/ 'Twas not thy woman's heart that spoke; / Thy heart was always true to me. / A duty, stern and pressing, broke / The tie which linked my soul to thee." On the abortive love affair that lies at the origin of Webster's song, see Ernest K. Emurian, *The Sweetheart of the Civil War: The True Story of the Song "Lorena"* (Natick, Mass.: W. A. Wilde, 1962), 10–15.

19. On Ford's scholarly knowledge of nineteenth-century American popular music, see Nugent's important letter to Anderson, in Anderson, *About John Ford*, 244; cf. 242.

20. See Kalinak's essay in this volume, establishing for the first time and in detail, from material in the John Ford Archive at Indiana University, that Ford was in total control over the music for *The Searchers*.

21. On the significance of the social meaning of "Lorena" for the psychological dilemmas of *The Searchers*, see Eckstein, "Darkening Ethan," 16; cf. Buscombe, *The Searchers*, 55–56.

22. On Wayne's 1974 statement, see Roberts and Olsen, *John Wayne, American*, 420. On Wayne's 1976 fantasy, see Macklin, "I Come Ready," 30–31.

23. Gallagher, *John Ford: The Man and His Films*, 338. Gallagher, of course—like Wayne—meant his comment innocently.

24. For Ford's characterization of *The Searchers*, see Mitry, "Interview," 197.

25. See Eckstein's introductory essay in this volume as well as "Darkening Ethan," 3–24.

26. On this issue, see the essay by Lehman in this volume.

27. Mannoni, *The Psychology of Colonization*, 19 (my emphasis). Compare here the quote on Ford in Maltby, "A Better Sense of History," 36.

28. For this important and pessimistic aspect of the problems raised in *The Searchers*, see Eckstein, "After the Rescue." On the social fate of the sexually abused, cf. esp. the comments of Judith L. Herman, *Trauma and Recovery* (New York: Basic Books, 1992), 62, 67–68, 143, 145.

29. Debbie and her stepbrother Marty in bed at the end of LeMay's novel: LeMay, *The Searchers*, 271–72. "From always": 235.

30. Debbie's locket a gift from Marty (substituted with the war medal from Ethan in the film): LeMay, *The Searchers*, 140. For LeMay's novel as focused on Marty, see Card, "*The Searchers* by Alan LeMay and John Ford," 5.

31. These lobby photographs—startlingly sexual for 1956—can be seen on the website for the Motion Picture Arts Gallery (New York City): www.mpagallery.com.

32. *Playboy*, April 1971, 100–101.

33. Marty is established as Mrs. Jorgensen's adoptive son in a marvelous moment during the first arrival of the weary searchers back at the Jorgensen's ranch: Mrs. Jorgensen (Olive Carey) walks right past Ethan and takes Marty into her arms. In LeMay's novel, her feelings for Marty are explicit (*The Searchers*, 70–71).

34. On the ideological importance to Ford's film of Marty as part Indian, see the essay by Henderson in this volume.

35. See Eckstein, "After the Rescue," esp. 37–45. "Rescue-and-romance" imposed because of audience-response testing: see Ritchie's letter to Eckstein, "After the Rescue," 46.

36. Ritchie's letter to Eckstein: "After the Rescue," 46–48.

37. See the comments of John Ford's grandson Dan Ford in *Pappy*, 273–74, and of Wayne's wife, Pilar Wayne, in *John Wayne: My Life with the Duke*, 88–89.

38. See John Huston, *An Open Book* (New York: Knopf, 1980), 283–84.

39. See the interview with Maddow in Pat McGilligan, *Backstory 2: Interviews with Screenwriters of the 1940s and 1950s* (Berkeley: University of California Press, 1991), 190–91. Huston actually thought the script was pretty good (he worked on it with Maddow) and blamed the film's faults on the producers: see Lawrence Groebel, *The Hustons* (New York: Scribner's, 1989), 472.

40. See Buscombe, *BFI Companion*, 307, compared with the briefest of notices in Slotkin's *Gunfighter Nation*, 472 (who, however, gives *The Searchers* a full-scale discussion: 461–73), and its complete absence from Tompkins, *West of Everything*, and from Kitses and Rickman, *The Western Reader*.

41. For a classic exposition of this methodology, see David Ehrenstein, "*Desert Fury*, Mon Amour," *Film Quarterly* 41 (1988): 2–12.

42. See Huston, *An Open Book*, 283. No doubt the fact that the film was financed by Hecht-Hill-Lancaster helped the idea that it would be a showcase for Burt Lancaster's acting talents.

43. See Nugent, "The Searchers," 33.

44. Martha secretly caresses Ethan's grey Confederate greatcoat, expressing her forbidden love in a famous scene (see Eckstein's introductory essay in this volume); Ethan will later use the Confederate greatcoat to bury his older niece, Martha's daughter Lucy, after he finds her raped and killed by the Comanches.

45. It is worth noting that Rachel's racial identity is left more unclear in Alan LeMay's novel than it is in Huston's film. In the film, a reading of the Kiowa Chronicle painted on deerskin finally forces Ben and his brothers to acknowledge the racial "fact" about their sister; but in LeMay's novel, the Zacharys throw the Chronicle into the fire to avoid reading it, and thus the novel comes to an end with Rachel's racial origins strongly hinted at but never resolved: see LeMay, *The Unforgiven*, 244–45.

46. For discussion of the racism of all of white society, not just Ethan, in *The Searchers*, see Eckstein's introductory essay in this volume.

47. The use of this shocking epithet is historically authentic and demonstrates (if more proof were necessary) that in western films of the 1950s, Indians are often substituting for the social question of black-white relations. On this aspect of the westerns, see Eckstein's introduction and Henderson's essay in this volume.

48. Lana Wood, who played Debbie as a nine-year-old, later gave an interview in which she claimed that though John Ford wanted her to display fear in the famous scene where she first sees Scar in the family cemetery in *The Searchers*, the actual emotion she felt (and which appears on the screen) was fascination—fascination with the massive, bare-chested and war-painted Henry Brandon. "He was magnificent!" Wood's interview appears in the documentary "A Turning of the Earth" (dir.: Nick Redmond), which appears at the start of the current Warner Bros. release of the video of *The Searchers*.

49. The depiction of Comanche and then Kiowa raiding is accurate, both in terms of fighting at night and the charismatic war chief; see Wallace and Hoebel, *The Comanches*, 245–57. Also accurate is the appearance of the full moon in the very first moment of *The Unforgiven:* this was the favorite raiding time both for Comanches and for Kiowas, both for religious and for practical reasons (Wallace and Hoebel, *The Comanches*, 256–57). LeMay, a native of Texas, had clearly done his homework.

50. On the sociopolitical situation under which films such as *The Searchers* and *The Unforgiven* were being filmed, see Michael Walker "The Westerns of Delmer Daves," in *The Book of Westerns*, ed. Cameron and Pye, 127–28.

51. See the discussion in David Grimsted's essay in this volume. Two classic examples: Debra Paget as the young Apache girl Sonsee-aray, eventually married to (a much older) Jimmy Stewart in Delmer Daves's *Broken Arrow* (1950—but then she is killed); Debra Paget as the Cheyenne girl Appearing Day, eventually married to Robert Wagner in *White Feather* (1955; dir.: Robert Webb—and this time they live happily ever after).

52. Huston, *An Open Book*, 283: *The Unforgiven* was partly a parable on current American race relations (i.e., white vs. black).

53. Tompkins, *West of Everything*, 6.

54. The inscription cannot be seen very clearly in the videos that most people now use to watch the film, but was clearer in the original release print, and the inscription appears, with capital letters as in the text above, in the shooting script, 33.

Incest and Miscegenation in *The Searchers* and *The Unforgiven*

55. For Ethan as suffering the fate of Oedipus, see Winkler, "Tragic Features," 201.

56. See the stimulating essay on *Mandingo* in Robin Wood, *Sexual Politics and Narrative Film,* 265–82.

57. The catastrophe is set in train by the discovery that a black slave girl is wearing a piece of jewelry, a love gift from Susan George's husband: this leads the infuriated wife (named Blanche), rejected by her husband because of incest with her own brother, to institute the sexual affair with a male black slave. The bit of jewelry as a token of (perhaps illicit) love plays an important symbolic role, of course, in *The Searchers* too (Ethan's war medal to Debbie in the film; Marty's gold locket to Debbie in the novel—with whom, as we have seen, he is in bed at the novel's end).

58. One wonders whether the emotional relationship between the mother and the violently racist older brother in *The Lover,* depicted as overly close, also helps us to understand both Ethan Edwards and Ben Zachary—men who have never married (like the older brother in *The Lover*), and who are only attracted to women who are socially forbidden them because of family ties (Martha/Debbie, and Rachel).

59. Note that here *The Unforgiven* once more parallels *The Searchers* in that the character in the traditional position of hero is in both films deprived of the traditional confrontation ("duel"; "shoot-out") with the main adversary: Ethan in *The Searchers* does not kill Scar (Marty does); Ben Zachary in *The Unforgiven* does not kill Rachel's Kiowa brother (Rachel does). This is unusual dramatic structure for narratives in the western genre—a fact commented on now by Winkler in his essay in this volume.

60. This was Huston's "liberal" intent: see *An Open Book,* 283.

61. Despite the liberal purposes of *The Unforgiven,* Buscombe rightly points out that the film is not as liberal as it wishes to be, for the Kiowa are not presented as in any way a legitimate alternate culture for Rachel; they are merely violent, raiding males, a totally alien Other: see *BFI Companion,* 472. By contrast, *The Searchers*—though it certainly has its own problems in terms of the depiction of Indians (see the comments of the Native Americans in Tom Colonnese's essay in this volume)—nevertheless presents a far fuller picture of Comanche life: we see many women and children, and Debbie has clearly been treated well and has adapted easily.

62. See Henderson's essay on *The Searchers* in this volume.

63. We now know that John Ford personally supervised the lyrics to the title song, which verses of the song would be used, and when: see the essay by Kay Kalinak in this volume. It is another indication of how important *The Searchers* and its themes were to him.

64. *The Psychology of Colonization,* 111. In terms of how widespread the fantasies discussed above are, and how powerfully these two films speak to them, it is interesting that both *The Searchers* and (far more surprisingly, given its relative obscurity) *The Unforgiven* can be found for rent at almost every Blockbuster video store.

Double Vision:
Miscegenation and Point of View in *The Searchers*

Douglas Pye

The history of the western is littered with movies that attempt to develop literal perspective on the historical treatment of Native Americans. However, the racism that is inherent in the traditions of the genre makes almost any attempt to produce an antiracist western a paradoxical, even contradictory, enterprise. It is, in effect, impossible to escape the genre's informing white supremacist terms.

The Searchers (dir.: John Ford, 1956) is no exception. But it is different in a number of ways from most other westerns which attempt to look critically at racism. Although it offers critical perspectives, it is not a liberal movie in any significant sense: its representation of a deeply racist and obsessive western hero and of the vicious attitudes to miscegenation located at the heart of white civilization is disturbing in ways that go far beyond the traditional liberalism of, say, *Broken Arrow* (dir.: Delmer Daves, 1950) or even the much later *Little Big Man* (dir.: Arthur Penn, 1970). *The Searchers* allows no comfortable identification with or disengagement from its hero (who is both monstrous *and* John Wayne) or easy detachment from other expressions by white characters of racial fear and hatred. The film probably goes further than any other western in dramatizing and implicating us in the neurosis of racism. But in wrestling as a western with the ideological and psychosexual complex that underlies attitudes to race, it is working *within* almost intractable traditions of representation. Much of what is fascinating about *The Searchers* lies in the resulting struggle to control point of view—in fact, in its multiple forms of incoherence.

This essay is not intended as a revisionist account of *The Searchers*, an attempt to challenge its critical standing. I share the widely held view that the film is one of the great westerns. Rather, I want to look at aspects of the film which have been noted by some writers as troubling or in some way problematical but which have tended (with one or two exceptions) to be marginalized within wider analyses. In particular, I want to consider them not as failures of realism or artistic control but as problems rooted in the film's engagement with generic tradition.

As many critics have noted, there are several important ways in which the film develops clear and critical perspectives on racism in white society. Almost from the outset, when Ethan (John Wayne) greets Martin Pawley (Jeffrey Hunter)—"Fella could mistake you for a half-breed," he scowls—Ethan's obsessive hatred of Indians and of the idea of mixed blood are presented in ways designed to distance us from him. The film develops this aspect of Ethan while simultaneously implying the ways in which at times Ethan demonstrates a kinship with the objects of his hatred. Increasingly, and in ways that seem entirely controlled, the film detaches us from Ethan so that we are required to perceive the neurotic and irrational nature of his attitudes and actions. Martin's letter to Laurie (Vera Miles), which functions as a kind of embedded narrative in the middle of the film, acts partly in this way by framing in a condemnatory voice-over Ethan's shooting of buffalo to deny winter food to the Comanches. (In other ways, the containing framework of the letter is less clear in its implications of point of view, as I will argue later.)

The interruption of Ethan's slaughter of the buffalo by the cavalry bugle and the cavalry's entrance—straight, as it turns out, from the massacre of a Comanche village—also marks eloquently the way in which Ethan's racist hatred is repeated at the institutional level in the genocidal actions of the U.S. Cavalry. Later, as it becomes clear that Ethan intends to kill, not rescue, Debbie once she has been taken as a squaw, the film's distance from Ethan is again unambiguous. The final and in some ways most extraordinary moment of this strand of the film's treatment of racial hatred comes in Laurie's appalling outburst to Martin, just before the last movement of the film, in which she describes Debbie as "the leavings of a Comanche buck, sold time and again to the highest bidder," and declares that Martha, Debbie's dead mother, would want Ethan to put a bullet in her brain. The speech is particularly shocking coming from Laurie, apparently one of the film's sanest and most sympathetic characters. But that is clearly the film's point: Laurie's hideous outburst locates the disgust and loathing of miscegenation not simply in Ethan but at the heart of the white

Miscegenation and Point of View in *The Searchers*

community. Ethan is, in this respect at least, not an aberrant but a representative figure.

These perspectives are in themselves coherent and remarkable. The film traces a network of racist loathing from Ethan, into white society in general, and out to the implementation of government policy by the genocidal cavalry. Particularly extraordinary in the film's context are the creation of a hero obsessed by racial hatred and the perception that such attitudes, rooted deep both in society and in the psyche, are found not only in the villainous, ignorant, or aberrant but in people like Laurie who are in other respects sympathetic and caring.

Other aspects of the film are consistent with its critical distance from Ethan's attitudes. In part, both Martin and Debbie seem to offer much more positive and rational perspectives on relationships between the races. In the early parts of the film, Martin's identity is created very strikingly in relation to his Cherokee ancestry ("an eighth Cherokee, the rest's Welsh and English")—bareback riding, moccasins, darkish skin and hair color, the ability to read a trail. He embodies the possibility of integration, of harmonious mixing of the races. In Natalie Wood's early appearances as the grown-up Debbie, too, cross-cultural assimilation, living contentedly with another race, is raised as a real possibility. The Comanches are not monstrous but a people with whom Debbie identifies: "These are my people. Go, Martin—go."

But in many other ways, as I have suggested, the film's point of view on this material is far less clear. Take two pivotal episodes, both contained within the narrative of Martin's letter to Laurie: that involving "Look" (Beulah Archuletta), the young Indian woman whom Martin inadvertently marries as he trades with her tribe, and the slightly later scene involving the white women recaptured from the Comanches by the cavalry. The fact that each is contained in Martin's letter invites the thought that Martin's sceptical and questioning attitude toward Ethan might govern the ways in which we are invited to respond to the two scenes. Certainly, there are parts of the letter's narrative in which Martin's voice signals a cognitive and evaluative distance from Ethan, as in his introduction to the shooting of the buffalo as part of "Something . . . I ain't got straight in my own mind yet." But the episodes of Look and the white female captives are much less obviously framed. Point of view proves much more fugitive in this case.

The only words of Martin's that we hear in the Look section give little away. The initial lines that Laurie reads about Look come *after* we have been shown the scene in which Ethan tells Martin that he has inadvertently bought a wife and are in fact quite misleading: Martin proposes to tell Laurie "how I got myself a wife." Nothing in the language here or later corresponds to his response to Look in the dramatized, as opposed to the narrated, version of events. When we witness the events with Look, there is nothing in the treatment which suggests a mediated or partial view: the episodes are presented in ways consistent with other episodes in the film, including those outside Martin's letter. The next voice-over, which comes after Ethan and Martin discover the next morning that Look has gone, leaving the sign of an arrow made with small stones, acts as a bridge to the shooting of the buffalo. Here Martin's voice begins with "Maybe she left other signs for us to follow, but . . ." There is a cut to Laurie, who continues in her own voice, " . . . we'll never know, 'cause it snowed that day and all the next week." Another cut introduces the two men, on foot, approaching the buffalo herd in a snowy landscape. The only other voice-over about Look comes after they have found her dead in the Comanche village following the cavalry attack. As Martin leaves the tepee containing Look's body, his voice picks up the narration and concludes: "What Look was doing there—whether she'd come to warn them or maybe to find Debbie for me—there's no way of knowing." Look and her actions, in other words, remain enigmas to Martin; his words in the letter convey little in the way of attitude.

In the wider structure of the film, one determinant in the presentation of Look is that she has the function of paralleling Charlie McCorry (Ken Curtis), each being constructed as a comically (even grotesquely) inappropriate potential partner for Martin and Laurie respectively. To cement that link, Ford dresses each in a bowler hat (Charlie as part of the outfit he wears to marry Laurie), one of a network of linking details between characters that permeates the film. One function of the grotesquerie, at any rate in Charlie's case, is as part of a wider vision of marriage and its possibilities that is central to the film's critical perspective on civilization. The implication is of women becoming tired of waiting for the desirable men who refuse to settle down, and marrying the available Charlie—in the way, perhaps, that Martha married Ethan's dull and worthy brother Aaron. For the parallel to work, both Charlie and Look have therefore to be created in ways that invite us to laugh at them, though this cannot fully account for the way in which Look is represented and treated.

She is from the outset a figure of fun—fat, comically modest, and, in conventional terms, sexually unattractive. Martin's dismay at the fact

Miscegenation and Point of View in *The Searchers*

that he has unwittingly bought her, and his frustration at being unable to make her understand what he is saying to her, are also comically treated, his discomfort underlined by Ethan's laughter at Martin's embarrassment. If the terms of Look's representation are in themselves problematical (though in line with the structural role assigned to the character), the episode creates more intense difficulties when Martin literally kicks Look down the sand hill as she settles down to sleep beside him under the blanket. What are we to make of the film's point of view? Ethan's laughter, his sexual wisecrack ("That's grounds for dee-vorce in Texas!"), and the conventionally funny image of Look rolling down the sand dune—all might suggest that we are intended to share Ethan's response.

But it is difficult (now, at any rate) not to experience the treatment of Look as brutal and painful. If it is intended as comic (even grotesquely comic), the effect seems ill-calculated, the humor unpleasant and misogynistic. If, on the other hand, we are being invited to be critical of Ethan's response, or indeed of Martin's action, it is difficult to account for the decisions that have gone into the construction of Look as a character. In terms of the way the episode is organized—narratively, within Martin's letter, as well as visually and dramatically—it is hard to mount an argument that will convincingly show how point of view is being *controlled* here. We may want to suggest that the episode is intended to be suffused by Ethan's distorted way of seeing, but evidence for such a view is, as Peter Lehman argues in his article on the Look episodes, hard to find.[1] It becomes difficult not to suspect that Ford can treat Look in this way because in terms of the traditions within which he is working, sex between a white man and a Native American woman is unthreatening, and so capable of treatment as comedy, while sexual contact between a white woman and a nonwhite man is an entirely different matter—tragic, and demanding of vengeance. This is, of course, Ethan's view, and in this respect, as in the whole presentation of Look, the film seems uncomfortably close to attitudes of which elsewhere it is critical.

In almost the next sequence, Look is found dead in a tepee, killed in the cavalry's attack on the Comanche village. We might consider that in this chilling moment there is an implicit rebuke to our previous attitude to Look, as well as to Ethan's and Marty's. It certainly confirms a presentation of the U.S. Cavalry (now killers of innocent women) very different from that in Ford's earlier films. But the sentimentalization of Look's death can also seem a conventional way of evading the problems of her continued presence in the narrative.

Ethan and Marty question Look about Scar.

Peter Lehman accounts for the uneasy treatment of Look in psychoanalytical terms. "Ford has 'let too much' into the film . . . there is too much dangerous, repressed, sensitive material being dealt with"—material, that is, about interracial sexuality. "The almost unbearable tensions raised by *The Searchers* need an outlet . . . Ford needs to be able to behave like a high-school kid. *He* needs to kick Look down the hill—*he* needs to laugh at it."[2] This argument perhaps makes the matter too individual. If it is plausible to speak of "repressed material" here, it is the nature of representation within the tradition that needs addressing rather than (or at least, as well as) the psychology of John Ford. In Ford's films, after all, sex is frequently deflected into horseplay. What makes this scene different is its focus on a Native American woman, a character who can be constructed and treated as she is, a way few other women are treated in Ford—though aspects of the treatment of the Indian barmaid Chihuahua (Linda Darnell) in *My Darling Clementine* (1946) offer uncomfortable parallels—because the tradition allows it.[3] In other words, the film *is* complicit with Ethan here because, in terms of the genre, it does not matter that Look is pre-

Miscegenation and Point of View in *The Searchers*

sented in this way, and it is highly unlikely that the filmmakers in 1956 would have considered their decisions in any way problematic.

In this sense the Look episode may be a moment "profoundly and symptomatically out of control," as Peter Lehman suggests,[4] but it is a moment representative of, rather than out of line with, the film's negotiation of its material. It is certainly not, as Lehman argues, the sole exception to the film's otherwise mature and complex handling of the sexual and racial themes.

Comparable but even more extreme problems of interpretation surround the white captive sequence. Ethan and Martin ask at the army camp to see the white women recaptured in the cavalry raid on the Comanche village. Martin produces Debbie's rag doll, in the hope that one of the women or girls will recognize it. Although the episode is still taking place within Martin's letter, narrative voice is suspended throughout this section, so that no perspective is offered through voice-over (either Martin's or Laurie's). That is, the sequence is presented "objectively." Two recaptured women are seen initially, one seated on a bench against the wall, a wide-brimmed hat masking her face, a dark blanket round her shoulders. She is never shown in close-up, does not speak, and acts only by leaning forward to pat the more obviously distressed woman seated at her feet. This second woman seems not only upset but, as we see her and we hear her cries in the course of the scene, appears to have been mentally unhinged by her experiences. In the way she cradles something in her arms, and later hysterically snatches the doll from Martin, there seems an implication that somewhere along the way she has lost a baby. The other two women are much younger— one perhaps in her mid-teens, the other younger still. The younger girl clings to her companion and stares fearfully up at Martin as he holds out the doll. The older girl smiles almost maniacally, and her equally directly look at Martin carries strong sexual overtones. The representation of the women carries powerful connotations of *at least* traumatic shock; in two cases—the woman on the floor and the older girl—of experiences that have driven them mad.

The scene is presented simply, in six shots. The first frames the door at the rear left of the frame and the first pair of women. The woman on the floor croons softly to herself or to something she is holding in her arms. She turns toward the door and screams as the men enter, until a soldier (Ford regular Jack Pennick) gives her what seems to be a child's rattle on a peace of leather or cloth, and she quiets, comforted by the other seated woman. Martin walks forward, looks down at the women, and turns frame

Blonde captives driven crazy by the Comanches.

right; the camera adjusts right to reveal the backs of the two girls, wrapped in a red blanket. As they begin to stand, helped to her feet by two soldiers, there is a cut to almost a reverse angle, showing the two girls from the front and from Martin's left (his shoulder is just in the shot). Martin produces Debbie's doll, but the girls make no response. Cut back to the first set up; Martin turns to leave and the camera moves left with him, excluding the two girls and reframing the woman on the floor, who snatches the doll and screams. At the rear of the shot, the army officer says, "It's difficult to believe they're white." Ethan takes a step or two toward the camera and the woman, and replies, "They ain't white—not anymore. They're Comanch." As he moves back toward the door, there is a cut to a shot of the doorway. Ethan walks into frame from the left, turns suddenly and looks back out of frame toward the woman on the floor. The camera dollies in, into medium close-up. The next shot (five) is Ethan's point of view of the woman on the ground, holding and crooning at the doll. Shot Six returns to Ethan and he turns toward the door.

This is to say that Ethan's point of view (in the limited, visual sense of the term) is given in one shot (shot five), and the scene ends by stress-

Miscegenation and Point of View in *The Searchers*

ing the effect on him of seeing the captives. The other shots, however, are spatially quite independent of Ethan—in fact, he is a significant visual presence in one (shot three), and then at some distance from the camera.

What does Ethan think he sees when he looks back, and how does it relate to what we are shown? His dialogue is clear and brutal: "They ain't white—not anymore. They're Comanch." For Ethan, the horror of miscegenation is so great that he perceives it as producing a racial change—a change *in nature*. It seems clear from its context within the film that Ethan's appalling belief is intended to distance us even further from him. He takes what has happened to the women as a vindication of his hatred of Indians and of his attitude to miscegenation. Following the dialogue as they do, the last three shots seem to underline this, but also, in the shots of Ethan's face, make graphically clear that Ethan himself is on the verge of madness caused by his obsessive hatred. In other words, the detached and critical point of view on Ethan developed in the scene is consistent with what the film has been doing in its representation of Ethan ever since Martin's first appearance.

Yet the presentation of the women themselves is much more puzzling. If Ethan's response to them is to be rejected, their trauma and madness nevertheless seems to be given to us objectively, independent of any informing and potentially distorting view. They *have* been traumatized and driven mad. If the implication is that captivity inevitably produces such effects, this again seems rather too close to Ethan's view for comfort. Even if we stand back from the distressing, even horrific effect of the scene, and try to ask whether any explanation of the women's states are possible other than from their sexual experiences, the scene offers us no significant help. Details may imply fear of the soldiers (with the possibility that it is the cavalry attack on the village which has traumatized them), or loss of a child, but there is no real support for a view markedly different from what Ethan thinks he sees. This seems a different case from the wider pattern of what Peter Lehman calls the film's epistemological theme—the network of moments in which actions or their consequences are not shown, or significant questions of perception or knowledge are posed.[5] We may be distanced here from Ethan, but there seems little or no ambiguity in the presentation of the women.

These sequences create perhaps the most obvious questions for interpretation in a film which is full of such questions. The representations of Look and the female white captives sit very uncomfortably, in their apparent complicity with Ethan's attitudes, with the film's analysis of racism in white society.

Douglas Pye

There is a further apparent contradiction between the implication of the captive scene and the very different outcome of Debbie's captivity and her experiences as one of Scar's wives. How has Debbie escaped the fate of the other white female captives? Given the above scene, there is no convincing explanation. There is no evidence, for instance, that she was captured younger than the others (a frequent suggestion by students in class discussion) and therefore has been able to assimilate more easily, or that her experience has been qualitatively different. The film is silent on these matters—and in any case the second of the two young girls confronted by Martin is as young as Debbie was when she was captured. It is finally as difficult here as it is in the other problem moments that I have mentioned to square this contradiction with the sense of the film's viewpoint being complex but also under control. This is what Joseph McBride and Michael Wilmington attempt, in proposing that the representation of Debbie enables us to *place* the white female captive scene: "The scene in which Ethan finds the mad White women is so disturbing that the spectator may momentarily wonder whether Ford is not succumbing to the same fear of miscegenation.... But our first glimpse of Debbie as a woman makes it clear that the fear has a purely neurotic base.... Miscegenation has not destroyed her identity, but deepened it."[6] The problem with this, I think, is that the way Debbie is represented can extend our sense of the different impulses at work in the film's treatment of miscegenation but it cannot change the way in which the captive sequence is realized, or the problem of viewpoint it contains. If the fear *is* neurotic, then the neurosis is not wholly confined to the film's characters.

Each of these problems points to a highly fraught negotiation of issues that cannot be resolved, in the film's context, into a coherent set of perspectives. At the heart of this troubled and troubling process of negotiation is miscegenation itself, the sexual act which is the focus of Ethan's and Laurie's fear and hatred, but which the film, in its commitment to dramatizing its material, has itself to confront imaginatively. It is much to the film's credit that it refuses to take refuge in easy liberal attitudes, but tries to engage with the horror that the act or the thought of it generates in the society Ford is representing. The consequences of doing this, however, is to produce these fundamental inconsistencies. In the material we have looked at here, two attitudes are present: in one, interracial marriage can produce the well-balanced Martin and apparently well-integrated Debbie; in the other, miscegenation can be imagined only as rape, and its results are madness, violence and death. The film might wish at one level of inten-

Miscegenation and Point of View in *The Searchers*

Debbie at Scar's camp in New Mexico: a survivor.

tion to embrace the first and distance us from the second, but the imaginative power of the latter in the traditions of the captivity narrative on which the film draws is such that it blurs the more rational discriminations at which the film seems to aim.

The two attitudes are in themselves intimately linked to the dual vision of the Indians which is central to the genre of the western as a whole: they are historically wronged peoples with legitimate grievances against the whites (for instance, Scar's two sons have been killed by white men), but they are also the "Other," the monstrous eruption of forces feared and denied in white civilization. The first offers a historical perspective, represented perhaps marginally in *The Searchers*, with the Comanches as a community, like the white settlers. In the second, they have only a symbolic function; they are not an autonomous people but, in effect, terms in the generic equation. It is at this second level that the frequently discussed idea of Scar and Ethan as "alter egos" makes sense in the symbolic economy of the film. Its divided vision of miscegenation is rooted in the severe constraints of the western's way of seeing.

How deeply the film is informed even by the details of traditional representation in these areas can be seen in the striking difference of appearance between Debbie and the other captive women. Debbie is the only white woman in the film with black hair and dark coloring. All the white captive women at the fort are blonde; Debbie's sister, Lucy, has fair hair and pale coloring. Once perceived, the pattern seems emphatic. In realist terms, it would of course be absurd to suggest that Debbie comes through unscathed because of her hair color, or that the other women go mad because they are blonde. Yet at another, less literal level, and in the context of the traditions on which the film draws, these decisions have a different order of significance.

The division between dark and fair women is deeply rooted in the western. As in so many other aspects of the genre, James Fenimore Cooper provides an early and telling example. Much of the action in *The Last of the Mohicans* (1826) centers on Colonel Munro's two daughters: Alice, of the "dazzling complexion, fair golden hair, and bright blue eyes," and Cora, whose "tresses . . . were shining and black. Her complexion was not brown, but it rather appeared charged with the color of rich blood, that seemed ready to burst its bounds." They are half sisters, and Cora's "rich blood" signifies mixed race. Character traits are developed in a corresponding way. Alice is delicate and fearful, characteristically "veiling her eyes in horror," and Cora is stronger and, crucially, more sensual. She can respond, for instance, to the beauty of the Mohican Uncas: "Who that looks at this creature of nature, remembers the shade of his skin?" This remark produces from her white companions "a short, and apparently embarrassed silence." The archetypes are very clear, and Alice and Cora have thousands of descendants in the genre, among them Ford's women in *The Searchers*.

The association of sensuality with the dark woman remains very powerful, though the link with mixed race that is made in *The Last of the Mohicans* is not consistently maintained in the genre—Debbie, for instance, is as "white," racially, as the other women in *The Searchers*. Something of its force and meaning remain, however, as though some explanation is required to account for the phenomenon of the sexual white woman. The fair woman is the essence of white womanhood, unable to withstand contact with the alien other. As Richard Maltby has written, "The dark heroine is doomed by her knowledge of the hero's sexuality, but the fair, for instance the blonde women captives in *The Searchers*, can be degraded out of their skin color."[7] Maltby also offers a broader perspective on Ford's use of this system: "The female survivors of Ford's captivity narratives are dark

Miscegenation and Point of View in *The Searchers*

women, physically unmarked by their ordeal, unlike their fair counterparts. To survive as a woman in the wilderness, to be degraded and yet unblemished, is to embody a contradiction in patriarchy's construction of true womanhood, to indicate, perhaps, a forbidden desire."[8] It is in relation to this tradition of representation and its cultural implications that Ford's treatment of Debbie and the other captives "makes sense," though it is not a sense that can be integrated into the film's powerful but partial analysis of racial hatred. It is impossible to know what the filmmakers intended by the decisions they took in creating these women, how consciously or unconsciously they drew on the tradition, but the resulting contradictions suggest that in this fraught area of representation the material is in a sense out of control, and that the tradition, powerfully internalized by generations of filmmakers and writers, "speaks through" the film in spite of the presence of other, conflicting intentions.

The kinds of tensions that the film has generated are highlighted starkly by its final movements. Here, in a number of ways, the contradictions inherent in the film's conflicting relationships to tradition are exposed in the evasions that come with the push toward resolution. In two key ways these relate to the dual vision of the Comanches and of miscegenation. The need to close down ambiguity in these areas can account, for instance, for the treatment of the final battle. In the overall pattern of the film, the attack on the Edwards ranch at the beginning is paralleled by the cavalry's massacre of the Comanche village, and logically the final attack on Scar's camp could become the third in a series of massacre and countermassacre that embodies one aspect of the film's view of the destructive relationship between the races. In fact, the treatment of the attack is partly but crucially deflected into comedy by the inept young lieutenant (Patrick Wayne), his sabre, and the undignified wound suffered by Sam Clayton (Ward Bond). Although we have no choice but to *understand* what is happening as a massacre, very little that we *see* offers us this view. Strongly related to this is Debbie's sudden willingness to go with Martin when he enters Scar's tent. Earlier she had refused; the Comanches were her people. When she responds, "Yes, Marty—yes!" to his waking her with the prospect of rescue, her conversion seems to relate less to psychologically motivated change than to the need to switch the Comanches into their "Other" mode prior to the final attack on their camp, in order to move the film toward its resolution. Unlike our view of the aftermath of the cavalry attack in which Look was killed, it is clearly important that in this final battle we should be left with no sense of outrage or of human loss.

Equally, it is vital in terms of the need to achieve some kind of affirmative ending to the search that Debbie should be returned safely to white society. Her wholly unmotivated change of heart is the more or less desperate strategy that will enable her to go willingly. The film simply has to drop its earlier suggestion of her contented assimilation. Along the way, it is important to note, the signifiers of Martin's Indian ancestry have also been dropped; when he wraps himself in a blanket to enter Scar's camp, it is simply a disguise—there are no implications about his cultural identity.

This simplifies the complex connotations of the last section of the film. There are, for instance, very uncomfortable undercurrents, after Laurie's outburst, to Debbie's return, though the film chooses not to foreground these in the way that, several years later, Ford's *Two Rode Together* (1961) does. And whatever the contortions of the last movement, the ending, as it refocuses on Ethan, remains remarkably moving. The film sustains complexity around Ethan, but finds it impossible to sustain other complexities that it has generated.

It is tempting to refer these various aspects of incoherence in *The Searchers* to Ford himself—there is after all plenty of biographical evidence to suggest that he was as contradictory as any of us. But as I have written elsewhere, much of what is of major interest in Ford's films, as well as many of the deepest contradictions, come from his recurrent encounter with generic material and traditional images.[9] Ford's personality as a filmmaker was formed in considerable part by the forms and meanings of the tradition, and, in turn, his films have become part of what we understand the western to be. This is not quite to say, as Richard Maltby does, that "Every western is a palimpsest, a manuscript written on the pages of an earlier, partially erased book, carrying traces of its previous inscriptions."[10] Although the metaphor is extremely evocative, it implies too inert a model of the relationship between individual film, filmmaker, and the tradition. Perhaps it would be more accurate, though equally metaphorical, to say that Ford internalized the "language" of the western and, however unconsciously, its accumulated resonances.

The tradition remained an active presence, not an underlying, partly suppressed layer, in his films, which might be seen, as his career develops, as a dialogue both in and with the "language" he inherited. The films make clear—none more so than *The Searchers*—that some parts of the "language" became more visible to him than others, more amenable to engagement and inflection. He could respond "to a problem he had found in tradition," the words used by E. H. Gombrich to describe Raphael engaging with inherited ways of painting the Virgin and Child.[11] Some problems, however, are less tractable than others, and in 1950s America, tackling miscegenation in popular cinema and particularly in the western was probably as intractable a problem as one could find. It is hardly surprising that the film contains both material that has been critically worked on and given forceful dramatic form, and material that seems barely to have been engaged with imaginatively at all. The aspects of the film I have discussed can be seen as offering available solutions from the repertoire of the genre to problems the film cannot solve or even fully articulate. The particular contradictions of the film are testimony to the intensity with which Ford and his collaborators wrestled with the ideological complex of racism and sexuality within a genre the basic terms of which exist to incorporate rather than to criticize racist fears and phobias. It is an attempt which is as perverse as it is admirable—in fact admirable partly because it is perverse.

There is perhaps a further perversity in claiming that the film's incoherence is an essential aspect of its greatness. But this is actually to say that the greatness of *The Searchers* lies in what it achieves within its context and its traditions.

NOTES

1. Lehman, "Looking at Look's Missing Reverse Shot."
2. Ibid., 68.
3. In *My Darling Clementine*, the heroic protagonist Wyatt Earp (Henry Fonda) deals with Chihauha's sexuality by pushing her into a horse trough. This is clearly meant to amuse the audience.
4. Lehman, "Looking at Look's Missing Reverse Shot," 68.
5. Lehman, "There's No Way of Knowing," 134.
6. McBride and Wilmington, *John Ford*, 162.
7. Maltby, "A Better Sense of History," 43.
8. Ibid.
9. See *Movie* 22 (1976).
10. Maltby, "A Better Sense of History," 40.
11. E. H. Gombrich, *Norm and Form* (London: Phaidon, 1966), 69.

"You Couldn't Hit It on the Nose":
The Limits of Knowledge in and of *The Searchers*

Peter Lehman

Being a clergyman and a military officer appear to be incompatible roles. The former ministers to people, bringing them comfort and urging them to live peacefully by the word of God, even attempting to save those who live outside the knowledge of his God's law. The latter, by contrast, frequently brings pain and death to people—punishing them as enemies if they live outside his laws. Yet, in the Reverend Captain Samuel Johnson Clayton, *The Searchers* contains a character who combines both functions. Near the end of the film, he quotes scriptures as he leads a military charge.

Like the Reverend Captain Clayton, *The Searchers* is something of a paradox. It is, in one sense, a classical film in terms of its narrative structure. In the influential terms of Roland Barthes's study *S/Z*, the hermeneutic code of the classical narrative tradition ensures that the "classical" text (and classic Hollywood cinema conforms to this) will pose and answer a series of questions, in a manner designed to maintain an interesting pace while at the same time delaying the answer to the major question until the end of the text—when, with the revelation of the truth, the text is finished, used up.[1] Yet while *The Searchers* employs this basic structure, it is also true that the film *denies* the audience the knowledge of precisely what has happened and why.

The Searchers on one level clearly conforms to the "classical" imperative toward the revelation of narrative truth. Near the beginning of the film, the major question is posed: Will Ethan Edwards find his niece Debbie, kidnapped by Indians, and if he does, what will he do to her?

Predictably enough in the classical Hollywood cinema, he does find Debbie, and we learn her fate when Ethan decides to overcome his murderous rage, cradle the adolescent girl in his arms, and return her home. He does not kill her. The end.

But the closure in *The Searchers* is actually far less clear-cut than such a brief summary indicates. Why has Ethan reversed his five-year-long, near-maniacal commitment to killing his niece? Indeed, why did he ever develop the obsessive need to hunt her down and kill her in the first place? The fact that these questions can still be posed by the end of the film, and that *any* possible answers to them involve some ambiguity and uncertainty indicates how unusual *The Searchers* is. It is a film with a classical narrative structure that nevertheless resists classical narration.

The fundamental issues involved in a classical Hollywood film are usually spoken about and discussed by characters in that film. In other words, someone tells us what's going on and why. In *The Searchers*, however, fundamental issues about central characters's actions are never spoken about by anyone. This unusual state of affairs may help explain why the film has become such a cult favorite among an entire generation of filmmakers: the film in one sense is the ultimate "director's" film (and perhaps the ultimate "critic's" film as well), because all the vital clues to many important questions are purely visual. No dialogue tells us anything about the answers to those questions. The cult status surrounding *The Searchers* as one of the greatest movies ever made grew out of a late 1960s and 1970s aesthetic which stressed film as a "visual medium." But, as I will show, this uniquely fascinating aspect of *The Searchers* is part of a larger epistemological concern in the film. Indeed, at the center of *The Searchers* lie a number fundamental questions about the nature of knowledge: How much can we ever know about events that have transpired at which we were not present? How fully can we understand the motives for the actions of others? How do we gain such knowledge, both of events and motives? Finally, and perhaps most surprisingly: What is the relationship between how the spectator of the film gains knowledge of events in the film, and how characters within the film gain knowledge of what transpires within the world they inhabit?

Even the song heard over the opening credits of the film, stresses unanswered questions:

> What makes a man to wander?
> What makes a man to roam?

The Limits of Knowledge in and of *The Searchers*

What makes a man to leave bed and board,
And turn his back on home?

Remarkably, even the very first word uttered by a character within the film once the film actually begins is *also* a question. A man, soon to be identified as Aaron Edwards, stares into the desert at an approaching rider and utters in disbelief, "Ethan?" The questioning (including mistakes by the questioner) continues in the following scene, showing Ethan's homecoming. Mistaking Debbie for her older sister Lucy, Ethan says, "Lucy, you ain't much bigger than when I last saw you." "I'm Deborah. There's Lucy over there." "Deborah? Debbie! And you're Lucy?" A bit later, Ethan is asked how California was. "California? I ain't been to California!" The family was under the mistaken impression that that's where he'd gone. When his nephew Ben asks Ethan to tell him about the Civil War, his father intervenes by informing the boy that the war ended three years ago. "It did? Then why didn't you come home before now?" Ben asks Ethan. It is a question that makes everyone uneasy—and one to which no answer is given. Instead, Martha tells Ben to go off to bed.

The questioning of names—"Ethan?" "Debbie?" "Lucy?"—is in fact a theme that echoes throughout the entire film: as if characters cannot trust who they see, or do not know who a name is supposed to designate, or do not know what their own name is, or have forgotten a name, or are not aware of different names for the same person or place, or do not even know if the person designated by a name is alive. Scar, Martha, Futterman, Debbie, Lucy, Marty, Captain Clayton, Colonel Greenhill—all have their names uttered at some point in an interrogative fashion, or somehow questioned. Scar is not recognized by the name Cicatrice; Seven Fingers (where Scar is finally located) is not identified as a known place by whites; the meaning of the name Nawyecka has to be explained—and so it goes. When Mose Harper tells Ethan he has found a man who has seen Debbie, Ethan asks, "Who is this man?" "I am this man," a voice answers and a man steps forward and introduces himself as Emilio Fernandez y Figueroa. The question "Who is this man?" and others like it haunt the characters in *The Searchers*—though much of the time they will never get such a clear-cut answer.

In his introduction to this volume, Arthur Eckstein refers to a scene from *The Searchers* which was included in the script of the film and a version of which was shot, though never included in the release print. The scene involves Ethan overhearing a Custer-like general relate one of his military campaigns to newspaper reporters. I shall return later to how the scene relates to the film's concern with how we can ever know what has happened at an event that is narrated to us and at which we were not present. But for the moment, I wish to bring attention to one of the correspondents. When Ethan mentions Scar's name and tribe, the script is as follows:

Corr.: (Fascinated) Scar? What a wonderful name!
Gen.: (to his aide) Are you getting this Keefer?
Corr.: (to E) How do you spell that word Nawyecka?[2]

The correspondent's response is the third questioning of Scar's name. When during the search Marty first encounters the name, he asks "Scar?" and when Laurie, reading a letter from Marty, comes across it, she pauses, looks up, and eerily repeats the name in a questioning tone before continuing with the letter. But Scar's name is not the only name which is questioned in this scene—the name of the tribe is also brought into question when the reporter asks how it is spelled.

Nawyecka, Ethan explains, means "Round about, fella says he's going to go one way, means to go t'other." Names in *The Searchers* share something in common with the meaning of Nawyecka, continually sliding into ambiguity. This is nowhere more clear than with the character who comes to be known as Look. Marty has inadvertently traded some trinkets to the Comanches for a wife (he thought he was trading for a blanket), and now the Indian woman follows him and Ethan from her camp. Later, when the searchers stop for the night, Marty attempts to explain the bizarre circumstances to the Indian woman. In an attempt to clarify, he says "Aw look" and "Hey look" as he speaks to her. When he repeats the phrase "Aw look," she takes (mistakes) the word "look" as his name for her. Ethan, in explaining to Marty what has happened, tells him, "She says her name is Wild Goose Flying in the Night Sky, but she'll answer to Luke if that pleases you." Mimicking the Indian woman's pronunciation, Ethan pronounces the name as the common name Luke. The mistaken and even mispronounced name Look is particularly provocative in that is arises out of a failed attempt on Marty's part to give knowledge to the Indian woman of what has transpired. And looking, of course, is one of the ways we gain knowledge of the world.

There seems to be no end in this film to the slippage of certainty surrounding names. Indeed, the Indian woman has at least four names: her Comanche name; the English translation of that name as Wild Goose

The Limits of Knowledge in and of *The Searchers*

Flying in the Night Sky; Look; and Luke. Several other characters have more than one name or are given additional names during the film: Ethan is also Big Shoulders; Scar is also Cicatrice; Marty is also He Who Follows; and Captain Clayton is also Reverend Clayton.

In this essay, I will trace the movement in *The Searchers* toward conventional narrative structuring leading to the revelation of the truth of what has happened, as well as the countermovement in the film to resist and question that very revelation. In some ways, *The Searchers* tests the limits of epistemological assumptions within the classical narrative style.

Several scenes make clear for the spectator of the film that characters within the film are frequently fooled and misled in their efforts to understand what has transpired at events at which they were not present. Perhaps the clearest example involves Jerem Futterman's attempt to kill Ethan and Marty. First, Ford establishes a distinction between the men who are present within the scene: Ethan possesses knowledge that Marty doesn't. He tricks Marty into believing that he is cold so that he can build up the fire as the two men prepare to go to sleep. Ethan then prepares his blanket as a decoy and sneaks off. Futterman who has been following them is fooled by what he sees and shoots the empty blanket. Ethan then kills Futterman and explains to an outraged Marty that he knew all along that they were being followed and that stoking the fire was part of his scheme to entrap whomever was following them.

At this level, the scene draws simple distinctions between how much the characters within the scene know: neither Marty nor Futterman have the knowledge Ethan does and, in Futterman's case, his error of "seeing is believing" leads to his death. He literally does not know what he sees. Even though he suspects it, Marty does not know they are being followed nor does he know why Ethan builds up the fire and his ignorance, as the scene makes comically clear, could have led to his death. When Marty, who has been lying by the fire as bait, asks Ethan what would have happened to him if Ethan had missed Futterman, Ethan replies that the thought never occurred to him.

After killing Futterman in self-defense, Ethan takes the coins from the man's body that he had earlier used to pay for information concerning Debbie's whereabouts. Later in the film, we learn that Marty and Ethan are now wanted for murdering and robbing Futterman and his men. Indeed, from the perspective of the law, the crime scene supplies clear evidence and motive: Futterman was murdered as part of a robbery attempt. The missing gold coins are the key. Yet we, the spectators of the scene, know that this, however logical, is a false account. We have seen with our own eyes an event that stands in stark opposition to an account of it constructed by those that were not present.

The deleted scene with the cavalry general relates to this epistemological issue: How do we know what has happened at events at which we were not present? The general is being interviewed by eastern newspaper correspondents. He paints a dramatic picture of men outnumbered four to one courageously attacking a Cheyenne camp. Ethan interrupts, "That camp you hit was Nawyecka Comanch . . . Chief Scar's bunch." When Ethan inquires about his niece, the general informs him that the "hostiles" murdered four girls. Ethan cynically asks whether the general is sure they weren't killed by the cavalry, whom he accuses of killing "squaws" rather than engaging in battle with men.[3]

The presence of the reporters indicates how the version of the story the general narrates will circulate as the official version of what happened. Yet, once again, something we as spectators of the film have seen contradicts this account. We have seen Marty and Ethan ride into the decimated camp where they find the bodies of women and children, one of whom is Look. Much like we "know" what happened to Futterman, we "know" what happened to the Indians and, had Ford left this scene in the film, the spectator would have once again been aware of the epistemological confusion of characters within the film—and how a sordid history becomes a glorious myth.

Indeed, the only way to understand the complex narrational structure of a major sequence in the film including Marty's inadvertent marriage to Look is within this epistemological framework. The sequence in question involves Charlie McCorry who delivers a letter to the Jorgensens. Ford intercuts the scene of Laurie reading the letter to her mother, father, and Charlie with the scenes of Marty and Ethan we are hearing about—that is, we have Laurie's voice-over narration of scenes we the audience see as they occurred. This structure is further complicated by various responses to the letter offered by Laurie and her listeners and by the fact that, at crucial times, it is Marty's voice-over narration that accompanies the scenes of his and Ethan's actions.

There are two sets of epistemological issues raised in the sequence: one involves Marty's attempts to understand the events he describes and the other involves the attempts of those reading or hearing Marty's letter to interpret what Marty is describing. Within the first category, we see Marty's surprise and confusion when Look follows him away from the

The Limits of Knowledge in and of *The Searchers*

Indian camp and Ethan explains to Marty that he has unknowingly traded for a wife; Marty's later questioning as to why Look has disappeared; and finally Marty's confusion and effort to understand Ethan's senseless slaughter of a number of buffalo in a herd they encounter. Marty acknowledges his confusions by saying such things as, "Something happened that I ain't got straight in my own mind yet."

Some of his confusions are quickly cleared up for him such as when Ethan explains why Look is following them and when he explains that he has killed the buffalo so that the Indians can't eat them. Marty's questioning Look's disappearance is, however, more complicated. When her absence is first discovered along with an arrow formed of rocks on the ground, Marty remarks, "Maybe she left other signs to follow, but we'll never know 'cause it snowed that day and all the next week." Finally, when Look is found dead in the Indian village, he concludes, "Whether she'd come to warn 'em or maybe find Debbie for me, there's no way of knowin'." Here neither Ethan nor anyone else can ever help Marty as he repeatedly emphasizes the limits of his knowledge.

If Marty is first temporarily and then permanently confused by the events he narrates, the letter readers are even more confused. They each respond to news of his "marriage" in a different manner, before they understand that Marty had no knowledge of what he was doing. In other words, Marty did not know what he was doing when he got married, and the letter readers do not know that he didn't know when they react to the surprising news. Then, when he reveals that he married a "squaw," Laurie, who reads the letter, gets so upset to have lost Marty to an Indian rather than a white woman, that she throws the letter in the fire. After it has been retrieved, she continues to read.

Marty's narrational style within his letter is a comic commentary within the film on the film's narrational style. Out of sheer ineptness, Marty constructs a plot that confuses his readers as to what has occurred, as well as to how and why it has occurred. He could, for example, have made clear at the beginning of his account that he inadvertently married an Indian woman because of his ignorance of Indian customs while engaged in a trade. Ford similarly constructs a plot in *The Searchers* which confuses us, the spectators of the film. Marty does so unwittingly, but Ford does so with great skill. One of the most remarkable aspects of *The Searchers* is that the film's audience is put into a position like that of the characters in the film—the limits of our knowledge are tested to the extreme and when it's all said and done, there is much that we do not know. The epistemological theme of the film, in other words, doubles back on the audience in a complex and unusual manner for a 1956 Western or, for that matter, any classical Hollywood film.

Before examining this aspect of the film, however, one other dimension of the letter-reading scene warrants attention—its gender structure. The song heard over the opening credits in the film speaks exclusively of men, both in the questions it asks of their behavior and the description it gives of their actions—men must search their whole life through. While being unusual in some regards, a conventional aspect of the film's narrative structure involves the place of men and women within it: men are active and women passive. Men search and women wait at home. Martha at the beginning of the film and Mrs. Jorgensen and Laurie throughout the film are all confined to the home and to waiting to see what will happen. Ethan and Marty, on the other hand, go where they want when they want. Indeed, after Martha's death Mrs. Jorgensen ineffectively attempts to stop Ethan from going on his search and, when the searchers temporarily return to the Jorgensen homestead, Laurie similarly ineffectively attempts to block Marty's resumption of the search. The women not only do not participate in the search but also cannot even stop the men from undertaking it.

The only men tied primarily to the home are Aaron Edwards and Mr. Jorgensen and neither one represents a masculine ideal—Aaron is represented as a failed man who cannot satisfy his wife, cannot see what is going on between his brother and wife, and cannot adequately defend his family from Indian attack. Mr. Jorgensen is represented as comic, elderly and past the peak of manhood. Though he accompanies the men at the beginning, he becomes hysterical when they discover they have been tricked and that his family is in danger. At the end, he waits at home when the others go off to fight Scar.[4]

Within their comparatively passive place in the narrative structure, the women are allowed a certain limited active role. Laurie, for example, has to choose between two rivals for her affections. This is, of course, a highly conventional position for a female character, her field of action being restricted to a romantic choice between two men—precisely what happens to the young woman who chooses between cavalry officers who vie for her affections in Ford's *She Wore a Yellow Ribbon* (1949). The fight that takes place between Charlie and Marty after Charlie's planned marriage to Laurie is interrupted further underscores the limited, passive nature of such a position for the women in *The Searchers*. The men will settle who

The Limits of Knowledge in and of *The Searchers*

gets her via active fighting while the women are relegated to the role of onlookers. Indeed, this latter point is further highlighted when Ethan ineffectively attempts to block the view of the fight from Mrs. Jorgensen by keeping her in the house behind closed doors. She joins the other women, however, who have rushed to the window to watch: They may not be active in controlling this form of masculine behavior but they relish being active onlookers.

In addition to the domestic and romantic spheres, women in *The Searchers* are also, however, associated with reading and writing. Much is made of Mr. Jorgensen's donning of his glasses while Laurie reads the letter because he appears to be illiterate. Twice he proudly boasts of his wife in such words as, "She was a school teacher, by-golly." Laurie is the one who reads the letter and while this certainly makes sense since it is addressed to her, her doing so has further ramifications. Her sphere of knowledge, like her mother's is that of the teacher—reading and writing. Marty's letter is not only awkwardly written but, as Laurie complains in near disbelief, he doesn't even know how to spell her name. Marty can only haltingly and partially read and understand Ethan's will. The men, or more accurately the truly masculine men, move through a world of direct experience and involvement. They do not read about things; they witness them and participate in them.

Once again, the deleted scene that Eckstein brings attention to has an interesting place in relation to these issues. The script specifically identifies the correspondent as being from the East. This eastern reporter who "knows" nothing about the West is, of course, part of the world of reading and writing, a world which if not feminine is, implicitly, less masculine than that of the western hero. And also a world that creates false "knowledge" wherein, like those confused by Marty's account of his marriage, the reading public will be fooled by the reporter's account of the general and the cavalry.

All in all, the world of *The Searchers* is a world in which what people can know is highly qualified and one in which what they think they know is frequently false. Which brings us to the spectator of the film.

Like those gathered around as Laurie reads her letter, the spectators of the film hear about events at which they were not present. This, of course, is not unusual in classical cinema. In *The Searchers*, however, much of what we hear about (and, as we shall see later, much of what we learn about visually) raises questions that the film never answers. What, for example, has Ethan been doing since the end of the Civil War? His brother notes with puzzling emphasis that the gold coins Ethan produces upon his arrival are freshly minted and we also learn that Ethan may have been a bank robber after the war. In most films that might be enough to make us conclude that he is guilty. Even though these things are strongly suggested in the dialogue, we cannot be sure of their validity precisely because if we did arrive at such a conclusion, we would be like those in the diegesis of the film who are convinced Ethan murdered Futterman for the purposes of robbing him. Ethan, as the Reverend Clayton says, fits "a lot of descriptions"—and we are never certain which ones are accurate.

Much about Ethan we learn solely from visual information resulting from Ford's careful shot compositions and his near dazzling use of visual motifs. First and foremost, we learn about an illicit relationship between Ethan and Martha. This is first indicated as Ethan and Martha exchange a long, intense look accompanied by ominous music when Ethan arrives at the beginning of the film. Once inside the home, she takes Ethan's coat into her bedroom and we see Ethan's lingering stare at her. Later, Ethan sits next to her at the dinner table and in many two-shots, they look like husband and wife while Aaron sits isolated at the other end of the table. After dinner, the reality of an illicit relationship between the two becomes more overt when Aaron says he never could understand why Ethan stayed around as long as he did before the war. Unobserved by Aaron, Ethan and Martha exchange charged glances and Martha looks terrified that her husband will discover the truth. Finally, Reverend Captain Clayton inadvertently discovers the truth when he glances into the bedroom of the Edwards home and sees Martha lovingly stroking Ethan's coat. Deeply troubled, he looks away as Martha comes out of the bedroom and gives the coat to Ethan. They stand behind Clayton and as they engage in their intense but silent exchange, he continues to drink his coffee and eat his doughnut, pretending to be unaware of what transpires behind him.

But what exactly *is* the truth that Clayton discovers and that Martha and Ethan fear Aaron might discover? Did Ethan and Martha have an affair? If they did, did it occur before or after Martha's marriage to Ethan's brother? Or are their feelings for each other part of an unfulfilled, unconsummated relationship?[5] Indeed, is it possible that Ethan is the father of one of the Edwards children? We learn the answers to none of these questions and while the latter might seem far-fetched, it is precisely because of the impossibility of knowing so many other things in the film, combined with the ambiguous nature of the knowledge we do have of certain actions,

The Limits of Knowledge in and of *The Searchers*

events and character motivations, that makes it even plausible to raise such a question.

Over the years that I have taught this film some of my students have interpreted Ethan as Debbie's father and others have interpreted him as Marty's father. Those believing the former offer as evidence Ethan's irrational commitment to the search and those believing the latter offer as evidence the manner in which Ethan recognizes Marty's mother's scalp when it is displayed with many others by Scar. Others have concluded that Ethan murdered Lucy on the basis of his strange behavior after he reports he has found her body. The searchers split up; Brad and Marty go off together and Ethan goes alone. When he reappears, he is agitated and behaves bizarrely, repeatedly stabbing his knife in the dirt as if he were cleaning it. When questioned, he explains to Marty and Brad that he found Lucy's body and buried it. Yet, it is clearly possible that Ethan found her alive and killed her himself before burying her. That is not only consistent with his racist abhorrence of sexual relations between Indian males and white females but also with the distracted manner in which he plunges his knife into the dirt—he could be cleaning Lucy's blood from it.

Alternative explanations, of course, exist for any of these speculations. Ethan could be stabbing his knife in the ground as a reenactment of the traumatic act of burying Lucy and he might be lying about recognizing Marty's mother's scalp as a ploy to convince Marty not to enter Scar's camp.

When students first offered these various readings of the film, I dismissed them as far-fetched. It has become clear to me, however, that something else is happening here. The fact that such extreme formulations about Ethan's behavior occurs to so many spectators of the film only makes sense within the epistemological framework I have described. The film pulls the rug out from so many epistemological certainties of both the characters within it and the spectators of it that it almost encourages this kind of speculation. Most classical Hollywood films are so clear about everything that there is no room for, or at least no motivation to engage in, such speculation. We know what we need to know about what the characters do and why they do it. Even though Ethan is the main character in this film, the fact remains that there are many things we do not know about him or his motivations. Ethan does indeed fit a lot of descriptions and while a composite character sketch of him as a bank-robbing, murdering, incestuous man who has fathered two illegitimate children is absurd, any one or even combination of those things is certainly possible, indeed probable.

It is, of course, the concluding action of the film that seems most puzzling to many spectators. Why is Ethan maniacally driven to find Debbie and kill her and why, when he has the opportunity, does he suddenly change his mind and return her home safely? There is an answer, of sorts, to this question but it points to the related issues of how much that is central in the film is never spoken about or even hinted at in the dialogue and how the visual information that cues our formulation of an answer to those central questions is inherently ambiguous—we simply do not see enough to know.

Visual clues to the romantic involvement between Ethan and Martha certainly enable one to hypothesize a motivation for Ethan's obsessive commitment to the search: His love for his sister-in-law poses a threat to the sanctity of the family. Scar's physical destruction of the family enacts the ruin lurking within Ethan. He then transfers guilt from within himself onto the racial "Other." If this, as Joseph McBride and Michael Wilmington among others have asserted, helps explain the motive for the search, an astonishing interweaving of two visual motifs helps explain the resolution of it: one involves doorways and the other a lifting gesture.

The doorway motif with its elaborate use of both outer and inner doorways as well as tepee openings and mouths of caves is elaborately complex. Throughout the film Ethan is established as an outsider to the homes and inner spaces represented by the doorways through which he is frequently framed and into which he frequently gazes. We first see him after we have seen Martha framed standing in the doorway of the Edwards home, gazing out at him as he approaches. After dinner on the night he arrives home, he sits on the front porch and peers through the outer doorway as Aaron closes the inner bedroom door. Upon returning to the Edwards homestead after the Indian attack, we see him framed through a doorway and then kneeling by it, realizing that her violated body lies within. When he similarly discovers Look's body, he stands framed through the opening of a tepee, gazing in at her. At the end of the film, a shot through the doorway shows everyone enter the Jorgensen home except Ethan, who approaches, turns, and walks away as the door closes on him.

Ethan's quest for Debbie takes him into the Native American culture where doorways are replaced by tepee openings and into a state of nature removed from any culture, represented by cave openings. When at the end of the film he catches up with Debbie, this series of motifs is invoked when Ford cuts to a shot of Ethan pursuing Debbie framed by the mouth of a cave.

The Limits of Knowledge in and of *The Searchers*

Martha: The first opening doorway shot.

The shot from within the cave is only briefly held and Ford cuts back to an exterior shot as Ethan dismounts and approaches Debbie who cowers by the cave.

He approaches her but, instead of killing her, he lifts her high in the air, then cradles her in his arms and says, "Let's go home, Debbie." The shot framing the action from within the cave is motivated entirely by the visual motif—the characters never enter it. Rather than cutting on action and reaction by simply showing Ethan gain on Debbie and her frightened response, in other words, Ford foregrounds the primary function here of the motif. When the action continues with the camera outside the cave, another visual motif is emphasized when Ethan lifts Debbie above his head and holds her in that position momentarily before cradling her in his arms. The lifting action seems to serve no practical purpose and indeed when viewed entirely with the action of picking her up and cradling her in his arms is downright illogical.

As with the shot viewing the action through the mouth of the cave, the manner in which Ethan lifts Debbie is entirely motivated by the visual rhyme of the composition: earlier we saw him similarly lift Debbie as a

Doorway shot: Ethan sees raped and dead Martha.

Doorway shot: Ethan sees dead Look.

Doorway shot through cave: Ethan pursuing fearful Debbie

Ethan lifting Debbie: "Let's go home, Debbie."

Ethan lifting Debbie as a child.

little girl when he entered his brother's home after years of absence. Much like the shot of the cave recalls the previous shot through the mouth of a cave when Ethan and Marty seek shelter from Indian attack, the lifting gesture recalls the previous occurrence. That much is clear. But how do these visual motifs help us know what motivates Ethan's actions?

I have always believed that the combination of the motifs explains Ethan's actions, since the shot of the cave is a reminder of his atavistic regression during the five-year search. In this state of nature, Ethan and Marty are far removed from all cultural laws and constraints. Earlier, when they seek shelter in a cave, Ethan speaks with inhuman coldness to Marty about how he has cut Debbie, his niece, out of his will. He no longer even considers her a person, at least not a white person, and to Ethan the two are synonymous. Marty responds to this outrage by losing all control and threatening Ethan with a knife while he wishes him dead. These are men who, as they journey through the wilderness and come into contact with another culture, are becoming increasingly barbaric. When they return again to the Jorgensens' home and hear a party, Marty wonders whether it is for them. Ethan bitterly replies, "That'll be the day," indicating he knows

The Limits of Knowledge in and of *The Searchers*

Doorway shot through cave: Ethan and Marty fleeing the Comanches

they have become unwelcome pariahs due to their antisocial behavior. The shot through the mouth of the cave at the end of the film is a reminder of that barbarism, the logical conclusion of which would be Ethan's killing Debbie.

Clearly, the cave shot can be read in other ways. The previous shot through the mouth of the cave showed Ethan and Marty fleeing toward it, seeking safety from the attacking "savages." In the later shot, Debbie, who may be seeking shelter in the cave, is in the position Ethan was in and Ethan is now in the position of the deadly "savage," which is underscored by the fact that we have just seen him scalping Scar. This reading places emphasis not on the brutal behavior Ethan and Marty engage in within the safety of the cave but, rather, on the reversal of Ethan's position within the two shots of him framed through the cave openings: in one he seeks shelter from savage attack and in the other he savagely attacks one who seeks shelter. Both of these readings, however, are closely related in that the cave shot is a reminder of Ethan's barbaric behavior.

The shot of Ethan lifting Debbie high in the air recalls neither savagery nor an atavistic removal from all cultural laws and constraints but, rather, the opposite—an act of love within the sanctity of his brother's home directly in front of the hearth that symbolizes the center of that sacred unit. The images are at opposite extremes and together they imply that while, on the one hand, Ethan's journey has been one of increasing depravity, on the other hand, he recalls at the last minute his earlier civilized, culturally sanctioned behavior. The gap between the two is too extreme, even for Ethan, and he cannot fulfill his murderous rage.

While I still believe the validity of this account, it now seems important to me to complicate it in at least three ways. I mentioned that the shot of the cave via its visual rhyme with a previous cave shot and various doorway shots triggers important associations. But an obvious question arises: for *whom* does the shot trigger these associations? A certain logic would dictate that for what we see in the shot to have any explanatory force for Ethan's behavior, he would also have to see it. But, of course, he does not. He not only never enters the cave and looks out but, when Ford cuts to the shot through the mouth of the cave, there is no indication that Ethan is even aware that there is a cave. His attention is fully devoted to pursuing Debbie. Thus, it would seem, that the shot only triggers associations for the spectator of the film. But if this so, how can it help explain a change in character behavior? We in other words seem to be aware of Ethan's atavistic regression but there is no evidence that *he* is.

Although I never commented on it, perhaps for fear that it weakened my argument, I have always been struck by the incongruity of the fact that Ethan has decided not to kill Debbie *before* he dismounts and approaches her. The proof is that he speaks her name in a kindly, reassuring fashion, not a threatening, hateful one, while still on his horse. Thus, he not only never sees out of the cave, nor enters it nor even acknowledges he is aware of its existence, but, also, he has already decided to return Debbie home *before* he lifts her high in the air. Thus, how can the lifting gesture trigger an association that explains something that has already occurred? Ethan has, in other words, already changed his mind before he lifts Debbie. The gesture is a *result* of his decision not to kill her, not the *cause* of his decision not to do so. It is worth adding, however, that this change is all the more mysterious in that it takes place very quickly and at the last moment. Before Marty goes into Scar's camp, Ethan tells him that he is counting on the fact that the Indians will kill Debbie during the Ranger attack. Furthermore, when he begins his final pursuit of her after scalping Scar, he appears to be in a murderous rage; the change, for whatever reason, occurs during that brief pursuit.

The Limits of Knowledge in and of *The Searchers*

Nevertheless the cave shot and the lifting gesture can still be read as ways of, if not explaining what *causes* Ethan's behavior, at least *understanding* it. If Ethan, while still intent on killing Debbie, entered the cave and then as he prepared to kill her had a memory triggered when he lifted her up, we could say that the cave setting and the lifting gesture caused him to change his mind and, thus, account for his surprising behavior. Instead, however, the spectator of the film constructs an account of Ethan's already changed behavior. While the cave shot seems solely for the spectator, the lifting gesture can be read as cathartic for Ethan; that is, instead of the lifting gesture triggering anything that changes Ethan's intentions of killing Debbie, it simply enables Ethan to enact what he has already remembered doing in the past. It is, in a sense, a cleansing gesture rather than one that changes his intended actions. That we see him do it by a cave after witnessing the events through the mouth of the cave enables us to formulate a connection between the two.

Even if we accept something like the reading above as a way of understanding Ethan's behavior, how precise is it? Put another way, can these purely visual clues have the specificity that would come from spoken explanations? Even if we should take the cave shot and the lifting gesture seriously as having explanatory force for comprehending Ethan's behavior, the explanation remains somewhat vague. Different spectators, in other words, who see these motifs will, nevertheless, read them differently than I have. For some, the cave and such related images as the opening shot and the shot of Ethan framed through the doorway behind which he knows Martha's dead body lies might be primarily a Freudian vaginal or womb image. These openings are all so darkly lit that the reminder of the screen is black. In a film so obsessed with rape and the home such a reading takes on added significance. These images, in other words, are open to quite a range of interpretation, as even my first two readings of the cave shot indicate. It would be entirely different if Ethan explained to someone in a final scene, "I couldn't kill her because when I lifted her up by that cave and remembered the way I had lovingly lifted her years earlier in her home, I realized how barbaric I was." While such a thing may seem preposterous in this movie, it is in fact commonplace in classical Hollywood cinema to have a character explain his or her own thoughts, emotions, motivations, and actions in just such a manner (which was the case in the script of *The Searchers*) or to have another character (a doctor, a close friend, a detective, etc.) do so.

Peter Lehman

It is instructive in this regard to briefly compare the ending of *The Searchers* with that of *Citizen Kane* (1941) and *Psycho* (1960). Critics have long argued about the endings of both of these highly praised films. For my purposes, what is particularly helpful about them is that they employ opposite strategies in explaining the actions of their central characters: *Citizen Kane* uses a purely visual image and *Psycho* has a psychiatrist offer a purely verbal account. The visual image to which I refer in *Citizen Kane* is, of course, the sled with the word "Rosebud" written on it, burning in the incinerator. Although none of the characters in the film see it, the spectators of the film do. Furthermore, the entire narrative of the film is motivated by a reporter's efforts to learn what "Rosebud," Kane's dying word, means. When we find out that his childhood sled was called Rosebud we have an explanation: this wealthy, powerful, unhappy man dies thinking back to the lost pleasures of his simple childhood. Some critics have always rejected this explanation as being inadequate and too simple. Nevertheless, the film clearly offers it.

Similarly, at the end of *Psycho* a psychiatrist explains to someone in the film and to the audience of the film both what a transvestite is and why Norman Bates had a psychological need to become his mother after killing her and his stepfather after discovering them having sexual intercourse years earlier. Once again, some critics have dismissed the account as inadequate and too simple. But as with *Citizen Kane,* it leaves the spectator of the film with a clear-cut, plausible explanation of what have been baffling events. The explanations may border on parody within the classical Hollywood cinema's need for closure and clarity, but nevertheless the films offer them.

Although entirely visual and available only to the spectator of the film rather than characters in the film, the ending of *The Searchers* is much more complex than that of *Citizen Kane.* First, *Citizen Kane* places the Rosebud image prominently in the frame where no one can miss it. Second, the image is extremely specific and concrete. In *The Searchers,* by contrast, the multiple images are complex and anything but obvious (over the years many students have told me that they totally missed both the rhymes of the cave shot and the lifting gesture) and, even if they are seen by the spectator, the motifs lack concrete meaning and specificity. The images are provocative and suggestive, not precise.

The Searchers also lacks any dialogue comparable to that in *Psycho* which could offer us any possible explanation for why Ethan behaves as he does. Thus, we do not even hear a hypothesis, paradoxical or otherwise, to

The Limits of Knowledge in and of *The Searchers*

help us understand this enigmatic character. Perhaps predictably, the script for the film includes dialogue in this scene where Ethan tells Debbie after lowering his gun and deciding not to shoot her, "You sure favor your mother."[6] By cutting that dialogue, whether out of a trust in the visual image or out of a desire to mystify the events or even because he did not think such a simple explanation adequate or even correct, Ford ensured the film's profound ambiguity. Indeed, the notion that Ethan couldn't kill Debbie because she reminded him of his beloved Martha does not fit with the lifting gesture, which recalls not Martha, but Debbie as a little girl. Ethan cannot kill her, the gesture implies, because of remembering something he did with *her* in her home as a little girl. (Perhaps also predictably, the script contains neither the lifting gesture nor the cave shot that are so central in the film.)

The only thing to suggest that Ethan is thinking of Martha in the film is the "Lorena" theme that Eckstein discusses in his introduction and that Kalinak also refers to elsewhere in this volume. Although as Eckstein points out, the theme has been called "Martha's theme" by Ford scholars, such use of a musical motif is just as ambiguous as the visual motifs in the scene. As I have indicated, Martha is strongly associated with the home, the doorway of which she stands in during the opening shot of the film when we first hear the music. Ethan's feelings for her are, in other words, intertwined with the home and family that he wants but can never have. Because of the theme's association with home and family, we hear it when the searchers return to the Jorgensen home with Debbie at the end of the film. Hearing the musical theme associated with Martha is not equivalent to hearing Ethan tell Debbie she reminds him of Martha; it (like the images of the cave and the lifting gesture) is more ambiguous than any such dialogue. *The Searchers* is such an unusual film that Frank Nugent, its writer, may have had a more specific and somewhat different understanding of Ethan's actions than Ford had.

A brief consideration of two other Ford films helps brings this unique aspect of *The Searchers* into focus. Ford dealt with similar epistemological issues throughout his career. *Fort Apache* (1948), for example, contains a scene much like the scene Ford cut from *The Searchers*. A cavalry officer (played by John Wayne), commenting on a painting depicting his predecessor Colonel Thursday, answers a question from a reporter by describing Thursday's death as having been gallant and honorable. Although the reporter, as we have heard, will spread an heroic account of what happened around the country, we the audience have seen the actual events; and we know that though Wayne's words bear some truth (Colonel Thursday did die courageously), they also give a fundamentally false impression of what had happened. The film has previously made crystal clear to us Colonel Thursday's arrogant mistakes and the dark motives for which he leads his men to their doom. Thursday comes to his isolated western outpost envisioning a glorious career for himself as an Indian fighter, and he maniacally pursues that self-serving goal. Furthermore, part of his failure as an officer comes from his lack of knowledge of and contempt for the Native American culture he encounters and the strange environment in which he finds himself. He disastrously misreads both his Indian enemy (to whom he in fact acts treacherously) and his environment. Yet, while we the audience possesses full knowledge of what has happened and why, we watch as John Wayne as Thursday's successor praise a man he had despised, allowing the reporter to spread the heroic legend: the reporter and, presumably his readers, will all be fooled.

Similarly, *The Man Who Shot Liberty Valance* deals with the question of who shot the title character. Everyone believes that Ransom Stoddard shot the outlaw Liberty Valance in a fair fight. Stoddard himself not only believes it but has built a successful political career on it. It thus comes as a shock both to him and the audience when we learn that Stoddard did not kill Liberty Valance. A flashback shows us that Tom Doniphon (played by John Wayne), hidden in a dark alley, fired the fatal shot with his rifle. Once again, a reporter is involved. Unlike the reporters in *Fort Apache* and the deleted scene in *The Searchers,* however, this reporter does learn the truth, yet he decides not to print it. In an oft-quoted line he says, "When the legend becomes fact, print the legend." The difference among the three films is thus minimized by the fact that while (unlike the two earlier films) in this one the reporter actually does get to know the truth, he nevertheless contributes instead to the legend: he tears up the story of what really happened; and falsehood will therefore continue to be accepted as truth by the general public. For them, Stoddard, not Doniphon, shot Liberty Valance; and Stoddard's political career continues unharmed by what has been revealed.

But if *The Man Who Shot Liberty Valance* deals with questions of knowledge and ignorance, once again (as in *Fort Apache*) those questions are limited in the film to the characters, not the spectator. Even though, remarkably, Stoddard himself doesn't know the truth until it is revealed to him years later, when it *is* revealed both he and the spectators of the film know exactly what happened and why. The flashback we see within the

The Limits of Knowledge in and of *The Searchers*

flashback has full explanatory force for us. We are even allowed to fully understand Doniphon's *motives* for killing Valance; he sees that Hallie, the woman he plans to marry, has fallen in love with Stoddard and he knows that Stoddard is no match for Valance in a fast-draw contest. In a self-sacrificing act, he kills Valance so that Stoddard can marry Hallie. Doniphon is a hero—but a hero fated to remain unknown to the general public in the film, because the reporter decides to keep his mouth shut. But Doniphon's secret act *is* at least known to the film's audience, the spectators in the movie theater—to whom in fact *everything* becomes known.

We can now see how dramatically different the audience's situation is in *The Searchers*. The distinction between *The Searchers*, on the one hand, and *Fort Apache* and *The Man Who Shot Liberty Valance*, on the other, is quite simply that only in *The Searchers* does the theme of the nature and limits of knowledge double back onto the spectator in the movie theater. It is this formal strategy that makes *The Searchers* such a unique and complex film.

A moment does occur in *The Searchers* during which for a fleeting instant spectators may think things are about to change and where, in the manner typical of the classical Hollywood cinema, they are about to hear the truth spoken in the dialogue. It is typical of this film, however, that any such hopes are quickly dashed. During their first return to the Jorgensen ranch, Ethan begins to confide some fact of crucial importance, telling Marty, "Marty, there's something I want you to know." But Marty, misunderstanding Ethan's tone and message, responds angrily: "Yeah, I know what you want me to know . . . so shut your mouth." And Ethan does. We never learn what this crucial fact was or even who it was about (that Ethan has paternal feelings for Marty? that he is in fact Marty's father? something about Debbie, or Martha?)—there's just no way of knowing. In a film where so much of Ethan's dark past and interior motives are only hinted at, and never spoken about directly, it is remarkable that, at the moment that he offers to do so, he is told to shut up! It is almost as if Ford teases the spectator, knowing precisely what he or she wants to know and expects to know—but withholds it.

Like Ethan Edwards its main character, *The Searchers* therefore turns out to be a film that "fits a lot of descriptions." Like Marty, we can conclude there is no way of ever knowing which of them truly fits. What strikes me most about *The Searchers* nearly half a century after its release is not how much we know about the film but, once again in Marty's words, how much we'll never know. The film itself is both like the arrow Look leaves on the ground (a clear sign to follow) and like the snowy weather that covers any other possible signs Ford might have left. If Ethan is condemned to wander forever, the thoughtful spectator is condemned to wonder forever.

In a well-known exchange, Peter Bogdanovich asked Ford whether there was a past romantic relationship between Ethan and Martha. Predictably, Ford's answer is outrageous and designed to cut off further discussion. "Well, I thought it was pretty obvious," he begins—and then adds, "You couldn't hit it on the nose."[7] Virtually nothing I am aware of in the history of American cinema is less obvious than that relationship. Within industry jargon, Ford simply means that a past romantic relationship between Ethan and Martha is obvious (which it isn't), and he doesn't want to be heavy-handed. But the phrase "You couldn't hit it on the nose" reverberates further within this context. Perhaps unintentionally, Ford implies he couldn't hit it on the nose because an explicit adulterous relationship with incestuous overtones would upset the audience and John Wayne fans, and also that such explicitness would rob the film of the ambiguity he desired.

With statements like the above, it seems as if Ford were saying to us as well as to Bogdanovich what Ethan says during the film: "What d'ya want me to do . . . draw you a picture, spell it out? Don't ever ask me, long as you live, don't ever ask me more." As critics and historians, we will of course continue to ask questions of this film. Like the characters in it, however, there is much we can never know. And most unusually, this is a film that makes clear to us the limits of our knowledge of it. We will never be able to fully draw a picture of it nor fully spell it out. We'll never be able to hit it on the nose.

NOTES

This essay draws on, revises, and adds to aspects of *The Searchers* that I have discussed in a number of previous publications. I have minimized repeating any points that are not in some manner reformulated here. Readers interested in a much more detailed account of those aspects of the film are referred to those publications. I initially analyzed *The Searchers* in a chapter of "John Ford and the Auteur Theory" (Ph.D. diss., University of Wisconsin, 1978), a version of which was published in Luhr and Lehman, *Authorship and Narrative*. It includes discussion of epistemological issues and has a detailed account of the letter-reading sequence as well as an illustrated analysis of the film's visual motifs, including the doorways and Ethan's lifting of Debbie. The book also includes chapters from my dissertation devoted to *The Man Who Shot Liberty*

The Limits of Knowledge in and of *The Searchers*

Valance and to a career overview of Ford's work. My doctoral dissertation also includes a chapter on *Fort Apache*. All of these sources take up issues related to the theme of knowledge in Ford's films. For a close examination of questioned names in *The Searchers* as well as a discussion of race and gender issues, see my essay "Texas 1868/America 1956," 387–415. For an insightful discussion of *The Searchers* that has influenced several of my points, see Joseph McBride and Michael Wilmington, *John Ford*.

1. Roland Barthes, *S/Z*, trans. Richard Miller (New York: Hill and Wang, 1974).
2. Nugent, "The Searchers."
3. Ibid.
4. Even traditional masculinity is, however, somewhat undermined in this film. The active searchers fail in many of their goals. Much like Mrs. Jorgensen cannot stop Ethan from going on the search and Laurie cannot stop Marty from returning to it, Marty cannot stop Ethan from pursuing Debbie when he throws himself at Ethan's horse. At the end of the film, Ethan finds Scar and Debbie again only when Mose, an old "fool," reveals where the tribe is camped. After five years of actively searching the entire territory, now Scar has come to Ethan. Ethan, however, fails to kill Scar and ends up scalping a dead man. From this perspective, he even fails to kill Debbie. Ethan accomplishes virtually nothing he sets out to do in this film. Much like he lost Martha years earlier to Aaron, Ethan is a character beset by loss and failure.
5. In his introductory essay to this volume, Eckstein suggests that since Martha's theme is an orchestral version of the nineteenth-century song "Lorena," it indicates that the affair was never consummated. Eckstein's identification of the song makes an important contribution to our understanding of music in *The Searchers* but I do not believe it eliminates the ambiguity surrounding Ethan's and Martha's past relationship. Such an interpretation is too literal an application of the song's lyrics that are never even heard in the film. Even when song lyrics are heard in films they seldom correlate in precise ways to character relationships or plot developments. "Lorena" is about a woman whose "duty, stern and pressing" breaks her romantic "tie" with the male narrator of the song. Even if Ethan and Martha had consummated their relationship, these lyrics would still apply in spirit for Martha has broken whatever tie she had with Ethan and chosen Aaron. I would argue that Ford's use of the song contains precisely the same kind of ambiguity that the visuals do and that any meaning it offers is open to a range of interpretation—it is suggestive without being explicit.
6. Nugent, "The Searchers."
7. Bogdanovich, *John Ford*, 93.

"That Don't Make You Kin!":
Borderlands History and Culture in *The Searchers*

James F. Brooks

John Ford's film *The Searchers* (1956) is a singular work of fictional art. As fictional art, however, its relationship to history is highly problematic, and historians (as opposed to film scholars) should approach it cautiously. Nevertheless, in this essay I intend as a historian to demonstrate how *The Searchers* has much to offer on important issues of race, gender, culture, and (especially) kinship as they actually existed in the historical and culturally complex Southwest borderlands of North America—and still do exist, in a broader sense, throughout the present United States.

As to the latter point: Annette Kolodny has observed that captivity narratives and their modern filmic treatments have a particular resonance with students in her courses on American literature, because students confront in these texts their own insecurities, discomfort and fascination with racially mixed and ethnically diverse classroom environments. The historical captivity narratives, whose particular subject is "the trauma of losing a secure cultural identity" while simultaneously gaining access to cultures once exotic and foreign, "feel very familiar to those who are themselves trying to communicate across the barriers of custom, tradition, religion, and language."[1] I find this similarly to be true in the course I regularly teach titled "The American West in History and Imagination." The course attempts to get students to think about "history as social process" vs. "history as narrative production" in a topic area to which they bring a good deal of cultural presupposition.[2] The general thrust of my teaching is to unsettle the triumphalist notion of a westward marching, democratizing Anglo American nation (prevalent in American thinking since Frederick

Jackson Turner more than a century ago).[3] Instead, an alternate framework of the West is suggested, a framework in which the West is a cultural borderland where Native American, Spanish, Mexican, African, Asian, and Anglo-American peoples collided in continual contests, accommodations, and confusions over cultural and political power.

Viewing John Ford's *The Searchers* is a key moment in this effort. The film continually employs notions of "kin" and "anti-kin" to comment on Ethan Edwards's racial and sexual obsessions. As Brian Henderson has persuasively argued, the film exposes in indirect fashion Americans' fears of black-white miscegenation in the 1950s, with Native Americans substituted for African Americans. Though reference to Levi-Straussian kinship theory, Henderson even addresses the tensions between the Ethan Edwards–Martin Pauley adoption motif and that of Debbie Edwards's assimilation into her captor Scar's Comanche family.[4] But I extend Henderson's insights to include a detailed treatment of the ways in which the concepts of kin and anti-kin can be used to examine the differences between Anglo-Texan society and Native American society in the Southwest, especially their different notions of race, gender, human bondage (a practice they shared)—and family. Such a focus highlights important cultural conflicts along American intercultural frontiers, and suggests some new hidden narratives within *The Searchers* itself. Kinship and its antithesis appear to lie at the crux of the painful and immutable obsessions fueling this extraordinary film, just as notions of kinship and its antithesis also underlie much of the broader ethnoracial history of our country.

Kinship Dilemmas in *The Searchers*

Early in Ethan Edwards's and Martin Pauley's long quest to recover Debbie from Comanche captivity, the two men confront one of the central dilemmas that will remain unresolved throughout the course of the film. This is the relative power of blood descent vs. affinal ties and fictive kinship in the creation of family boundaries and responsibilities. Readying for sleep in the Jorgensen family's bunkhouse, Ethan—who now as before has no home of his own—declares that he will henceforth go forward in the search for Debbie (his niece) alone. Marty replies that family loyalty requires that he, too, be included in the search for Debbie:

"Why?" Ethan asks.
"Why? Because she's my . . . ; she's my . . . "

Borderlands History and Culture in *The Searchers*

"She's your *nothin'*," Ethan responds. "She's no kin to you at all."
"Well, I always *thought* she was—the way her folks took me in and all, they raised me—"
"That don't make you no kin!"

Marty, the adopted son of the Edwards family, fires back "Maybe it don't!"—but that he intends to keep looking anyway. Ethan sneers that doing so may be difficult, since Marty has no horses, money, or even ammunition. Ethan then says, "Marty, there's something I want to you to know." Marty shouts, "Yeah, I know what you want me to know—that I got no kin, no money, no horses. All I got here is a bunch of dead man's clothes to wear. Well, you told me that already . . . so shut your mouth!"[5]

This is not the first time that Ethan has denied any kin relation to Marty. In the film's opening scenes, Ethan, returning home from fighting for the South in the Civil War, greets all his brother's family: his sister-in-law, his nephew, his two nieces; but when Marty arrives Ethan glares at him and sneers that he looks like an Indian: "A fella could mistake you for a half-breed." Marty admits that he partly is, and Ethan continues to glower at him through the rest of the scene. When Martha Edwards then tries to point out that Ethan had been the one who found Marty when Marty's own parents were massacred—an attempt to establish a fictive kinship through saving action—Ethan is unmoved, and replies bluntly, "It just happened to be me—no need to make more of it." Thereafter, Ethan refuses Marty's attempts to address him as "Uncle Ethan": "I *ain't* your uncle!" The Edwards family indeed had adopted the boy in infancy, and for them, this adoption is equal to the power of blood—even if Marty has mixed blood—in establishing the obligations of kinship. Likewise, Marty's ongoing quest to rescue Debbie from captivity among the Comanches is driven by his own sense of his fraternal obligation to her: they had been raised as brother and sister and he feels it.

The film's perspective is that Ethan is clearly wrong to reject Marty's kinship, and that—as every other Texan figure does in the film—Ethan should accept that Marty really is a member of his family. But Ethan's rejection of Anglo-Texan kinship customs—and their normative restrictions and obligations—extends even to his real brother Aaron and his sister-in-law Martha. His affection for Martha dangerously exceeds the properly fraternal. He restrains himself—barely—from acting on those feelings while Aaron and Martha are alive. But Aaron's death and Martha's rape and death at the hands of the Indians allows him now to engage in a stepwise projection of those desires onto the youthful Martha-looking Debbie (and to punish her for them).[6] In order to complete that shift in desire, of course, Ethan must at some point reject the existence of any kin affiliation with Debbie at all. This he accomplishes in two steps. First, he claims that captivity among the Comanches has the general capacity to erase whiteness itself—and, as he demonstrated with Marty, he cannot be kin to anyone who is not fully white. Second, he implicitly recognizes the power of Comanche affinal and/or fictive kinship systems, and their capacity to erase the specific blood-kin relationship he has with his niece.

The first step occurs when he and Marty examine three rescued captive girls in the U.S. Cavalry fort, on the chance that Debbie might be among them. When asked for whom they're searching, Marty again tries to claim kinship with Debbie:

Marty: "She's my . . ."
Ethan (interrupting): "My niece."

Debbie turns out not to be among the redeemed captives. But their terrified, hysterical, or catatonic responses to Ethan's and Marty's presence (or perhaps it's the presence of the cavalrymen, who in the film have just gotten through brutally massacring their Comanche "families") prompts one of the cavalrymen to comment:

"It's hard to believe they're white."
Ethan (grimly): "They're not white—not anymore. They're . . . *Comanch*."

The scene ends famously with the shot of Ethan, his faced convulsed with hatred and horror, staring back at the girls.

Indian captivity, and probably Ethan's presumption that the girls have suffered sexual outrage, are powerful enough in Ethan's mind to reconstitute the girls' race. This scene must be counted as one of John Ford's boldest critiques of the irrationality of American racism. The biological consequences of miscegenation, the transformative symbolic potency of interracial sex itself, have, in Ethan's obsession, made the girls not just nonwhite, but nonhuman. The implications for Debbie's fate at Ethan's hands are horrendous—by this point in the film the audience has been repeatedly told that Ethan is intent not on rescuing Debbie but on murdering her if he can find her.

Borderlands History and Culture in *The Searchers*

With this theme of reracialization through sexuality in place, Ethan is then free to take the next step, and to claim the erasure of his specific blood kinship with Debbie. Having found Debbie dressed in Comanche clothes at Scar's camp in New Mexico, and living in Scar's own tepee, Ethan attempts to kill her; but instead he is wounded in the shoulder by a Comanche arrow as he attempts to do it. Later, nursing the shoulder wound, Ethan delivers to Marty his written out last will and testament:

Marty reads: "I, Ethan Edwards, being of sound mind and body (as Henderson points out, this is one of the film's "little jokes"), *and without blood kin,* do hereby bequeath my property to . . . Martin Pauley" (my emphasis).

Marty: "What do you *mean*—you don't have any blood kin? Why, *Debbie's* your blood kin!"

Ethan: "Not no more she ain't."

Marty throws the will back in Ethan's face, and warns him, "Don't think I've forgotten what you were fixin' to do to her back there. What kind of a man *are* you, anyway—?"

Ethan: (*fiercely*) "She's been livin' with a buck! She's nothin' but a—"

Marty: (*equally fiercely*) "Shut up! I hope you die!"

The great irony of the uncertain kin and anti-kin tangle, the kinship dislocations that make up so much of the story of *The Searchers,* lies here: in Ethan's new willingness to reject his blood kinship with Debbie and to *accept* the creation of kinship between Debbie and the Comanches as real instead, though it is a fictive kinship based merely on her sexual relationship with her captor and presumed "husband" Scar. This comes from the man who earlier in the film had posited that blood ties were the *only* true kinship, and hence Marty was to be rejected—both as an adopted child and more broadly because he was part Indian (which of course Debbie is not). And at the same time, by making *Marty* now his heir, Ethan accepts some sort of (fictive) kinship with him—even though he has previously insisted that Marty is not his blood kin and therefore has no relationship to him, and has previously rejected him because he is part Indian. Ethan's actions thus reveal the deep confusions and dislocations created by the conditions of the borderlands world. That world is what I wish to enter now. How might the complicated and fluctuating web of kinship relations played out in *The Searchers* look in the historical and cultural context of the true Southwest borderlands?

Historical Indian Captivity in the Southwest Borderlands

In the last decade or so, scholars of Indian-European relations in colonial North America have begun to turn from broadly framed "conquest-and-resistance" narratives to analyses that attempt to embrace the very real uncertainties faced by both Native Americans and Euro-Americans. Although historical hindsight makes clear the inevitable violent swing of the pendulum of power from the indigenous to the Euro-American pole, we understand now that daily life at any one time offered few hints as to this ultimate outcome. In the Southwest borderlands, as elsewhere in North America, people rose each day within a complex situation, to deal with the worries of keeping the family, clan, or village fed, sheltered, and reproducing across the generations. In this essay we deal most explicitly with the latter anxiety—the problem of "making kin" (*numu'aitu'* in Comanche), whether in the literal sense of arranging those sexual unions which in turn created children, or in the more figurative sense of creating emotional and symbolic ties between families, clans, and villages that counted as "kinship." In either case, though, the goal of action was to foster longer-term security and prosperity. *The Searchers*, I believe, is as much about the confusions of "making kin" in the unstable conditions of the frontier, and the often-tortured historical consequences of the instability, as it is about the more mainstream theme of "conquest and resistance" in the history of the American West.

With this in mind I now address two aspects of "making kin." First, I propose that the seizure and subsequent cultural assimilation of captives from "outsider" groups could be Indian or Hispanic or Euro-American, and must be understood as part of a larger borderlands political economy. That is, it was part of a larger pattern of exchange of goods that offered tangible *economic* rewards to many participants (especially men). Second, the practice of captive trade went along with the cultural assimilation of the victims; and this is indeed an understudied aspect of kinship creation on the Southwest frontier.[7] We can illustrate these two points with two cases, nearly two centuries apart, which suggest both the situational complexity and remarkable persistence of this customary practice across the Southwest borderlands. I will anchor the discussion on these two cases,

Borderlands History and Culture in *The Searchers*

while providing in between a broader historical examination of the scale and economic-cultural meaning of the multisided trade in captives.

Just what do we mean by a "borderlands political economy"? The term "borderlands" indicates the culturally heterogenous character of this society, the many opportunities for misunderstanding that haunted daily life, and the transformative potential of exchanges between indigenous and colonial peoples who were at this point roughly equal in power. Linking "borderlands" to "political economy," however, induces a paradox: despite profound cultural differences, Native Americans, Hispanic people, and Euro-Americans in the region came to *share* a larger understanding of the production and distribution of wealth, as conditioned by the social relations of power. In the Southwest these shared understandings had to do with *converging* patriarchal notions about the productive and exchange value of women and children, as well as livestock such as sheep, cattle, and horses.[8] The situation points to a regional economy in which struggles for power and prestige both within and between indigenous and colonial societies resulted in meaningful mutual forms of commerce, exchange, and accumulation. This was actually part of parallel developments within the larger Atlantic world.

Let us take one example of how this "political economy" worked, and the impact it had. While in *The Searchers* the focus is on obsessive white worry about Comanche raiders kidnapping white women for sexual purposes, we know that while increasing the size of the kin unit was certainly an important Comanche motive, the larger reason for Comanche kidnapping was the need for slave labor, especially female labor, in the horse, cattle, and bison robe business. The point of the slave labor regime for all the Plains tribes was to produce goods (horses, cattle, hides, buffalo robes) which could then be exchanged for the advanced industrial products of Hispanic or Euro-American culture: finished cloth garments, steel tools, and weapons of all sorts (e.g., knives and hatchets), luxuries such as whiskey and gin, and finally firearms—and especially rifles. The rise of the trade in bison robes with the whites had a special impact upon women in the Comanche bands. The Comanche were profiting significantly in the 1830s–60s from their quickly growing trade in bison hides with whites; but the curing of bison hides was a severely gendered occupation, "women's work" (as the killing of the bison was "men's work")—and eventually more women workers were needed than the bands had available. Thus the historical "Debbie Edwardses" were not so much sexually enslaved as forced into sweatshops of production. Rachel Plummer's Comanche master (late 1830s) even set her a monthly bison hide quota, and beat her if she did not achieve it. But to concentrate on the Rachel Plummers is in itself an Anglocentric act, and misses the complexity of the ethnic story. Native American raids for slaves were often conducted intertribally rather than toward the outside; and among the Comanches the primary outside target of raiders was not in any case the Texas (Euro-American) frontier to the southeast of the *Comancheria* but rather the Mexican frontier directly to the south, across the Rio Grande. It is true that many captives did eventually become "kin" of their captors (as Debbie Edwards does). But the main impact of the *numu'aitu'* process in the Comanche lands by 1860 was to increase the percentage of "Comanches" who were ultimately of *Hispanic* descent.[9]

John Ford had a scholarly knowledge of the American West; he was well aware of the importance of Hispanic captives among the Comanches, and that they far outnumbered Anglo captives. In 1961 Ford in fact made *Two Rode Together,* a new version of *The Searchers,* this time with a Hispanic woman, Elena de la Madriaga (played by Linda Crystal), held captive by the Comanches. *Two Rode Together* is a far lesser work of art than *The Searchers,* less psychologically profound (though still an exploration of racism)—but it is more in line with main historical reality.[10]

Now to the two cases of complex cross-ethnic "kin-making" on the complex southwestern borderlands. In the 1740s, Fray Carlos Delgado, a Franciscan missionary into the Navaho lands of northwestern New Mexico (in Navaho, the *Dinétah*) found a Navaho band at a location he termed *Pueblo Españoles.* The story was that the name of the location derived from two Spanish women, Augustina de Peralta and Juana Almassán, each taken captive by Navahos in 1680, during the Great Southwest Revolt against Spanish rule. The band received Fray Carlos very enthusiastically—a sharp contrast to the usual hostile reception of Spanish missionaries among the Navaho in this period.[11] The Spanish records unfortunately fail us at this point; but two other sources do not. In the 1890s the Smithsonian ethnographer Washington Matthews was able to collect the "legends" of the Navahos, including tales of the creation of the various Navaho clans. Matthews's informants recalled that the *Nakaidiné* or "Mexican" Clan, derived from either one or two captive Spanish women. The women were seized by the *Notadiné* or "Ute" clan in a raid into southern New Mexico in the early Spanish period. At first, these captive Spanish women served the Ute Clan as *naalté* or "slaves," but their mixed-blood Spanish-Navaho descendants later became free among the Navahos. The descendants eventually formed a separate clan, which was prohibited from intermarrying with the Ute Clan, their former captors. Washington Matthews was unaware of the discoveries of Fray Delgado, and assumed that the two founding women of the *Nakaidiné* were mythic figures; but with our fuller knowledge, we need not think this.[12] An unusual archaeological discovery confirms the pattern. In narrow Cañon Largo in northwestern New Mexico lie the remains of an early Navaho settlement which researchers call the "Hooded Fireplace" site (LA5662). In many ways an ordinary settlement of both *hogans* and masonry buildings, the site derives its name from the unusual existence of two fireplaces in Spanish style in one of the buildings: not central hearths but in a corner, and hooded with cedar lathes which retain traces of adobe plaster. Tree ring dating places the date of the settlement as 1694, and the Spanish-style fireplaces here predate the beginning of the use of such fireplaces among the Navaho by at least a generation. Furthermore, Hooded Fireplace is the only Navaho site where sweat lodges, still so profoundly important to Navaho spiritual practice, are missing.[13]

It is very tempting to conclude that Hooded Fireplace is Fray Delgado's *Pueblo Españoles,* home to the descendants of the captives Augustina de Peralta and Juana Almassan—the Navaho clan called the *Nakaidiné*. In their captivity, the Spanish women may have constructed a reminder of their earlier lives in the Spanish-style hearths over which they daily labored. They may even have taught their mixed-descent children some elements of Catholicism—which would explain both the striking absence of sweatlodges at Hooded Fireplace, and the unusually warm welcome Fray Delgado received.

The story of Augustina de Peralta and Juana Almassan and their "Navaho" descendants demonstrates that captivity and cultural transformation in the Southwest is more than a literary or filmic novelty. It was a real and complex phenomenon of the borderlands. But there is quantitative evidence that can move the story of Augustina and Juana and the *Nakaidiné* out of the realm of the merely anecdotal.

The fact is that captures of Hispanic settlers in New Mexico by Indian raiders such as the Navahos *never* reached the numbers that characterize the reciprocal side of the captive trade—that is, captures of Indians by New Mexican colonists. Several hundred New Mexicans disappeared into Native American hands during the two centuries between 1680 and 1880. But by contrast nearly four thousand and probably closer to five thousand

Hooded fireplace site, northern New Mexico.

nomadic Indians entered New Mexican society as captives. Primarily these captives were produced by intertribal warfare and raiding, and the victorious Native American groups then sold the captives in New Mexico markets in exchange for finished goods. The result was a social group called by the New Mexican colonists the *indios de rescate,* or Indian captives "redeemed" from the captivity of other Indians—"redeemed" to be raised up as slaves in colonial New Mexican households. At any given time, these "redeemed" Indian captives represented some 10 to 20 percent of the colonial New Mexican population.[14]

That 10 to 20 percent of the New Mexican population were Indian slave laborers produced by the Plains Indian slave trade may not appear to be an overwhelming number when compared to more intense "slave societies" such as the American South, but it was sufficient to affect the overall social structure of New Mexico in significant ways. Thus Ramon Gutierrez has argued that the caste category into which many of these Indian captives were eventually inserted—*genízaros*—served the fundamental ideological role in New Mexican society of defining via contrast the high status, honor, and dignity of their masters the *españoles.* "Spaniards,"

Borderlands History and Culture in *The Searchers*

Gutierrez claims, "whatever their estate, were men of honor in comparison to the vanquished Indians."[15] I have argued elsewhere, however, that the *genízaros* should be seen as much more than a central ideological symbol (though they were that too). Because of their numbers they were an important material force in New Mexican society, and played important active roles: as "slave soldiers," as laborers in the expanding textile trade in wool, and even as rebels who fomented social unrest in the colony at several key junctures.[16]

Let us return now to the Hispanic captives who, like the Euro-American Debbie, found themselves forced into the Native American societies of the borderlands. If we look not at New Mexico alone, but take a larger view of the borderlands as a whole, including now the provinces of northern Mexico, yet a different picture emerges. The scale of captures during raiding into Mexico proper by Comanches, Kiowas, and southern Apaches in the eighteenth century was still relatively modest. When Spanish authorities took up a short-lived plan for collecting alms in churches in northern Mexico to create a fund to ransom captives in the 1780s, the number of Hispanic captives among the Indians was thought to be only about 150. The situation changed dramatically, however, as the Plains groups began to increase their participation in hide and horse commerce with advancing Euro-American purchasers and entrepreneurs. Northern Mexico, with hundreds of thousands of cattle and horses watched by poorly armed *peones*, became the southern Plains peoples' prime source of goods to trade: bluntly, the prime raiding ground. Because successful horse and cattle raids resulted in livestock wealth that in turn required additional labor—herders and/or hide-processors—the scale of human captures in turn escalated. As we have seen, when the Plains people also entered the buffalo robe trade in full force, the need for labor (especially female labor) increased even further. It was thus in the early and mid–nineteenth century that northern Mexico suffered severely. The Mexican records indicate that hundreds of thousands of horses and cattle disappeared in these raids; probably close to 18,000 citizens died at the hands of the Plains raiders; and at least 3,000 Mexican citizens were carried away into captivity.[17]

American Texas also experienced the new violence of the borderlands economy in the mid–nineteenth century. The great rancher Charles Goodnight estimated that Texans lost 300,000 cattle and 100,000 horses to Plains raiders during the 1860s (it was the new Anglo ranchers in New Mexico who were buying much of this livestock from the Indians). And perhaps as many as 1,000 Texan citizens were taken by the Kiowas and Comanches between 1860 and 1875.[18] Cynthia Ann Parker, seized in 1836 and recovered in 1860, and upon whose story Ford based *The Searchers*, was therefore only one of hundreds (though, again, Hispanic captives were three times more common). When an attempt was made to redeem these captives via purchase from the Plains peoples by U.S. government Indian agents, this only *increased* the numbers of captives taken on the frontier—for the shrewd and profit-minded borderlands warriors now had the additional incentive of hard cash for their raiding. Quaker missionaries such as Lawrie Tatum soon discovered they were making the same mistake: their $100 reward for each surrendered captive quickly resulted in Kiowas and Comanches showing up with dozens of newly captured Mexican boys to barter, and the missionaries' coffers were drained. But in fact redemptions of captives, especially Mexican captives, were not the rule—because their labor was needed by the Plains bands; and enough "outsiders" (primarily Hispanics) eventually found adoption within Indian groups that we may project their numbers as roughly equal to their Indian slave counterparts in New Mexican society, or some 10 to 20 percent of any given "tribal" population.[19]

To some extent, such incorporation of non-Indians helped offset the demographic disasters to the Plains peoples caused by the increasing epidemics among them, epidemics in turn caused by their increasing interaction with non-Indian populations.[20] But again, the extent of the population offset is not large, and therefore the primary motive for capture seems to have remained the gaining of slave labor. This can be shown in a specific way: the continued inferiority of status of even those captives who were admitted into Plains societies as "kin."

"Foreign" captives did become tribal members, but many did so at statuses that suggest emergent severe stratification of status within cultures which are nowadays usually celebrated by the ignorant for their "egalitarian" social organization.[21] The Kiowas, for instance, maintained a social category called *dapóm* into which many captives were assimilated. Kiowas translated this term to American ethnographers as "people without property, accomplishment, or honor."[22] Likewise, Comanches called their captive laborers *tiri'aiwapi*, "those who work for another."[23] Jicarilla Apaches declared that a captive woman could be sexually used, and sent from camp to camp to do heavy labor; her mixed-blood children, while accepted as Apaches, were considered to be Apaches of a lower social status.[24] This evidence suggests that the growing power of commercial relations and their

Borderlands History and Culture in *The Searchers*

associated labor needs (stock herders, hide processors, robe curers) fostered the creation of permanently subordinated castes within many Indian societies. And if we step back a bit, we can see a gradual transformation under way as *all* the borderlands societies—Indian, New Mexican, and of course American Texas (with its many African American slaves)—became more internally stratified because of their increased interactions with the capitalist Atlantic economy.

For each faceless number cited above, however, there went a private story of terror and personal transformation. Not many of these stories remain to scholars, but we do have a few to which we can turn to recreate those images and feelings that must have dominated the historical borderlands. This brings us to my last case, which illustrates the continuing role of assimilated captives in cultural adaptation and survival.

This story begins on October 6, 1866 (not far distant from the dramatic date on which *The Searchers* begins), when ten-year-old José Andres Martín set out with his younger nephew Pedro to graze his family's cattle on the pastures above the village of San Gerónimo, just west of Las Vegas, New Mexico. They were captured by Mescalero Apaches, who had earlier killed three men of the village and run off thirty or forty head of livestock. The Apaches killed Pedro within a few days, but José Andres came under the protection of "a little lame Apache woman," for whom he did chores during the next several months. In late winter 1867 a raiding band of Kiowas led by Set-daya-ité (Many Bears) appeared in the Apache camp. After a night of fierce bargaining, Many Bears purchased José Andres for "one mule, two buffalo robes, and a red blanket." Using the interpretive services of "Santiago," an adult Mexican captive who was now a Kiowa warrior, Many Bears explained to the boy that he had purchased him for his daughter Etonbo, whose son of similar age had recently died. Renaming the boy "Andali" (there is no "r" in the Kiowa-Tanoan language; the name can be Hispanicized to "Andele"), Many Bears adopted him as his grandson, and Andali grew to adulthood among the Kiowas.

As a "Mexican-Kiowa captive," Andali participated in the twilight years of Kiowa freedom on the southern Plains. Unlike less fortunate captives, his adoptive status in Many Bears's family gave him full social mobility. After a successful horse raid into Texas (one of the last Kiowa livestock raids, as it turned out) he was invited to join the *Tsatanma,* or "Rulers of Horses" age grade. As an adult, he married four times. His first wife abandoned him for a higher-status warrior, while he "put away" his second wife "because she was too old." Such were the businesslike ways of the Plains peoples. Andali found temporary happiness with the Kiowa woman White Sage, but she, to his great sorrow, died in 1886.

Andali's story comes down to us as a consequence of great historical changes in the borderlands. After the final Comanche-Kiowa defeats in the Red River Wars of 1874–75 (the dramatic date of the recovery of Debbie from Scar, incidentally; and indeed the final assault on Scar's camp in the film is a replication of the historical Battle of Palo Duro Canyon), the Kiowas were confined by the U.S. government to a Comanche-Kiowa Reservation in Oklahoma; there they found themselves assigned, under the civilizing mandate of the "Peace Policy," to Methodist missionaries. In the early 1880s Andali requested and received training as a blacksmith. Although originally he had refused Agent Lawrie Tatum's offers of "rescue" and return to his family in New Mexico, Andali now asked the government to contact his brother Dionicio. After several years of searching, he was reunited with his brother and aged mother, who wept when she recognized her "muchachito" ("My little boy!"). Andali lived in New Mexico for several years but in 1889, like Cynthia Ann Parker with her Comanches some thirty years before, he realized that "his interests were all identified with the Kiowa, and that he had learned to love them." But whereas Cynthia Ann was held prisoner by her Euro-American relatives who forbade her to return to her Comanche adoptive kin—she committed suicide—Andali (as a male) simply abandoned New Mexico again and returned to the Kiowa-Comanche Reservation.

Andali converted to Methodism upon his return, and began teaching industrial arts in the Kiowa Agency school. The Reverend J. J. Methvin wrote down his story in 1899, using it as evidence that "a people . . . in whom there was so little upon which to base a hope of building a civilization" could nevertheless be brought to salvation through God's works. On the surface, Andali's conversion seemed complete. Since White Sage had died during his absence in New Mexico, he wooed and married the Methodist Mission Matron, Miss Emma McWhorter, in 1893. After three Kiowa wives, the Mexican-Kiowa Andres/Andali now married an Anglo woman—yet another example of the complexity of borderlands kin making.

In fact, though, Andali's conversion was not complete, and he continued to straddle the three cultures to which he was heir. Although a regular member of the Methodist church, he also attended meetings of the Native American (or Peyote) Church. The Church was itself a syncretistic religious expression of Christianity combined with traditional Plains mysticism and drug taking; it saw Christ represented in the cross-shaped peyote

Borderlands History and Culture in *The Searchers*

Andele, the Hispanic captive of the Kiowas.

button. (One of the biggest proponents of this religious movement was Quanah Parker, the great Comanche war chief, now a prosperous Oklahoma rancher—and the Comanche son of Cynthia Ann Parker.) Andali also protested the U.S. government's destructive imposition of individual and sellable landholding (the Dawes Act) among the more communal-minded Kiowa. In 1915 Andali served as anthropologist Ralph Linton's principal informant on Kiowa culture—evidence of his continuing pride in his adoptive people, and in turn an important source of information for modern scholars on how the Plains people actually lived. Finally, in a poignant reenactment of his own assimilation experiences, the Mexican-Kiowa Andali and his Euro-American wife adopted two orphan girls: one was a Cherokee and the other a Mexican-Kiowa mixed-blood girl.[25]

Although separated by nearly two centuries and hundreds of miles of territory, Andali's story resonates with that of Augustina de Peralta and Juana Almassan, and, at a metaphoric level, with that of Cynthia Ann Parker and "Debbie." All the stories begin in acts of violence and terror. But the captives move to assimilation into a new kinship nexus, first as adoptive relatives and then as marriage partners. In the Spanish women's case, they seem ultimately to have been the ancestors of an entire Navaho clan, the *Nakaidiné*. At first glance Andali might seem a sell out to advancing Euro-American cultural pressure, but there is clear evidence that he felt deeply torn by the end of traditional Plains life, and while he was attracted both to aspects of Euro-American culture as well as his childhood New Mexican culture, he sought to salvage what dignity he could for his Kiowa people.

Reading Kinship in *The Searchers*

With this historical and cultural framework in mind, let us return to the film, and play out some alternative scenarios available to us as if this were a story told from the Comanche point of view. If we take Comanche kinship systems and lay them like an alternative cultural template over what we have seen from the Anglo-Texan perspective, some useful differences in relationality and motivation are revealed. The crucial relation, of course, is the one between Debbie and her captor Scar. But one other deserves our attention before we reach our closing interpretation.

The most objectionable sequence in *The Searchers* from our perspective today is clearly Ford's treatment of Marty's "purchase" and "marriage" to the chubby Comanche girl Wild Goose Flying Across the Night Sky. We know her as "Look," from Marty's repeated attempts to impose upon her his understanding of the situation by using that verb ("Look—can't you understand?"). Trading with a Comanche band with close ties to Scar, Marty believes that he has bargained for a blanket, but finds that he has inadvertently bestowed bride-price upon her father. "Look" then trails dutifully after Marty as his "bride," enduring jokes and physical assaults that must have struck audiences even in 1956 as minstrel-show tastelessness. The viewer is jarred out of racist amusement, however, by Ford's suddenly sympathetic representation of Look. Ethan and Marty had questioned her fiercely about the whereabouts of Marty's *taibo nami* ("younger white sister");[26] at first denying knowledge, now—out of dutiful love of Marty— Look provides the searchers with a lead to Scar's camp. And then follows the discovery of her brutal death at the hands of U.S. soldiers during the cavalry assault on that camp. The discovery of her death moves even the stone-hearted Ethan to shake his head at the horror of the world.[27]

Ford uses the scenes of the ill-fated cross-cultural marriage of Look and Marty as a humorous interlude in what is a grim and tragic story, and as a way to move the story forward. But we can use it also to explore Comanche strategies for intertribal and interethnic diplomacy. Anthropologist Patricia Albers has recently argued that patterns of alliance-making within and between Plains Indian groups were often marked by marriages and adoptions (i.e., establishment of fictive kinship) that symbolized new, peaceful relationships. "It is likely," Albers argues, "that [marital] unions were arranged by fathers [or uncles or brothers, depending on the marriage system] and cemented by gift presentations committing both parties to a long-term cycle of reciprocal obligation." The Comanches partook of this strategy of peace-making and had a specific term for such a marriage for diplomacy's sake: *na'huturu kuhmaru*, "exchanging gifts marriage."[28]

Although presented in hideously poor taste, the Look-Martin Pauley marriage sequence may be read as one attempt to resolve the impending violence between the searchers and the "Noyeka" (*noy'uka'* [wandering, vagabond]) band of Comanches. Aware that Ethan Edwards harbors implacable hatred for Comanches, Look's father seeks resolution by binding the mixed-blood Martin Pauley to Comanche interests through a Comanche diplomatic marriage.

Albers's second sociopolitical mechanism, fictive adoption, leads us finally into a deeper examination of Comanche kinship systems and the relationship between Ethan, Debbie, and Scar (*Cicatrice*, as we learn, in Spanish; *Pikha* in Comanche). The Anglo-Texan characters in the film, and no doubt American audiences in general, assume that Debbie has at age fifteen become Scar's wife; she thereby serves as the focal point for Ethan's sexual envy and murderous rage. But what if the story is different?

Historical and anthropological evidence on Comanche kinship and captivity practices suggest a possible alternative reconstruction. Those few captivity accounts by and about women captives that remain available to us—Sarah Ann Horn (1836), Rachel Plummer (1838), Rosita Rodriguez (1846), Cynthia Ann Parker (1836–60)—suggest that marriage to the captor, though it did occur, was unusual. When a child—as opposed to an adult—was taken captive, almost immediately, and usually after a brutal and terrifying ritual of physical beating and clothes-stripping, the child would become "adopted." He or she would then come under the control and protection of a senior wife or elder sister of the captor. This adoption procedure, termed *tue'tunabinaru*, would allow for the captive's subsequent assimilation as fictive kin into Comanche culture: *numu'aitu* ("making kin"). But the ritual process of adoption invoked a parent-child incest taboo, hence prohibiting sexual relations between captor and captive. If the captive was a female child, this avoided any female versus female conflict caused by the eventual introduction of a new wife into the captor's household (which might contain several wives already, the Comanches being polygamous). But beyond this, the prohibition served a specific economic function of profit for the household. Under the Comanche matri-fraternal kin power system, females were given in out-marriage by elder brothers or by mothers' brothers (maternal uncles) in exchange for "bride price" gifts from their new spouses; therefore they served to bring to the household much wealth in ponies, robes, and service through bride-price.[29]

Is it possible, then, for us to reread our conventional understanding of the Debbie-Scar-Ethan relationship as one in which Debbie is not Scar's wife, but his adoptive daughter, whom he seriously considers giving to Ethan in a marriage for diplomacy's sake when Ethan finally arrives at his camp? A nineteenth-century Comanche could easily (perhaps naturally) interpret the sequence we see in the film in that fashion. And the fact is we do *not* know for certain what Scar's relationship to Debbie is. Let us look closely at the key scene in which Ethan and Marty are delivered to Scar's camp by the *Comanchero* merchant Emilio Fernandez y Figueroa. The old *Comanchero* announces that they have come "be'l a kwana kwé temué" (that is, to barter or trade). One of his men then demonstrates the swiftness and agility of the horse Ethan offers as a gift, and Ethan confirms his intent: "temué is right—we come to trade."

With everyone then invited into Scar's tepee, Fernandez y Figueroa explains that Scar's sons are dead, and his wives sit on the other side of his lodge. Ethan asks, "Are they *all* his wives?" A crucial question, but this question is never answered. Instead Scar remains focused on Fernandez's previous statement about his sons, declaring that "For each son I take many . . . [he has to ask Fernandez for the English word] . . . *scalps*." One of the women sitting on the other side of the lodge—it turns out to be Debbie—is then ordered to present Scar's scalp-laden lance to Ethan and Marty for inspection. Ethan and Marty start when they see Debbie, but Ethan then abruptly breaks off negotiations by saying, "We came to trade, not to admire his collection," and he rises and stalks out.

Ethan may have committed a critical mistake. His own question raises the possibility that *not* all the women sitting on the other side of the lodge are Scar's wives. Indeed, in the novel by Alan LeMay on which the film is based, young Debbie is *not* Scar's wife but—in fact—his adopted daughter. But Ethan assumes that Debbie *is* Scar's wife ("She's been living with a buck!")—as does the Anglo audience—and therefore his sexual envy and

Borderlands History and Culture in *The Searchers*

Ethan, Marty, Scar, and Fernandez: "Temué is right—we come to trade."

rage determine the violence that is to come.[30] If we replay this crucial scene in the tepee from the point of view of *Comanche* culture, however, it would be more likely that Scar had not married Debbie but had adopted her (as he does in the novel), and then perhaps Scar has had something else in mind all along. With Debbie as his adoptive daughter, and not knowing that Ethan is related to her as uncle and is driven by his own sexual fantasies, but simply that Ethan is an enemy of the Wanderers, the Noyeka Comanche, an offer of "exchanging gifts marriage" (*na'huturu kuhmaru*) between the two men would have the potential of placing Ethan safely within a Comanche kin nexus: according to Comanche marriage custom, Ethan would then become both Scar's fictively adopted male friend (*haits*) as well as his brother-in-law (*mo'napi*). Had Ethan's disturbed psychology and his impulsive hatred allowed him to ponder the possible complexity of the situation a moment longer, perhaps he might have realized that at least one aspect of his desires was right at his fingertips. As it is, his conduct in stalking off is ferociously insulting from a Comanche point of view.[31]

This alternative way of viewing the transactions in Scar's lodge accords well with Albers's analysis of how the institution of captive taking and assimilation functioned in southern Plains societies. Arguing that raiding for captive women and children not only helped fill demographic holes in Indian societies hard hit by disease and continual warfare but that these new kin connections also sometimes promoted new intertribal alliances and trade relations, she concludes that "the practice of abduction takes on new meaning, for not only did it contain the grounds for conflict, but it also embodied (quite literally) the terms of reconciliation. In other words, the capture of women and children was both a quintessential element of war and a fundamental opportunity for peace."[32] Viewing *The Searchers* in this manner casts in high relief the contradictory and mutually constituent relationship between war and peace as viewed by the Plains peoples who actually occupied the turbulent space of the Southwest borderlands in the nineteenth century. And it casts into relief the many possible mutual misunderstandings, including misunderstandings about kinship, that can occur even during peaceful cross-cultural contacts. I am reminded of the African proverb, "They are our enemies; we marry them."[33]

NOTES

1. Kolodny, "Among the Indians," 195.

2. See Michel-Rolph Trouillot, *Silencing the Past: Power and the Production of History* (Boston: Beacon Press, 1997), 1–30, for an insightful treatment of the relationship between these two aspects of "history."

3. See Frederick Jackson Turner, "The Significance of the Frontier in American History," American Historical Association *Annual Report* (1893), 199–227.

4. Henderson, "*The Searchers:* An American Dilemma," reprinted in this volume. I borrow "kin" and "anti-kin" from anthropologist Claude Meillassoux, who utilizes it to distinguish kin-based forms of subordination and exploitation in Africa from the institution of slavery—a distinction useful in thinking about differences between American Indian captivity and American chattel slavery as well. See *The Anthropology of Slavery: The Womb of Iron and Gold* (Chicago: University of Chicago Press, 1991).

5. Note that in this scene Marty has now received symbolic integration into the *Jorgensen* family, as a substitute for their dead son Brad (killed by Comanches during the search for Debbie), through the gift of the dead Brad's clothing to him. At the beginning of this sequence we have already seen Mrs. Jorgensen (Olive Carey) greet the returning Marty as if she were his biological mother—embracing him warmly and lovingly—while ignoring Ethan standing beside him. The artificially constructed and complex kinship relation of Marty to the Jorgensens is further developed (though doubly ambiguously, for he is both an adopted son and part Indian) in Marty's later marriage to Brad's sister Laurie. On the convergence of incest and miscegenation in *The Searchers,* see Eckstein, "Incest and Miscegenation in *The Searchers* and *The Unforgiven* (1959)" in this volume.

Borderlands History and Culture in *The Searchers*

6. For more on this theme, see Eckstein's introductory essay in this volume.

7. Jack D. Forbes proposed this idea some thirty years ago; see "The Eurindian: A Subject for Southwestern Studies," *New Mexico Historical Review* 34 (1961): 346–47.

8. For a more comprehensive treatment, see James F. Brooks, *Captives and Cousins;* for the specific role of women, see James F. Brooks, "'This Evil Extends Especially . . . to the Feminine Sex': Negotiating Captivity in the New Mexico Borderlands," *Feminist Studies* 22 (1996): 279–309.

9. By the 1840s, the Plains tribes were bringing in more than one hundred thousand bison robes a year to trade for Euro-American industrial goods. For more on this, see Isenberg, *Destruction of the Bison,* 93–94; for more on the severely gendered bison hunting and curing process, see 95–97; for more about Rachel Plummer, see 100. On the predominance, in raiding and trading for slaves, of inter-Native American actions; the annual great raids into Mexico; the growing Hispanic ethnicity of the Comanches, see this essay, 273–76. Note the portrait painting of the Quahada Comanche warrior "Hee Soo San Ches" (i.e., Jesus Sanchez) by George Catlin (1830s).

10. On *Two Rode Together* and its relationship to *The Searchers,* see Eckstein, "After the Rescue," 31–32.

11. See "Testimony Taken at Isleta in July, 1746" (pt. 1, doc. 32, New Mexico Archives, Coronado Library, University of New Mexico); for the context, see Frank D. Reeve, "The Navaho-Spanish Peace, 1720–1770," *New Mexico Historical Review* 34 (1959): 9–40. For the likelihood that the two women came from the Santo Domingo area, see Fray Angelico Chavez, *The Origins of New Mexico Families* (1954; reprint, Albuquerque: Museum of New Mexico Press, 1992), 4, 86.

12. Washington Matthews, ed., *Navaho Legends* (1897; reprint, Salt Lake City: University of Utah Press), 146.

13. See Michael P. Marshal and Patrick Hogan, *Rethinking Navaho Pueblitos.* BLM Cultural Resource Series no. 8 (Farmington: Bureau of Land Management, New Mexico State Office, 1991), 33–51.

14. See David M. Brugge, *Navajos in the Catholic Church Records of New Mexico, 1694–1875* (Tsaile: Diné College Press, 1985).

15. Ramon Gutierrez, *When Jesus Came, the Corn Mothers Went Away* (Stanford: Stanford University Press, 1990), 188.

16. James F. Brooks, "'Lest We Go in Search of Relief to Our Lands and Our Nation': Local Justice, Political Economy and Colonial Law in the New Mexico Borderlands, 1680–1821," paper presented at "The Many Legalities of Early America," Institute for Early American History and Culture conference, Williamsburg, Virginia, 1996.

17. Between 1832 and 1855 alone, the northern departments of Mexico suffered 11,704 citizens killed and 1,441 captured by Plains raiders: see Ignacio Pasto Rouaix, *Dictionario geografico, historico biografico del estado de Durango* (Mexico City, 1946): 34. Over the next twenty years, at least another 1,000 Mexicans were taken captive: *Informes que se complimiento del Decreto de 2 octubre de 1872 rinde al ejecutiva de la Union, le comision Pesquididora de la Fronera del Norte, sobre el desempeno de sus trabajos* (Mexico City, 1874), 83–88.

18. See Rister, *Border Captives*. Jack County alone lost more than two hundred settlers to Indian captures between 1859 and 1871: Rister, *Border Captives*, 141–43.

19. The data can be found in James F. Brooks, "Captives and Cousins: Violence, Kinship, and Community in New Mexico Borderlands, 1680–1880" (Ph.D. diss., University of California, 1995), 430–65. John Ford was—again—well aware of the importance of trade (business) to the southern Plains peoples: an impressive character in *The Searchers* is the New Mexican trader with the Comanches (a *Comanchero*, as they were called) who ultimately guides Ethan and Marty to Scar's camp, and there the cover story is that Ethan and Marty have come to trade; and in *Two Rode Together* Ford depicts Comanche leaders such as Quanah Parker (played by Henry Brandon, the grim actor who played Scar in *The Searchers*) as pragmatic businessmen.

20. On these terrible epidemics, see Isenberg, *Destruction of the Bison*, 53–62, 113–20.

21. Kevin Costner's film *Dances with Wolves* (Academy Award for best film, 1991) is the prime recent example of such romanticizing of the Plains peoples.

22. See Bernard Mishkin, *Rank and Warfare Among the Plains Indians* (1950; reprint, Lincoln: University of Nebraska Press, 1992), 44.

23. See Gladwin, "Comanche Kin Behavior," 82.

24. See Morris Opler, "A Summary of Jicarilla Apache Culture," *American Anthropologist* 38 (1936).

25. For Jose Andres Martin's life story, originally published in 1899, see James F. Brooks, ed., *Andele, the Mexican-Kiowa Captive* (Albuquerque: University of New Mexico Press, 1996).

26. *The Searchers* is almost unique among westerns in that when Comanches (or Anglos) speak "Comanche," it sometimes really *is* Comanche.

27. On the "Look" episode in *The Searchers*, see Lehman, "Texas 1868/America 1956," 395 ff. The massacre of the encampment in this sequence—uniquely and shockingly real for the 1950s—is a representation of the massacre perpetrated by Custer's Seventh Cavalry on the Cheyenne encampment on the Washita in November 1868: see Eckstein's introductory essay in this volume.

28. Albers, "Symbiosis, Merger, and War," 111.

29. For treatment of Comanche captivity and processes of cultural assimilation, see James F. Brooks, "'Negotiating Captivity in the New Mexico Borderlands," *Feminist Studies* 22 (1996): 279–309; Gladwin, "Comanche Kin Behavior." On Comanche marriage systems, see Jane F. Collier, *Marriage and Inequality in Classless Societies* (Norman: University of Oklahoma Press, 1988).

30. Debbie and Scar's relationship in LeMay's *The Searchers:* see the comments of Eckstein's introductory essay in this volume. It is typical of Ford's film, and part of its enduring fascination, that we *cannot* know for certain whether Debbie is Scar's wife or not. The widespread assumption that the teenager is having sexual relations with Scar merely appeals to a Euro-American audience's miscegenistic fears (and fantasies)—as it is certainly does to Ethan's. We must assume that the creation of this central mystery is intentional on Ford's part, because it fits the pattern of similar mysteries the film intentionally creates; see Lehman, "The Limits of Knowledge in and about *The Searchers*."

Borderlands History and Culture in *The Searchers*

31. McBride's biography of John Ford contains an interview with the actor Henry Brandon, who played Scar, in which Brandon says that on the way out to Monument Valley in spring 1955, Ford asked him how he felt about an Indian sleeping with a white woman; when Brandon answered that it wouldn't bother him, Ford indicated his approval, and Brandon's impression is that Ford didn't want Scar to appear as a villain: see *Searching for John Ford* (New York: St. Martin's Press, 2001), 566. The reference is evidently to Scar and Debbie. But this only shows what Ford was apparently thinking about the Scar-Debbie relationship two months before the scene in Scar's tepee was actually filmed, and my point is that what is actually on the screen is, like so many borderlands relationships, highly ambiguous.

32. Albers, "Symbiosis, Merger, and War," 128.

33. Max Gluckman, *Custom and Conflict in Africa* (Oxford: Oxford University Press, 1956): 12–13.

Re-searching

David Grimsted

God's got some mighty funny trails...
—William S. Hart's *The Disciple*, 1915

Shall we gather at the river...?
—Methodist hymn

Scholars are searchers, too, re-searching overgrown trails toward truth or thereabouts, riding long years after Jerem-Futterman facts through their chosen Monument Valleys. Nor are they sure that in the end the intellectual Debbies they hunt will be found alive, even to the few who will view their trophies. And the search goes on through terrain where lurk savages bloodthirsty enough—their fellow students and academics, always on the lookout for another scalp for their belts. Happily, there's enough meat in each of these essays to slake normal thirst for blood.

These studies show nothing more clearly than the variety of valuable searches that can occur over a single document's domain. They less contradict one another than follow happy trails that wend in different directions. Richard Hutson stresses how the film's geographic/geologic setting, Ford's beloved Monument Valley, places his people and society in the context of corresponding and contrasting beauty and threat, of overpowering grandeur and permanence that is in fact the remnant of huge change and disappearance. James Brooks explores the geo-historical terrain in which the film ostensibly is set, richly suggesting regional, racial, captivity, and cultural interweavings more complex than anyone, certainly including John Ford, has recognized.

Martin Winkler ties Ford's film to a more familiar context, that of classic literature and myths, particularly *The Iliad*, in a way that forces more serious consideration of stereotypes about the alleged divisions between the classical and modern, and between canonized high culture and popular culture. Another classical scholar, Arthur Eckstein, largely takes Winkler's arguments about archetypes for granted, going on to explore Ford's film in the context of incest and racial taboos and tying it in rich detail to other films with parallel themes. Winkler and Eckstein vitally demonstrate how close attention to the aesthetic and human detail of *popular* works is every bit as essential for understanding them as it is for texts deemed literary "classics."

Brian Henderson also uses the concept of myth to explore *The Searchers'* effectiveness, but moves to ground the film's power not in the traditional but the contemporary. Henderson interprets the story as one opposing a racist idea of "kinship by blood" to a tolerant notion of "kinship by adoption" that replicates the central question in the United States as it moved away from its traditional system of apartheid in the 1950s. William Luhr ties his analysis to another preoccupation of the 1950s, an uneasiness over conformity and other-directedness tied to insecurity about masculinity that helped make John Wayne a revered film icon. Luhr relates the film's success to both Wayne's popularity, and to his bravery in taking on this "dark" role in such an "iconoclastic" western.

Gaylyn Studlar's perspective is influenced not by issues given much attention in the fifties, but by the feminism that became a central social and academic concern after the early 1960s. She argues that Ford diverged from an alleged tradition in western films of rejecting the feminine values of "home, religion and society." Instead, Studlar contends Ethan is only the "ostensible hero" of the film and Ford made Martha, despite her relatively brief appearance, its moral center whose values dictate its action and conclusion. Kathryn Kalinak reaches near-opposite conclusions from her rich exploration of the film's music, "a kind of aural shorthand" guiding audience response. For Kalinak, the films "interrupted song" underlines "the failure of community." She also sees pro-Confederate sympathies in the musical choices, while the Indian music proves its "undeniable stereotyping" of the Comanche.

Tom Colonnese and his Native American colleagues make the same point about the stereotyping of Indians in the music, as well as in Ford's very limited concern about accurate portrayal of Comanche culture. Their central criticisms of the film, however, emphasize its conventionality as a western: a story where the good is tied to the triumph of civilization—white society—over Indians whose brutality and incompetence in battle

Re-searching

are repeatedly stressed. Douglas Pye argues similarly that Ford's desire to be socially fair crumbles because of traditions in western movies that make almost any attempt to produce an antiracist western a paradoxical, even contradictory, enterprise. Hence "fundamental inconsistencies" muddy "the more rational discriminations at which the film seems to aim." Despite argumentative similarities, the things that the Native Americans notice and which the liberal critic emphasizes are quite distinct. The Indians passingly mention the captive scene and not the Look comedy at all, sequences that Pye finds disturbing, and he doesn't mention the very traditional coming of "civilization" thesis and the fight sequences that the Native Americans rightly mock as the most wholly convention-ridden aspects of the movie.

Much of this interpretive divergence involves how far *The Searchers* violates traditional patterns in western film. Extreme differences are emphasized in the Luhr and Eckstein essays but perhaps most strongly by the film's leading academic analyst, Peter Lehman. Lehman stresses the film's epistemological "theme," its refusal to let the audience know certainly what happens, and more positively, Ford's use of visual motifs to suggest central significances.

"So what can you believe?" ask good students, readers, and movie fans. Not much, if you're wise, Lehman answers, a conclusion common enough for anyone noticing the wholly different and sometimes clearly antagonistic interpretive trails scholars or friends lay out. The essays all deftly broaden anyone's range of possible responses and questions about the film, in ways bound to create some insecurity about one's own judgements. Yet this expanding universe of possibilities does not imply a work of engulfing ambiguity or a world of equal ignorance where any opinion or approach is as good as any other. At its best, it leads to careful judgment about what rings most thoughtful and shallow, false and true in one's own statements and answers, and in those of others. Anyone who accepts *equally* the information of Jerem Futterman and Mose Harper deserves to end up dead wrong. One needs to listen carefully and critically to what people have to say, how they say it and why, as to all the tales and attempted truths that academics, teachers, the press, books, movies and you spin.

To illustrate this truism, I'll first suggest two additional trails, ones that I'd put near the center of a search for *The Searchers*' meaning and aesthetic quality, suggesting some complications in these essays' paths to truth, some byways especially hard to follow, and a few possible side paths that may aid the quest. Finally, I'll use these varied mappings of the intellectual terrain of *The Searchers* to ponder the more general question of what we can know, how we can judge, and whether we can judge or know better or finally.

My two recommended trails are more commonplace than some pursued in these essays. One, preferred often by historians, involves a historical integration of the text with contemporary events, concerns, uneasiness, and changes. The second path, the frequent preference of literary critics, involves integration of the work studied with earlier texts sharing important common contours with it—in this case, Ford's other films and, more generally, the western movie genre.

While possible paths involving integration with other contemporary realities are innumerable, the issue of race is the one most strongly suggested within the film and the one raging most openly in American society at the time it was made. Eckstein points out that Frank Nugent and John Ford wrote *The Searchers'* script in the months just after the nation's Supreme Court issued its landmark, and socially explosive, decision in *Brown v. the Topeka Board of Education.* Henderson circles complexly through the film toward this racial reality. My "search" here largely accepts Henderson's conclusion, and illustrates primarily the major differences that occur when a shared thesis is the start rather than the ending point of the intellectual journey.

Of course, by the mid-1950s there had already been much preparation for the huge change that *Brown* represented. The human horrors resulting from Nazi ideology had rendered suspect all racist theory, and the Cold War made embarrassing the American variant of this social viciousness. Harry Truman responded by deciding that racial segregation was no longer to be a central organizing principle in the American armed forces. He also proved in 1948 that his party might win elections—if very narrowly—while arguing that African Americans deserved full access to America's opportunities and facilities. On these issues, Truman diverged from his political predecessors, with some limited exceptions during the nations' earlier great division. In the 1950s, changing popular feeling, along with often reluctant federal compliance and good sense, were to make the "Massive Resistance" campaign against *Brown* a pale shadow of the earlier fight over states' rights to support gross exploitation of blacks. Yet this result was far from clear when the Supreme Court declared policies of segregation unconstitutional, and the white South began its counterattack.

Within this atmosphere of uncertainty about the nation's future, John Ford began making *The Searchers.* Most movies of the mid-1950s offered little suggestion of the racial controversy, but personal and structural real-

Re-searching

ities made Ford's film, and several other westerns, exceptions. Filmmakers were controlled by Hollywood's bottom line of not lessening profits by offending anyone, but they could obliquely address major issues, often attracting a larger audience by such limited venturesomeness. John Lenihan has well shown how westerns of the 1950s became increasingly popular because of their flexibility in incorporating contemporary concerns of all kinds within their distancing conventions.[1] John Ford knew this reality well. Indeed his long career had depended on an ability to unite his personal and social vision comfortably in Hollywood conventions that allowed him to make films steadily that were both reasonably successful and honestly suggestive.

By the mid-1950s several things encouraged him to focus on adding new themes to his familiar genre. Ford's "box office" had never been stronger. In 1952 he'd made *The Quiet Man,* the most critically and popularly successful of all his privately developed projects, and his 1954 *Mogambo* took in more money that any other Ford film, before or after.[2] Yet at this point in Ford's career, he was not receiving the critical reverence being lavished on all sorts of European directors—or on Charlie Chaplin and Orson Welles, whose genius seemed ratified by Hollywood's rejection of them. Ford was thought of as an old craftsman, working best in westerns, the decade's most popular, and hence critically suspect, genre.[3]

Ford's politico-social instincts had always been liberal in the twentieth-century American sense. He had had no greater earlier critical/financial successes than with heartfelt portraits of the costs of capitalism to poor people, *The Grapes of Wrath* (1940) and *How Green Was My Valley* (1941). In the former, while faithful to John Steinbeck's characters, incidents, and class sympathies, Ford substituted for Steinbeck's vague radicalism a fairly explicit endorsement of the New Deal as answer to the problems of America's poor. Presenting such problems with a degree of power unprecedented in Hollywood's big corporate era, Ford's "solution" was the government camp, switched from the novel's center to the film's end, presided over by an FDR look-alike (down to the cigarette in a long holder), where the government takes some responsibility for establishing an environment decent and protective enough to allow dignity, popular democracy, work, and self-development for all to be meaningful.

In Ford's return via *Stagecoach* to the western in 1939, he inserted his most partisanly explicit character, or caricature, by giving the most despicable of the coach's passengers the opinions of FDR's wealthy opponents of the post-1936 years. Played by Berton Churchill, Ford's favorite pompous twit of his 1930s films, this busily embezzling banker intones endlessly about government waste of taxpayer money, the need for a businessman as president, and the folly of government interference with banking, especially the idea that the government might protect citizens by auditing his accounts.[4] In the McCarthy era, he showed hostility to the witch hunts and successfully headed off an attempt by Cecil B. DeMille and others to use the scare to remove liberals from positions of influence in Hollywood. The quiet power of this, one of Ford's two known political speeches—with its famous beginning "My name's John Ford, I make westerns"—parallels in many ways lawyer Joseph Welch's restrainedly detonating one, put in terms of personal decency, later in the Army-McCarthy hearings.[5]

Ford's liberalism in fact predated the crash of 1929 and the New Deal. In what I judge his best film, *Three Bad Men* (1926), Ford made clear how deeply entwined his liberalism was with his Americana. Silent film's narrative voice encouraged creators and audience to talk comfortably outside the personal story, and Ford here told how his broad social vision was grounded in a populism of the common man rather than a religion of uncommon gain. Set in the 1870s, the decade Ford's Irish parents came to the United States, the film argues "that ships of hope bore thousands of emigrants to seek the realization of their dreams." We see a ship and then learn of the good and the vile motives that drew people across the ocean: "Some sought happiness—some only the horn of plenty—the chalice of gold—the Unholy Grail!" The anti-gold theme runs through the film, where the "rush" into Dakota territory is driven by mixed motives of finding gold and starting farms. As the rush begins, the good parson talks the men into putting plows, which they've removed to increase their speed, back in their wagons: "You'll find the real wealth of this land in its soil." Ford concentrates in the rush on two wagons that break down. In one the man and his hefty wife fix it and rush on for gold—forgetting to put their baby back in the wagon. The pursuit of wealth involves forgetfulness of all humanely nurturing virtues. In the second case, the wagon can't be fixed and the couple despairs—until the woman reaches down and sifts the soil between her fingers (the same gesture, its meaning reversed, that a defeated John Qualen was to use in *Grapes of Wrath* some years later) and says with conviction that the parson was right: "We'll stay right here. The soil is as rich as gold." It is the preacher-blessed plows that will bring the golden grain of life to build family and community, and those who seek only the unholy grail of wealth must be defeated lest they destroy all social and divine decencies.[6] Ford's lesson about the contradiction of gross wealth-

Re-searching

seeking to the truly good society was delivered to Calvin Coolidge's America, the time when there was most sanctified national worship of the Golden Calf and when other Hollywood products made having more the chief proof of virtue.

In 1954, with prosperity broadening faster than at any time in the country's history and the nation convulsed over "the Negro question," Ford, like other liberals, accepted that race was now the key to the nation's providing a social environment of equal dignity, decency, and opportunity. In 1949–50 Hollywood had released its first efforts to broach the question of the nation's color line in films such as *Home of the Brave*, *Lost Boundaries*, *Pinky*, and *Intruder in the Dust*. Perhaps most straightforwardly, *No Way Out* tied Richard Widmark's patented psychopathology to white racism, and Sidney Poitier became Hollywood's first major indication that the African American male might be educated, intelligent, competent, and good-looking.[7] Producers and directors were to return to black problem films in the late 1950s, but in mid-decade the topic was too hot for Hollywood handling. Hence filmmakers who wished to deal with racism safely distanced their message by substituting groups outside the contemporary controversy, as in *Giant*'s exposure of anti-Hispanic and *Bad Day at Black Rock*'s of anti-Japanese sentiment. Much more commonly used as stand-in were attitudes toward Native Americans in traditional late-nineteenth-century westerns.[8]

So in 1954, Ford had a property, Alan LeMay's novel *The Searchers*, that touched on race in a genre where a film might explore it. The aging Ford wished to make his possibly last film a masterpiece, a western that would be in the jargon of the day "adult," and, in Ford's words, a "psychological epic," the study of "the tragedy of a loner."[9] But it would also address the nation's racist flaws, just as some of his earlier films had exposed those tied to excessively exploitative capitalism. He hoped it would be his racial *Grapes of Wrath*—a film redolent with pride in the core of American folk and folkways, but critical of the racism now seen as the severest threat to it.

LeMay's book was ripe for this shaping, a best seller with no great critical following to make shifting the theme toward race difficult. It in fact had no strong theme to change at all. LeMay's contemporary target of interest in the novel was not racial but cold war: brief "Quaker" peace policies on the frontier worsened and prolonged savage destructiveness until get-tough realism and real bullets restored peace.[10] Ford chucked this idea out, as well as the book's central emphasis on Martin's coming-of-age. Marty remains key to the story, but now less for the way he changes than for the way he is changed at its beginning. He is given some Indian blood so that he can become a catalyst for the hero's racism. Ford's Marty is made partly comic by his extreme sexual naivete and passivity, while his mixed ancestry first introduces us to Ethan's tragic racist flaw, and assures us that the good society—always acomin' in westerns—will embrace the racial "others" whom the hero trains and saves.

Such seems to have been Ford's "idea" as the script and film developed, and it led to a deeply felt, richly visualized, powerfully interesting—and troubling—film. In the film's first scenes Ford efficiently sets up his situation and his theme in a way that's clear without any undue hammering on the obvious. Ethan enters after a long absence, with a past that probably includes some robbery. Martha's cutting off Ben's question about what Ethan's been doing leaves no one confused, but tells the audience what they need to know: that Martha knows enough about Ethan's dubious activities that she doesn't want the children to hear about them. The audience learns also about the problems of the present. That Martha and Ethan love one another is suggested from the beginning when she greets him and than backs toward the house smiling lovingly at him. Ford also makes clear how this relationship makes that between the two brothers tense and troubled, though confidence in Martha's steadfastness causes Aaron to assure Ethan he's welcome to stay as long as he wants.

Ethan's roughness is clear in this introduction, but also his tenderness, expressed especially to the children. To them he's happy to give his trophies—his Confederate sword and Maximilian medal—because, unlike Winkler's Homeric heroes, he cares nothing about the emblems and proofs of his glory and superiority. He is a liberal democratic hero whose worth relates to his superior abilities and his disinclination to use them for self-advancement or glorification. And Ford weaves his social theme into the warp of these personal ties, by bringing out that part of Ethan's past that in fact torments him and cuts him off from Martha and the good community: his racial hatred. The film's first shock comes when Martin enters, sliding off his horse Indian-style, and rushing in to greet "Uncle Ethan" as warmly as other family members—only to have Ethan rebuff him with cold taunts about his Indian appearance, blood, and non-kinship to him. Marty enters when the family is at table, Aaron at its head and Ethan in the place of honor on the woman of the house's right, as nineteenth-century, and even 1950s, practice dictated. This sitting allows Ford to underline quietly Ethan and Martha's closeness, but also what has separated

Re-searching

them. Aaron is not "isolated" but the opposing focus of interest when Martin sits down next to him. When Ethan spurns Martha's and Aaron's gentle attempts to encourage him to be at least polite to Marty, quiet shock unites the family and isolates Ethan. Martha for the first time looks at him, and at her plate, coldly. The audience also learns the why of Ethan's hatefulness, enough to understand but not to forgive fully his mean behavior to a sweet young man the rest of the family deservedly loves. Ethan had rescued him as a young child from an Indian massacre of his family. This past tragedy not only prefigures the one soon to come but also the divergent reactions: the corrosive racial hatred on Ethan's part and that of inclusive acceptance by the good family/community being born out of frontier hardships and tragedies. At the same time, Ethan's rescue, without his being wholly happy about it, of the part Indian Marty prefigures his coming rescue of Debbie.

To my mind there's nothing confusing, nor anything of importance omitted, in this opening sequence. It is instead a tribute both to Ford's aesthetic proficiency and to moviegoers' skill at catching meaning elliptically presented. Ford knew that good filmmaking wasn't a matter of hitting everything "on the nose" or the audience over the head with each point.[11] It was letting the audience hear and see enough to understand in a medium whose very movement demanded a lot of comprehending that had no time to be raised to consciousness. In watching any film, as in "hearing" the background music, persons grasp much more than they think about, and absorb the vital situation rather than catalogue and categorize it. Yet one can go back, on one's own or led by others, and catch the clues that created the subconscious sense of things. One hears the music, feels the camera angle, knows the personality of the well-known actor, hears the allusions, watches the repetition of image and grasps their unified significance without consciously noting any of these elements. Consider, for example, the closing visual structure of this sequence of scenes on Ethan's return. After dinner, as Ethan, Martha, and Aaron talk and send the children off to bed, we see Marty, excluded by Ethan's hate, alone on the porch with the dog. As the sequence nears its end, however, Martin enters, and is kissed by Martha with the restrained tenderness and much the same gesture as Ethan will be later. Marty goes off to bed with the others who belong, while Ethan is left alone with the dog on the porch. The way Ethan's hate has isolated him more permanently from the familial/communal circle is underlined by the film's first door closing. Aaron appears in silhouette through the open door to the warmly lit bedroom he

David Grimsted

shares with Martha—and the door closes, as firmly and quietly, on Ethan as another door will at film's end. The movie's sense of quiet sadness grows partly out of our already knowing that Ethan deserves his exclusion, though his very faults are a part of his strength, intensity, and capacity to care. He, alone in his black night, doesn't kick but abstractedly pets the pooch.

A sequence of under eight minutes as rich as this is a tribute to Ford's extraordinary craftsmanship, his faith in his art and his audience, the decency of his racial attitudes, and his sense of his genre's conventions and flexibility. And it's Ford's faithfulness to the conventions of the western genre and its ability to embody his social vision that critics miss when they stress *The Searchers*' uniquely dark and tragic dimensions: the unsavory characteristics and background of its hero; his parallelism to the villain; the bleakness of its social landscape; and the tragedy of its ending. That all of these things are comfortably within the tradition of western movies, and of Ford's work, a short trip down the trail of literary integration shows.

Western movie heroes, from their creation by Bronco Billy Anderson, William S. Hart, and Harry Carey, were often loners, men with a past who rode into the story bearing a lot of prior history, hatred, criminality, and destructiveness. Hart's characters were known as "good bad men": a hired gun who supports the crooked town sheriff or range boss, a professional train or bank robber, or a drunken gambler with bar girls on the side who loves to terrorize decent folk. In about half of Ford's early westerns with Carey, the hero is a crook, a kidnapper, a marauder, a hired killer, or a horse thief.[12] Ethan's social credentials at the beginning of *The Searchers*' are comparatively elevated: he fought for the Confederacy and Maximilian and maybe robbed a bank or stage or two later on.

In such morally dubious battles, western film heroes often honed their superior skills, their attractive assurance, and sometimes the moral ambiguities or furies they bring to the myth where they are tested. And the story is the test, often involving simply the events that flow from heroes' choosing the side of good, but frequently the struggle within them between their old demons and their new role or sensibility. Will Harry Carey in Ford's *Riders of Vengeance* (1919) kill the man he wrongly believes helped kill his wife, or really abuse the woman he kidnaps for revenge or profit (*The Scarlet Drop*, 1918; *A Gun Fightin' Gentleman*, 1919)? Will William S. Hart in *The Disciple* (1915) destroy the wife who betrayed him and kill her paramour after the latter saves the life of Hart's child? Will he continue to mock God? Will gentle country boy Tyrone Power in *Jesse James* (1939), driven to crime by railroad rapacity, come to enjoy murder and mayhem?

Re-searching

Will *Red River*'s John Wayne kill his "adopted son" who deposes him for gross brutality on a cattle drive (1948)? Will Gregory Peck bump off one of those callow, fame-seeking adolescents who taunt him in *The Gunfighter* (1950)? Will Gary Cooper abandon the town to evil as he learns how deeply cowardly and craven this community is in *High Noon* (1952)? Will bounty hunter Jimmy Stewart kill to make money in *The Naked Spur* (1953), or Henry Fonda desert the protection of a town that doesn't deserve him to resume his highly profitable business of murder for money in *The Tin Star* (1957)? Will charmingly genial career crook Glenn Ford let honest Van Heflin who's guarding him be killed in *3:10 to Yuma* (1957)? The answer to each question, like the one about Ethan's killing Debbie, is no, and audiences know it's going to be no. Yet the excitement and involvement in each film lies in keeping the option the hero can't take a vital possibility until the climax.

Given their often tarnished and tormented backgrounds and continuing moral weaknesses, its unsurprising that many heroes share deep affinity with the films' primary villains. In *The Toll Gate* (1920) William S. Hart and the villain differ only over the latter's desire to perform one more robbery. In *Blood on the Moon* (1948) hero Robert Mitchum and villain Robert Preston are old friends and gunhands who meet again when Preston hires Mitchum's gun. In *Drum Beat* (1954) the good Alan Ladd and the bad Indian alone understand and respect one another.[13] Only hero Stewart Granger fathoms and cares about villainous Robert Taylor in *The Last Hunt* (1956), in part out of their shared experiences as soldiers and buffalo hunters. Hero Jimmy Stewart of *Winchester '73* (1950) and the villain he's determined to kill almost tie in a shooting contest; no wonder since they were taught by the same man, their father. The moral opposites in western films fairly often are boyhood friends, old chums, former gang members, close relatives by blood or adoption, or products of similar experiences. Ethan and Scar, with their parallel speeches, hurts, and ferocities, are securely within this tradition.

One can readily trace the conventions of *The Searchers*' blacker and bleaker genre generalities to Ford's earliest extant westerns, which illustrate well the director's later contention that heroes "shouldn't be holier-than-thou and namby-pamby," that they need "feet of clay" to keep them from turning into "clay statues."[14] Ford established himself as a director in the teens working with actor Harry Carey to create a cowboy hero who was usually "a good bad man" like Hart, but in a more "modern," less highly sentimental mode: earthy, casual, lightly good-humored, as well as capable of viciousness. Carey's style and persona were remarkably like a combination of Ford's two most popular later stars: Will Rogers's bemusedly wise folksiness and John Wayne's down-to-earth granite simplicity, to which a "dark" past was usually attached.[15]

Of their many joint films, only the first feature-length Ford-Carey film is known to be extant, *Straight Shooting* (1917). It, like most films at this time, was quickly made and is uneven, but full of wonderful shots, details, and moral ambiguities showing much less distance than years would suggest between the John Ford of 1916 and of 1956, or between Cheyenne Harry and Ethan Edwards. Harry's "past" is prelude to his remarkable entry into the film. A man nails a wanted poster on a huge live oak, offering $1000 for Harry's capture. A moment later a hand emerges from a hole in the tree and then a smiling face. Harry, head turned from the viewer, reads the bill, scratches his head, and then turns to laugh with the audience. After letting the audience bond with the hero in this brief shot, Ford introduces him fully to the story much later and in much darker guise. We see him sprawled drunk on a barroom table, with the barman urging, "Let him be. Awake, he's a mean man." Awakened, he seems a tough crook or at least a surly and dangerous drunk. Harry moves on to more heavy drinking and abuse of the barkeep, now with his buddy, a fellow robber and hired gun for the bad ranchers. Fortunately both men get drunk enough so they miss when they try to gun down an unarmed young man they've been told to kill.

These buddies, too drunk to murder, are the film's hero and its villain, and no movie could work harder to underline pictorially their closeness of relationship and character. When they miss their prey, the two, guns in hand, are so mistrustful of each other that they awkwardly walk and go downstairs in tandem so no back will be exposed to the drunk and irritated other. Society, as the film shows it, is no more spotless than Harry. People in town for the shootout flit around wanting both to watch and to avoid injury, with the same combined curiosity and cowardice that 1950s westerns often used to scorn America's "townfolks." And in the end, the good farmers are saved not by Harry's courage nor their own, much less the cavalry or cops. Harry informs the farmers, "They're too many. We have to meet killers with killers"—and rides off to enlist his old gang of bandit-murderers who obligingly ride to the rescue of the nation's good farmer yeomanry.

At the end of this film, Harry, outside and alone, holds his arm in the gesture that Ford movingly had Wayne repeat at the end of *The*

Re-searching

Searchers, with its suggestion that the hero has only himself to hold. While the extant print has Harry finally getting the girl, this was an add on for the film's rerelease in 1925. Initially he rode off, "left facing the setting sun alone" after having left the heroine to her young suitor.[16] For all its dark, ironic, and sad elements, *Straight Shooting* remains a remarkably sweet, upbeat, and conventional western. If Carey "tutored" him as Ford later claimed in these early collaborations, Ford never forgot the lessons of how much personal and social moral ambiguity the western's positive structure allowed.

Straight Shooting also shows how early Ford came to some of his favorite and most effective visual tactics He already uses shots through doorways, men framed by a slit in monumental cliffs, or sentries silhouetted against the sky with dramatic intensity. His funny and loving fondness for family is a steady visual theme, as in the girl's tousling her brother's hair as she serves dinner. Ford constructs one of his touching burial sequences, has the audience see Harry watching it, and then has them see the mourners again, now blurrily through Harry's tears. When the girl clears the table where her brother will never eat again, she picks up his bowl, touches it to her lips and breast, and tenderly puts it away from the other dishes in a small drawer in the hutch, in poignant suggestion of private burial and memorial to her love for him.[17]

Ford's early films did well, but his first blockbuster came in 1924 with *The Iron Horse,* a handsome western rather heavily plotted and determinedly inclusive and epic. Two years later he made a more personal and aesthetically unified western, *Three Bad Men,* where Ford's sense of America and the frontier experience were joined to a story that gave full and wonderfully balanced rein to his sentimental, comic, and dramatic sensibility. This movie's three bad heroes have a history that makes Ethan seem saintly. Ford introduces them to the film by showing four wanted posters for them—one in Spanish—for varied crimes, and the camera's first shot of them duplicates that of the first wanted poster picture. All we ever learn of them is that their leader and the film's hero, Bull, "lived day by day on pluck, powder, and providence" and that his more comic companions "weren't exactly thieves—but they had a habit of finding horses no one had lost." Ford and the audience both know this is all any reasonable viewer need know: here are the heroes and they have enough of a past for this to be an "adult" western.

The good bad guys and the sheriff's evil gang meet in a way that underlines their basic unity. Both are about to swoop down on characters we've met earlier: an old Virginia colonel and his jaunty pretty daughter, Lee, who are bringing race horses to help them to get to the best gold lands when the Dakota strip is opened. The gang gets to these intended victims first; the bad men see them arriving just after they put on masks. Our heroes express moral outrage—"Why the low-down horse thieves"—before they ride down, not intending to rescue but to do the stealing themselves. They quickly drive off the gang, and the two begin to round up the horses; and Bull moves toward what looks like a young man grieving above the body of the father. Bull takes out his gun, and is about to shoot Lee—when her hat comes off: "By golly—he's a woman!" This revelation stays the execution, but not the intended theft—until the girl sees the hero, and, thinking him her rescuer, thanks profusely her almost killer. The moment of putting his gun near the girl's head is chilling; one's relief at the change palpable—the parallel with Ethan and Debbie clear. When Lee learns from the sheriff that her rescuers are really crooks, she knows, as do we, who's really decent. She tells the three she'd like to hire them, though she has no money at the moment and she knows they might have other business. "To tell the truth, miss" one answers for all, "our business ain't what it used to be."

At the end of the film, the three bad men have one last task: in sequence, with guts and good humor, they sacrifice their lives, Bull and the corrupt sheriff simultaneously killing each other in the last gunfire, so that Lee, her man and American society may flourish. There is a brief epilogue. "The years went on—The West was won—And those who came for treasure found it in harvests of golden grain!" The camera pans a vast wheat field and in on Lee and Dan by the wagon-wheel gate of their farm cottage, symbol that the mobility that brought them here has become the stability of the yeoman ideal. And there's a fat, somewhat obnoxious looking baby who's got out of his cradle—and is playing with a gun. Dan tells the baby "And someday I'll tell you of the best Three Bad Men that ever named a baby." As in most Ford's best films the personal tragedy is subsumed and sanctified in the decent communal process.[18]

At the end of *The Searchers,* the hero's fate is less tragic, and that of society less underlined but little less positive. The long missing member of the family is home, lovingly accepted, and the door closes in security on all those who wish to enter, whatever their race, creed, or previous experience. Civilization is a coming; the Edwardses' frontier soddy has been replaced by the Jorgensens' Victorian rural gothic house as the locus of family and community. Ethan, not ready for the rocking chair so genially readied for Mose, goes off alone, like Cheyenne Harry of *Straight Shooting*

Re-searching

or the Irish hero who protects home, country and girl that he himself must leave in *Hangman's House* (1928). In *Three Bad Men,* the Moses and exodus imagery is explicit. And in *The Searchers* Aaron's brother who has brought the community through the wilderness, cannot himself enter the promised land of the "Texicans," the good and decent place that has come to be, partly for his sins that are so entwined with his virtues. The power of both films—as in the best of Ford's canon and Americana—lies in his full faith in the meaningfulness of the process and of his film genre to express it. Ford's confidence allows him to accept fully the costs and tragedies and sadnesses involved with the process.

The uneasiness in *The Searchers* comes in Ford's racial "idea." His antiracism is as sincere as was his earlier anti–money seeking, but its expression is more befuddled. Ford in his first scenes makes Ethan's racist flaw clear and shocking, but racism seems non-existent outside him until well into the film. No one besides Ethan shows any concern about Marty's Indian blood. Martin needn't prove himself worthy of communal inclusion, as Henderson argues, because from the beginning he's included without question—in much the same way that Debbie is at the end of the film. The good society that the country will become has little troubling racism, but only the individual twisted by furious personal response to the harsh brutality of the process. The basic distinction between the situation of Native Americans, during the time of fierce conflict between cultures, and that of African Americans in "settled" America, limits the tellingness of the allegory by suggesting that racism is centrally a product of personal weakness and temporal circumstances.

When the Indians kill Aaron's family, except for the captured child Debbie, the long search begins. Through the years, Ethan keeps going, on his faith that Indians can't understand or handle someone who "just keeps comin' on"; and Martin accompanies him out of fear that Ethan wants not to rescue Debbie but to kill her. While Ethan's sharper competence and comprehension of the Native Americans are made clear, so is his netherside of hate. His violence that creates audience shock is not the expected killing of Indians in battle or ambushing bad guys while using Martin's living body as a decoy, but the unexpected. It climaxes in his scalping his dead Indian enemy and alter ego, and includes his shooting out the eyes of a dead Comanche so he will wander blind in the spirit world; his wish to slaughter dozens of buffalo so "at least they won't feed any Comanch this winter"; and his description of the recaptured and insane white females, "They ain't white—not anymore; they're Comanch." All of these scenes suggest racism made frightening, but also racism that grows from personal rather than social pathology.[19]

It's unsurprising that Ford would have more discomfort handling the problem of American racism than he had assaulting the excesses of capitalist graspingness and greed. The latter were major themes of the Progressive Era of Ford's young manhood and of the melodrama, the theater of Ford's youth in which the main early influences on his art directly honed their talents: D. W. Griffith, William S. Hart, and especially Harry Carey. In traditional melodrama, those who pursued money and power overtly were villains to be foiled by those happy to sacrifice self, and more readily pelf, for virtue, family, and community.[20] In Progressivism's intellectual turbulence, however, the problem of race was comparatively neglected. The decision that the 1954 *Brown* case finally overruled, *Plessy v. Ferguson* (1896), suggested, in a general way, the prevailing social consensus until after World War II: "separate but equal" was good—and few would show concern about the "equal." The New Deal never deeply engaged the issue of race, and the era's great social protest artifact, *Grapes of Wrath,* book and film, confined its sympathies to whites only.[21] The ablest aesthetic attempts to expose American racism, such as *Uncle Tom's Cabin* and *Huckleberry Finn,* made clear how hard it was to find the "correct" position—a difficulty especially great for an aging filmmaker who developed his American art and ideas over long years when he and his society gave little thought to racial injustice.

Ford expressed fury in his later life when people accused him of racism, and in lots of ways rightly so.[22] There was no suggestion in any of his films of hostility to blacks or of any tolerance for the grosser cruelties visited upon them. He had Harry Carey marry a heroine with some black blood in an early film made from a Ford story. In *Arrowsmith* (1931) he, with the support of the book, presented an able, attractive black doctor without condescension or any suggestion of anything out of the ordinary, perhaps Hollywood's only precedent for Sidney Poitier's character in *No Way Out* (1950). He fought hard, if unsuccessfully, to keep an anti-lynching sequence in *Judge Priest* in 1934 and emphasized it in his remake of 1953, *The Sun Shines Bright.* The NAACP awarded him a certificate of merit in 1937 for the pointed if mild anti-imperialism of *The Hurricane.*[23] Four of his films after *The Searchers* were, like it, grounded in antiracist themes.[24]

Yet there is the other side of the story, symbolized best in Ford's favorite African American performer, Stepin Fetchit, who appeared in five

Re-searching

Ford films and who would have appeared in more had producer Daryl Zanuck not been more attuned to post–World War II sensibilities than his director. Fetchit won wealth and popularity in the 1930s with the worst caricature of blacks: dumb, slow, lazy, and inarticulate to the point of being often literally unintelligible. The persona is socially indefensible, but aesthetically the stereotype is carried so far it circles back on itself. Someone slowly scratching an ear to get his brain—slowly—in motion is a caricature; someone reaching with his right hand over his head to scratch his left ear to get his brain to work broaches caricature of the caricature.[25] Whatever the case, Ford used Fetchit straightforwardly with affectionate humor. At the beginning of *Judge Priest*, Will Rogers has to wake Fetchit up—"If anyone's going to sleep in this court, it's going to be me"—to be tried for chicken theft. The trial erupts into genial argument about what Fetchit uses for catfish bait—and the scene is cut to a shot of Rogers and Fetchit strolling away side-by-side with fishing poles over their shoulder and pails of the preferred bait in hand.

Ford was too old after World War II to outgrow the sentimental and in some ways demeaning stereotypes that he worked into his films from the ethnic and vaudeville stages as well as movies of his youth. When briefly assigned to direct the "black problem film" *Pinky* in 1949, Ford clashed with Ethel Waters over the handling of her role, and Zanuck convinced him to withdraw in favor of Elia Kazan.[26] Kazan understood that, for all the "mammy" qualities of the character, the film depended on letting Waters transcend the role's comic possibilities with her strong, even steely, sense of self-definition.[27] Ford instead showed his older-style racial liberalism in *The Sun Shines Bright*, basically his earlier *Judge Priest* with the lynching restored. Ford's lynching sequence was very much of a piece with those in *Intruder in the Dust* (1950) and later *To Kill A Mockingbird* (1961). Ford's lynching is in one way superior to the parallel films: only he shows a dignified black man, quietly, non-aggressively, but bravely, standing between the mob and the terrified man they yearn to kill.

Group stereotypes fill Ford's—as most other—films. Ken Curtis's dumb hillbilly suitor is the most jarring example in *The Searchers*, and John Qualen's dumb but goodhearted Swede, with his "by golly" tag, fits the pattern, too.[28] Nor can one enter a Ford one-table Mexican bar without a hot senorita provocatively swaying her hips at the men to the clack of finger tambourines. At least she's not named Chihuahua in this film. Ford was equally ready to laugh at the stereotyped Irish taste for the battle and the bottle; a sequence in *The Rising of the Moon* (1957) has the whole nation happy at any delay-of-train as chance to belt down more booze. The alcoholic editor of the boomtown paper in *Three Bad Men* is, we're told, "half Scotch and half seltzer," and the town's hopeful haberdasher is Joe Minsk, who calls the preacher "rabbi" as he complains of poor business. Most fun is made of a city dude, a dapper little man who the two comic badmen briefly consider as a husband for the heroine. The fellow's terrified as the drunks make sure his hair is real, inspect his teeth, and philosophize, "If a man's heart is in the right place, it don't matter what sex he belongs to."[29]

The humor in *Three Bad Men* works almost perfectly; that in *The Searchers* reasonably well—as watching the film with any sizable audience always proves. It is not primarily relief to the tragedy or tension of the main action, but an integral part of Ford's vision of the inclusive American family and community that informs the more sentimental aspects of his vision. How audiences respond to stereotype humor is, of course, a different issue from how one should respond to it. A good case can be made for stern righteousness in casting out such socially sinful stuff. There's something to be said, too, for toleration and remembering how often groups were not only the butt of such jokes but creators and appreciators of them, too. The canny decency of the stereotyped figures, and their inclusion in the good community, gave at times to the comparatively marginal a comfortable feeling both of belonging and of superiority to their "simpler" representatives. Fetchit honed his "act," and won popularity, first in vaudeville for black audiences.[30]

Drums Along the Mohawk (1939) perhaps best represents Ford's racial sensibilities. The chief Indian character, Blue Back, is used for comedy—he drinks and gives advice about the wisdom of wife beating—but he is part of the good community, as is the black maid Daisy. The latter is treated straightforwardly; she gives out one Butterfly McQueen squeak at the birthing, but otherwise behaves sensibly and is active protecting the fort. Yet the comic Blue Back, not the hero, kills the villain (certainly an odder substitute avenger than Marty). And Ford at the film's very patriotic end does something perhaps no other director at the time would have done. As the American flag is raised after the victory, Ford highlights four groups, ending with hero and heroine. A salt-of-the-earth old white couple comes in between the Native American and the African American, both shot from below to suggest heroic stature. Ford believed in the dream and that no one stood outside it.

Because the "late" John Ford oeuvre was so much a piece with the early, Ford's use of Native Americans to attack the nation's antiblack racism was especially problematic. Ford always vehemently insisted that he'd never been anti-Indian; but in his early films he seems never to have given Native Americans a thought beyond the most common clichéd use of them in westerns. They simply were not involved in most of his Harry Carey collaborations. In *The Iron Horse* the Indians were simply the threat, the savage servants of the white entrepreneur villain, a device repeated closely in *Drums Along the Mohawk*. In *Three Bad Men* Native Americans have no real role other than dignifiedly standing by as the whites march by in their course of empire. There is a beautiful shot of a tree falling and then Indians in the foreground as the camera pans across the river and plain where settlers advance. It's a powerful image of the vanishing American—who in fact vanished from Ford's mind; he labels the new land a "trackless wilderness."[31] In *Stagecoach* Ford provided movies' most vivid enactment of whites holding off huge numbers of roaring savages, whom the audience knows only by the varied picturesqueness with which they are shot dead.[32]

Ford's *Stagecoach* and earlier filmic Indian baggage was surely no help to him when he began to consider that the Native American "threat" were people, too, in his postwar years. In *Fort Apache* (1949) Ford much changed the moral equation by making the white leader, pursuing his glory with Homeric intensity and fretting that it wasn't recognized sufficiently, responsible for an unneeded bloody conflict with the Apaches. And Ford certainly intended his *Cheyenne Autumn* (1964) as a mea culpa gesture to those people whom he recognized he'd had killed in numbers greater than most leaders of the United States' expansion west.[33] Yet in both films Ford's deep interest remains in the white experience. This makes *Cheyenne Autumn* Ford's least coherent film, coming close to a satire on his good intentions. Indian characters, culture, and conflicts are left almost unintelligible beyond the victimization theme, as Ford focuses on the good soldier hero, the heroine who serves as a protective nanny to the Cheyenne children on the long march, and the villain, made a Nazi-like German American. And at film's end, deus ex machina Edward G. Robinson drops in from Washington to announce permanent just peace, and offer cigars to all. The shoved-in puerile Dodge City sequence was for Ford escape back to the world of white choice he was comfortable exploring, the longest of many dusty detours *Cheyenne Autumn* took to avoid the Indian-centeredness of the book Ford was supposedly bringing to the screen.[34]

Some of these problems, in less debilitating form, enter *The Searchers*. The three episodes of general white-Indian battle are key illustrations. The first is beautifully shot and wholly conventionally structured: the whites chasing Indians find themselves surrounded, race to a river, and win, as the Native American contributors to this volume point out, by slaughtering lots of Indians while suffering one casualty. In such crises, Indians just can't shoot straight, convention decrees, anymore than the dumb savages of *Stagecoach,* falling dead in flocks while chasing whites, would think of shooting a horse to stop the stage.[35] The second battle, seen only in its aftermath, Ford uses to try to even the film's moral balance: Ethan and Marty come on the remnants of an Indian camp through which the U.S. Cavalry has swept, the destructiveness of this raid underlined in the oddly immaculate body of an Indian woman left behind. Here, as Pye argues, one gets real if muted sense of the nation's institutionalized racism. In the final battle, just before the film's climax, there is talk before it begins of how much slaughter there will be, but Ford shows only a few Indian men being shot—most run away—and these are given no emotive weight as the film hurries on to the Ethan-Debbie showdown and the farce of doctoring the sword wound to Reverend Captain Clayton's behind.

The middle scene, less plot needed, is Ford's gesture to equal justice, but stands out for that reason more than for any special power. Look's fate evokes pity, and perhaps a touch of audience guilt for having so recently laughed at her comic humiliation, but her body defies any sense of rape or gross brutality. She is a sadly innocent victim, but without hint of the awfulness of Martha's and Lucy's end, which the audience "sees" so memorably because Ford so effectively makes clear that their deaths were too horrible to look upon.

This scene is book-ended not only within the two "conventional" white-Indian battles but directly between two other sequences which Pye and others rightly find jarringly out of tune with an antiracist theme. The first and longest sequence deals with Look's entry into the film. Ford introduces her by injecting into the dumb Charlie's comic courting of Laurie a letter from the simple Marty explaining his comic "marriage" to Look. Laurie's reading of the letter with mounting exasperation is intercut, in classic film fashion, with the reality the letter, very stiltedly, is trying to describe.[36] Martin uses a bowler hat to buy, he thinks, a blanket—but he finds he has actually bought a plump, plain Indian wife. Martin is irritated when she persists in following him, and Ethan immensely amused: "Come on, Mrs. Pauley!" This comic duet continues as Look tries to do domestic work at a campsite, and climaxes when Marty kicks her out of bed, she rolls over and over down a sandhill, and Ethan jokes that in Texas that's cause for "dee-vorce." Disturbing to feelings of political correctness, the scene retains that humorous zest Ford usually brings to his low comedy sequences. Nor is there any sense of hostility and hurtfulness toward Look, who retains substantial dignity. She doesn't seem dumb like Ford's Anglo yokels like Charlie or irresponsible like the comic Irishmen Ford had Victor McLaglen often play.

Is Ford's crude but unhostile laughter at Anglo dudes and rubes all right, in contrast to his crude but unhostile laughter at other members of the American community? Clearly academic critics tend to think so, but their explanations of why Ford inserted the comic Look sequence are dubious. If, as Lehman has argued, the "almost unbearable tensions" in *The Searches* forces Ford to behave "like a high school kid," the bulk of his other films must fully share these "unbearable tensions."[37] Nor does Pye's argument about the traditions of the genre apply. There is no film precedent for Ford's use of a Native American woman for comic relief. It was a Fordian innovation toward integration, slightly increasing his huge repertory of laughable folk who populate his humorous Americana.

Pye also stresses the racism of the captive scene that follows the one revealing Look's death. Searching for clues about Debbie, Ethan, and Marty are shown four captive women rescued in the cavalry's murderous raid on the Indians. Two of them are clearly crazed, a young girl who has presumably been raped and an old woman who keens for a lost baby, presumably killed long ago. The scene is redolent with a sense of excess, of something a bit twisted entering from story-teller to story. Yet paired with the aftermath of the cavalry slaughter and roundup, the captive scene shows the costs of the brutal conflict to all sides. Parallel to the scene revealing Look's murder, Ford uses it, with subtle power, to underline Ethan's deep decencies and their ties to his shocking racism.

Over Look's body, Martin is given the liberal verbal message, "What'd them soldiers have to go kill her for? She never did 'em any harm." But he without a breath rushes on to what concerns him more, "We gotta catch up with them yellowlegs. Maybe they've got Debbie with them." The visual in fact instills what real sadness the scene conveys. Ethan gently covers the body with the blanket that began the long comic-tragic sequence, the way we imagine him covering Lucy with his rebel coat. Then as Martin talks, he stands delicately brushing Look's funny hat with something of the tenderness with which Martha brushed his rebel coat much earlier.

This is the response not of a man who simply hates Indians, but one whose racism is the product of knowing better and feeling more deeply the costs of an often horrifying conflict between races—and knowing whose

David Grimsted

Sadness: Ethan contemplating Look's death.

side he is on. The captive scene features terrible words that remind us of Ethan's half-crazed racism: "They ain't white—not anymore. They're Comanch." The words are what's remembered most vividly from the scene, a central hint that Ethan might kill Debbie. Yet Ford closes the scene with quiet reminder of the hero's compassion that is the source of his racism. Marty is only concerned about getting information about Debbie, and the soldiers show only casual racism: "It's hard to believe they're white." But just before he leaves Ethan looks back in torment—and makes the audience briefly recognize the human cost of the conflict that fuels his fury. His—and our—last look is at the older woman, whose recent experience of cavalry killings has sharpened memories of her long dead babe. This glance, like Ethan's gestures over Look's body, evokes compassionate sense of the woman's loss. She, like Ethan, has suffered too much to rejoin the white community. Linked by Ethan's tormented gaze, remembered tragedies unite the two as "others"—as Comanch, if you will: one keening in madness and one to scalp in triumphant fury.

Several westerns showed some commitment to melodrama's "fate worse than death" clichés; "the last bullet" or even the "last dynamite" to

Re-searching

At the fort: Ethan contemplating the crazy older woman.

save white womanhood was used enough, even as late as the 1950s, to become a joke.[38] Yet Ford's use of white captives seem uniquely fetid, a bit odd in *The Searchers* and demented in his later *Two Rode Together* (1961).

Here Ford returned partly to his anti-money grabbing theme with raunchy good humor. The flawed hero (Jimmy Stewart), like his Indian alter ego (Henry Brandon, who played Scar in *The Searchers*), enters the captive business strictly as an entrepreneur. Asked "What do you think human lives are worth?" he cynically replies, "Whatever the market will bear." This is perhaps the only western to move a captive story beyond the moral/psychological issues into its economic superstructure that Brooks makes clear. The film's problems come in its antiracism theme that centers on the bad treatment given a returned captive, a beautiful Spanish woman, Elena, who has been the wife of a chief. The centerpiece here is one of Ford's dances, this one not evoking the sweetness of the American community, but prejudice and coarse curiosity toward the "fallen" woman. She is given a strong speech about how white prejudice is worse than her terrible sufferings as a captive. The hero, whom love turns from a cynic seeking after the "unholy grail" of gold to a pursuer of romantic/humanistic

What Ethan sees.

happiness, then tells the assemblage more about Indian awfulness and that he knows they are all wondering why Elena didn't kill herself if she's decent. He has a good answer: she's Catholic. The suicide/insanity choice, thus, is truism applicable only to decent Protestant women.

Much of the film illustrates Ford's weird views about captives. In the Indian camp, the film shows two women, one skulking in horror, half-crazy at the degradation of having two children by an Indian, and the other older one explaining she's so debased she couldn't bear the embarrassment of return to civilization. Even odder is the young male white captive brought back because a businessman has offered the hero money for anyone he can pass off as his wife's long-lost child. This returned captive is depicted like an animal, so oddly crazed and savage he kills the woman who believes she's his mother. In this handling, Ford's fixations about captive debasement, unparalleled in other westerns, seem scarier than the social racism he attacks.[39]

Debbie, like Elena, lives and doesn't go mad, but Ford has little sense of how to treat her except as symbol of society's acceptance. She says at the first meeting with Ethan and Martin that she had long hoped for rescue, but now "these are my people," though her anxiety to protect her white relatives by strongly encouraging them to leave seems her main motive.[40] This supports Lehman's assertion that in *The Searchers* you can't often trust what people say. There is no indication that her life as Scar's wife has been terrible, but when Martin comes for her later, she smiles happily and says "O, Marty, yes"—and despite many critics, there is no serious contradiction if we examine her motives in the first scene. As Ethan carries her "home" and the Jorgensen family/community take her in, she says or does nothing: not a word said, not even a step taken until Ethan puts her on the sheltering porch. This has something to do with the nature of 1950s— and Ford's—racial liberalism, geared to society's generously admitting others rather than changing its own vision a bit to benefit from somewhat different perspectives. It was a dream, surely beautiful enough, of one truly inclusive culture, not many.

The film's clearest gesture suggesting personal racism beyond Ethan comes in Laurie's speech near the end of the film in which she says terrible things: that Debbie is now "the leavings of Comanche bucks, . . . with savage brats of her own," that Ethan will kill her if he gets a chance, and that Martha would so want it. The words are as snarlingly vicious as any of Ethan's, but they don't have the same impact. We know they are really voiced out of love of part-Indian Martin—to keep him home. She has waited six years for Martin; his letter that cemented Charlie's courting elicited her earlier angry, "A squaw!" Now, immediately after disrupting her wedding, Martin is off again on her chase. And she uses arguments that Martin himself implanted in his mind, his naive interpretation of Ethan's stance, last time he dropped by—five years ago. She says them to hold the man whose racial ancestry bothers her and her family not a jot. No one feels a touch of surprise when Laurie joins in leading Debbie— and Martin—back into the sheltering community.

There is little in the film that contradicts Ford's point in his opening sequence: Ethan's racism is what cuts him off from the rest of the family/society. No one else considers Martin's genes; nobody even shows great personal hostility to the Native Americans with whom tragic conflict is fought, except Brad briefly, in fear and then grief about Lucy's fate. Clayton pushes down Ethan's gun when he tries to shoot at departing Indians at the end of a fight, just as Marty tries to interfere with Ethan's shooting buffalo so they won't be there for Comanches to eat. Even at those points where some Indian-hating would seem humanly logical, Ford turns anger elsewhere. Jorgensen blames not Indians when he laments his only son's death, but "this country." And when Charlie, his marriage disrupted, tells Martin he has no right to marry Laurie, he explains it not in terms of Martin's blood but in those of prior Indian wives. Ford's society in the film, rather than racist, is notably free of racism even where circumstances would lead one to expect it.

Laurie's speech functions in the narrative not to condemn her, much less her family/community, for sharing Ethan's racial hate, but to help convince the audience that Ethan may really attempt to kill Debbie, on which partial belief depends the power of *The Searchers'* climax. Ethan's last minute change of heart is something critics, pretty unconvincingly, have long tried to explain in terms of some sudden moral epiphany. When I first saw the film, I thought that Ford cheated, offering no clues to the expected conclusion we have been led to believe just might happen differently. Closer inspection suggests how fairly, and cleverly, Ford leads and misleads his audience. Nowhere in the film does Ethan say or suggest he plans to kill Debbie. His hatred for Native Americans is repeatedly and chillingly underlined, though this is tied to his responsiveness to the tragedies of the conflict. And this is far different from planning to kill his niece. But the naive and impressionable Marty doesn't see this; he tells Laurie, and us, that Ethan plans to kill Debbie, with adolescent melodrama—explaining this conclusion wholly by Ethan's fury against Indians. He's apparently seen and heard no more than we have, but Laurie—and we—are encouraged to accept his leap of logic from one thing to the very different one. And when Laurie tells us what Ethan plans to do and what Martha would want, she elaborates the rumor she got from Martin in a way that supports our fears. But if we thought about the data, her only source of information about this comes from Martin, and from her fantasy, and ours, elaborating his interpretation—or rather misinterpretation.

Ethan says little about Debbie directly. At the end of the first journey, Marty despairs that now their search is hopeless, and Ethan quietly assures him he'll go on because "If she's alive, she's safe." He tells Futterman he'll get his reward only "if we find her and if she's safe." *Safe,* again. When the grown Debbie comes to ask them to go away, Ethan draws a gun on her, and there is dramatic music in the background. But we really have no indication of whether he intends to shoot her or to try to keep her from running away. Again Ford lets Martin—arms outstretched in front of Debbie and face terrified—impose his fears on us. After the rather grossly conventional battle where the two white men (one wounded), handily hold off hordes of Indians, Marty reminds Ethan that Debbie is his kin: "Not

Re-searching

no more she ain't. She's been livin' with a buck, she's no. . . . ." This parallels his initial rejection of kinship to Marty, but the young man interrupts to impose his fears on the audience: he knows Ethan was about to shoot her. Then we get the film's one explicit movement to kill within the "family"—it comes from Martin, who frenziedly takes out a knife to kill Ethan. Of course he doesn't, but the scene heightens the audience's "hearing" Ethan as intended murderer in Marty's, Laurie's, and now its own fantasy.

LeMay's book contains nothing about Ethan's plan to kill Debbie. Marty's fear in the book grows out of a sense that Ethan was more intent on revenge than rescue which might lead him to attack Indians in ways that would endanger the girl. Ford knew the hint of personal demonism that would consider intentional murder was much stronger stuff, and he and Nugent wrote Ethan planning this, and the script's climax comes complete with Ethan pointing a gun at kneeling Debbie's head. Yet during the filming Ford created a subtler story where audience misinterpretation would create the climatic excitement.[41] When the young man saves Debbie and kills the villain, Ethan scalps Scar to underline our hero's flaw, and the ties of suffering and of hate that connect the two men. Then he rides to rescue Debbie—and the audience from its fears that he would fail the film's basic test. Rightfully it is Ethan who brings Debbie home and on whom the door closes, still hero, still alone.

Ethan's status as hero which requires that he pass the "test" socially protectively rather than destructively comes also because we see him taking on that role steadily in regard to the character who is the catalyst for our initial recognition of Ethan's racism. He saves Martin as a child; he again saves his life by keeping him from following Brad to his death. He tries to protect Martin by getting him to stay behind when he renews the quest, and by trying to change his mind about going in alone to protect Debbie. He keeps him from drinking in good paternal fashion: "Wait'll you grow up." And he wills his property to Martin.[42] For all Martin's fears and Ethan's roughness of manner they are good buddies; Ethan's sobriquets—lunkhead or blankethead—and teasing about Mrs. Pauley shows that Ethan's racism doesn't destroy his developing protective affection for the boy.

There are Ford's visual touches that equally effectively underline the truth we felt about Ethan's caringness shown to the children in first scene. He says he counts on the raid killing Debbie, and Martin chastises him for it, but he actually shows no personal wish to do it—only brief opposition to Marty's plan to slip into Scar's camp to rescue Debbie. He pats Marty

David Grimsted

Sadness: Ethan contemplating the probable deaths of both Lucy and Debbie

affectionately on the arm as he leaves. Cinematographer Winton Hoch understood the emotive power of the black silhouette in a color film, and he and Ford first show Ethan in silhouette outside the destroyed Edwards home.[43] Ford has also revealed, in powerful closeup, Ethan's fear when he plumbs the Indians' intent and his fury when he sees its results. And we see his shadow kneeling before a smoking beam: the outlined head and hat bend downward slightly in powerful evocation of deep grief, touched with religious resignation. The Look/captive women sequences underline Ethan's already established traits of character, his responsiveness to suffering that goads his verbal racist virulence. Ethan's most shocking actions are tied also to his knowledge of, indeed respect for the traditions of the enemy: shooting out the eyes and scalping the dead opponents. If such acts are inhuman, Comanches were inhuman. Ethan is a multiculturalist in a mode more serious than the academic sentimental one. Even his shooting at the buffalo was clearly a gesture of fury at the costs and frustrations of the conflict. It is far from an exterminating plan like that which was briefly U.S. Cavalry policy, or its casual enactment as white man's sport. Ethan's flaws are made shocking but Ford lets us know, mostly though the quiet shots that punc-

Re-searching

tuate his fury, its deeply humane connections. These are to this democratic hero what the twenty-fourth book is to *The Iliad* in Winkler's analysis.

In this interpretation, the strength of *The Searchers* grows not out of its iconoclasm, but its faithfulness to the genre and the ideology in which Ford had honed great skill and rich vision. It makes Ethan much less vicious, though no less flawed. It's also faithful to Ford's desire to use his art to advance causes that he saw as essential to democratic decency and American values. That social, generic and personal weaknesses complicate Ford's wish to attack racism is clear. Yet Ford's struggle with his racial "idea" sharpens his love for the hard beauty of his landscape and hero, and of those folks he saw as earning entry, through hardship, into a decent society. In this film—and others—Ford is the warm, if never uncritical, poet of Americana, delicately affectionate, though always with some dose of fairly crude comedy and melodrama, much in accord with the country he loved.

Perhaps Ford sensed some of his problem. He tells us that the name of Scar's band, the "Nawyecka Comanch," means "kinda like 'roundabout'—fella says he's going to go one way, means to go t'other." This motto suits the film, as it does the nation whose growth the film celebrates and frets about. Yet the film, like Debbie, does hit home. Ford drew viewers into a story of comforting conventions and of a terribly flawed but deeply decent hero, with whom audiences could identify, while strongly feeling his racist excess and the sad necessity of his exclusion because of it. For a nation struggling both to slough off its racism and to stress an underlying virtue and inclusiveness in its traditions, it was a good and acceptable lesson when put in a form that was felt more than preached. In some ways, Ford's and his genre's strengths and limitations helped *The Searchers* reverberate as decently as Ford wished in the hearts of a troubled country in the midst of big change.

"Well, that's a big help," all intelligent readers should sneer. "We're supposed to get some answer about these varied interpretations, and instead we get another one! So what we needed was more confusion?" Yes, partly. Such is the process of intellectual growth, where more data and ideas help clarify some things and inevitably confuse others. If you were to write an essay on *The Searchers,* you would essentially try to figure out what others had seen in it and said about it, and find something that had been neglected or had been handled wrongly or limitedly. If the paper turns out well, it will bring up something that seems convincing or worth seriously considering, and also raise some questions and doubts one hadn't previously pondered.

For the readers, rather than the writers, there's a different problem. How decide between conflicting arguments, and how choose between different ways of looking at the document so as to strengthen sense of the film's meaning and quality?

One chooses between interpretations on a number of legitimate grounds: by proclivity, by consideration of fact, by coherence and richness of argument, and by re-searching the text with various interpretations in mind. The most personal of these criteria, proclivity, is as legitimate as any other, and underlines the right and need everyone has to bring one's own experience and interests to all intellectual questions. Those with complex ethnic heritage tied to the region might feel special affinity for Brooks's essay; set designers or those who care about the relation of broad setting to human mood would find special interest in Hutson's discussion of how Monument Valley effects the film; students of deconstruction might especially respond to Lehman's argument for the movie's indeterminacy; movie buffs might appreciate Eckstein's and Studlar's close tracking of personal and thematic influences between films, or my discussion of conventions/themes within the western genre and Ford's films; those fond of classical literature would be inclined to prefer Winkler's essay; persons with special concern about myth or American racism might be especially responsive to Henderson's approach; American Indians, and many others, might particularly welcome the first publication of Native American responses to the film; feminists would consider centrally significant Studlar's consideration of the gendering of the film's vision. Star watchers, especially John Wayne fans, would be most interested in Luhr's study. Kalinak's essay would fascinate those most responsive to music.[44]

Such prior interests are perfectly reasonable determinants of what you judge "best," though they well may create as much wariness as welcome to specific arguments. Proclivity to topic does not necessarily dictate preference. Some feminist scholars, I'm sure, would dispute Sundlar's quite generous evaluation of Ford's treatment of women, based as it is on woman's distinct role as upholder of domestic, religious, moral, and communal values. This sharp differentiation of gender roles is many feminists' locus of anger, what they see as the basic social mechanism keeping women in "their place."[45]

Often what we find most interesting or valuable is that which, for some reason, draws us into worlds of connection that prove engrossing because we have not much pondered them before. Kalinak's essay, for example, made me more thoughtful about the relationship of music to

Re-searching

film, and her detailed handling of the score and songs within it seemed steadily fascinating. Although I disagree with several of her central conclusions, the article makes me want to be more reflective about an element of film that I usually notice only when it seems insistently manipulative. To get stimulus like this from scholarship or conversation is the purpose and the gift.

Similarly valuable gifts come in smaller packages, observations or passing comments that help us to know or notice things to which we'd otherwise be blind. Lehman's pointing out the parallel Ethan-Debbie lifting gesture near the film's beginning and its close is sharp insight, one that I think underlines the continuities in the hero's decencies. Eckstein's long list of westerns centered on psychological complexes amusingly reminds us how absorptive pop culture is—and how many films could be titled *Oedipus Rides Again . . . and Again.* Studlar's pointing out the references to "what Martha thinks" helped me to better see the shape of the film, without inducing agreement with her claim that this makes Martha the central locus of interest.

Proclivities are equally capable of reasonably leading one away from particular analyses. I find irritating one of the commonplaces of *The Searchers'* scholarship: that Scar is Ethan's id, who, in raping and killing Martha, does what Ethan really wishes to do. For me, this Freudianism seems pasted on in a way that confuses rather than illumines anything. Ethan has plenty of clear faults without making him want to butcher the woman he deeply loves. Why not make this *Martin's* very secret wish? After all he shares the first four letters of name with Martha, and "complexes" toward adopted mothers may be especially twisted. Nor does Martin seem to give much thought to news about his real mother's scalp, while he's the person who rides off toward home right away so there's no chance he'll arrive in the nick of time to rescue the family. He also seems happy to go on any chase to avoid sex with a girl *not* his mother, and draws a knife wanting to kill his "adopted father" later on. My uneasiness with such easy Freudianism, and what strikes me as wayward readings of the text's signposts, create a proclivity to say "Nonsense." And my nonsense and others' "certainly" can't be wholly clarified by the text, because the decision depends on what kind of approach to interpretation one can swallow or grasp.[46]

Facts or evidence also can be brought to bear in weighing interpretations, though they usually less dictate answers than cast doubt on them. My journey into other westerns attempts to show that most things about the film's hero—dark background, deep flaws, vicious actions, close similarities to the villain, use of tricky tactics, exclusion from the society he protects—are common in the genre. I think I show that they are far from unprecedented: these elements are all clear, and most more strongly stressed, in *Straight Shooting*—which Ford made four decades earlier. Yet the question of "how common" is harder to answer, much less the key concern of "how uncommonly powerful." At times scholars neglect of relevant fact seems puzzling. In these papers, I find strange the stress on fears about miscegenation when the central romance in the film, which bothers no one including Ethan, is between the blonde heroine and a man whose Indian blood is emphasized.[47]

Sometimes interpretive differences center on verbal quibbles related to fact. Eckstein and others talk of Ethan's viciousness in relation to his "illicit" love of Martha that threatens to disrupt the family Ford always idealizes. Ford makes clear the love between Ethan and Martha, but does he suggest anything illicit or any real threat to the family? Martha has chosen Aaron, perhaps because of their shared values (made clear at the table) and there's no suggestion that she regrets that choice or her family commitment. Ford uses his framing exclamation points to make clear Aaron belongs in the bedroom and Ethan's place is outside. In broader terms, Ford's interest in family led him to stress often its negative potential, in villainous groups like the Plummers, the Clantons, and the Cleggs and in well-intended but destructive family choices in *Hangman's House, How Green Was My Valley*, and *Wings of Eagles* (1957). And any threat Ethan poses to family is faint compared to that of Ford's mother-hero in *Pilgrimage* (1933), who prevents her only son from marrying the girl he's made pregnant by sending him into the army where he's killed. Perhaps no image in film more strongly evokes the awful results that family love can have than the image of this strong and decent woman, after she hears of her boy's death, fumblingly trying to piece together a picture of him she tore up when she learned of his affair.

If one accepted Lehman's claim that "no dialogue tells us anything" about aspects of the story, one would have to chuck out his theory—all those questions are in the dialogue—and everyone else's. Still one appreciates his visual (like Kalinak's aural) observations, even if one doubts some of the conclusions drawn from them. From the start of his career, Ford used framing devices to concentrate viewers' vision and emotion in key scenes. I don't quite see how his moving from doorways to caves and tepees suggests Ethan's and Marty's "atavistic regression to barbarism," nor do I notice regression, but these visuals help integrate the film experience and powerfully underline Ethan's exclusion at the end. One can fully accept Eckstein's stress on Ford's special importance to the film western without agreeing that the highly popular *Searchers* helped end the genre, or that *Stagecoach* introduced the western as art form in 1939. The success of *The Plainsman* in 1936 encouraged the covey of strong "A" (for adult? for art?) westerns of 1939–40, several of them more popular than *Stagecoach*, that restored the serious western from the teens and twenties to its cinematic centrality.[48] The number and popularity of westerns declined a bit in the 1960s and sharply in the mid-1970s, but to attribute that to a strong critical and financial success made twenty years earlier seems odd.

Facts, too, may mislead. Kalinak's facts are rich, but that Ford had deep awareness of the complex origins and versions of the "oldies" he used effectively is dubious. That he uses these songs to show the impossibility of community in the film or to assure that "the antebellum South is ennobled in the process" seems contradictory to his clear verbal, visual, and structural stress on the coming good society whose door closes on Ethan's racism. And the latter's racism is tied to his Confederate loyalties, which are also linked to his fighting to keep a European usurper on the Mexican throne and to his robberies. In fact, the only Confederate music in the film is "The Bonnie Blue Flag" with its justificatory refrain of southern armies' "fighting for the property we've won by honest toil." Probably Ford didn't think of this, but if he was as deeply knowledgeable about nineteenth-century music as Kalinak and Eckstein suggest, this odd labor justification of slavery would have appealed to the sense of irony with which Ford leavened his sentimentalities. Probably here, as elsewhere, Ford thought the tune, and its vague ramifications in the audience mind, fit the mood. Lots of things may be true without being truly pertinent to proving a particular point. I accept Henderson's racial argument about the film, but if the "racial myth" conveys greatness on *The Searchers* there were at least nine other great westerns in 1956, and well over 50 in the decade.[49]

Arguments about fact also are entwined with personal experience. Kalinak argues the hymn "Shall We Gather at the River?" suggests "determinism and an overwhelming sense of fatalism." To me it sings of vibrant faith in communal salvation. There is the fact of Methodist faith: God's grace is readily available to all, directly contradictory to Kalinak's claim that the hymn teaches "a Calvinist notion of predestination." There also is the film fact: when the hymn is reprised in the wedding scene we hear it in the affirmative mode to which it moves: "Yes, we will gather at the river." And there's the personal memory of my grandmother singing it, the question wholly rhetorical and the happy communal result assured—despite her own (not to mention her family's) varied waywardnesses.

There are always questions about the generalizing facts people present about groups and genres. I doubt Studlar's argument that Irish Americans idealized home and family more than other groups. Kalinak's confidence that minstrel shows and songs were "created to reinforce white superiority" seems to me a limited explanation of the popularity of this first distinctively American theatrical genre, one rich in popular song in all moods, in expressive dance, in sharp wit and complicated word play that audiences, black and white, enjoyed for decades.[50] The form had deep racist elements, but it less demeaned African Americans—American laws and customs did that—than put them at the center of the American entertainment-aesthetic experience. Partly you can judge this argument by looking at the "demeaning" minstrel song that Kalinak reprints, "Yellow Rose of Texas." Does this jaunty paean to true love, about to be restored, of a beautiful woman denigrate blacks? Why does it not then denigrate the many other groups who eagerly appropriated the ballad?

Generalizations abound in these essays about western films, many of which I judge misleading. For example, Luhr argues that *The Searchers* was much more "iconoclastic" than *High Noon,* without considering what made critics and audiences of the 1950s—and John Wayne—find *High Noon* odd and/or shocking: its stress on the craven, cowardly, greedy nature of a society hardly worth saving since it preferred to accept rather than to fight evil, because that was safer and more profitable.[51] Pye argues that the "basic terms" of the western genre "exist to incorporate rather than criticize racist fears and phobias." Perhaps this is partly true for films like *The Iron Horse, Stagecoach,* and *The Searchers* where Indians provide a basic threat. Yet Native Americans and race enter little or not at all in about half of all westerns, and in another quarter Indians are treated with substantial gestures of respect, or sorrow at their fate, or of anger at the white injustices or attitudes toward them.

One can develop collective facts with a bit less guesswork, though statistics seldom "solve" arguments. My doubts about one theme that laces these essays, American society's and western movies' horror at miscegenation, led me to develop some generalizing facts about sexual unions between whites and Native Americans in cowboy films.[52]

These "facts" suggest a world of attitudes quite different from those Octave Mannoni described.[53] The country in a sense began with the Pocahontas story, and never lost some enthusiasm for interracial romance

Re-searching

Native American / White unions

		Native American woman	Native American man	Half-Breed	Totals
1909–29	happy	13	5	3	21
	tragic	9	1	5	15
	bad	1	—	—	1
1929–45	happy	8	—	—	8
	tragic	1	—	2	3
	bad	—	—	—	—
1946–60	happy	9	5	7	17
	tragic	7	—	—	7
	bad	2	—	—	2

between Indians and whites. No novel in the late nineteenth century was more popular than Helen Hunt Jackson's story of complicated interracial mixing, *Ramona*, nor was any story more frequently adapted to the nation's earliest movies. American audiences had long seen red-white interracial sex as readily acceptable, or titillating, or telling about social injustice, rather than taboo.[54] *The Searchers* offers clearly the same evidence—and about white women and Indian men, where Pye insists the true phobia lay. Most of the interracial romances that ended tragically blamed white injustice and/or prejudice for the result, and most of the "happy" ones suggested more problems than does *The Searchers*.

Westerns proved a good place in the 1950s to decry racism, not only because of their distance from the contemporary controversies over African American status but because predominant social prejudice had long accepted white and Native American unions. In fact, these western miscegenist romances proved popular enough that Daryl Zanuck, always quick to catch public readiness for new film themes, produced Hollywood's first foray into romances between whites and blacks. The success of *Island in the Sun* (1957) began the small but significant number of films dealing sympathetically with white-black miscegenation in Hollywood's late 1950s return to films directly handling African American characters and issues.[55]

For most questions about a specific work, a return to the text offers most hope of forming better answers or choosing between alternative ones.

David Grimsted

Look at the first scene, and decide if Ford leaves the viewer in a morass of uncertainty about what's going on as Lehman claims, or if he with brilliant economy sketches in all that anyone needs to know about his characters and his themes to ready them for the search ahead. Go over the scenes related to the letter Laurie reads and see if you think that her *imaginings* are what we see, or does Ford use the letter to integrate major aspects of what we are to accept as really happening at home and on the search.[56] Consider what Ford presents that leads us to think Ethan plans to kill Debbie, and how reliable that information is. Take a look at those shots and scenes that I think show Ethan's decent caringness, and judge if I describe them accurately, or if you agree with Eckstein's assessment that Ethan steadily shows "a stony lack of all human decency." Consider the *context* of Laurie's racist screed and decide if you think these words prove basic viciousness. Look at the bleak beauty of Ford's setting and decide if you agree with Kalinak that Ford uses it to show unsuitableness for settlement or with Hutson's argument that it "stands for the generalized or mythologized harshness of the American frontier experience." Ponder Ford's "Texicans"—Aaron's family, the Jorgensens, Marty, Mose, Clayton, Charlie—and see if you find them "greedy, hypocritical—and grotesquely racist." Look (as I have often done) at Ethan's look back at the older captive woman and decide if you see the villainy and hatred that most of these writers describe, or tormented grief that guides us back to our most compassionate sense of the woman's tragedy. Pick out anything in these essays that strikes you as particularly right or wrong, and go over the "evidence" for the claim and any other evidence that you notice related to it. Such work may not provide an absolutely clear answer or any "final" truth, but, if done honestly, it should settle your, and most viewers', opinions about some questions, and lead everyone to a richer sense of the film's truth.

Because of lack of finality, some scholars argue that all texts are Rohrsach tests, blanks on which everyone writes their peculiar passions and propensities. In this world, there's no reason for not believing Ethan fathered all the young people in the story, killed Lucy *and* Martha, and laughed so uproariously at Look's being kicked out of Marty's bed because this meant he could get back into it. Even those who assert such principles philosophically pay them no real heed. If they did, they'd have no reason for rejecting the convictions of those who assert absolute truths and values in order to deify wholly contradictory opinions and conclusions. That we see through the glass of self darkly and limitedly is surely true, but that doesn't mean we can't see at all—or see better.

Re-searching

The problem, especially for a cultural historian, involves not only what a cultural product says but what its consumers thought it said. The desirability of glimpsing the special understanding of others is clear, but, since the bulk of this remains unconscious and unrecorded, one is driven back to the text as the trigger of collective response.[57] You may have noticed in my essay I often use "we" and "our" to suggest that audience response would parallel mine—a kind of democratic "we," if you will. This requires a large leap of faith, and the only honest answer to the question "How can you be sure others see and respond as you?" is "I can't." Yet there is some evidence that the film was accepted more comfortably and straightforwardly by audiences than later critical emphasis on its confusing, dark, and tragic nature would suggest. Critics in 1956 found it a strong and beautiful movie—"a rip-snorting western as brashly entertaining as they come," said the *New York Times*—and audiences liked it.[58] With good notices that suggested nothing highly unusual or genre-shattering about it, the American public made *The Searchers* the most successful of the Ford westerns. Ford's own comment on it—"It made a lot of money"—is far from the whole story, but an important part of it, and one that indicates the accessibility and acceptability of the film to the ordinary moviegoer. Of course, popular audiences are no more dependable guides to truth than are scholars.[59]

We properly judge arguments by aesthetic standards as well: how deep, caring, graceful, perceptive, honest is the argument? Since argument/criticism/history depend on factual as well as aesthetic accuracy, verbal and formal grace can mislead as well as they surely lead us toward conclusion. In regard to works of art, where aesthetic truth and depth is all that matters, the standards are always so amorphous that commitment to one's own taste is essential. Others' enthusiasm should make everyone want to look at *The Searchers* closely, but without any commitment to concurring in the choruses of praise to it. After all, those self-appointed judges who compose the popular fodder of "ten best lists" or solemnly announce their discovery of the "great" claimed in the 1950s that *The Informer* was Ford's best work and one of the great films of all time, a position that few now take seriously.[60]

I'd place *The Searchers* in the select company of a second group of Ford films behind *Young Man Lincoln*, *The Grapes of Wrath*, *The Man Who Shot Liberty Valance* and especially *Three Bad Men*, where Ford seems to me to maintain fuller integration of his special commitment to excitement, comedy, the coming of a good community, and his moral theme (in this case the vileness of a central commitment to greed) than he does in *The Searchers*. See it some time and try to "see" what you think. Of course, you shouldn't take my word for what's good in film, if I refuse to take that of Martin Scorcese or Stephen Spielberg or of the writers of these essays, most of whom have studied it longer and more closely than I. With art, as with all kinds of love, take the word of your heart.

Lots of things in *The Searchers* strike me as much less dark, morally and intellectually, than its scholarly fans usually suggest. I'd guess almost every enthusiast of western movies knows the answer to that "existential" question, "What makes a man to wander?" Yet lots of questions and answers should be richer and clearer from looking over these essays' maps of Ford's crisscrossing trails. Certainly they amply warn: don't expect to untangle the mysteries without getting entangled in them. We researchers keep gathering, but not by rivers that flow by the throne of God or Perfect Answer. Yet that always distant shore of truth should be just across some "beautiful river." And maybe since we're "critters that just keep comin' on."

Those who go on searching, guessing, learning, wondering are often left alone, cradling their own right arm, the one that usually wields the gun or the pen. The door closes on them behind the happy community of modern Jorgensens, entering the house to bond over TV and sports and stock market listings—and maybe some videos of good old films. Ford kept learning, too, enough to wonder deeply, at age sixty-six, whether those who came to John Wayne's funeral in *The Man Who Shot Liberty Valence* (1962) were better off in the world they'd won than was the deceased in the world he'd lost.

NOTES

1. Lenihan, *Showdown*.

2. None of Ford's films were among the biggest moneymakers, but the great majority were solidly profitable and several seemingly in the "top ten" for their years, though figures are often uncertain. I use the figures Gallagher gives in his useful appendix in *John Ford: The Man and His Films*, 497–500. Also very successful were *The Iron Horse* (1924), *Arrowsmith* (1932), *The Hurricane* (1937), *How Green Was My Valley* (1941), *They Were Expendable* (1945), *Fort Apache* (1948), *The Searchers* (1956), and *The Horse Soldiers* (1959). Just below these, Gallagher ranks *Salute* (1929), *Judge Priest* (1934), *Steamboat Round the Bend* (1935)—both Will Rogers-Stepin Fetchit films—*Mary of Scotland* (1936), *Wee Willie Winkie* (1937) with Shirley Temple, *Drums Along the Mohawk* (1939), *Grapes of Wrath* (1940), *My Darling Clementine* (1946), *She Wore a Yellow Ribbon* (1949), *Rio Grande* (1950), *The Long Gray Line* (1955), *The Man Who Shot Liberty Valance* (1962), and *Donovan's Reef* (1963). The standard top

Re-searching

ten lists suggest that Gallagher underrates the box office of the Will Rogers-Stepin Fetchit and the Shirley Temple films and *Stagecoach* (1939) and overstates that of *The Hurricane*. From Cobbett Steinberg, ed., *Reel Facts: The Movie Book of Records* (New York: Vintage Books/Random House, 1982). Ironically, if one credits *Mr. Roberts* (1955) to Ford, where it partly belongs, it becomes his biggest box office success, as well as his most troubled shoot.

3. Critic Sarris sets up Ford's postwar reputation—competent but uninteresting—among cultural arbiters in the 1950s and 1960s (*John Ford Movie Mystery,* 12–15). This image Sarris set out to change, as did Anderson in *About John Ford* and Bogdanovich, *John Ford*. The last work has Bogdanovich's interviews with Ford about his films: comments cryptic and cantankerous but also the most revealing and generally honest available from Ford, 36–108. Bogdanovich's documentary film *Directed by John Ford* (1971) richly suggests the continuities in Ford's themes and images that Sarris denies.

4. Churchill appeared in four earlier Ford films, notably as a less partisanly political pomposity in *Judge Priest,* and as a frontier revivalist, the New Moses, in *Steamboat Round the Bend*. Edward Buscombe, *Stagecoach* (London, 1992), 28–32, comments on the political intent of this character, added by Dudley Nichols and Ford to the original story. Warshow's use of *Stagecoach* as a prototype western free from any contemporary concerns suggests the way critics neglect close analysis of westerns prior to the ones they see as "iconoclastic." *The Immediate Experience* (New York: Doubleday, 1962), 149.

5. Davis describes and quotes this speech well, *John Ford: Hollywood's Old Master,* 234. Gallagher quotes the 1933 speech to the Screen Actors Guild where Ford blamed studios cutting workers and salaries on a "crisis" that "big finance" engineered "so that wages and wage-earners can be pushed back to where they were in 1910" (Bogdanovich, *John Ford,* 340).

6. *Three Bad Men* has a subplot that sharpens this anti-gold emphasis: an old prospector who discovers gold is killed by those who put it first.

7. Thomas Cripps provides the best analysis of these films' strengths and limitations in his *Making Movies Black: The Hollywood Message Movie from World War II to the Civil Rights Era* (New York: Oxford University Press, 1993), 220–49.

8. Lenihan covers the 1950s westerns that preached antiracism in *Showdown,* 55–87, as does Philip French, *Westerns: Aspects of a Movie Genre* (London: Viking, 1973), 76–99. In *The Hollywood Indian,* 45–49, O'Connor offers an interesting brief history of the changes in the script for Anthony Mann's *The Devil's Doorway* (1949) to make it a "historical allegory on American racial issues." George Sherman's 1956 *Reprisal* reset a novel about a black lynching in a white/Native American western context.

9. Qtd. in Bogdanovich, *John Ford,* 92, and, from a McBride interview, in Gallagher, *John Ford: The Man and His Films,* 333.

10. LeMay, *The Searchers*. The only Ford western to evoke the politics of containment was *Rio Grande* (1950), filmed at the beginning of the Korean war. Here the John Wayne hero, "sick of diplomatic hide and seek," finally gets tacit approval to "cross the river" to destroy the Apache. Lenihan points out that this followed the 1947

David Grimsted

James Warner Bellah story, but that Ford wholly expunged this perspective from the earlier Bellah story he made into *Fort Apache* (Lenihan, *Showdown*, 30–31).

11. The larger quote makes clear Ford thought there was no ambiguity about what he told the audience: "Well, I thought it was, pretty obvious. . . . You couldn't hit it on the nose, but I think it's very plain to anyone with any intelligence" (Bogdanovich, *John Ford*, 93).

12. Bronco Billy Anderson, an outlaw hero in many films, made the first version (1910) of the Peter Kyne story that was remade five times, twice by Ford, as *Marked Men* (1919), Ford's favorite of his silents, and as *Three Godfathers* (1948), dedicated to Harry Carey's memory. Kim Newman, *Wild West Movies: or How the West Was Found, Won, Lost, Lied About, Filmed and Forgotten* (London: Wrigley-Cross, 1990), 100. George Fenin and William S. Everson, *The Western: From the Silents to the Seventies* (New York: Bonanza, 1973) offer rich tribute to Hart's films, though their praise of his "realism" limits thematic considerations. I rely on the plot summaries of the Carey films in Bogdanovich, *John Ford*, 115–22.

13. Michael Walker, "The Westerns of Delmar Daves," in *The Book of Westerns*, ed. Cameron and Pye, 133, describes the hero and villain in *Drum Beat* as linked homoerotically, "with some highly phallic gestures with the weapon." This is currently a popular interpretative stance, related often, as here, to Leslie Fiedler's analysis of the ties of race in American westerns to sex and especially homosexual urges (Fiedler, *Return of the Vanishing American* [New York: Stein and Day, 1968]). This is one interpretive approach not explored in our collection of essays here with regard to Ethan-Marty's long journey or the Clayton-Lieutenant Greenhill comic interlude so centered on the youth's saber in the old man's face and behind. Ford plays with the notion by having someone ask, "What was it? Bullets? An arrow?" Clayton growls, "No."

14. Ford, qtd. in Davis, *John Ford: Hollywood's Old Master*, 40.

15. Several Ford biographers suggest the ties between Carey, Rogers, and Wayne, while Gallagher quotes from John Wayne about how Ford urged him to pattern his acting on Carey's (*John Ford: The Man and His Films*, 23).

16. *Motion Picture Weekly*, August 18, 1917. The film was found in a Czech film archives in the 1960s, so the titles are translations from Czech. The arm-holding gesture is also in a still of Carey in a pre–John Ford Universal western, probably from 1916. Here Carey is standing and looking away from his costar and future wife, Olive Fuller Golden, who plays Mrs. Jorgenson in *The Searchers*. Reproduced in Buck Rainey, *Saddle Aces of the Cinema* (Stamford, Conn.: Barnes), 125, where the author points out that Carey usually loved the heroine "in silence—often riding away, heartbroken from a feeling of unworthiness to make his love known."

17. Martha in *The Searchers* makes the same gesture with Ethan's Confederate coat (noted by Eckstein in his introductory essay in this collection). Place, *Western Films of John Ford*, 12–29, offers the best account of Ford's silent westerns, especially their visual vitality.

18. Calder points out Ford's "unrivalled ability" to make us see "the individual within the collective, and the collective beyond the individual" (*There Must Be A Lone Ranger*, 5, 189). Of the many books defining the western generally, Calder most successfully avoids insistence on a formula that short-sheets the flexibility of the genre.

Re-searching

19. The buffalo killing illumines well Ford's dramatization of "personal" racism. Richard Brooks's *The Last Hunt* (of the same year) connects such vicious motive for slaughter, correctly, with U.S. Army policy which at one time put a bounty on buffalo skins to help starve the Indians into submission.

20. On the Hart and Carey early ties to melodramatic theater, see Michael K. Schoenecke "William S. Hart," *Shooting Stars*, 1–6; Rainey, *Saddle Aces*, 123–34. For my attempt to define the politics of melodrama, see Jacky Bratton, Jim Cook, and Christine Gledhill, eds., *Melodrama: Stage, Picture, Screen* (London: British Film Institute, 1994), 199–213.

21. Howard Sitkoff suggests well how Roosevelt centrally tried to duck racial issues. In the North, most New Deal agencies operated racially fairly, and hence helped—and helped win the votes of—blacks greatly. Under pressure from Eleanor Roosevelt and a few other egalitarians, FDR spoke out gingerly against lynching and the poll tax, but his concern rarely moved beyond the complicated political calculus of keeping the black vote *and* that of "solid" South (Harvard Sitkoff, *A New Deal for Blacks: The Emergence of Civil Rights as a National Issue*, Vol.1: *The Depression Decade* [New York: Oxford University Press, 1978]). King Vidor's "radical" film *Our Daily Bread* (1934) involved all groups except racial others, and Clifford Odets's radical plays left out questions of race. Steinbeck's *Of Mice and Men* (1937) included some pointed evocation of the isolating realities of American racism.

22. Gallagher quotes a 1967 interview between Ford and French Communist Samuel Lachize where Ford talked at length about his liberalism and vehemently insisted on his racial egalitarianism.

23. For Bogdanovich's summary of *the Scarlet Drop* (1918), see *John Ford*, 114. See Cripps, *Slow Fade to Black: The Negro in American Film, 1900–1942* (New York: Oxford University Press, 1977) on the *Arrowsmith* black doctor, 300, and on the NAACP citation, 68. Anderson in *About John Ford* talks of Ford's anger at the deletion of the lynching scene in *Judge Priest*, 60–61.

24. *Sergeant Rutledge* (1960), *Two Rode Together* (1961), *Donovan's Reef* (1963), and *Cheyenne Autumn* (1964).

25. Cripps catches well how the two southern Will Rogers films offer "a mossy sentimental version of Southern life" with "wisps of racial satire," though his claim that Fetchit's character offered "a covert, unstated metaphor for insurrection" seems much stretched (*Making Movies Black*, 285–86). Donald Bogle offers a quieter positive assessment of the "subterranean" message that Fetchit delivered in his *Toms, Coons, Mulattoes, Mammies and Bucks: An Interpretive History of Blacks in American Films* (New York: Bantam, 1973), v, 57–59. Robert Benchley in 1929 called Fetchit "the best actor that the talking pictures have produced" (qtd. in Richard A. Maynard, ed., *The Black Man in Film: Racial Stereotyping* [Rochelle Park, N.J.: Hayden Books, 1974], 47).

26. Cripps, *Making Movies Black*, 233–35, presents the complicated negotiations/changes in *Pinky*, arguing at one point that Zanuck's problem came from "having hired [Dudley] Nichols, a frequent collaborator with the Catholic conservative, John Ford, whom he had engaged as director."

27. The central problem may not have been racial, but Ford's zest for low comedy, which was surely the trigger for Ford's bitter battles with his longtime friend and star, Henry Ford, over *Mr. Roberts* (1955).

28. As a Nordic American, maybe I should have sufficient dignity to decry the "dumb Swede" portrayal, but I thoroughly like and enjoy Jorgenson as representative of "my people"—especially when he puts on glasses to help others read letters.

29. This character, whom Minsk soon outfits in western garb identical to the sheriff's, seems to me presented as a dandy rather than a gay, but it's a bit dubious. Asked his age by the two bad men inspecting him, he says he's just reached manhood, and they reply "Then you better reach again."

30. Cripps, *Slow Fade,* 166. In *Melodrama Unveiled* (Berkeley: University of California Press, 1981), 183–95, I point out how Yankee, frontier, rural, city, Irish, and black stereotypes had special appeal to the groups represented.

31. Ford introduced Indians comparatively rarely and briefly in his early films, and never within the progressive-sympathetic context that was common at the time. The standard works on Indians in films are very condemnatory of Hollywood, but show a broad range of sympathetic as well as hostile stereotyping from the earliest silents. See esp. Hilger, *From Savage to Nobleman.*

32. To some degree the Indians in *Drums* and *Stagecoach* were, as in many 1939–41 films, stand-ins for another group, the Nazis, as demonic threat, but Ford never emphasized the tie as did King Vidor's *Northwest Passage* (1940), where a war of "extinction" became the only safeguard for "western civilization." Similarly in the 1950s, Indians sometimes became stand-ins for the communists who had to be fought and defeated (Lenihan, *Showdown,* 24–54).

33. Bogdanovich, *John Ford,* 104. Gallagher presents the most glowing brief for Ford's treatment of Indians, claiming he always "tended to ally himself with blacks or Indians" (*John Ford: The Man and His Films,* 339). Tuska presents the negative, including the claim that *The Searchers* was "Ford's most vicious anti-Indian film yet"—and that "Mart" is made part Indian so it's unacceptable for him to mate with Debbie (*The American West in Film,* 41–61).

34. Mari Sandoz, *Cheyenne Autumn* (New York, 1953). To read Sandoz's moving account, and to see how little heed Ford paid to it, is to catch the depth of his incapacity to see his "west" from a nonwhite perspective. Sandoz understandably was "terribly disappointed" in the film, which in fact travestied the book's perception. Colonnese argues in our collection that *Cheyenne Autumn* was a great improvement, showing Ford becoming "civilized." It was an improvement in broad intent, in the sense that it involved not simply an attack on virulent racism, but on the costs to native Americans of American imperialist settlement. But this was, I judge, an intent really at odds with Ford's lifetime western myths, as *The Searchers'* antiracism was not.

35. Ford's response to this criticism was that, if the Indians had acted with sense, "that would have been the end of the picture, wouldn't it?" (Bogdanovich, *John Ford,* 72).

36. Luhr and Lehman suggest the interplay of cultural misunderstandings in the two "courtships" in their *Authorship and Narrative,* 112–17.

37. Lehman "Looking at Look's Missing Reverse Shot," 68. Scholars of nineteenth-century culture routinely denounce the "vicious" low comedy stage stereotypes of African and Irish Americans, neglecting how much actors and audiences from those

Re-searching

groups contributed to/enjoyed them. They pay no attention to the similar Yankee/frontier stereotypes that set the general pattern. Stepin Fetchit is—at best—controversial, but no one worries about Gabby Hayes's—another Ford favorite—patented dumb/cowardly rube; Amos and Andy are highly suspect, but not the parallel whites, Lum and Abner.

38. *Winchester '73* (1950) and *War Arrow* (1954). Joseph W. Reed finds this cliché in *Stagecoach* "one of the most powerful and disturbing shots, and one of the most remarkable *coups* I know in film" (*Three American Originals: Ford, Charles Ives and Faulkner* [Middletown, Conn.: Wesleyan University Press, 1984]), 97). Coups of this kind were far from unprecedented. The threat (but never the enactment) of "last bullet" heroics to "protect" white woman went back to the early silents, though it was a cliché used rather rarely.

39. Maltby, "A Better Sense of History," connects Ford's treatment of Indians with earlier American stories, especially those of James Fenimore Cooper (as does Pye), in illustration of "the three dominant terms of the western mythos, the three Rs of the western: Racism, Rape, and Repression," 35. That these elements are present in westerns is certainly true, but, if one looks only for or at these aspects, one also often misses the strong Reconciliation, Regret, Realization, and anti-Racist themes in these manipulations of Native American characters toward satisfying white myths. There is a problem, too, with Ford as exemplar. I know of no films so involved with captivity-degradation themes as Ford. Ford's last film, *Seven Women* (1966), made in the wake of Betty Friedan's *The Feminine Mystique*, handles a "new woman" well, though the conclusion centers on women captives and savage barbarity again. The humanist new woman here saves the community by self sacrifice and prefers suicide to "degraded" sex, but—given her advanced views—kills the villain simultaneously.

40. Critics often miss Debbie's protective motive here; she says things to get them to leave because she knows the Comanches are about to strike. Natalie Wood had no doubt about what she was doing. In a promotional program, she told Gig Young as introduction to this speech: "In this scene I've come to warn Jeffrey Hunter and John Wayne."

41. Sometimes shooting scripts express what the filmmaker wanted to do, but which time, studio executives, or other circumstances prohibited. In this case, Ford had full control, so that discrepancies between script and film reflect things Ford intentionally rejected or changed. See Eckstein's introductory discussion in this collection.

42. Critics of the "dark" school see this, again following Marty's lead, as proof of Ethan's determination that the "degraded" Debbie never get anything. In fact, should Debbie return to white society, the Edwards property would belong to her, as Martin explains clearly earlier in the film.

43. Ford never expressed appreciation of Hoch's large contribution to the five films he photographed, starting with the beautiful *Three Godfathers*, including *She Wore a Yellow Ribbon* and *The Quiet Man*, and concluding with *The Searchers*, perhaps because he considered black and white a more demanding and rewarding aesthetic. He told Bogdanovich that he considered Gregg Toland, Joe August, and Artie Miller "great cameramen," omitting Hoch and George Schneiderman, who beautifully filmed most of the best Ford films, 1920–35 (*John Ford*, 75).

44. There are always additional valuable perspectives. For example, missing here is consideration of Fords' Christian symbolism, less apparent in *The Searchers* than in many Ford films, but certainly a much more overt reference point for Ford than classical texts.

45. Lehman's alternative view—in Ford's films "men act and women stay home"—is also partially true, though Ford sees women's acts and attitudes within the home, or in nurturing extensions outside it, as comparably significant. And he does have heroines like Lee in *Three Bad Men* who direct the action, though neither she nor her somewhat Aaron-like beau/husband takes part in the gunfights.

46. Of course, some films work self-consciously within a Freudian framework, and others evoke connections almost inevitably to Freudian theory. Yet Freud offers such a flexible and reversible set of ideas that they, by providing facile explanation of everything, often tell us little.

47. Some books seem written with determination to neglect the basic relevant data. Studlar wholly convincingly points out how Ford's westerns defy the definition of the genre Tompkins offers in *West of Everything*. Almost all westerns disprove Tompkins's claim that the genre glorifies escape from the feminine sphere of religion, family, and community. It's a rare western where the hero's action does not save or promote the coming of communities, families, churches, schoolhouses, and nurturing women.

48. Ford's *Drums Along The Mohawk* along with *Jesse James* (1939) and *North West Mounted Police*, *Northwest Passage*, and *Santa Fe Trail* (all 1940) outgrossed narrowly *Stagecoach* (1939), *Destry Rides Again* and *The Westerner* (both 1940) (David Pirie, ed., *Anatomy of the Movies*, 206). On the many westerns of 1939, see the good article by Peter Stanfield, "Country Music and the 1939 Western," in *The Book of Westerns*, ed. Cameron and Pye, 22–33.

49. Westerns presenting antiracist ideas in 1956: *Giant*, *The Last Hunt*, *The Last Wagon*, *Reprisal*, *The Lone Ranger*, *White Squaw*, *Walk the Proud Land*, *The Last Frontier*, and *Ghost Town*. Of the era's films attacking social racism in a western setting, particularly strong are *Devil's Doorway* (1949) *Apache* and *Broken Lance* (both 1954), *The Last Hunt* and *Reprisal* (both 1956), *Run of the Arrow*, *Trooper Hook* and *The Tin Star* (all 1957)—written by frequent Ford collaborator Dudley Nichols—and *Flaming Star* (1960). Cripps reports that this last, the best of Elvis Presley's films, was especially well received by black youths (*Making Movies Black*, 282–83).

50. Kalinak, in her essay in our collection, could refer to much of the recent literature on minstrelsy to back up her position: Robert Toll, *Blacking Up: The Minstrel Show in Nineteenth-Century America* (New York: Oxford University Press, 1974); Alexander Saxton, *The Rise and Fall of the White Republic: Class, Politics and Mass Culture in Nineteenth-Century America* (London: Verso, 1990); David Roediger, *The Wages of Whiteness: Race and the Making of the American Working Class* (London: Verso, 1995); Eric Lott, *Love and Theft: Blackface Minstrelsy and the American Working Class* (New York: Oxford University Press, 1993). All these books are intelligent, but suffer from preconclusions about racism, and too little attention to both the texts and audiences of minstrelsy. For me, the best and richest study of the wide variety of things on the minstrel stage remains the oldest (despite some underanalysis): Carl Wittke, *Tambo*

Re-searching

and Bones: A History of the American Minstrel Stage (Durham, N.C.: Duke University Press, 1930).

51. Wayne, in a *Playboy* interview (May 1971, 90) raged that *High Noon* was "the most unAmerican thing I've seen in my whole life." Like most Wayne "ideas" this is ludicrous, but I think most 1950s audiences and critics were right to see *High Noon* as more iconoclastic and *The Searchers* as comparatively conventional, though both are comfortably within the flexible genre. *High Noon* has the most unusual character in either film, Katy Jurado as the dark and discarded mistress of the hero: economically shrewd and independent, intellectually astute, and morally strong and perceptive. Like the hero she is anxious to leave this sick and—she emphasizes—racist society. The antiracist theme in *High Noon* is less stressed and quieter, but is argued in broader and more social terms. In no film I'm familiar with is the "dark woman" convention used, and mocked so intelligently.

52. These figures are compiled from the plot summaries provided by Hilger, *From Savage to Nobleman,* supplemented in a few places by references from Phil Hardy, *The Western* (New York, 1983), an evaluative encyclopedia of sound westerns. The categories are crude, and mistakes are likely when one reads a film from a brief verbal summary, but the numbers indicate general realties, I think. "Bad" means that the film suggests the union is undesirable, "happy" means that it is approved and of long duration, and "tragic" means that the relation is portrayed sympathetically, but that one partner quickly dies, is killed, commits suicide, or leaves.

53. Henderson's general position and his stress on American miscegenation laws not applying to Native American/European American unions reinforces this cultural argument. The pride Americans often took in Native American ancestry is also clear. In a publicity piece on the filming of *My Darling Clementine* in *Collier's* (April 1946), for example, much was made of Linda Darnell's Cherokee ancestry. Ford's joking ambiguity about how much Indian Marty is—Ethan says "half," Marty says "eighth," and Ethan compromises on "quarter"—may have owed something to Will Rogers's proud handling of his Native American ancestry. His father was one-eighth Indian, his mother one-quarter—and he wasn't good enough at arithmetic to figure out his percentage, but he was emphatically proud of it all (*Autobiography of Will Rogers* [Boston, 1947], 6).

54. I think, too, the popular American definition of incest was strictly genetic, and not applied to people simply raised as siblings. *Pursued* (1947) takes this about as far as it can go, and still the hero and heroine go off happily together at the end. Not only were they raised as brother and sister but the hero's father was killed by the family of the heroine's mother, because she was having an affair with him. There's surely more than a soupçon of Freudian frisson in all this, but the accepted "rules" seem clear. What makes *The Unforgiven* such a poor film—the worst Huston film I've seen—is that neither director nor audience sees "incest," race, or age as a real problem, and the film's various exposures of American racism are by this time too formulaic to have sharp bite.

55. Cripps, *Making Movies Black,* 263–66; Daniel J. Leab, *From Sambo to Superspade: The Black Experience in Motion Pictures* (Boston: Houghton Mifflin, 1976), 212–19.

56. Stowell, *John Ford,* 139–40, used the theory that what we see is what Laurie imagines to handle his embarrassment about the use of Look for comic farce, the

motive I'd guess of most subsequent stress on it. Pye shows the difficulty of "reading" the scenes interposed with the letter as a transcript of Laurie's thoughts.

57. There has been much interest in "reader response theory," of judging the meaning of works by what readers or watchers say the works meant to them. The desirability of knowing this is clear, but the problematics of the results of determining this are equally clear, even when scholars happen on to a good source of "reader response," as in Janice Radway's *Reading the Romance: Women, Patriarchy and Popular Literature* (Chapel Hill: University of North Carolina Press, 1984).

58. *New York Times,* March 31, 1956. Of the ten reviews I've read, only three were negative, one by Anderson arguing Ethan was too dark a figure for a hero. The other two rather superciliously mocked the film for its conventionality as "another excursion into the patented Old West of Director John Ford" (*Time,* June 25, 1956, qtd., and *New Yorker,* June 9, 1956).

59. Qtd. in McBride and Wilmington, *John Ford,* 45. The full reply, in answer to "Do you like *The Searchers?*" was "I enjoyed doing it. Yeah, *The Searchers* is a good picture. It made a lot of money, and that's the ultimate end." The whole McBride interview, like those with Bogdanovich and Anderson, suggest how shrewd and how impossibly cantankerous Ford was. In David Pirie's ranking of all westerns' box office, indexed to inflation, *The Searchers* comes in number 16; *Fort Apache*-22; *My Darling Clementine* and *She Wore a Yellow Ribbon*-31 and 32; and *Drums Along the Mohawk*- 40 (*Anatomy of the Movies,* 206.) I wonder if figures for *The Iron Horse* are available; the other smash epic of the twenties, *The Covered Wagon* (1923) is ranked seventh. *How the West Was Won* (1962), of which Ford directed a very short third, comes in fourth, making it ironically the biggest money maker of all the westerns on which Ford worked, as well as the worst.

60. Anderson, *About John Ford,* 63.

Native American Reactions to *The Searchers*

Tom Grayson Colonnese

When historian Art Eckstein of the University of Maryland contacted me and told me he was putting together a book of essays about John Ford's *The Searchers*, he definitely caught my interest. When he went on to tell me that he wanted me to write an essay on "the American Indian reaction" to the film—and that no such essay had ever been written before!—he had me hooked. Later phone calls about the specifics of this exciting project just "reeled me in." For years, *The Searchers* had intrigued me. My best friend is novelist and critic Louis Owens (Choctaw/Cherokee), and he and I had many conversations about the movie during camping and fishing trips in Arizona and New Mexico. Louis calls it "the best Indian movie ever made." It is odd, but whenever the movie comes up among Indian people, it turns out that it is very special to them. It is a movie that most Indian people remember as "the fairest Indian movie."

In order to attempt to respond to Professor Eckstein's request, I called up several of my Indian colleagues here at the University of Washington at Seattle and asked them if they would watch *The Searchers* with me, so that I could record their reactions to the movie to put into a book of essays about the film. To my surprise, no one said "No." I thought they might, because asking Indians to watch a John Wayne western is like asking someone if they would like to go back and visit the schoolyard where they used to get beat up every day. No—that's too unserious a comparison, though the connection to our childhoods and bad childhood memories is important. Rather, for Native American people, watching westerns is like Jews watching movies about the Holocaust. It's that painful. It's that real: between 1850 and 1875, for instance, the Comanches lost 905 of their population. But even this comparison misses the mark, because for Indians, watching westerns would be like Jews watching films about the Holocaust in which the Jews themselves were presented as the violent, aggressive villains! *We* were the ones who were slaughtered and destroyed, but that's not usually how we've been depicted.

So we gathered together to watch the movie. Besides myself (a Santee Sioux), there was Bernice Elke (Oglala Sioux), Augustine McCaffery (Comanche), and Scott Pinkham (Nez Perce).

As soon as the movie began, we were aware, of course, that John Ford's "West" is not the "real West." The screen reads "Texas 1868," and then the door opens onto Monument Valley in far northern Arizona, which with its spectacular cliffs and spires and buttes is just about the opposite of the flat Texas plains. We are in a fictional world. We may be reminded, as well, that John Ford "discovered" Monument Valley for white America, and introduced it to white Americans in his films. Monument Valley lies in the northernmost part of the Navajo Reservation. Prior to World War II, the Navajo Reservation was one of the most isolated places in the United States, and Navajos had to have written permission to leave it. Few white Americans had ever been to Monument Valley then: if it is a popular tourist spot now, it is because John Ford made it one by identifying this most unusual and beautiful place as the symbol of "*the* West." Before the war, the Navajo language had never even been placed in written form, a factor that led to the success of the Navajo Codetalkers—World War II Navajo soldiers who were employed as radio men between U.S. units because no enemy could possibly decipher their language or even know what it was.

By 1956 the Navajo Reservation had become a little less isolated than before; but as Indian viewers, we were immediately aware that we were watching a movie that was filmed "on the reservation" and employed Indians as "extras." That made it all the more ironic that we expected the movie to portray Indians in a negative manner. It is another piece of irony that the Navajo "extras" were happy to be involved in the movie, since Indian people were poverty-stricken even though the Eisenhower years were prosperous ones for most of white America. The Navajos needed the money, desperately—even if it was only minimum "extras" pay, and even if Indians were going to be portrayed negatively. And it is a final irony that Indians were the "extras" in a movie about their own subjugation by whites. The term "extras" speaks for itself as to the usual place of Indians in American history.

An initial element of the movie that bothered us, as Indian viewers, was the ordering of events in the film. As *The Searchers* begins, the non-

Native American Reactions to *The Searchers*

Indian audience may have a sense that they are there just as the story is starting and events are beginning to unroll. They are witnessing the return of Ethan Edwards to the ranch from which he has been absent for many years. The Indian audience, however, is quite aware that this story has begun far "in medias res." I mean: where did that ranch *come from*? Indian viewers are aware that these supposedly peaceful ranchers, interested only in making a living through raising cattle, are living on land that has been *seized*. The "first attack," here, does *not* come from the Comanches; the first attack has already taken place, though we are not permitted to see it: it was a white attack, a successful white attack, that captured this land from the Indians by violence. Scar's attack, in which the Edwards ranch is destroyed, much of the Edwards family killed, and Lucy and Debbie captured, is in fact a *counterattack*. But for white audiences, it appears to lack clear motivation, and is merely an act of senseless cruelty. ("It's a murder-raid," says Ethan grimly.) The full cycle of white/Indian conflict and warfare is not shown.

As we continued to watch the movie, Bernice said that she was being flooded by old emotions. "I remember how I used to feel as a child," she said. "I remember how angry I used to get when I would watch them depict us so negatively. It hurts to feel this all again." Augustine, a Comanche himself, said, "I know what you mean. I used to think, 'Oh, no—what are those bad Indians going to do now?' None of us wanted to be Indians when we played. I used to make my younger brother be the Indian." As we watched the scene of the fight at the river, where several Comanches are killed by white gunfire while only one white character is wounded by the Indians, Augustine said, "I used to think, too, 'Why can't those Indians shoot better? Why are those whites so accurate?' It confused me, because my uncles and my dad were all good shots." The previous fight, at the Edwards ranch, had been similar: there was only one adult white male present (Aaron Edwards, Ethan's weaker brother), helped only by one young boy barely in his teens and two semi-hysterical women (that's how they are portrayed)—and yet he kills *seven* warriors! Gee—just imagine what Ethan could have done in that situation (as the teenage boy actually says)! This doesn't conform to any historical reality, either, as you can see if you look at any account of the Comanche raid on the Parker family compound near Waco which is the basis for Alan LeMay's novel and then the film. But in this movie, as in most other westerns, the Indians aren't just *bad*—they are, in battle, *incompetent*. (Ethan shoots Scar off his horse *twice*.)[1] All of us also cringed as we watched *The Searchers* at the stylized "Indian music,"

337

"Oh, no, what are those bad Indians going to do now?" Scar's first appearance.

with its sinister overtones, that was always played when the Comanches appeared. We kept expecting Ted Turner and Jane Fonda to appear next, leading a "tomahawk chop."

I told the other Indian people watching the film that I became confused when I looked at the attempts by Ford at "balance." The sequence displaying the brutal genocide of the cavalry at the winter camp of the Comanches is certainly striking, and the audience even in 1956 was clearly being directed by Ford to have a negative reaction to it, because Martin Pauley says explicitly when the searchers find the dead Comanche girl Look, "Aw, Ethan, why'd them soldiers have to go and *kill* her for? She never did nobody any harm!" The next scene, with the pitiful Comanche survivors—mostly women and children—being herded along with whips by the U.S. soldiers, was historically accurate regarding what actually happened to the Cheyennes at Custer's hands at the Washita in November 1868 (which this sequence in *The Searchers* clearly represents). But while this scene was painful for us Indians to watch (just as the scenes with the Nazis herding innocent Jews along in *Schindler's List* must be painful for Jews to watch), we thought that perhaps it was a bit too subtle for the orig-

Native American Reactions to *The Searchers*

inal white audiences in 1956 to get. The killing of Look, and Ethan's respectful covering of her with a blanket, seemed to mirror what we'd been told about the killing of Lucy, and Ethan's actions when he found her. The Comanche lance in Lars Jorgensen's dead prize bull at the beginning of the film (but what is anyone doing trying to raise cattle in the Monument Valley desert anyway?) seemed to be intentionally and shockingly echoed later in the film by a cavalry saber left sticking in a dead Comanche. Ford's point seemed to be: was this scale of retribution necessary? And late in the movie we finally learn that Scar's actions are not motivated by sheer senseless cruelty and brutality but by the fact that whites had murdered his sons—though of course we never *see* this atrocity or its physical and emotional results, while we do emphatically see the results of the atrocity at the Edwards ranch committed by Scar. Scar is even allowed to match wits with Ethan when he stands chest to chest with him and counters Ethan's "You speak pretty good English. Somebody teach you?"—an obvious reference to sexually enslaved Debbie—with "You speak pretty good Comanche. Somebody teach YOU?," implying that Ethan himself had actually had a Comanche woman as a lover (or even "wife") at one time.

But these elements in the scene at Scar's camp in New Mexico are joined with the preceding winter sequence at the cavalry fort where the white female captives have quite literally gone mad just from *being* with Comanches—and Ford plays that scene absolutely straight. And though it is an element taken directly from Alan LeMay's novel which is the source of the film, throughout *The Searchers* the factor that blocks Debbie's rescue, and Lucy's rescue earlier, is that the Comanches will kill their prisoners, innocent though those prisoners are, if they are attacked. This is repeated even late in the film when to all appearances Debbie has become completely part of the tribe: and frankly, it is pretty hard to accept it as anything but slander. It was a mystery, too, why Ford worked so hard to depict some elements of the movie with great historical accuracy (such as the fact that the cowboys wear blue jeans and suspenders, rather than anything fancy), yet he is so haphazard in his depiction of the Comanche. Scholars often point out that Ford was widely read, a real scholar of the nineteenth-century American West, but he obviously has not studied *them* much, and knows little specific about them. He does, rightly, have them both as polygamous and as divided into separate and independent wandering bands, but basically they are just generic Indians, as is shown by the fact that the costumes they wear were made in Hollywood (as the promotional short subject for the film proudly proclaims).

Generic Indians: why, I wondered, were the Navajos in *The Searchers* (i.e., "the Comanches") allowed to speak Navajo? Navajo and Comanche belong to completely different language groups, and are not mutually comprehensible. This is not a small point to Indians. It would be as if when we meet the Jorgensens, they have Italian accents, or as if the Hispanic Comanchero who finally leads the searchers to Scar speaks with a heavy Swedish accent. Would the (Euro-American) audience put up with that kind of bizarre inaccuracy? Then why are Indians supposed to put up with it? Any Comanchero who came up and greeted a Comanche war chief with the Navajo greeting "Ye-to-hay!," as "Emilio Fernandez" does to Scar in *The Searchers*, wouldn't have stayed alive long on the Llano Estacado! But clearly, for Ford any Indian language would suffice. I suppose we should be "grateful" that at least a real Indian language is being spoken by the Indians in this film, instead of just gibberish. But even the one fully realized male Indian character in *The Searchers*, Scar—as opposed to all those faceless guys getting shot off their horses by the whites—was played by a white man (Henry Brandon, actually a *German*).

There was another thing in the film that was a mystery to us Indians. "There is just so much that goes unanswered," Scott said. "Debbie first says that she won't leave the Comanches. 'These are my people,' she says. But then she changes her mind and does leave. I find myself wondering why." Especially because the historical woman upon whom Debbie is based, Cynthia Ann Parker, did *not* want to leave the Comanches—not ever. It is true that in December 1860 she was recaptured from Peta Nokona's band on the Pease River by Texas Rangers under the command of Captain Sul Ross (we see a version of this event—a sanitized version—in the final Ranger attack on Scar's camp in *The Searchers*). Later, in April 1861, Cynthia Parker was even displayed to the Texas State Legislature as an example of the superiority of "white civilization," in the form of the recovered white female captive, as the Legislature prepared to secede from the Union and join the racist Confederate States of America. But Cynthia Parker was recaptured in the course of a murderous Texas Ranger raid on a Comanche camp consisting mostly of women and children (the men were out hunting buffalo), and Cynthia herself was saved from the general slaughter only by the sight of her blond hair—which she immediately cut short, a Comanche sign of mourning, as we see her in the famous photograph taken right after her capture. It is a signal to us, across 150 years, of her despair. Later, as is well known, she was so mistreated and mistrusted by her white Parker relatives that she tried to escape back to the

Native American Reactions to *The Searchers*

Comanches, pleading with a passing frontier scout (in Comanche) that Peta Nokona would pay many horses for her—which was true; he loved her. The legend is that she soon committed suicide. The son Cynthia Parker left behind among the Comanches became the great Kwahada Comanche war chief Quanah Parker, and after his surrender to the whites in 1875 he spent long years trying to find her. Clever man that he was, and a man who quickly adapted in important ways to white culture, he used attorneys. In 1911, he was able to gain the legal return of Cynthia's body to his own custody and that of the Comanche people, and she was transferred from a cemetery in Texas to the Comanche Reservation in Oklahoma, where she was greeted with great ceremony. Later, Quanah and Cynthia were buried side by side. He said that was what she would have wished. "These are my people," Debbie says. Later still, in 1957, the graves had to be moved when the U.S. Army confiscated the Comanche cemetery to use as an artillery testing ground.

But this story, though a true story, will never be made into a film. Here, too, John Ford in the end took the easy, traditional, and fictional way out, and the white female captive, after initial hesitation, happily returns to white "civilization." On the other hand, I suppose we have to be grateful that at least Ford was willing to depict Debbie as perfectly sane and calm, and well cared for by the Comanches, and respected by them, and not degraded by them. In that sense, Debbie in *The Searchers* points forward to the far more rounded character Stands-With-A-Fist (Mary McConnell), the white female captive of the Sioux, integrated totally into the community, in *Dances with Wolves* (1990). And I suppose that, in that limited sense, Ford—as with his shocking scene of U.S. Cavalry brutality in the winter attack on the Comanche camp—was decades ahead of his time in what he put on the screen.

Of course—shocking to *whom*? For all of us Indian people who watched *The Searchers* out here in Washington, the film is both promise and disappointment. Admittedly, *The Searchers* does show the terrible effect of hate and prejudice, and seems to say that life can only go on if one triumphs over these emotions. Scar cannot lessen his hatred, and he dies. Ethan is able to soften his heart, though only at the very last moment, and that allows him to survive. But Ford simultaneously seems very limited by his own prejudices, or by his own limited ideas of what he can do in the film. *The Searchers* is *filled* with prejudicial images: not only of Indians but also of women, and—in the case of Futterman, the trader who has important information about Debbie—of Jews. Art Eckstein himself has told me that watching the scenes involving the greedy, amoral, treacherous Futterman is extremely painful to him. In sharp contrast to Futterman, the Hispanic Comanchero Emilio Fernandez is a man of honor, pointedly returning the money Ethan has paid him to guide the searchers to Scar's camp when he realizes that Scar knows who Ethan and Marty are, and intends to kill them ("I do not want blood-money," he says with dignity, and rides off.) Yet the Hispanic saloon girl who tries to seduce Marty just a couple of scenes earlier, dancing toward him with her clicking castanets, is an offensively stereotypical "hot-blooded" Hispanic woman (bluntly, a slut).

That's what we mean. *The Searchers* is engaging because it goes further than any other western of its day in the direction of truth and fairness; but finally *The Searchers* was frustrating to us because it stops well short of being truly fair. Ford pushes the limits that apparently existed in 1956, with portrayals of Indians, Mexicans, and women which are sympathetic, or at least partially sympathetic, but he doesn't "go the distance"—not at all. We wondered why that was. Did Ford fear that his film would not be marketable if he went too far? Did he go just as far as he was able? After all, in *Cheyenne Autumn* (1964), made eight years after *The Searchers*, he would go much farther in the presentation of Indians as real people, and sympathetic people, not just faceless enemies to be shot off their horses. But by then, times had changed.[2] And perhaps Ford had changed, too: his films in his last period were much more overtly attacks on white racism. We had one line of thinking wherein Ford was "educated" by filming so many movies in Monument Valley, making so many films working closely with Indian people. Slowly, he was becoming "civilized."

NOTES

1. In the climactic battle in the cavalry movie *A Distant Trumpet* (1964), directed by the great Hollywood veteran Raoul Walsh, the Indians are so incompetent that they do not get off even a single rifle shot; they just ride around wildly on their horses until shot from them by the white soldiers, like toy targets at a carnival.

2. And perhaps not only among the whites. In his crime novel *Sacred Clowns* (New York: HarperCollins, 1993), 120–21, Tony Hillerman has a scene in which a Navajo audience at a Gallup drive-in watches *Cheyenne Autumn* in order to laugh at the obscene jokes which the Navajos speak in Navajo, unknown to the whites, as they play Cheyennes for Ford. Sometimes being an "extra" can be a site of resistance as Hillerman, *Sacred Clowns*, 119, says.

Credits

The Searchers

USA 1956
Filmed on location in Gunnison, Colorado, and in Monument Valley, Arizona,
 spring-summer 1955; interiors: Burbank, California, summer 1955
Distributor: Warner Bros. Pictures, Inc.
Production Companies: C. V. Whitney Pictures; Warner Bros. Pictures, Inc.
Filmed in Technicolor and VistaVision
Length: 119 minutes; 10,681 feet
U.S. release date: May 26, 1956
Director: John Ford
Executive Producer: Merian C. Cooper
Associate Producer: Patrick Ford
Screenplay: Frank S. Nugent, from the novel by Alan LeMay
Photography: Winton C. Hoch (Monument Valley and interiors); Alfred Gilks
 (second unit, Colorado)
Film Editor: Jack Murray
Assistant Directors: Wingate Smith; Edward O'Fearna (second unit)
Production Supervisor: Lowell Farrell
Script Supervisor: Robert Gary
Art Directors: Frank Hotaling and James Basevi
Set Decorator: Victor Gangelin
Technicolor Color Consultant: James Gooch
Location Scout: Robert Lee "Lefty" Hough
Music: Max Steiner
Title Song: Stan Jones, sung by The Sons of the Pioneers
Sound: Hugh McDowell and Howard Wilson
Men's Wardrobe: Frank Beetson
Women's Wardrobe: Ann Peck
Makeup: Web Overlander
Hairdresser: Fae Smith
Props: Art Cole

Film Credits

Stunts: William J. Cartledge, Chuck Hayward, Slim Hightower, Fred Kennedy, Frank McGrath, Chuck Roberson, Dale van Sickle, and Henry Wills, Terry Wilson

Wranglers: Glen Holly, Desmond Lane, Logan Morris, Robert Reeves, and Ellsworth Vierelle

Cast

John Wayne: Ethan Edwards
Jeffrey Hunter: Martin Pauley
Vera Miles: Laurie Jorgensen
Ward Bond: Reverend Captain Samuel Johnson Clayton
Natalie Wood: Debbie Edwards
Dorothy Jordan: Martha Edwards
John Qualen: Lars Jorgensen
Olive Carey: Mrs. Jorgensen
Henry Brandon: Chief Scar
Ken Curtis: Charley McCorry
Harry Carey, Jr.: Brad Jorgensen
Antonio Moreno: Emilio Gabriel Fernandez y Figueroa
Beulah Archuletta: Look/Wild Goose Flying in the Night Sky
Hank Worden: Mose Harper
Lana Wood: Debbie as a Child
Walter Coy: Aaron Edwards
Pippa Scott: Lucy Edwards
Patrick Wayne: Lieutenant Greenhill

Uncredited Cast

Peter Mamakos: Futterman
Cliff Lyons: Colonel Greenhill
Ruth Clifford: Deranged Woman at Fort
Mae Marsh: Woman at Fort
Carmen D'Antonio: Dancer at Cantina
Robert Lyden: Ben Edwards
Comanches: Away Luna, Billy Yellow, Bob Many Mules, Exactly Sonnie Betsuie, Feather Hat Jr, Harry Black Horse, Jack Tin Horn, Many Mules Son, Percy Shooting Star, Pete Gray Eyes, Pipe Line Begishe, and Smile White Sheep

Role Filmed but Cut

Peter Ortiz: General Custer

SELECTED BIBLIOGRAPHY

Compiled by Arthur M. Eckstein

PRIMARY SOURCES

LeMay, Alan. *The Searchers*. New York: Harper, 1954.
———. *The Unforgiven*. New York: Harper, 1957.
Nugent, Frank S. Shooting script of *The Searchers*. John Ford Papers. Lilly Library, Indiana University, Bloomington; Warner Brothers Archive, University of Southern California.
For scholars of Ford and *The Searchers*, the material in the John Ford Papers and the Warner Brothers Archive are indispensable. They cover in detail all aspects of the film's production history.

CONTEMPORANEOUS REVIEWS

Newsweek, May 21, 1956, 116.
New York Times, May 31, 1956, 21.
America, June 6, 1956, 272.
Commonweal, June 15, 1956, 274.
New Yorker, June 9, 1956, 34
Nation, June 23, 1956, 54.
Time, June 25, 1956, 58.
Sight and Sound (autumn 1956): 94–95.

BOOKS AND ARTICLES

Albers, Patricia C. "Symbiosis, Merger, and War: Contrasting Forms of Intertribal Relationship Among Historic Plains Indians." In *The Political Economy of North American Indians*, ed John H. Moore, 94–132. Norman: University of Oklahoma Press, 1993.
Aleis, Angela. "A Race Divided: The Indian Westerns of John Ford." *American Indian Culture and Research Journal* 18 (1994): 167–86.
Anderson, Lindsey. *About John Ford*. New York: McGraw-Hill, 1981.
Axtell, James. "The White Indians of Colonial North America." *William and Mary Quarterly* 32 (1975): 55–88.
Baxter, John. *The Cinema of John Ford*. London: A. S. Barnes, 1971.
Berg, Charles Ramirez. "The Margin as Center: The Multicultural Dynamics of John Ford's Westerns." In Studlar and Bernstein, *John Ford Made Westerns*, 75–101.
Blake, Michael F. *Code of Honor: The Making of Three Great Westerns*. New York: Cooper Square, 2003.

Selected Bibliography

Bogdanovich, Peter. "The America of John Ford." In *Pieces of Time: Peter Bogdanovich on Movies*, ed. Peter Bogdanovich, 291–305. New York: Arbor House, 1985.

———. *John Ford*. Berkeley: University of California Press, 1978.

Brooks, James F. *Captives and Cousins: Slavery, Kinship, and Community in the Southwest Borderlands*. Chapel Hill: University of North Carolina Press, 2002.

Budd, Michael. "A Home in the Wilderness: Visual Imagery in John Ford's Westerns." In Kitses and Rickman, *The Western Reader*, 133–48. Originally published in *Cinema Journal* 16 (1976): 62–75.

Buscombe, Edward. *The BFI Companion to the Western*. New York: Da Capo Press, 1988.

———. "Critics and *The Searchers*." *Screen Education* 17 (autumn 1975): 49–51.

———. *The Searchers*. London: British Film Institute, 2000.

Byron, Stuart. "*The Searchers*: Cult Movie of the New Hollywood." *New York Magazine*, March 5, 1979, 45–48.

Calder, Jenni. *There Must Be a Lone Ranger: The Amercian West in Film and Reality*. New York: 1975.

Cameron, Ian, and Douglas Pye, eds. *The Book of Westerns*. New York: Continuum, 1996.

Card, Andrew. "*The Searchers* by Alan LeMay and John Ford." *Literature/Film Quarterly* 16 (1988): 1–9.

Carey, Harry, Jr. *Company of Heroes: My Life as an Actor in the John Ford Stock Company*. Metuchen, N.J.: Scarecrow Press, 1994.

Clauss, James J. "Descent into Hell: Mythic Paradigms in *The Searchers*." *Journal of Popular Film and Television* 27 (1999): 1–17

Corliss, Richard. *Talking Pictures: Screenwriters in the American Cinema*. Woodstock, N.Y.: Overlook Press, 1974.

Coyne, Michael. *The Crowded Prairie: American National Identity in the Hollywood Western*. London: Tauris, 1997.

Crouch, Stanley. "Bull Feeney Plays the Blues." In *Always in Pursuit: Fresh American Perspectives, 1995–1997*. New York: Pantheon, 1998. 268–88.

Darby, William. *John Ford's Westerns: A Thematic Analysis, with a Filmography*. Jefferson, N.C.: McFarland, 1996.

Davis, Ronald L. *John Ford: Hollywood's Old Master*. Norman: University of Oklahoma Press, 1995.

Dempsey, Michael. "John Ford: A Reassessment." *Film Quarterly* 18 (1975): 2–15.

Eckstein, Arthur M. "After the Rescue: *The Searchers*, the Audience, and *Prime Cut* (1972)." *Journal of Popular Culture* 28 (1994): 35–52

———. "Darkening Ethan: John Ford's *The Searchers* from Novel to Screenplay to Screen." *Cinema Journal* 21 (1998): 3–24

Ellis, Kirk. "On the Warpath: John Ford and the Indians." *Journal of Popular Film and Television* 8 (1980): 34–41

Eyman, Scott. *Print the Legend: The Life and Times of John Ford*. New York: Simon and Schuster, 1999.

Flanagan, Thomas. "John Ford's West." *New York Review of Books*, December 20, 2001, 73–74

Ford, Dan. *Pappy: The Life of John Ford*. Englewood Cliffs, N.J.: Prentice-Hall, 1979.

Selected Bibliography

———. "The West of John Ford and How It Was Made." *Action* (September/October 1971).
Gallagher, Tag. "Angels Gambol Where They Will: John Ford's Indians." In Kitses and Rickman, *The Western Reader*, 269–76. Originally published in *Film Comment* 29 (1983): 68–72.
———. *John Ford: The Man and His Films.* Berkeley: University of California Press, 1986.
———. "John Ford's Indians." *Film Comment* 29 (1993): 68–72.
Girgus, Sam B. *Hollywood Renaissance: The Cinema of Democracy in the Era of Ford, Capra and Kazan.* Cambridge: Cambridge University Press, 1998.
Gladwin, Thomas, "Comanche Kin Behavior." *American Anthropologist* 50 (1948): 73–94.
Gorbman, Claudia, "Scoring the Indian: Music in the Liberal Western." In *Western Music and Its Others: Difference, Representation, and Appropriation in Music,* ed. Georgina Born and David Hesmondhaigh, 234–53. Berkeley: University of California Press, 2000.
Greenspun, Roger. "John Ford, 1895–1973." In *Film 73/74,* ed. Jack Cocks and David Denby, 333–41. Indianapolis: Bobbs-Merrill, 1974.
Hacker, Margaret S. *Cynthia Ann Parker: The Life and the Legend.* El Paso: Texas Western Press, 1990.
Henderson, Brian. "*The Searchers:* An American Dilemma." *Film Quarterly* 34 (1981): 9–23.
Hilger, Michael. *From Savage to Nobleman: Images of Native Americans in Film.* Lanham, Md.: Scarecrow Press, 1995.
Hutson, Richard. "Sermons in Stone: Monument Valley in *The Searchers.*" In *The Big Empty: Essays on Western Landscapes and Narrative,* ed. Leonard Engle, 187–205. Albuquerque: University of New Mexico Press, 1994.
Hutton, Paul A. *The Custer Reader.* Lincoln: University of Nebraska Press, 1994.
Isenberg, Andrew. *The Destruction of the Bison.* Cambridge: Cambridge University Press, 2000.
Kennedy, Burt. "Burt Kennedy Interviews John Ford." In Gerald Peary, *John Ford Interviews,* 118–23.
Kindem, Gorham. "Towards a Semiotic of Color in Popular Narrative Film: Color Signification in John Ford's The Searchers." *Film Reader* 2 (1977): 78–84.
Kitses, Jim, and Gregg Rickman. *The Western Reader.* New York: Limelight, 1998.
Kolodny, Annette. "Among the Indians: The Uses of Captivity." *Women's Studies Quarterly* 21 (1993): 184–95.
Lalich, G. "John Ford's *The Searchers:* Capitalist Claptrap." *Filament* 4 (1984): 50–53.
Lehman, Peter. "Looking at Look's Missing Reverse Shot: Psychoanalysis and Style in John Ford's *The Searchers.*" *Wide Angle* 4 (1981): 65–70. Reprinted in Kitses and Rickman, *The Western Reader*, 259–68.
———. "Texas, 1868/America, 1956: *The Searchers.*" In *Close Viewings: An Anthology of New Film Criticism,* ed. Peter Lehman, 387–415. Tallahassee: University of Florida Press, 1990.
———. "'There's No Way of Knowing'—Analysis of *The Searchers.*" In Luhr and Lehman, *Authorship and Narrative.*

Selected Bibliography

Lenihan, J. H. *Showdown: Confronting Modern America in the Western Film.* Urbana: University of Illinois Press, 1980.

Luhr, William, and Peter Lehman. *Authorship and Narrative in the Cinema: Issues in Contemporary Aesthetics and Criticism.* New York: Putnam, 1977.

Lusted, David. "*The Searchers* and the Study of Image." *Screen Education* 17 (autumn 1975): 14–26.

Macklin, F. Anthony. "'I Come Ready': An Interview with John Wayne." *Film Heritage* 10 (1975): 1–32.

Maltby, Richard. "A Better Sense of History: John Ford and the Indians." In Cameron and Pye, *The Book of Westerns*, 34–49.

Mannoni, Octave. *Prospero and Caliban: The Psychology of Colonization.* Ann Arbor: University of Michigan Press, 1990.

May, Larry, ed. *Recasting America: Culture and Politics in the Age of Cold War.* Chicago: University of Chicago Press, 1989.

McBride, Joseph. "*The Searchers.*" *Sight and Sound* (spring 1972).

———. *Searching for John Ford: A Life.* New York: St. Martin's Press, 2001.

McBride, Joseph, and Michael Wilmington. *John Ford.* New York: Da Capo Press, 1975.

———. "The Prisoner of the Desert." *Sight and Sound* (autumn 1971).

Mitchell, Lee Clark. *Westerns: Making the Man in Fiction and Film.* Chicago: University of Chicago Press, 1996.

Mitry, Jean. "Interview with John Ford." In *Interviews with Film Directors*, ed. Andrew Sarris, 193–201. New York: Avon, 1969. Originally published as "Rencontre avec John Ford," *Cahiers du Cinema* 45 (March 1955): 3–9.

Mortimer, Barbara. *Hollywood's Frontier Captives: Cultural Anxiety and the Captivity Plot in American Film.* New York: Garland, 2000.

Neale, Steve. "Vanishing Americans: Racial and Ethnic Issues in Interpretation and Context of Post-War 'Pro-Indian' Westerns." In *Back in the Saddle Again: New Essays on the Western*, ed. Edward Buscombe and Roberta E. Pearson, 8–28. London: British Film Institute, 1998.

Neely, William. *The Last Comanche Chief: The Life and Times of Quanah Parker.* New York: John Wiley, 1995.

Nolley, Ken. "The Representation of Conquest: John Ford and the Hollywood Indian, 1939–1964." In Rollins and O'Connor, *Hollywood's Indian*, 73–90.

Nowell-Smith, Geoffrey. "Six Authors in Pursuit of The Searchers." *Screen* 17 (spring 1976): 26–33.

O'Connor, John E. *The Hollywood Indian: Stereotypes of Native Americans in Film.* Patterson: New Jersey State Museum, 1980.

Oldmeadow, H. "Tracking *The Searchers:* A Survey of the Film's Critical Reception." *Continuum* 11 (1997): 132–62.

Peary, Danny. *Cult Movies.* New York: Simon and Schuster, 1981.

Peary, Gerald, ed. *John Ford Interviews.* Jackson: University of Mississippi Press, 2002.

Peek, Wendy Chapman. "Cherchez la Femme: *The Searchers, Vertigo,* and Masculinity in Post-Kinsey America." *Journal of American Culture* 21 (1998): 73–87.

Place, Janice A. *The Western Films of John Ford.* Secaucus, N.J.: Citadel Press, 1974.

Selected Bibliography

Pratts, Armando José. *Invisible Natives: Myth and Identity in the American Western.* Ithaca, N.Y.: Cornell University Press, 2002.
Pye, Douglas. "Double Vision: Miscegenation and Point of View in *The Searchers.*" In Cameron and Pye, *The Book of Westerns,* 229–35.
———. "*The Searchers* and Teaching the Film Industry." *Screen Education* 17 (1975): 34–48.
Quart, Leonard, and Albert Auster. *American Film and Society since 1945.* Westport, Conn.: Praeger, 2002.
Rister, Charles Coke. *Border Captives: The Traffic in Prisoners by the Southern Plains Tribes, 1835–1875.* Norman: University of Oklahoma Press, 1940.
Roberson, Chuck. *The Fall Guy: Thirty Years as the Duke's Double.* North Vancouver, B.C.: Hancock House, 1980.
Roberts, Randy, and James S Olsen. *John Wayne, American.* New York: Free Press, 1995.
Rollins, Peter C., and John E. O'Connor, eds. *Hollywood's Indian: The Portrayal of the Native American in Film.* Lexington: University of Kentucky Press, 1998.
Roth, Marty. "'Yes, My Darling Daughter': Gender, Miscegenation, and Generation in John Ford's *The Searchers.*" *New Orleans Review* 18 (1991): 65–73.
Sarris, Andrew. "Andrew Sarris on *The Searchers.*" *Film Comment* 7 (1971): 59–61.
———. *The John Ford Movie Mystery.* Bloomington: University of Indiana Press, 1975.
Sinclair, Andrew. *John Ford: A Biography.* New York: Lorrimer, 1979.
Skerry, P. J. "What Makes a Man to Wander? Ethan Edwards of John Ford's *The Searchers.*" *New Orleans Review* 18 (1991): 86–91.
Slotkin, Richard. *Gunfighter Nation: The Myth of the Frontier in Twentieth-Century America.* New York: HarperCollins, 1993.
———. *Regeneration through Violence: The Mythology of the American Frontier, 1600–1860.* Middletown, Conn.: Wesleyan University Press, 1973.
Smith, Henry Nash. *Virgin Land: The American West as Symbol and Myth.* Cambridge: Harvard University Press, 1970.
Stowell, Peter. *John Ford.* Boston: Twayne, 1986.
Studlar, Gaylyn, and Matthew Bernstein. *John Ford Made Westerns: Filming the Legend in the Sound Era.* Bloomington: Indiana University Press, 2001.
Swindell, Larry. "Yes, John Ford Knew a Thing or Two about Art." In Gerald Peary, *John Ford Interviews,* 145–50.
Thomas, Deborah. "John Wayne's Body." In Cameron and Pye, *The Book of Westerns,* 75–87.
Thomson, David. "Open and Shut: A Fresh Look at *The Searchers.*" *Film Comment* 33 (1997): 28–31.
Tompkins, Jane. *West of Everything.* New York: Oxford University Press, 1992.
Travers, P. "*The Searchers* Rides Again." *Rolling Stone,* June 10, 1993, 74.
Tuska, John. *The American West in Film.* Westport, Conn.: Greenwood Press, 1983.
Walker, Janet. "Captive Images: Traumatic Events and the Historiographic Function of the Film Western." In *Westerns: Films through History,* ed. Janet Walker, 219–51. New York: Routledge, 2001.

Selected Bibliography

Walker, Michael. "Melodramatic Narrative: *Orphans of the Storm* and *The Searchers.*" *Cineaction* 31 (1993): 62–72.

Wallace, Ernest, and E. Adamson Hoebel. *The Comanches: Lords of the South Plains.* Norman: University of Oklahoma Press, 1952.

Warshow, Robert. "The Westerner." In *The Immediate Experience: Movies, Comics, Theater and Other Aspects of Popular Culture,* ed. Robert Warshow, 135–54. New York: Atheneum, 1979.

Wayne, Pilar Pallete. *John Wayne: My Life with the Duke.* New York: McGraw-Hill, 1987.

Whissel, Kristen. "Racialized Spectacle, Exchange Relations, and the Western in *Johanna d'Arc of Mongolia.*" *Screen* 37 (1996): 41–67.

White, Hayden. *Metahistory: The Historical Imagination in Nineteenth-Century Europe.* Baltimore: Johns Hopkins University Press, 1973.

Whitfield, Stephen J. *The Culture of the Cold War.* Baltimore: Johns Hopkins University Press, 1996.

Wills, Garry. *John Wayne's America: The Politics of Celebrity.* New York: Simon and Schuster, 1997.

Winkler, Martin. "Tragic Features in John Ford's *The Searchers.*" In *Classics and the Cinema,* ed. Martin Winkler, 185–208. Lewisburg, Pa.: Bucknell University Press, 1993.

Wood, Robin. *Sexual Politics and Narrative Film.* New York: Columbia University Press, 1998.

———. "Shall We Gather at the River? The Late Films of John Ford." *Film Comment* 7 (1971): 8–17.

Young, Robert J. C. *Colonial Desire: Hybridity in Theory, Culture and Race.* London: Routledge, 1995.

Contributors

JAMES F. BROOKS is an ethnohistorian specializing in the gendered aspects of violence and identity formation in colonial borderlands. His monograph, *Captives and Cousins: Slavery, Kinship, and Community in the Southwest Borderlands* (University of North Carolina Press, 2002) won the Frederick Jackson Turner Award for best first book in American history, the Bancroft Prize for distinguished book in American history, and the Francis Parkman Prize for best book in American history. He is currently a member of the research faculty at the School of American Research in Santa Fe, New Mexico, and director of the SAR Press.

TOM GRAYSON COLONNESE (Santee Sioux) is the director of American Indian Studies at the University of Washington. His areas of research include American Indian military history and American Indian novels. He is the coauthor of *American Indian Novelists* with Louis Owens. Colonnese was an adviser to President Clinton on American Indian tribal college education. He has directed several American Indian education grants funded by the Department of Education, NASA, Hewlett Foundations, and Microsoft. He also taught at Arizona State University, Northern Arizona University, and was a Libra Professor at the University of Maine.

ARTHUR M. ECKSTEIN is professor of history at the University of Maryland at College Park. He is the author of two books and thirty-five articles, mostly on ancient and modern imperialism. His article "Darkening Ethan: John Ford's *The Searchers* from Novel to Screenplay to Screen" was nominated for the Society for Cinema and Media Studies Katherine Kovacs Award as best scholarly article on Film, 1998.

DAVID GRIMSTED, who teaches history at the University of Maryland, is interested in American popular culture and its ties with the people who consume it so generously. His enthusiasms are primarily antiquarian, for he has written a book on melodrama and another book on that other popular

Contributors

American art form, rioting (before the Civil War). But sometimes he watches movies to see what he can see in them about more recent developments.

BRIAN HENDERSON is currently professor of film theory and history in the Department of Media Studies at the State University of New York at Buffalo. He is the author of *A Critique of Film Theory* (1980), the editor of two volumes of screenplays by Preston Sturges (1986 and 1995), and the editor of *Film Quarterly: Fifty Years—A Selection* (1999).

RICHARD HUTSON is in the English department at the University of California, Berkeley. He is also a member of the affiliated faculty of the American Studies Program. He is interested in American popular culture and has written about a number of film westerns. He is working on a study of various writings from, and about, the cattle trade and ranch life from the Civil War to 1940.

KATHRYN KALINAK is a professor of English and Film Studies at Rhode Island College. She is the author of *Settling the Score* as well as numerous articles on the role of music in film. She is currently at work on a book-length study of music for westerns titled *How the West Was Sung*.

PETER LEHMAN is director of the Interdisciplinary Humanities Program at Arizona State University. He is author of *Roy Orbison: The Invention of an Alternative Rock Masculinity* and *Running Scared: Masculinity and the Representation of the Male Body*. He is coauthor of *Thinking about Movies: Watching, Questioning, Enjoying* and editor of *Defining Cinema* and *Masculinity: Bodies, Movies, Culture*.

WILLIAM LUHR is professor of English at Saint Peter's College and Co-Chair of the Columbia University Seminar on Cinema and Interdisciplinary Interpretation. Among other works, he is author of *Raymond Chandler and Film*, 2nd ed. (1991); editor of *World Cinema since 1945* (1987), The Maltese Falcon: *John Huston, Director* (1995), and *The Coen Brothers's* Fargo (2004); and coauthor of *Thinking about Movies: Watching, Questioning, Enjoying* (2003). He is currently writing a book on film noir.

DOUGLAS PYE is senior lecturer in film at the University of Reading (UK). He co-edited (with Ian Cameron) *The Movie Book of the Western*

Contributors

(Continuum, 1996), and his edited volume of essays on Fritz Lang is forthcoming from Cameron and Hollis. He has had a long association with the journal *Movie*.

GAYLYN STUDLAR is Rudolf Arnheim Collegiate Professor of Film Studies at the University of Michigan, Ann Arbor, where she has directed the program in film and video studies since 1995. She is widely published on issues of gender in Hollywood cinema. Her scholarship on the Western has appeared in the anthologies *Back in the Saddle, Stagecoach,* and her own volume coedited with Matthew Bernstein, *John Ford Made Westerns*.

MARTIN M. WINKLER is professor of classics at George Mason University. His publications include books and articles on Roman literature, on the classical tradition, and on classical and medieval culture and mythology in the cinema. He has also edited the essay collections *Classical Myth and Culture in the Cinema* (Oxford, 2001) and *Gladiator: Film and History* (Blackwell, 2004).

INDEX

Page numbers in italics refer to figures.

Academy Awards, 33, 117
adoption, intertribal, 52, 61, 64, 66, 71
"adult westerns," 83, 90, 301
African Americans, 8, 9, 65–66, 132–37, 323; absence from *The Searchers*, 69; actors, 304–5; antimiscegenation laws and, 65, 67; civil rights movement and, 66–68; in Cold War era, 292; in Ford films, 17; minstrel music and, 139, 322; as slaves in Texas, 277; stereotypes of, 305; in western genre, 12
African Queen, The (film), 205
Albers, Patricia, 281, 283
Almassen, Juana, 272, 273, 279
alter egos, 15, 153, 200, 202, 215, 233
altruism, as female virtue, 175, 176, 178
American Film Institute, 1, 35
Anderson, Bronco Billy, 298, 328n. 12
Anderson, Lindsay, 33, 48
Angel and the Badman (film), 79, 86
Annaud, Jean-Jacques, 214
anthropological analysis, 51–52, 53, 64, 198, 279, 281
Apache tribe, 11, 12, 188; historical captivity narratives and, 275, 276, 277; in Mexico, 275
Archuletta, Beulah, 2, 189, 225
Argosy Pictures, 22, 32
aristeia, 146, 147, 148, 152, 156
Armendarez, Pedro, 12
Arness, James, 76
Arrowsmith (Ford film), 304
Asians, as villains, 10, 11
audience response, 64, 190, 297, 325; depiction of white racist brutality and, 13; to Ethan Edwards character, 3, 70; to final scene, 28; identification with hero, 213; limits of knowledge and, 239, 245–46; Marty's fears and, 314–15; musical scores and, 114, 115; Native American audience, 340; rescue-and-romance fantasy and, 204; to stereotype humor, 306; unconscious fantasies involved in, 54, 213
Autry, Gene, 90

Back to Bataan (film), 76
Bad Day at Black Rock (film), 295
Baker, Carroll, 175
Bancroft, George, 178
Barbarian and the Geisha, The (film), 84
Barthes, Roland, 49, 239
Baxter, John, 48, 163
Bend of the River (film), 83
Berg, Charles Ramirez, 130
BFI Companion to the Western (Buscombe), 205
Big Jim McLain (film), 76, 88
Big Wednesday (film), 47
binary oppositions, 51, 72n. 8, 172
Blood on the Moon (film), 299
Boetticher, Budd, 97, 155
Bogdanovich, Peter, 29, 110, 125, 262, 327n. 3
Bond, Ward, 5, 6, 120, 175
Bonner, Priscilla, 176
"Bonnie Blue Flag, The" (song), 112, 123, 136, 139, 321
Boom Town (film), 79
Born on the Fourth of July (Kovic), 77

355

Index

Borzage, Danny, 110
"brainwashing," fear of, 10, 11
Brando, Marlon, 5, 84
Brandon, Henry, 2, 13, 174, 287n. 31, 311, 340
bricolage principle, 68
"Bringing in the Sheaves" (song), 110
Broken Arrow (film), 11, 223
Brooks, James F., 16, 115, 311, 318
Brown, Marshall, 100
Brown v. Board of Education, 8, 9, 39n. 27, 217, 292; judicial precedent and, 304; in Northern and Southern states, 73n. 24; social upheaval over, 66–68
Buffalo Bill's Wild West, 130
burial ritual, 148
Buscombe, Edward, 48, 51, 205
Buttolph, David, 111
Byron, Stuart, 47

C. V. Whitney Pictures, 117
Cagney, James, 78, 84, 87
Cahiers du cinéma, 50, 51, 54, 55
Canutt, Yakima, 88, 91n. 9
capitalism, 293, 295
Capra, Frank, 23
Captive Mind, The (Milosz), 10
captivity narratives, 10–11, 119, 165, 173, 233, 265; borderlands culture and, 270–80; circular structure in *The Searchers*, 94; Native Americans captured by colonists, 273–74; variety of, 190
Carey, Harry, Jr., 2, 19, 120–21, 174, 186
Carey, Harry, Sr., 29, 298, 299, 301, 304
Carey, Olive, 19, 29, 186
Carradine, John, 188
catharsis, 160, 257
Cavalry (U.S. Army): as agents of the law, 54; as killers of women, 227; massacre of Indians by, 82, 224, 235, 308; racist social network and, 225

Ceiling Zero (film), 79
censorship, 177, 178
Chaplin, Charlie, 293
Charge at Feather River, The (film), 10
Charge of the Light Brigade (film), 118
Cherokee tribe, 52, 59, 65, 225, 279, 335
Cheyenne Autumn (Ford film), 12, 24, 40n. 37, 342; critical response to, 330n. 34; female pioneering spirit in, 175; Native Americans depicted in, 307; racism condemned in, 199; view of scalping, 155
Cheyenne (television series), 90
Cheyenne tribe, 10, 11, 22, 338
China Seas (film), 79
chivalry, 21, 23, 188
Christianity, 172, 183, 184, 185, 278, 321; female captivity narratives and, 312; Ford's use of symbolism and, 332n. 44
Christy Minstrels, 134, 135
Churchill, Berton, 293–94, 327n. 4
Cimino, Michael, 47
Citizen Kane (film), 258
civilization, 28, 29, 82, 153, 226, 302; corrosion of knowledge by, 103; Ethan's exile from, 160; imperial narrative and, 30; inhospitable frontier and, 126; Jorgensen house as symbol of, 199; models of, 172; Monument Valley and, 100; renunciation of violence and, 162; "savages" and, 202; as triumph of white society, 290–91; violent price of, 164; women as representatives of, 171, 174–75, 179, 186. *See also* "white civilization"
civil rights movement, 8–9, 129, 132
Civil War, 4, 6, 68, 69, 241, 247; popular music of, 121, 123, 135–37; Texas settlement after, 73n. 28
Clayton, Rev. Capt. Samuel Johnson (character), 5–6, 102, 128; as butt of humor, 23, 308, 328n. 13; Ethan-Martha relationship and,

356

Index

248; Martin's attempt to rescue Debbie and, 62; paradoxical functions of, 239; restraint on vengeance and, 187; as symbol of authority, 69, 151
Close Encounters of the Third Kind (film), 47, 48
Cochise (Apache chief), 11, 12
Colbert, Claudette, 175
Cold War era, 106, 292
Colonnese, Tom, 290
Comanche (film), 119
Comanche Station (film), 155
Comanche tribe, 1, 2, 275; depiction in *The Searchers*, 11–13, 54, 126–27, 221n. 61, 225, 227–28, 233, 337–41; as "empty signifiers," 9; historical captivity narratives and, 43n. 89, 275, 276; losses in Indian Wars, 335; massacred by U.S. Cavalry, 12–13, 22; sexual division of labor among, 271–72
comedy, 206, 235, 245, 280, 309, 330–31n. 37
Communism, 10, 11, 39n. 22
community, 126, 127, 199, 313
Confederate States of America, 135, 136–37, 188; music of, 290, 321; Texas as part of, 340; in *The Unforgiven*, 207, 208
Conqueror, The (film), 83–84
conquest-and-resistance narratives, 270
Coolidge, Calvin, 295
Cooper, Chris, 215
Cooper, Gary, 5, 76, 299; male body display and, 87; undermined western hero and, 82, 83; Wayne's body language and, 78
Cooper, James Fenimore, 234, 331n. 39
Cooper, Merian C., 19, 22, 67, 117
corpse, mutilation of, 4, 148, *153*, 155, 160, 316
Costner, Kevin, 11, 81
coup de theatre, 100, 103
Covered Wagon, The (Ford film), 334n. 59

Cowboys, The (film), 88
Coy, Walter, 7, 173
critics and criticism, 1, 3, 204, 314, 325; African American critics, 9; on the happy ending, 20, 30; on imperial narrative, 30; methods of, 50; music in *The Searchers* and, 109; reputation of *The Searchers* and, 33–36
"Critics on *The Searchers*" (Buscombe), 48
Crystal, Linda, 272
cultural studies, 36
Curtis, Ken, 19, 226, 305
Custer, George Armstrong, 31, 163, 189, 338; in scene cut from *The Searchers*, 22, 23, 199; search-and-destroy missions of, 40n. 37, 286n. 27
Cutter, Murray, 123

Dances with Wolves (film), 11, 22, 45n. 118, 341
Darby, Ken, 117
D'Arc, James, 117
Darnell, Linda, 120, 228, 333n. 53
Daves, Delmer, 5, 11, 12, 13, 223
Dead Man's Walk (McMurtry), 155
Dean, James, 84
death, meaning of, 183–84
Deer Hunter, The (film), 47, 48
Delgado, Fray Carlos, 272, 273
DeMille, Cecil B., 294
Dempsey, Michael, 172
desire, deferment of, 54
Dillinger (film), 34, 47
Disciple, The (film), 298
Dodge City (film), 118
Donovan's Reef (Ford film), 193, 199
doorway visual motif, 250–51, *252–53*, 255, *255*, 298
Double Indemnity (film), 81
Douglas, Gordon, 10
Douglas, Kirk, 83, 84
Dru, Joanne, 176
Drum Beat (film), 299, 328n. 13

Index

Drums Along the Mohawk (Ford film), 175, 176, 185, 306, 307
dualism, structural, 54
Duras, Marguerite, 214

Earp, Wyatt, 24, 155, 184
Eastwood, Clint, 89, 90
Eckert, Charles, 51
Eckstein, Arthur M., 82, 112, 247, 290, 318; criticism of, 321; Native American response to *The Searchers* and, 335; on portrayal of Futterman character, 341–42; on song "Lorena," 123; on western genre, 319
Edwards, Aaron (character), 4, 19, 55, 182, 297; adoption of Martin Pauley, 13, 52; death of, 7, 28, 80, 173; as dull and passive presence, 181, 226; as failed masculine figure, 246; on living in Monument Valley, 104; relationship with Ethan, 15, 119–20
Edwards, Amos (Ethan character in LeMay novel), 20–21
Edwards, Ben (character), 7, 28, 80, 211
Edwards, Debbie (character): abducted by Scar, 80, 194n. 18; attitude toward captivity, 312–13; in captivity, 10, 12, 15, 190–91, 232, 266; as child in opening scene, 181, 201, 254, 254; choice overridden by white society, 53; as Hollywood "valuable woman," 15; infantilization of, 191–92; judged by white pioneer community, 177; kinship relations and, 18, 59, 60–62, 154; in LeMay novel, 67–68, 203, 282; rag doll (Topsy) of, 132–33; refusal to leave Scar, 55, 173, 174; rescue of, 2, 25, 124, 185, 191, 235, 297; resemblance to Martha, 17, 20, 191, 200, 202; return to white society, 27–28, 43n. 89, 124, 191–92, 192, 236, 313; as Scar's wife, 16, 21, 52, 61, 190, 202,

269; as sexual war trophy, 183; spared by Ethan, 19–20, 25, 31–32, 125, 159–60
Edwards, Ethan (character), 2, 210–11; as Achilles, 145, 151–57, 159–63; adoption of Martin and, 57; ambiguous aspect of, 224, 249–51, 254–57, 324; attempt to kill Debbie, 29; background of, 247–48, 339; beaten to the punch by Scar, 15; as Captain Ahab, 165, 170n. 43; Comanche marriage practices and, 282–83; as Confederate veteran, 97, 123, 137, 151, 173, 182, 298; critics' focus upon, 48–49; darkening of, 21–22, 43n. 81, 82, 152–57, 153, 154, 165, 199–200; desire to murder Debbie, 7, 10, 13, 19–20, 23, 30, 53, 59, 97, 179, 224; doorway motif and, 250, 252–53; kinship dilemmas and, 266–69; knowledge of Comanche ways, 58, 59, 72n. 11, 115, 152, 153, 303, 316; in LeMay novel, 20–21, 67, 112, 165, 202; love for Martha, 4, 5–7, 55, 122–23, 127, 179, 181, 182, 200, 248, 263n. 5; Martha's wishes and, 186–90; military medal of, 182–83, 202, 203; mother killed by Comanches, 207; as multiculturalist, 316–17; as Oedipus, 214; in opening scene, 79, 119–20, 181; as outlaw, 3–4, 21, 69–70, 102, 120, 248; racism of, 3, 4, 13, 27, 81, 98, 136–37, 199, 309–10; reaction to death of Look, 309, 310, 339; redemption from hate and rage, 159–60, 189–90, 240, 256, 259, 280, 341; rejection of family by, 28; relationship with children, 296; relationship with Martin Pauley, 13–14, 52, 57–60, 58, 296; as remnant or ghost, 98, 99; as representative of his society, 14, 28, 224–25; repudiation of kinship with

358

Index

Debbie, 61, 154, 254; scalping of Scar, 24, 31, 62, 155–56, 157, 255, 315; sparing of Debbie's life, 25, 31–32, 125, 159–60; structural foregrounding of, 50; as suppressor of knowledge, 102; tilt toward madness, 24–25, 231; as tragic outcast, 26–28, *27,* 32, 70, 154, 160–61, 163, 192, 199; Wayne's established persona and, 81–82; in white captives scene, 21–24, 189, 229–31, 268, 303, 309–10, *311;* wounded arm of, 25, *27,* 28–29, *30,* 61, 160, 199, 269

Edwards, Lucy (character), 6, 14, 28; abducted by Scar, 80; death of, 7, 58, 173–74, 190; Ethan questioned about fate of, 249; Ethan's Confederate jacket as shroud for, 182, 220n. 44; fate contrasted to Look's, 308; in opening scene, 181; paleness of, 234

Edwards, Mark, 159, 160

Edwards, Martha (character), 4, 19, 28; adoption of Martin Pauley, 13, 52; death of, 7, 80, 124, 173, 267; Debbie's resemblance to, 16, 17, 20, 191, 200, 202; doorway motif and, 250, *251, 252;* Ethan's dedication to, 97; fate contrasted to Look's, 308; fear of rape, 14; feminine values and, 173, 179–82, *182, 185, 192,* 193; on frontier life, 116; as incarnation of ideal Law, 55–56; invocation of wishes of, 224; in LeMay novel, 21; love for Ethan, 122–23, 127, 179, 181, 182, 248, 263n. 5; musical score and, 113; as pioneer mother, 176; as suppressor of knowledge, 102

Ehrenstein, David, 206

El Dorado (film), 88

Eliot, T. S., 49

Elke, Bernice, 336, 337

Emancipation Proclamation (1863), 66, 136

Englishman's Boy, The (film), 155
epic poetry, 145
Euro (Anglo)-Americans, 265–66, 270, 271
Eurocentrism, 175

families: adoption and, 64; Comanche, 12; Debbie's captivity and return, 191–92; Ethan's mean-spiritedness and, 297; Ethan's rejection of, 28, 29; Ford family, 18–19, 294; Ford's vision of family on the frontier, 174, 320; as future of the nation, 174; as sacred institution, 199; threat of illicit sexual desire and, 20; in *The Unforgiven,* 206–7
femininity, 171–72, 174, 177, 183, 247
feminists, 318
Fernandez y Figueroa, Emilio (character), 131, 282, *283,* 340, 342
film noir, 75, 83
film studies, academic, 67
Fistful of Dollars, A (film), 89
Fleischer, Richard, 214
Flying Leathernecks (film), 76
Flying Tigers (film), 76, 79
Flynn, Errol, 87
folk song, 133, 134, 135
Fonda, Henry, 184, 185, 299
For a Few Dollars More (film), 89
Ford, Glenn, 5, 299
Ford, John, 1, 3, 35, 130; as auteur, 31–33, 44n. 100; career, 5, 32, 37n. 3, 75, 205; depiction of African Americans, 17; depiction of Euro-Americans, 12–13; depiction of Native Americans, 11–12; directorial intentions, 4; editing process and, 23, 32; family in vision of frontier, 174, 320; family of, 19–19, 294; gender values and, 185–86; heroes in films of, 54, 162–65, 163, 199; interviewed about *The Searchers,* 262, 327n. 3, 334n. 59; knowledge of American West, 272, 286n. 19, 339; LeMay

359

Index

Ford, John (*continued*)
novel and, 20–21; liberal politics of, 9, 39n. 28, 293–95; memory and, 98, 103–4; Monument Valley landscape and, 93; music and, 109–13, 137, 139, 201, 321; as "poet of civilization," 14–15; problematic antiracism of *The Searchers* and, 306–10; ritual behavior patterns in films of, 99, 101–2; sexuality as horseplay in films of, 228; silent films of, 176, 177; stereotypes in films of, 305–6; we stern genre and, 2, 5, 11, 156, 178–79, 192, 236–37, 293, 298, 299–302, 317, 321; white racism condemned in films of, 7–9, 11, 12, 199, 268, 272, 303–5; women in films of, 97, 172–73, 174–80, 193n. 4; working relationship with John Wayne, 25, 31, 38n. 18
Ford, Patrick, 18–19, 31, 112
Fort Apache (Ford film), 12, 22, 85; as Custer story, 163; knowledge and ignorance in, 259–60, 261; Native Americans depicted in, 307; women's values in, 172
Foster, Stephen, 110
Fourteenth Amendment, 66
Four Wives (film), 118
Frankenheimer, John, 10
Freudian criticism, 51, 71, 257, 319, 332n. 46
Friendly Persuasion (film), 59
frontier, 105, 106, 126, 129
Futterman, Jerem (character), 69, 156, 166n. 11, 243, 291, 341–42

Gable, Clark, 79, 87
Gallagher, Tag, 99, 126, 202, 330n. 33
Garfield, John, 78
George, Susan, 214, 221n. 57
Geronimo: An American Legend (film), 155
Giant (film), 295
Gish, Lillian, 205, 207, 209, 211

Glory (film), 12, 199
Gone with the Wind (film), 118, 121, 139
Good, Bad, and the Ugly, The (film), 89
Goodnight, Charles, 275
Gorbman, Claudia, 130
Granger, Stewart, 299
Grant, Cary, 79, 84
Grapes of Wrath, The (Ford film), 293, 294, 295, 304, 325
Griffith, D. W., 304
Guion, David, 135
Gunfight at O.K. Corral (film), 83
Gunfighter, The (film), 299
Gun Fightin' Gentleman, A (Ford film), 298
Gunsmoke (television series), 76, 90
Gutierrez, Ramon, 274–75

Halttunen, Karen, 184
Hamilton, Annette, 129
Hanging Tree, The (film), 5
Hangman's House, The (Ford film), 303, 320
happy endings, 32, 215
Hardcore (film), 34, 45n. 112, 47, 48
Harper, Mose (character), 43n. 83, 59, 98, 291; as holy fool, 156, 263n. 4; racial ambiguity of, 133
Hart, William S., 298, 299, 304
Hawks, Howard, 82, 165
Hayward, Susan, 83
Heflin, Van, 299
Hegel, G. W. F., 94
Henderson, Brian, 28, 132, 266, 290
Hepburn, Audrey, 207, 212
heroic code, 21, 23, 25, 146, 147, 156–57
High and the Mighty, The (film), 79
High Noon (film), 82, 83, 299, 322; antiracist theme in, 333n. 51; John Wayne's opinion of, 322, 333n. 51; music in, 118
High Sierra (film), 81
Hill, Walter, 155
His Girl Friday (film), 79

360

Index

Hispanics, 131, 271; Hispanics in Indian captivity, 270, 272–75, 277–80, *279*; Hispanics portrayed in Ford films, 305, 342
history, 48, 54, 104, 265
Hitchcock, Alfred, 2, 84, 161
Hoch, Winton, 31, 33, 44n. 98, 316, 331n. 43
Hollywood film industry, 11, 87, 257, 261; Baby Boomer generation and, 34, 35, 36, 76–77; blacklist, 39n. 28, 205; closure and clarity in, 258; hermeneutic code of, 239, 240; musical scores, 110, 114; racial controversy and, 292–93, 295, 323; studio system, 23, 110; "valuable woman" stereotype, 15
Home of the Brave (film), 295
Hondo (film), 76, 79, 88
Hooded Fireplace site, 273, *274*
Horn, Sarah Ann, 281
Horse Soldiers, The (Ford film), 38n. 22, 111, 112, 124, 139
How Green Was My Valley (Ford film), 118, 293, 320
Hunter, Jeffrey, 2, 13, 31, 120, 173
Hurricane, The (Ford film), 304
Huston, John, 23, 198, 205, 206, 212, 215
Hutson, Richard, 126, 289, 318, 324

ideology, 54, 128–29
Iliad (Homeric epic), 145–70, 289, 317
imperialism, 30, 43n. 94, 198
incest, 32, 197, 198, 206, 281–82, 333n. 54
"Indian Idyll" (song), 118
"Indian" music, 129–30, 131–32, 290, 337–38
individuality, 75, 82, 172
Informer, The (Ford film), 117, 125, 325
interracial sexuality, 7, 67, 197, 228, 268–69, 322–23. *See also* race; sexual/racial "defilement"
interruption, structural, 126, 127–28
Intruder in the Dust (film), 295, 305

Invasion of the Body Snatchers (film), 10
Iron Horse, The (Ford film), 121, 176, 301, 307, 322
Island in the Sky (film), 76
Island in the Sun (film), 323

Jackson, Helen Hunt, 323
Jackson, Howard, 111
Jackson, Jesse, 72
Jackson, John Brinkerhof, 105, 106
"Japanese war-bride films," 9
Jefferson, Thomas, 65
Jews, 335–36, 341–42
Johnson, Ben, 178, 186
Jones, Buck, 89
Jones, Stan, 109, 110, 112–13, 115, 121
Jordan, Dorothy, 19, 31, 124, 173
Jordan, Winthrop, 65
Jorgensen, Brad (character), 6, 58, 84–85, 315; attitude toward Indians, 313; death of, 14, 104, 120, 125, 174, 186; Marty as substitute for, 284n. 5; suicidal action of, 102
Jorgensen, Lars (character), 101, 104, 127, 246, 247, 313–14
Jorgensen, Laurie (character), 15, 25, 116; attempt to keep Marty home, 313; "false marriage" of, 19, 37n. 7, 61, 128, 246; kinship relations and, 18; in LeMay novel, 68; marriage to Martin Pauley, 52, 62–64, 127, 203–4; Martha's importance and, 55, 180; Marty's letter and, 324; masculine (patriarchal) values and, 173, 186; racist outburst of, 3, 14, 20, 28, 62, 187, 224–25, 313, 314; wait for Marty, 246
Jorgensen, Mrs. (character), 21, 25, 29, 43n. 89, 120, 180; Debbie's return and, 191; on living in Monument Valley, 94, 101, 104, 116, 126; Martha's wishes and, 186–87; relationship with Marty, 219n. 33, 284n. 5
Jubal (film), 5

361

Index

"Jubilo" (song), 111, 112, 128, 133, 134, 135–36, 137
Judge Priest (Ford film), 304, 305

Kael, Pauline, 33
Kalinak, Kathryn, 201, 259, 290, 318, 321–22, 324
Kazan, Elia, 305
Kearney, William, 120–21
King, Martin Luther, Jr., 9
King Kong (film), 117
kinship relations, 17–18, 51, 160, 195n. 34; blood versus adoption, 64, 66, 70, 290; borderlands culture and, 266–70; Ethan's relationship with Martin and, 58; reading in *The Searchers*, 280–84
Kiowa tribe, 205, 207, 208–10, 215–16; historical captivity narratives and, 275, 276, 277–79, *279*; in Mexico, 275
Kitses, Jim, 205
Klinck, Richard, 95
Kolodny, Annette, 265
Korean War, 10, 327n. 10
Kovic, Ron, 77
Kristopherson, Kris, 215

Lacan, Jacques, 71, 198
Ladd, Alan, 26, 299
L'Amour, Louis, 97
Lancaster, Burt, 206, 210, 213
Last Hunt, The (film), 299
Last of the Mohicans, The (Cooper), 234
Laura (film), 118
law, 53–54, 54, 55–56, 56, 68
Left-Handed Gun, The (film), 5
Legend of the Lost (film), 88
Lehman, Peter, 99, 116, 124, 291; on epistemological theme, 231; on lifting gesture motif, 319; on Look episode, 227, 228, 229; on structural interruption, 127
LeMay, Alan. *See Searchers, The* (LeMay novel)
Lenihan, John, 293

Leone, Sergio, 89, 90
Leung, Tony, 214
Lévi-Strauss, Claude, 49, 51, 65, 68
liberalism, 223, 232
libido, unrestrained, 54, 55
Life and Legend of Wyatt Earp, The (television series), 90
lifting gesture (visual motif), 250, 251, *253–54*, 254, 255–56, 257, 259, 319
Lincoln, Abraham, 50, 55, 135, 184
Linton, Ralph, 279
Little Big Man (film), 11, 22, 223
Logan, Joshua, 9
Lone Ranger, The (television series), 26
Lone Star (film), 215
Look (character), 2–3, 18, 21, 104, 262; alternate names of, 242–43; comic treatment of, 226–27; death of, 132, 164, 189, 226, 227, 338; described in Martin's letter to Laurie, 225–26, 244–45; historical kinship alliances and, 280–81; meaning of, 116; musical score and, 132; problematic representation of, 226–29
"Lorena" (Civil War ballad), 6, 111, 128, 132, 259; ambiguity of Ethan-Martha relationship and, 263n. 5; Debbie's relation to Martha and, 191; as favorite of Confederate soldiers, 136; function of, 121–25; historical background of, 38n. 22, 200–201; as "Martha's Theme," 6, 19, 20, 191, 200; popularity of, 139; used in other films, 124, 139; woman as object of desire in, 116
Lost Boundaries (film), 295
Lost Patrol, The (Ford film), 117
Lover, The (film), 214–15, 221n. 58
Lucas, George, 34, 35, 45n. 112, 47, 77
Luhr, William, 290, 318, 322

Macarthy, Harry, 136, 143n. 67
MacLaglen, Victor, 117
Maddow, Ben, 205

Index

Maltby, Richard, 198, 234, 236
Maltese Falcon, The (film), 81, 205
Manchurian Candidate, The (film), 10
Mandingo (film), 214, 221n. 57
Man from Laramie, The (film), 5, 83
Manifest Destiny, 101, 129
Mann, Anthony, 4–5, 83
Mannoni, Octave, 197–98, 202, 213, 217, 322
Man of the West (film), 5
Man Who Shot Liberty Valance, The (Ford film), 2, 111, 260–61, 325
Man without a Star (film), 83
March, Jane, 214
Marked Woman (film), 51
marriage, 51, 96, 127; civilization and, 226; "false" and "natural," 208; interethnic diplomacy of Plains Indians and, 281, 283
"Martha's Theme." *See under* "Lorena" (Civil War ballad)
Martin, Dean, 53
Martín, José Andres (Andali), 277–79, *279*
Marvin, Lee, 204
Marxist criticism, 51
Mary of Scotland (Ford film), 117
masculinity, 75–76, 77, 79, 158; associated with action, 246–47; feminine values and, 185–86, 191, 193; repression of masculine prowess, 171; shirtless actors, 86–87; undermined, 263n. 4; western landscape and, 96–97
Matthews, Washington, 272
Maximilian, emperor of Mexico, 4, 16, 202, 298
McBride, Joseph, 35, 48, 105, 180; on Debbie's captivity, 190; on motive for the search, 250; on white female captives scene, 232
McCaffrey, Augustine, 336, 337
McConnell, Mary, 341
McCorry, Charlie (character), 37n. 7, 61, 63, 208; attitude toward Indians, 314; delivery of Marty's letter, 244; "false marriage" to Laurie, 128, 135; in LeMay novel, 68; as parallel to Look, 226; as "singing cowboy," 90
McMurtry, Larry, 155
McWhorter, Emma, 278
Mean Streets (film), 47
Melville, Herman, 165
"Method" actors, 84
Methvin, J. J., 278
Mexico, 131, 173, 272, 275
Miles, Vera, 3, 224
Milius, John, 34, 45n. 112, 47, 77
Miller, Mitch, 112, 135, 137, *138*
Milosz, Czeslaw, 10
minstrelsy, 133–35, 280, 322
miscegenation, 7–8, 20, 174, 193, 231, 320; antimiscegenation laws, 65, 67, 333n. 53; colonial elites obsessed by, 197; as comic or tragic, 227; different types of, 190, 232–33; incest and, 198, 203, 206, 209, 212–15; kinship relations and, 17–18; Motion Picture Production Code and, 3, 8, 211; point of view and, 223; rescue fantasy and, 203; sensuality of the dark woman, 234–35; social acceptance of Native-white unions, 322–23; white fear of, 13–14
Mitchell, Margaret, 121
Mitchell, Thomas, 178
Mitchum, Robert, 4, 299
Mix, Tom, 89
Mockridge, Cyril J., 111
Mogambo (Ford film), 293
Monument Valley, 2, 25, 78, 93–108, *96–97, 101, 106,* 289; Ford's "discovery" of, 336; harsh desert not compatible with "civilization," 104, 318; Native Americans and Ford films made in, 342
Motion Picture Herald, 67
Motion Picture Production Code, 3, 8, 211
mourning, 183–84

363

Index

Murphy, Audie, 209
music, use of, 6, 177, 318–19; audience response and, 297; in classical Hollywood, 118–19; darkness of Ethan's character and, 24–25; in final scene, 25, 26; Ford's artistic control and, 109–13; leitmotifs, 119–20, 121, 123, 125, 130; limits of knowledge and, 240–41; in other Ford films, 111, 112, 114–15, 120–21; parlor arrangement, 123–24; race and, 128–39; sense of danger and, 186; "silent" cinema and, 32; title song ("The Searchers"), 15, 50, 109–10, 112–14, 115, 117, 119–20. *See also specific song titles*
My Darling Clementine (Ford film), 111, 120, 131, 175, 184, 228
myth, 50–51, 68, 72, 106

national identity, 129, 134
"national imaginary," 129
Native American (Peyote) Church, 278–79
Native Americans, 9, 52, 130; antimiscegenation laws and, 65; depiction in western genre, 11–12, 142n. 51, 153, 223, 233; integration into American society, 64–65; kinship and captivity among, 270–77; massacres of and by, 82, 104–5, 152, 163–64, *164*, 173–74, 235, 337; responses to *The Searchers*, 318, 335–42; sexual unions with whites, 322–23; as stand-in for African Americans, 8–9, 66–68, 132, 212, 220n. 47, 266; white women in captivity by, 10–11. *See also specific tribes*
Natwick, Mildred, 175
Navaho tribe, 272–73, 280, 336, 340
Nazism, 292, 330n. 32, 338
New Deal, 293, 294, 304, 329n. 21
Newman, Alfred, 111, 118
Newman, Paul, 5, 84

New Mexico, 273–75
Nineteen Eighty-Four (Orwell), 10
Norton, Ken, 214
No Way Out (film), 295, 304
Nugent, Frank S., 6, 8, 14, 15; adaptation of LeMay's novel, 67; Ethan character and, 82, 165, 259; Ethan-Scar confrontation and, 16; final scene and, 199; Ford's artistic control and, 32, 111; "happy ending" of, 32; LeMay novel and, 20–21; musical score and, 112; narrative opacity and, 99; opening scene in *The Searchers* and, 180; on rough cut of *The Searchers*, 23; scalping scene and, 25; white captives scene and, 24; working relationship with Ford, 27, 31, 32. *See also* shooting script *(The Searchers)*

Oedipal themes, 5, 28, 213–14, 319
Oklahoma Kid, The (film), 118
Oliver, Edna May, 175
One-Eyed Jacks (film), 5
Only Angels Have Wings (film), 79
Operation Pacific (film), 76
"organization man," 76
Orwell, George, 10
Other, the, 16, 129, 131, 233; masculine domination over, 171; projection of sexual fantasy and, 197, 198
overdetermination, 53
Owens, Louis, 335
Ox-Bow Incident, The (film), 83

Paint Your Wagon (film), 90
Palo Duro Canyon, Battle of, 278
Parker, Cynthia Ann: Comanche kinship practices and, 281; fate of, 43n. 89, 278; as historical basis for "Debbie," 1, 276, 340; son of, 40n. 38, 279, 341
Parker, Quanah, 279, 286n. 19, 341
patriarchy, 178, 235, 271
Pauley, Martin (character), 2, 25; adoption of, 56; confrontation with

Index

Ethan over Debbie, 132, 154, 159; "false marriage" to Look, 21, 59, 280–81, 308–9; feminine values and, 173; innocence of, 95–96, 128, 243, 296; integration into Jorgensen family, 283n. 5; interaction with Martha, 183; killing of Scar by, 20, 26, 62, 156; kinship relations and, 18, 59–64, 68–69, 266–69; in LeMay novel, 67–68, 203, 295; letter to Laurie, 116, 224–27, 244–45, 308; loyalty to white society, 71; marriage to Laurie, 62–64, 127, 203–4; Martha's importance and, 55, 180, 184–85; in opening scene, 181; as part Indian, 13–14, 28, 52, 56, 57, 64, 184, 225, 269; reaction to death of Look, 338; relationship with Ethan, 57–60, 58, 166n.11; rescue of Debbie and, 53, 187; shedding of Indian signifiers, 236; struggle for soul of, 185–86; unconscious symbolic function of, 64; in white captives scene, 229–31
Peary, Danny, 34
Peck, Gregory, 299
Pena, Elizabeth, 215
Penn, Arthur, 5, 11, 22, 223
Pennick, Jack, 229
Peralta, Augustina de, 272, 273, 279
Perkins, Anthony, 59
Peta Nocona (Wandering Wolf) (Comanche war-chief), 1, 340, 341
Pilgrimage (Ford film), 320
Pinkham, Scott, 336
Pinky (film), 285, 305, 329n. 26
Pisani, Michael, 129–30
Pittsburgh (film), 79
Place, Janice A., 48
Plainsman, The (film), 321
pleasure, postponement of, 54, 55, 71
Plessy v. Ferguson, 304
Plummer, Rachel, 272, 281
point of view, 223–37

Poitier, Sidney, 295, 304
Pollack, Sydney, 155
polygamy, 282, 339
postmodernity, 89
power, social relations of, 271
Power, Tyrone, 298
Pratt, Louise, 177, 188
Preston, Robert, 299
Prime Cut (film), 204, 209
progress, idea of, 94
Progressive Era, 304
projection, psychological, 197
Propp, Vladimir, 49, 53, 70, 71
psychoanalytic criticism, 54, 197, 198, 228
Psycho (film), 258–59
psychological novels, 48
"psychological" westerns, 15–16, 20–21, 26, 31, 36. See also western genre
Psychology of Colonization, The (Mannoni), 198
Puhvel, Jaan, 164
Pumphrey, Martin, 171
purity, sexual, 175, 177, 180, 187, 208
Pursued (film), 4, 83, 118, 333n. 54
Pye, Douglas, 136, 137, 189, 291, 308

Qualen, John, 305
Quiet Man, The (Ford film), 79, 83, 85, 88, 118, 293

race, 9, 51, 110, 265; minstrel song and, 133–34; music in construction of, 128–39; "Negro question" in 1950s America, 295; sexual purity of white female, 185, 187. *See also* interracial sexuality
"racial problem" films, 9
racism, 3, 4, 70, 72, 193; absence of, 313–14; America's struggle to discard, 317; audience implicated in, 223; depicted as pervasive in white society, 14, 82; limited critique of, 303–4; minstrelsy and, 135, 280; origins of, 16–17; psychoanalytical

365

racism (*continued*)
    interpretation of, 197–98, 198; sexual issues and, 214; white racist violence, 12–13
Raft, George, 81
Raksin, David, 118
Ramona (Jackson), 323
rape, 58, 85, 143n. 64, 187, 188, 308; colonial fear of miscegenation and, 197; Freudian analysis and, 257; racism and false accusation, 17; sign of, 14
Reap the Wild Wind (film), 79
Reconstruction, 68
Red River (film), 79, 83, 88, 165, 299
Red River Wars (1874–75), 278
religion, 3–4, 175
representation, 54, 223, 235
Rickman, Gregg, 205
Riders of Destiny (film), 90
Riders of Vengeance (Ford film), 298
Rio Bravo (film), 53, 82
Rio Grande (Ford film), 5, 12, 83, 327n.10; female pioneering spirit in, 175; music in, 112, 121; romantic interests in, 85
Rio Lobo (film), 88
Rios, Elvar, 121
Rising of the Moon, The (Ford film), 305–6
Ritchie, Michael, 204
RKO studio, 117
Robinson, Edward G., 307
Rodriguez, Rosita, 281
Rogers, Roy, 90
Rogers, Will, 65, 305, 329n. 25, 333n. 53
Roosevelt, Franklin D., 293, 329n. 21
Roth, Marty, 174
Rowlandson, Mary, 10, 193n. 6
Run for Cover (film), 84
Rutledge, Ann, 111

Salmi, Albert, 207
Sands of Iwo Jima (film), 76, 78, 83
Santa Fe Trail (film), 118

Santschi, Tom, 176
Sarris, Andrew, 48, 174, 177, 327n. 3
Sayles, John, 215
Sayonara (film), 9
scalping, 4, 20, 24, 62, 155; as castration, 55; doorway motif and, 255; Ford's attitude toward, 24–25; narrative function in *The Searchers*, 315; as pretext for annihilating vengeance, 102; Scar's collection of scalps, 282
Scar, Chief (character), 2, 3, 70; alternate name of, 242, 243, 281; as "bad nigger," 71; Comanche point of view and, 11, 281, 282–83; death of, 13, 20, 26, 62; Debbie as sexual war trophy of, 183; as Ethan's alter ego, 15, 153, 200, 202, 215, 233; as Ethan's id, *17*, 319; musical letimotif of, 132; played by white actor, 340; as racially mixed, 13; raid on Edwards homestead and, 7, 80, 152, 174, 194n. 18; scalped by Ethan, 24, 31, 55, 62, 81, 155–56, 157, 255, 315; sexual relationship with Debbie, 16, 21, 281–82; sons killed by whites, 104–5, 233, 282, 339; speaking lines, 11, 12, 16; as unrestrained criminal libido, 54
Scarlet Drop, The (Ford film), 298
Schindler's List (film), 338
school desegregation, 66–67, 68
Schrader, Paul, 34, 47
Schwarzenegger, Arnold, 87
Scorsese, Martin, 33–34, 47, 77, 326
Scott, Dred, 66
Scott, Pippa, 39n. 28, 173–74
Sea Chase, The (film), 76
Searchers, The (Ford film): ambivalence and ambiguity in, 2–3, 17–20, 133, 134, 173, 225–27, 242, 248–49, 324; canon of great films and, 1, 34–35; as captivity narrative, 119, 165, 173–74, 270–72, 276, 277; cast and credits, 343–44; cine-

Index

matography of, 31; contemporary popularity in video rental, 221n. 64; critical reputation of, 1, 34–36, 77, 223–24, 240, 325–26; Custer scene eliminated from, 22–23, 199; "dark" western genre and, 5; differences from LeMay novel, 14, 16, 20–21, 41n. 49, 67–68, 315; doorway visual motif in, 250–51, *252–53*, 255, *255*; final scene, 25–29, 160–62, 167n. 25, 199; gender roles in, 246–47; historical events contemporary with, 8–10, 11, 51, 65, 67–70, 132; *Iliad* and, 145–70; incest theme in, 198–217; influence on contemporary film directors, 33–34, 45n. 112, 47–48, 76–77, 240; kinship in, 266–70, 280–84; lifting gesture (visual motif) in, 250, 251, *253–54*, 254, 255–56; limits of knowledge and, 239–63; Monument Valley landscape in, 93–108, *96–97, 101, 106*; music in, 109–43; narrative opacity in, 99, 103, 124–25, 241–43; Native American "extras" in, 336; Native American responses to, 335–42; opening sequence, 180, 241; plot, 2, 4, 99, 107; point of view in, 223–37; portrayal of Jewish character Futterman, 341–42; problematic antiracism of, 307–10; production of, 18–19, 31, 32; as psychological study, 3; racism seen in, 130, 189, 195n. 31, 231–32; rehearsal of scenes, 2; rough cut of, 22–23; structural themes in, 94, 180–82, 226; time frame in narrative, 2, 8, 37n. 7, 48, 93, 100, 126, 173, 190, 336; visual pleasure of, 1–2, 33; western genre and, 30, 223, 228–29, 291; white captives (winter fort) scene, 189, 229–31, *230*, 268, 309–10, *311*. *See also names of characters in film;* shooting script *(The Searchers)*

Searchers, The (LeMay novel), 14, 16, 20–21, 31, 67, 339; Comanche language in, 115; comparison with *The Unforgiven* (LeMay's other novel), 198, 204–5, 208, 210, 216; Debbie character in, 282–83; differences from Ford's film, 14, 16, 20–21, 41n. 49, 67–68, 315; Ethan character in, 82, 165; Ford's adaptation of, 295; historical background of, 1, 337; incest-miscegenation theme and, 213

Sea Wolf, The (film), 81

Sergeant Rutledge (Ford film), 12, 17, 111, 137, 175, 199

Set-daya-ité (Many Bears) (Kiowa warchief), 277

Seven Women (Ford film), 193, 331n. 39

sexuality, 53, 177–79

sexual/racial "defilement," 2, 7, 16; Debbie equated with her sexuality, 53; Ethan and Scar as doubles, 15–16; fantasies about, 14, 15. *See also* interracial sexuality

"Shall We Gather at the River?" (hymn), 127–28, 177, 321

Shane (film), 26, 49

Sherman, George, 119

She Wore a Yellow Ribbon (Ford film), 12, 83, 108n. 12, 185–86; female pioneering spirit in, 175; limits of female action in, 246; mourning in, 184; music in, 121; romantic interests in, 85

shooting script *(The Searchers)*, 31, 180, 315; contemporary events of 1950s America and, 292; deleted scenes, 247, 260; dialogue cut from, 124; Ford's artistic control and, 33, 185, 199–200

Shootist, The (film), 88

Siegel, Don, 10

Sight and Sound (journal), 1, 34, 35

silhouette, 94, 105, 316

"singing cowboys," 90

Sioux tribes, 11, 336

Index

"Skip to My Lou" (song), 128
slave labor, 271–72, 274, 276
Slotkin, Richard, 172, 205
Smith, Henry Nash, 155
Smith, Wingate, 19
Sons of Katie Elder, The (film), 88
Sons of the Pioneers, 111, 113, 117, 135
Spacek, Sissy, 204
Spanish language, 131
Spielberg, Steven, 33, 34, 45n. 112, 47, 326
Spirit of America, The (film), 165
Stagecoach (Ford film), 3, 12, 78–79, 85, 188; liberal politics in, 293–94; model of civilization in, 172, 177, 178; Monument Valley in, 93–94, 126, 130, 131; music in, 111, 114, 115, 121, 130, 131, 140n. 9; Native Americans depicted in, 307, 322; popularity of, 321; stunts in, 88; western genre and, 327n. 4; women in, 177, 178, 190
star actors, persona and, 81
Star Wars (film), 34, 45n. 112, 47
Star Wars II: Attack of the Clones (film), 35
Steiger, Rod, 84
Steinbeck, John, 293
Steiner, Max, 56, 110, 111, 112; career, 117–18; Ford's artistic control and, 116, 201; "Indian" music and, 129; minstrel songs and, 137, 139
Stepin Fetchit, 304–5, 306, 329n. 25
stereotypes, 172, 175, 290, 305–6; Hispanic women, 342; "Indian" music, 129–30; "valuable woman," 15
Stevens, George, 26
Stewart, James, 4–5, 83, 84, 299, 311
Stolen Life, A (film), 118
Stone, Robert, 165
Straight Shooting (Ford film), 199, 300–301, 320
studio system, 23, 110
Studlar, Gaylyn, 116, 290, 318, 322

stunt men, 31, 88, 91n. 9
Sun Shines Bright, The (Ford film), 17, 180, 304, 305
Supreme Court, 66–68, 292
Suspicion (film), 84
S/Z (Barthes), 239

Tall in the Saddle (film), 79
Tatum, Lawrie, 276, 278
Taxi Driver (film), 34, 47, 48
Taylor, Robert, 299
television, 76, 83, 89
Temple, Shirley, 175
temporality, 105
Texas Rangers, 3, 5, 187; as agents of the law, 54; final assault on Scar's camp, 19, 24, 29, 62, 102; historical raid to rescue Cynthia Ann Parker, 340; "Yellow Rose of Texas" sung by, 135
They Died with Their Boots On (film), 118
They Were Expendable (Ford film), 76
Third Man, The (film), 118
Thomas, Deborah, 77, 78, 87
Thomson, David, 162
Three Bad Men (Ford film), 12, 301–2, 303, 306, 325; liberal politics in, 294; role of Native Americans in, 307; women in, 176
Three Godfathers (Ford film), 85, 121, 131
3:10 to Yuma (film), 5, 299
3,000 Miles to Graceland (film), 81
Todorov, Tzvetan, 49
To Kill a Mockingbird (film), 305
Toll Gate, The (film), 299
Tompkins, Jane, 96, 171, 172, 205, 213
Torrid Zone (film), 79
Towers, Constance, 124
tragicomedy, 19
Treasure of the Sierra Madre, The (film), 118, 205
Trevor, Claire, 177
Trouble Along the Way (film), 88
True Grit (film), 88, 89

Index

Truman, Harry S., 292
Turner, Frederick Jackson, 105, 265–66
Twentieth-Century Fox studio, 118
Two Rode Together (Ford film), 12, 40n. 38, 199, 236; as captivity narrative, 272, 311–12; family in, 175; racial conflict in, 192–93, 195n. 35
Tycoon (film), 79

Ulzana's Raid (film), 47
Uncle Tom's Cabin (Stowe), 133
unconscious, the, 51, 56, 64
Unforgiven, The (film), 198, 204–17, 333n. 54
United States, history of, 103–4, 105, 145, 265–66

"valuable woman" stereotype, 15
Van Damme, Jean-Claude, 87
Vanderhaeghe, Guy, 155
vaudeville, 305
Vertigo (film), 84, 161, 167n. 27
Vietnam War, 77, 90
violence, 2, 3, 12, 104, 150; catharsis in western genre, 83; epic poetry and, 145, 146, 149; figure of the Mother and, 55; John Wayne's screen image and, 77; masculine vengeance and, 172; slavery of African Americans, 65–66; tribal exchange relations and, 52; women as victims of, 36
Virgil, 164
Virginia City (film), 118, 137
visual images, 5, 29
visual pleasure, 2, 33
voyeurism, 64

Wagon Master (Ford film), 112, 175, 176, 178, 186
Walsh, Raoul, 4
Wandering Wolf, 1, 40n. 38
Warner Brothers, 22–23, 112, 117
War of the Wildcats (film), 79
Warshow, Robert, 145, 149, 150–51, 152

Washita massacre (1868), 22
Waters, Ethel, 305
Wayne, John, 19, 67, 166n. 13, 206, 217, 322; acting of, 33, 34, 78–79; age and screen roles, 86, 86–87, 88; associated with western genre, 69, 78; body image and language, 78, 80, 91n. 9; box office appeal of, 49; career, 75, 76, 83–84; as cultural icon, 31, 77–78, 80; decline of western genre and, 89; evolution of screen persona, 78; interviewed about *The Searchers*, 17, 29, 162, 201–2; masculine image of, 77; in other Ford movies, 5, 12, 78–79, 83, 85, 88, 176, 178, 259–60, 299, 326; performance in *The Searchers*, 2, 77, 79–82, 84–87, 162, 201; posthumous reception of, 90; romantic involvements on screen, 85, 87; star status, 75, 90; in unsympathetic role, 3–4, 154, 223; western (established) persona, 79; working relationship with Ford, 25, 31, 38n. 18, 83
Wayne, Patrick, 19, 235
Wayne, Pilar Pallete, 33
Webster, H. D. L., 201
Webster, J. P., 122, 123
Welles, Orson, 293
western genre, 1, 2, 82–83; adaptation to changing times, 293; "adult" westerns, 83, 90, 301; as children's movies, 20; clichés of, 310–11, 331n. 38; conventions of, 23, 26, 156–57, 190, 291; "dark," 4–5, 11, 13, 15 (*See also* "psychological" westerns); death of, 13; decline of, 89, 321; denigration of femininity, 171–72; domination of television in 1950s, 76; heroes in, 298–99; Homeric epic and, 149–51; miscegenation in, 174; racism issue in, 7, 136, 223, 228, 322; villains in, 24; white triumphalism in, 2, 198; women's role in, 116, 175

369

Index

Western Reader, The (Kitses and Rickman), 205
West of Everything: The Inner Life of Westerns (Tompkins), 205
"white civilization," 2, 19; erasure of whiteness, 268; female sexuality and, 185, 187; fragility of white identity, 10–11; harshness of Monument Valley and, 104; law and, 53–54; obsession with miscegenation and, 223; recovered female captives and, 340; repressed forces in, 233. *See also* civilization
"white conquest" genre, 36, 45n. 119
White Sage (Kiowa woman), 278
white violence, 12–13, 163–65
white women: captives (winter fort) scene in *The Searchers*, 168n. 29, 189, 225, 229–31, *230*, 309–10, *312*; in captivity narratives, 10–11, 13; colonial obsession with miscegenation and, 197; dark and fair, 234; frontier masculinity and, 171; interracial sexuality and, 7; killed by U.S. Cavalry, 22; sexual purity and, 190, 192, 214; traditional social roles of, 175; tribal relations and, 52. *See also* women
Whitman, Cedric, 151
Whitney, C. V., 67, 111
wide-screen theaters, 33
Widmark, Richard, 295
Wild Goose Flying in the Night Sky. *See* Look (character)
Wills, Garry, 31, 166–67n. 20
Wilmington, John, 35
Wilmington, Michael, 48, 105, 180, 190, 232, 250
Wilson, George M., 98
Winchester '73 (film), 5, 299

Wind and the Lion, The (film), 47
Wings of Eagles, The (Ford film), 42n. 79, 88, 320
Winkler, Martin, 24, 28, 289, 290, 317, 318
Wiseman, Joseph, 205, 207
women: as amateur musicians, 123–24; in borderlands political economy, 271–72, 275; "fallen," 311; Hispanic, 342; as representatives of civilization, 171, 174–75, 179; role in classical cinema, 53, 318; waiting passively, 246. *See also* white women
"women's pictures" genre, 53
Wood, Lana, 19, 41n. 54, 174, 181, 203, 220n. 48
Wood, Natalie, 2, 15, 19, 124, 174, 225; beauty of, 203; motives of "Debbie" character and, 331n. 40
Wood, Robin, 164, 174
Work, Henry Clay, 135
Workman, Chuck, 165
World War II, 75
Wyler, William, 23

"Yellow Rose of Texas, The" (song), 112, 128, 322; history of, 133–37, *138*, *139*, 142–43n. 64; woman as object of desire in, 116
Young, Robert J. C., 198
Young, Victor, 118
Young Mr. Lincoln (Ford film), 54, 55, 56, 325; music in, 111, 118; spectators' knowledge in, 50
youth culture, postwar, 77

Zanuck, Daryl, 305, 323
Zizek, Slavoj, 98

www.ingramcontent.com/pod-product-compliance
Lightning Source LLC
Chambersburg PA
CBHW051535230426
43669CB00015B/2601